The American Social Experience Series
GENERAL EDITOR: JAMES KIRBY MARTIN
EDITORS: PAULA S. FASS, STEVEN H.
MINTZ, JAMES W. REED, PETER N.
STEARNS, & ALLAN M. WINKLER

THE ORIGINS OF BEHAVIORISM

American Psychology, 1870–1920

JOHN M. O'DONNELL

NEW YORK UNIVERSITY PRESS
NEW YORK *and* LONDON
1985

Library of Congress Cataloging in Publication Data

O'Donnell, John M., 1945–
The origins of behaviorism.

(The American social experience series ; 3)
Bibliography: p.
Includes index.
1. Behaviorism (Psychology)—History.   2. Psychology—
United States—History—19th century.   3. Psychology—
United States—History—20th century.   I. Title.
II. Series
BF199.O38   1985   150.19'43   85-7094
        ISBN 0-8147-6162-3 (alk. paper)

Book design by Ken Venezio

For my father and
his daughter-in-law

Contents

Preface

In the American college of 1870, psychology—true to its etymology—was virtually indistinguishable from the philosophy of the soul. A quarter-century later, academic institutions possessed not only psychology but psychologists, experimental scientists dedicated to pure research and seeking to explicate through introspective analysis of conscious experience the general laws of mental organization. Twenty-five years later, many psychologists justified their activities in terms of practical utility. For them, psychology had become an objective science that purported both to predict and to control human behavior.

From the consciousness of man to the behavior of men: surely this marked if somewhat schematized shift of focus represents more than the process of cumulative empirical inquiry. Any integral account of this reorientation must consider not only intellectual currents, both philosophic and scientific, but also institutional and cultural change. Psychology, of course, is not only a body of knowledge; it is also an organization of knowers, individuals who, in the words of Laurence Veysey, "thought abstractly, but only for portions of each day."[1] Legislation as well as logic, social influences as well as scientific insights shape the course of disciplinary development. Like other cogitating creatures, psychologists enlist ideas not only for their intrinsic intellectual appeal or plausibility but also because these ideas appear conducive to shifting professional needs, institutional mandates, social roles, and cultural values. In the phrase "intellectual community" the adjective modifies but does not exclusively govern the noun.

What follows is an attempt to explain the transformation of American academic psychology from the science of consciousness to the science of behavior. Like any historical problem, this one is fraught with difficulties; accordingly, it might be convenient to delineate a few of them at the outset. First, the categories of consciousness and behavior never constituted exclusive foci for distinct generations of psychologists at the chronological extremes of the half-century under consideration. In the 1870s and 1880s students of psychology drew distinctions between "rational" and "empirical" psychology, between the study of mind and the investigation of human conduct. Some academicians attended to the latter. Conversely, quite a few twentieth-century psychologists continued to be interested in the former. This study assumes that there are continually alive a number of conceptions of psychology's purpose, methods, and scope and that other than strictly intellectual forces determine which of these conceptions will at any particular moment reign supreme.[2] The historian's task is to uncover those forces.

Second, there is the problem of relating the study of behavior as a scientific endeavor to the broader philosophic movement known as behaviorism. B. F. Skinner has illuminated the distinction as follows: "Behaviorism, with an accent on the last syllable, is not the scientific study of behavior but a philosophy of science concerned with the subject matter and methods of psychology."[3] Behaviorism as a philosophy of science is commonly considered to have begun in 1912–13 with John Broadus Watson's radical formulations.[4] It involves assumptions of materialistic monism and positivistic insistence on viewing man as a stimulus-response machine and consciousness as epiphenomenon. My concern is with those scientists who did not necessarily accent behaviorism's last syllable. Few psychologists were inclined to agree with Watson's parsimonious philosophy, yet many called themselves behaviorists simply because they eschewed introspective analysis, concentrated on human performance rather than on human experience, and sought at times merely to predict human behavior (e.g., as intelligence testers) and at times actually to change it (e.g., as clinicians). Watson's manifesto did not revolutionize psychological endeavor; rather, an entrenched pattern of disciplinary activity emboldened Watson to make his pronouncement. The object of this inquiry is not to trace the intellectual sources of Watson's formulations but to provide a history of the emergence of the disciplinary pattern that supported those formulations.[5]

In a marvelously succinct account of the intellectual foundations of Watsonianism, John C. Burnham has concluded that "the evolution of Watson's thinking, on the one hand, is not necessarily relevant to the origins of behaviorism, on the other hand." Burnham suggests that historians look to "the actions of the psychological community" in order to account for their adoption of the central tenets of his declaration.[6] Commentators have sought explanations for Watson's manifesto and its apparent success in the broad contours of American culture.[7] While not oblivious to such interpretations, my investigation has centered upon the specific subculture of the academic psychologist. The socioeconomic and cultural pressures to which psychologists responded were, after all, mediated by the institutions within which they worked. The shift from the study of consciousness to the study of behavior can be largely explained by viewing psychological thought within the context of a patterned system of social and intellectual relationships significantly circumscribed by academic discipline, professional association, and institutional affiliation. The shift did not occur overnight, and no account of it that fails to consider the impact of psychology's institutional and professional development upon its fundamental intellectual postulates can possibly be complete. What holds together an account of the professionalization of American psychology, on the one hand, and an analysis of the origins of behaviorism, on the other hand, is my contention that ultimately the two phenomena are but aspects of a single, though hardly linear, process.

Though the writing of this account has likewise been hardly linear, many individuals have helped me to see straighter. Donald H. Meyer at the University of Delaware gave initial encouragement to me and my project. At the University of Pennsylvania, Riki Kuklick, Rob Kohler and Bruce Kuklick were simultaneously teachers and colleagues whose acumen, energy and care I found sustaining. Especially I must thank Charles Rosenberg for his wise counsel, acute criticism and lasting influence. John Burnham not only publicly set the terms of the debate for the historical problem of behaviorism but privately introduced me to Cheiron, a group whose collective knowledge has saved me from many misinterpretations. Mike Sokal finally convinced me to publish the manuscript, and the promise of Jim Reed's editorial supervision constituted an offer I could not refuse. The University of Pennsylvania supported this study in the form of a University Fellowship at a critical juncture. Among the many helpful librarians who aided me in my research, I must particularly thank Ferenc Gyorgyey of the Historical Library of the Yale Medical Library, William Koelsch and Suzanne Hamel of the Clark University Archives, and John Miller of the Archives of the History of American Psychology in Akron, Ohio. The Archives' founders and codirectors, John Popplestone and Marion White McPherson were gracious and knowledgeable hosts. Clark University Press, Little Brown and the American Psychological Association are also gratefully acknowledged for giving permission to reprint from their publications. Shirley Anderson typed the original manuscript with amazing accuracy, speed and cheer.

Finally, there is Kate O'Donnell, whose support meant everything and always will.

CHAPTER I

Introduction: The New Psychology in America

In the last quarter of the nineteenth century, as science came to occupy ever larger portions of the Western world's cultural terrain, psychology secured recognition as a separate academic discipline by promoting its status as an experimental laboratory science. Research advances in the fields of sensorimotor physiology, neuroanatomy, and brain physiology were showing that mental processes and neuromuscular functioning seemed to operate interdependently. The philosophically battered but resilient belief of British empiricism that mind could be studied introspectively by analyzing how physical elements called sensations produced acts of perception and cognition was reinforced by the scientific promise that the introspective data of conscious experience could now be experimentally controlled and mathematically measured.[1] This combination of assumptions would be distilled in the science that came to be called physiological psychology. Its appearance heightened expectations for the field as a whole. It was time, the British journal *Mind* straightforwardly editorialized in its first issue in 1876, "to procure a decision on . . . the scientific standing of psychology."[2]

That same year in England, Sir David Ferrier fortified this impatient conviction with the publication of his classic monograph, *On The Functions of the Brain.* Ferrier proved conclusively that mind's cortical organ is a differentiated system of sensory and motor centers responsive to electrical stimulation and susceptible to physiological laws. "In their subjective aspect," declared the London physiologist, "the functions of the brain are synonymous with mental operations, the consideration of which belongs to the science of psychology."[3] Could there be an objective science of subjective experience? In Germany a Heidelberg physiologist named Wilhelm Wundt had just published a persuasive affirmative in his *Grundzüge der physiologischen Psychologie (Principles of Physiological Psychology)*.[4] In America, a Harvard physiologist named William James, who had once attempted to study with Wundt, concurred. In 1876, the year of the nation's centennial celebration of technological growth and scientific progress, James urged young men with professorial ambitions to study recent trends in scientific psychology. He predicted that they would soon find in departments of philosophy "a number of vacant places calling for their peculiar capacity."[5] Months earlier he had exhibited his own exemplary capacity in that regard by establishing a rudimentary demonstration laboratory at Cambridge, Massachusetts.

But "a metronome, a device for whirling a frog, a horopter chart, and one or two other bits of apparatus" tucked in a stairwell closet do not a discipline make. Though James's prediction was realized, his ambitious though not quite youthful student Granville Stanley Hall was to become the acknowledged spearhead of psychology's academic professionalization in America.[6] In 1878, the year James began writing his celebrated *Principles of Psychology*,[7] Hall received Harvard's first Ph.D. in philosophy, which was also the country's first degree awarded specifically in psychology. In order to augment and further certify his own "peculiar capacity," Hall immediately traveled to Leipzig, where Wundt had just established his Institute of Experimental Psychology and, in 1879, would create the world's first research laboratory in experimental psychology. Returning to the United States, Hall secured in 1881 a temporary three-year appointment at Johns Hopkins University's Department of Philosophy as lecturer in psychology and pedagogics and a permanent post in these same fields in 1883, the year in which he set up his own laboratory.

Established in 1876, Johns Hopkins was self-consciously patterned upon the German research-oriented university. There psychology took shape as a scientific discipline as Hall's students, who included John Dewey, Joseph Jastrow, James McKeen Cattell, Edmund Clark Sanford, and the physiologist Henry Herbert Donaldson, engaged in experimental research.[8] The results of their scientific investigations were published, first in *Mind* and then in Hall's *American Journal of Psychology*, created in October 1887. Hall's students supplemented their experimental training with seminars, received doctorates, and as certified psychologists went on to introduce their new discipline into other American institutions. In 1888 Jastrow assumed the chair of psychology at the University of Wisconsin, as did Cattell, who had received his doctorate from Wundt, at the University of Pennsylvania. Three years later Cattell moved to Columbia University. Dewey became instructor of physiological psychology at the University of Michigan. When Hall left Hopkins to become president and chairman of the psychology department at the newly founded Clark University in 1889, he took with him Sanford and Donaldson. By 1898 Hall's departments at Hopkins and Clark had conferred thirty Ph.D.'s, more than all the other American universities combined.[9]

Meanwhile, the final member of American psychology's founding triumvirate that included James and Hall brought the new psychology to Yale. While professor of mental and moral philosophy at Bowdoin College from 1879 to 1881, George Trumbell Ladd was characteristically attendant to trends in physiological psychology. Moving to Yale in 1881 at the age of 39, he began working in the physiologist J. K. Thatcher's laboratory at the Yale Medical School as James had worked in H. P. Bowditch's laboratory at the Harvard Medical School a decade earlier. The Yale philosopher and theologian began formally teaching physiological psychology in 1884, and three years later he published his *Elements of Physiological Psychology*.[10] American students finally possessed an exhaustive exposition of the principles of German experimentalism and of nerve physiology in one accessible volume. In 1892 Ladd delegated the direction of his psychological laboratory to Edward Wheeler Scripture, who had secured his doctorate from Wundt the previous year.

The year 1892 represents an important watershed for the history of American psychology. Hall founded the American Psychological Association (APA), manifestly dedicated "to the advancement of psychology as a science" and no less obviously to the professional advancement of psychologists as scientists. That year Americans made their premier showing at the Second International Congress of Psychology in London. Perhaps more important than such organizational bench marks were subtle changes in departmental structure. In 1892 the "founders" of the American discipline, more interested in the philosophic and theoretical aspects of their science than in performing actual research, surrendered control of their laboratories to a second generation of aspiring experimentalists. Ladd imported Scripture to Yale; James induced the German psychologist Hugo Münsterberg, another product of Wundt's institute, to Harvard; and Hall formally turned over his Clark laboratory to Sanford. In 1892 also, Edward Bradford Titchener, who would become the so-called champion of Wundtian orthodoxy in America, assumed command of Cornell's recently established facilities. Simultaneously, Jastrow was laying plans for a public exposition of the new experimental psychology at the Chicago World's Fair. Psychology was claiming philosophic, scientific, and popular attention.

Because of psychology's broad appeal and the promise of professional opportunities for investigators interested in the philosophic, scientific, and practical aspects of the new science, Leipzig continued throughout the 1890s to attract students who returned to the United States to establish laboratories purportedly patterned after the German model. In the year of the APA's founding there existed formal research laboratories at Harvard, Pennsylvania, Wisconsin, Clark, Columbia, Yale, and Cornell. By then demonstration facilities created for teaching and training could be found at Indiana, the University of Nebraska, Michigan, the University of Iowa, Wellesley, Brown, the University of Illinois, the University of Kansas, and Catholic University of America in Washington, D.C.[11] When the association celebrated its twenty-fifth anniversary in 1903, psychology produced more doctorates in America than all other sciences save chemistry, zoology, and physics; over forty laboratories had been founded; and the APA's original membership of thirty-one had quadrupled.[12] In 1913, the year Watson published his manifesto, the membership had doubled again; Americans had just surpassed Germany in the quantity of research publications; and the British *Who's Who in Science* listed among the world's leading psychologists 84 Americans and only 31 Germans.[13] In 1929, when Edwin G. Boring reviewed the science's intellectual development in his massive *History of Experimental Psychology*, there were approximately 1,000 psychologists in the United States representing well over 300 academic institutions.[14] James's prophecy had indeed come to pass.

The apotheosis of the laboratory and the emergence of a scientific discipline of psychology from a religiously based tradition of academic philosophy should come as no surprise to anyone passingly familiar with the history of American higher education in the late nineteenth century.[15] According to the accepted wisdom, as science came increasingly to be associated with inductively acquired evidence, European experimental research attracted the attention of scientifically minded Americans. Lacking opportunities to pursue such studies in the United States, students by the 1870s ventured abroad, especially to the German universities, where they assimilated not only specific laboratory techniques but also a broad philosophic rationale for the pursuit of science for its own sake. Returning home, they proceeded to reconstruct the institutional pattern of the German university as they perceived it. "In an imitation of these institutions as such," comments Laurence Veysey, "certain Americans saw their only hope for secure / support and personal advancement."[16] The introduction of the German seminar and laboratory, together with the creation of graduate schools such as those at Hopkins and Clark, provided the mechanisms that enabled nascent scientific disciplines to perpetuate themselves and set the stage for a developing intellectual argument designed to safeguard their professional gains and to justify their scientific attitudes and endeavors. By the 1880s the practice of research had been elevated to the level of an academic ideal accentuating the growth rather than the mere diffusion of knowledge; German scholarship had become a fetish; graduate schools and scientific departments proliferated; and pure science, according to Veysey, "was clearly on the ascendant as a source of academic inspiration."[17] By 1900 the American universities, in the words of Hunter Dupree, had become "the homes of disinterested pure science."[18]

Those who have equated the beginnings of academic professionalization and the rise of research science with the emergence of the modern university tend to regard the new discipline of psychology as an ideal embodiment of the transformation of American scholarship.[19] Returning from Leipzig in the 1880s and 1890s, successive cohorts of newly minted Ph.D.'s forcefully maneuvered physiological psychology into the academic syllabus as they moved their elegant brass instruments into the attics of ivy-covered halls of classical learning. Soon they would occupy the ground floors. The new psychologists, so the argument runs, quickly wrested psychology from the clerical grasp of conservative moral philosophers who had employed a "mental science" called Scottish Realism as an epistemological rationalization for Christianity's normative categories of right conduct and character. In short order, religious speculation gave way to experimental science; laboratory research replaced textbook indoctrination. The history of American psychology prior to 1880, quipped Cattell, is as brief as the chronicle of serpents in Iceland: "There are no snakes in Iceland."[20]

While it is useful to see that "the spread of the new psychology in American colleges is an indicator of the extent to which the new education had replaced the old,"[21] this historiographic great divide possesses little analytic usefulness.[22] It fails to explain, for example, why many moral philosophers welcomed the new psychology with open arms or why later so-called modern university presidents discountenanced it. The persistent notion of "the academic revolution" that occurred in the last quarter of the nineteenth century deflects attention from the essential continuities between the new psychology and the old moral philosophy. Furthermore, the identification of the new psychology with a pure, esoteric experimental science withdrawn from worldly concerns obviates the need to seek institutional, intellectual, and ideological connections between the laboratory and society. By taking as their starting point the creation of laboratories and the academic establishment of a generation of experimenters dedicated to science for science's sake, standard histories of psychology have constricted our conception of the enormous breadth of the new psychology.

In 1887 Joseph Jastrow warned of the restricting tendency to equate the new psychology with experimentalism. Uncertain of the prospects of the laboratory, Jastrow cautioned against "raising 'physiological psychology' to a separate and independent science when it is simply a convenient term for referring to a characteristic attribute of modern 'scientific psychology.'" Admitting that physiological psychology represented "perhaps the most scientifically developed part of it," this founding member and future president of the APA insisted that "the 'new psychology' includes much more than is usually termed physiological."[23]

Jastrow's perspective was assumed by the vast majority of nineteenth-century Americans who professed to study the subject. Even Cattell knew that there was always psychology in America. It existed within social and political philosophy, metaphysics and ethics; it informed pedagogy, medicine, and criminology. Within the collegiate curriculum a pervasive psychologism in the form of "Common Sense" Realism constituted the intellectual keystone of moral philosophy. Outside the college, psychological thought—especially phrenology— informed amateur social science and popular social thought about the mental aspects of human behavior and personality. As the new psychology was fashioned, it could not have been more novel than the ageless questions it would have to confront: How do we obtain and retain valid knowledge? Why are some people bright and others dull? Some mad, others sane? Some fitted for tasks others could not master? Older answers were becoming increasingly unsatisfactory in an emerging secular, industrial, and urban culture. The discipline developed and flourished not primarily as a community of pure scientists but as a scientistic response to this search for social and philosophic order. It did not seek to supply new answers; on the contrary, in most cases it won its place in the curriculum as an empirical science that promised to use new methods to reinforce and to modernize old beliefs.

Physiological psychology constituted the most conspicuous but not the most characteristic aspect of the new science. The esoteric laboratory provided its practitioners with a scientific passport to professional autonomy, an entering wedge into an academic world that offered status, security, and financial support for pursuits that often bore little substantive relation to experimental endeavor. The new psychology in America did not spring full-blown from German experimentalism. It evolved from, and retained ties with, philosophy, medicine, positivistic social reform, educational interests, and those secularized "social science" aspects of academic moralism concerned with the development of an appropriate political and social order. Celebratory accounts of scientific psychology's emergence from epistemological and metaphysical speculation to pure scientific investigation ignore this institutional complexity.

Nevertheless, if one looks at the discipline as a whole, the laboratory remained psychology's vital center. Throughout the period of this study it housed the elite representatives of the science's "community of the competent" whose status derived not only from scientific accomplishment but also from their power to invest nonexperimental activity with authenticity by association. Yet, at the same time, if one examines the pattern of individual careers within the discipline, one discovers that the laboratory represented not a stable community of the competent but a springboard for a vocationally mobile profession. For most psychologists the laboratory represented not the workshop where they spent their professional lives but the seminary in which they were originally trained. Psychologists involved with practical questions never tired of explaining that the problems with which they dealt might eventually become susceptible to experimental solutions. Yet whether this attitude could be translated in specific instances into actuality or whether it remained an unfulfilled expectation, nonexperimental endeavor continued apace and partook of the aura of scientific legitimacy that the laboratory bestowed.

In 1903 Edward Franklin Buchner complained that in spite of what might constitute a statistically impressive "experimental showing . . . somewhere answers must be found for the questions persistently raised by the fact that the laboratory of psychology has not held its men like the other types of laboratory developed by science."[24] The psychological laboratory resembled a sort of academic train terminal where student travelers acquired sheepskin tickets to a variety of professional destinations. Portions of this study intend—if I may extend the metaphor—to follow the tracks and to explore the outlying stops (the clinics, classrooms, asylums, industries, etc.), for what went on beyond the laboratory had a significant impact on what transpired within. Buchner had provided a compelling answer to his own question when he claimed that his profession "has a solemn duty to perform in keeping in touch with the changing social and educational conditions of our national life and in seeing to it that the interests of psychology are adjusted to them."[25] To examine these adjustments is to see why psychology became the science of behavior.

The new psychology originated as a volatile mixture of philosophy, physiology, and social science. As such, its development into a distinct academic discipline was complex and controversial. Finding a fundamental conception of psychology that would sidestep philosophical considerations damaging to psychology's scientific reputation; that would justify experimental psychology as a science distinct from physiology in both purpose and method; and that would simultaneously permit experimentalism to legitimate educational, therapeutic, and managerial objectives would be no easy task. This search for autonomy was essential to psychology's institutional survival and constitutes the keystone of its intellectual development after 1892. In the United States prior to World War I, three major varieties of experimentation successively arose in response to these demands: structuralism, functionalism, and behaviorism.[26] It is worthwhile briefly to describe these "schools," which represented rival conceptions of psychology's purpose and scope, for their development mirrors the intellectual and institutional pressures facing the discipline as a whole.

In the late 1890s structuralism became the label for that version of Wundt's physiological psychology upheld by E. B. Titchener, America's thoroughly Germanized Englishman.[27] He left Oxford to receive his doctoral degree from Wundt in 1892 and immediately accepted the post of laboratory director at Cornell, where he remained until his death. Titchener's psychology was the science of "mind." "Mind" he defines as "the sum total of human experience as dependent upon the experiencing person." When he refers to "consciousness," he is speaking of "the sum-total of mental processes *now*, at any given 'present' time." Consciousness is thus a portion of mind. While the subject matter of psychology is mind, "the direct object of psychological study is always a consciousness."[28]

In order to study the elements and workings of the mind, psychology utilizes the experiment, that is, "an observation that can be repeated, isolated, and varied." The method of psychological investigation, says Titchener, is introspection. The experiment (which will be treated more technically in the next chapter) involves an attempt to observe by means of an intensive, carefully prepared act of introspection the effects upon consciousness of a controllable stimulus. Just as physical science tries to reduce the world to its various chemical elements, psychology must endeavor to discover the composition of mental elements. Having solved the chemical "what," physical science proceeds to trace how these elements react in various combinations. Similarly, the psychologist "takes a particular consciousness and works over it again and again, phase by phase and process by process, until his analysis can go no further. He thus learns to formulate 'the laws of connection of the elementary mental processes.' " Why these reactions occur posed a greater puzzle to Titchener, but he managed to skirt the issue by insisting that it not be taken up until the first two questions had received more adequate attention.[29]

Titchener offered a compelling justification, both intellectual and professional, for concentrating on mental "structures" or contents rather than on mental functions or activities. Experimental psychology was, after all, modeled after experimental physiology, whose remarkable scientific progress and institutional success followed upon the work of scientists who had made physiology a "vivisectional" science. As Karl Rothschuh has remarked:

The kind of questioning inherent in this approach . . . was a "what is it?" rather than "how does it actually happen?" In other words, the performance of individual organs and tissues was of more interest than the determination of the physico-chemical forces responsible for these functions.[30]

Psychologists assumed with the physicists and physiologists whom they sought to emulate that "valid explanations must always be in terms of small, elementary units in regularly changing relations."[31] Asking what forces accounted for physiological activity, preexperimental biological science in Germany leaned speculatively toward vitalistic explanations. Experimentalism's physicalist approach to its data enhanced its scientific image by eliminating such embarrassingly metaphysical questions from its purview. Furthermore, asking what an activity is *for* can become a dangerously teleological endeavor. Structuralism in physiology offered—at least in some respects—metaphysical agnosticism. Titchener, who sought to put as much ground as possible between philosophy and psychology, demanded a similar dispensation.

Titchener likewise eschewed practical psychology. His conception of psychology involved the notion that science proceeds cautiously and incrementally. He cautioned against the naive expectation that such a new psychology might soon offer anything useful to contemporary society. To Titchener the distinction between the psychology of content and the psychology of act was the difference between pure and applied psychology or, as he once put it, between science and technology.[32] Structuralism refused to be either philosophic or practical, which is why it did not prevail. Titchener had managed to divorce psychology from philosophy by developing an intellectual system that justified scientific asceticism. But the same agnosticism that eschewed metaphysics also isolated his program from the demands of more immediate utilities. While Titchener viewed psychology in terms of a systematic theory of logic, both philosophers and practically oriented psychologists were looking at mind in the light of Darwin's theory of adaption. In his influential *Principles of Psychology* William James had treated mind not as an entity, as had Titchener, but as a functional activity of the organism. If consciousness had no practical value, it would not have survived biologically. By invoking Darwinian biology, James restored respectability to the functionally oriented empiricist tradition of psychology. John Dewey and James Rowland Angell, James's former student at Harvard, reinforced that respectability with an experimental framework. Both arrived at the University of Chicago in 1894, Dewey as a professor of philosophy and Angell as director of the new psychology department. Together they transformed Chicago into the new center of American psychology, a psychology that was to become known as functionalism.

In 1906 Angell formalized the functional position in his presidential address before the APA.[33] Functionalism, announced Angell, is concerned with the "how" and "why" of consciousness, whereas structuralism merely investigates the "what." Functionalism conceives of mind "as primarily engaged in mediating between the environment and the needs of the organism. This is the psychology of the fundamental utilities of consciousness."[34] Angell also noted that the functional viewpoint was basic to contemporary experimentation: "We find nowadays both psychologists and biologists who treat consciousness as substantially synonymous with adaptive reactions to novel situations."[35] It is important to note, however, that there was really little difference in experimental design or procedure between structuralism and functionalism. Both used introspection and considered psychology the study of consciousness. The difference came in their respective motives for the experiment and in their different attitudes toward the interpretation of results.[36]

Significantly, functionalism was never as systematic or as dogmatic as structuralism. Angell recognized the broad philosophical context of pragmatism, of which functional psychology was only one aspect. He acknowledged furthermore that the functional viewpoint had existed in psychology prior to the Chicago formulation. He insisted that it must remain "a broad and flexible and organic point of view in psychology."[37] Functionalism was an attitude that encouraged and—in a very real sense—legitimized heterogeneous developments that had already taken root in America (which will be explained more fully in subsequent chapters).

Unlike Titchener, Angell did not withhold his blessing from American interest in applied psychology. On the contrary, functionalism encouraged its development and regarded as evidences of functional psychology's vitality the transfer of attention from static consciousness to "accommodating activity." One of the most compelling examples of this reorientation, claimed Angell, could be found in the rejuvenation of interest in animal psychology, "surely among the most pregnant movements with which we meet in our own generation."[38] When Angell made these remarks in 1906, he had little notion of how pregnant this movement would become. Less than two years later his foremost student of animal psychology, John Broadus Watson, would leave Chicago for a post at Johns Hopkins and there in 1912–13 preside over the birth of behaviorism—the vindictive offspring of animal psychology, a child that had nothing favorable to say about its intellectual godfather, functionalism.

The Chicago functionalists were naturally interested in animal psychology because it furnished objective procedures for observing the capacities that help the organism to succeed. But there was a rub. To the extent that functionalism preserved the method of introspection it violated the old anthropomorphic taboo against interpreting by analogy or empathy. The investigator could attempt to put himself in the place of the animal he was observing, but such a procedure came unscientifically close to intuitive supposition. Functional psychology was biologically oriented, but its standard procedure demanded that the observer use the results of his observations of animal behavior to draw inferences about animal consciousness. Watson adopted a radical parsimony, reasoning that after he had explained functional behavior his job was done. Why drag in consciousness post facto? [39]

Watson communicated his views to his colleagues at Chicago in 1904, but they were unreceptive. Later Angell advised him against advancing a psychology without reference to consciousness. [40] Yet Watson could not tolerate this superfluous requirement even though his co-workers often recognized the perfunctory nature of their post hoc speculation. He accepted from Hopkins an offer of full professorship in experimental and animal psychology and the directorship of the laboratory as well. In 1908 he left Chicago for Baltimore and for freedom from his associates' sanctions.

Watson's revolutionary manifesto appeared five years later. Psychology would no longer be a science of consciousness; rather, it would be a science of behavior. Watson announced:

Psychology as the behaviorist views it is a purely objective experimental branch of natural science. Its theoretical goal is the prediction and control of behavior. Introspection forms no essential part of its methods, nor is the scientific value of its data dependent upon the readiness with which they lend themselves to interpretation in terms of consciousness. The behaviorist, in his efforts to get a unitary scheme of animal response, recognizes no dividing line between man and brute. The behavior of man, with all its refinement and complexity, forms only a part of the behaviorist's total scheme of investigation. [41]

These three brands of experimentation—structuralism, functionalism, and behaviorism—arose at specific junctures of psychology's growth toward professional autonomy. In order to attain such independence, psychology had to separate itself from philosophy, to distinguish itself from physiology, and to promise that it could make practical contributions to a demanding society. Structuralism met the first two requirements; functionalism, the second two. When psychologists returned from the Great War, they thought they had found a conception of psychology that would meet all three criteria in the science of human behavior. "Behaviorism"—though not necessarily the Watsonian variety—was hailed after World War I with as much hopeful enthusiasm as an older generation had received the new psychology after the Civil War. Then, what was new about the new psychology was its experimental basis, and experimentalism—according to the received wisdom—began in Leipzig, Germany.

CHAPTER 2

The Rise of
Experimental Psychology

[P]sychology is passing into a less simple phase. Within a few years what one may call a microscopic psychology has arisen in Germany. . . . This method taxes patience to the utmost, and could hardly have arisen in a country whose natives could be *bored*. Such Germans as Weber, Fechner, Vierordt, and Wundt obviously cannot; and their success has brought into the field an array of younger experimental psychologists, bent on studying the *elements* of the mental life, dissecting them out from the gross results in which they are embedded, and as far as possible reducing them to quantitative scales. . . . There is little of the grand style about these new prism, pedulum, and chronograph-philosophers. They mean business, not chivalry.

—William James
The Principles of Psychology (1890)

We ought never to doubt that Humanity will continue to produce all the types of thinker which she needs.

—William James
"A Plea for Psychology as a 'Natural Science'," *Philosophical Review*
(1892)

Although Titchener regarded Wilhelm Wundt "the founder, not of experimental psychology alone, but of psychology,"[1] Leipzig was hardly the first place psychology was studied. It was, however, where psychology was initially manufactured. The central role accorded Wundt in the development of the modern discipline derives not from any scientific discovery that bears his name eponymously but rather from his heroic propagandizing for experimentalism.[2] He organized the first disciplinary pursuit dedicated to the analysis of a clearly defined set of problems and certified doctorally a professional progeny capable of perpetuating his research agenda.[3] Wundt's career is worth examining briefly, for his endeavors significantly shaped the rhetorical contours of the new psychology in America.

When Wundt was twenty years old he matriculated in 1852 at Heidelberg, where, intent on a medical career, he studied anatomy, physiology, chemistry, and materia medica.[4] Four years later he shifted his vocational interests from medical practice to physiological research and journeyed to Johannes Müller's famed Berlin institute. Returning to Heidelberg, he completed his requirements for the M.D. degree but became *Dozent* and later *extraordinarius* in physiology. In 1858 Herman von Helmholtz arrived at Heidelberg, and Wundt worked under the celebrated experimental physiologist for thirteen years.

In 1873, two years after his failure to obtain Helmholtz's vacated chair, Wundt published the first half of his *Grundzüge*. What he had done in this work was to select those psychological problems which emerged in the course of physiological investigation and then fuse them with the epistemological questions that derived from the associationist tradition of philosophical psychology. Associationists argued that complex mental phenomena could be reduced to sensations, the repetition and compounding of which produced ideas. As early as 1749 the British empiricist David Hartley had furnished associationism with a systematic if speculative physiological basis. A century later Alexander Bain had provided associationism with a refined sensorimotor perspective. By establishing experimental conditions under which stimuli could be controlled and sensation measured, Wundt sought to make psychology an exact science. His effort was rewarded in 1874 by a call to the chair of inductive philosophy at Zürich. The next year, following the publication of the second half of his *Grundzüge*, he accepted the chair of philosophy at Leipzig. There he established his Institute of Experimental Psychology, thus founding, in a very real sense, the modern discipline of psychology.

The Foundations of Experimentalism

Intellectual and ideological imperatives as well as institutional mobility played a part in Wundt's transmutation. His call for a systematic experimental psychology must be seen within the philosophical and scientific context of the debate between vitalists and reductionists in biological circles. In the early nineteenth century, German idealists attempted to reunite the noumenal and phenomenal worlds that Kant had dichotomized on logical and epistemological grounds. The paucity of knowledge about the nature of certain physiological processes encouraged them to postulate the existence of a vital force immanent in the natural world and directing it toward the gradual unfolding of some higher spiritual purpose. Explicit in the work of the embryologist Ernst Haeckel, this *Naturphilosophie* provided teleological explanations for biological processes and led to conclusions potentially damaging to the stature of university-based natural scientists.[5]

In the 1840s Emil du Bois-Reymond and Ernst Brücke, representing a new breed of experimental physiologists trained by Müller, undertook a reductionist campaign against vitalism.[6] In 1847, Helmholtz, another Müller student, published *On the Conservation of Force* in which he brought physiology under the canopy of theoretical physics and viewed the entire world, including living beings, as a closed physical system.[7] He argued that to assume such a force as psychic power distinct from physical energy was to violate the principle of "closed physical causality" and to undermine the possibility of reducing the phenomenal world to a predictable, law-bound order. In 1848–49, du Bois-Reymond identified the vital force of *Naturphilosophie* with negative electrical waves.[8] In the 1860s—by which time Wundt had been trained by Müller, du Bois-Reymond, and Helmholtz—*Naturphilosophie* had been effectively repudiated.[9]

This is not to say, however, that the idealistic underpinnings of that philosophy gave way under the pressure of mechanistic reductionism.[10] In common with most German intellectuals, Wundt subscribed to the view that the activities of the mind determined the structure of physical reality. He was unwilling to accept the deterministic implications of reductionism that would seem to deny free will and human responsibility. For centuries Cartesian dualism—the doctrine that matter is extended, divisible, law-bound, and inert and that mind is unextended, indivisible, free, and active—protected cherished notions of voluntarism. Even Johannes Müller, the "father of experimental physiology," found it difficult to discard dualism. When Müller elaborated Charles Bell's ideas about specific nerve energies in his classic *Handbuch* of 1838, he claimed that the "fibres of all the motor, cerebral and spinal nerves may be imagined as spread out in the medulla oblongata, and exposed to the influence of the will like the keys of a piano-forte."[11] Mind remained the musician; and mind's cortical organ, the brain, was excepted from those physicochemical laws developed to explain sensorimotor action. As Geoffrey Jefferson put it, "The hemispheres were the seat of the 'will': they excited movements by playing on these motor mechanisms. But how they did no one knew and no nice man would ask."[12] By the last quarter of the century, however, the law of the conservation of energy, the demonstrable fact that the cortical areas responded to stimulation, and the theory of evolution that discountenanced the notion that mind could be somehow "superadded" to the biological organism forced psychologists to attend to the findings of neurophysiology. The institutionalization of experimental physiology that threatened to abolish dualism necessitated the invention of an experimental psychology to defend it. Wundt would plead the case for "psychic causality" (and hence for idealism) in rigorously experimental terms, thus borrowing not only the methods but the prestige of modern physiological science. Wundt, the experimentalist, eschewed the "grand style" of philosophical speculation that James admired, but he nevertheless intended a very precious chivalry.

Wundt maintained the familiar doctrine of psychophysical dualism according to which physical and psychological processes are held to be distinct and inexplicable in terms of each other. Psychology, he argued, differs from physiology because it considers different phenomena from a different point of view. Physiology deals with the phenomena of the external "mediate" world, whereas psychology concerns itself with "the facts of immediate experience in relationship to the perceiving subject himself."[13] Physiology seeks to discover the physical and chemical connections between objective occurrences within the neuromuscular system and sees human behavior as a physical phenomenon objectively describable. Introspective analysis of consciousness, however, illustrates that the connection between elements of a subject's "immediate experience" is explicable not in terms of physicochemical relations but in terms of the subject's motivation. Psychology seeks to explicate the subjective aspects of human experience by viewing it as

a succession of representations of movements [not, in other words, of movements themselves], together with feelings, sensations, and representations of ends which precede the action as motives—elements all of which are immediate contents of consciousness. Since these contents constitute a connected whole . . . we get here a purely psychological causal connection which, like the purely physiological one, is homogeneous.[14]

Because psychology deals with the actual material "which our own consciousness presents to us" it is, according to Wundt, concrete and phenomenal. Physiology, on the other hand, succeeds by ruling out the subjective from experience and so is "abstract" and "conceptual."[15] While Wundt does not defend the ontological dualism of mind and matter, he can still maintain that psychology represents an autonomous field because of its distinctive viewpoint. Nevertheless, as Theodore Mischel has perceptively pointed out, Wundt adheres to the essential feature of Cartesianism: the notion of "an 'inner' realm that is epistemologically and psychologically prior to the 'outer' physical world."[16] In this respect, Wundt's conceptualization does not differ significantly from the philosophic tradition of commonsense psychologizing. What makes Wundt's systematic psychology innovative is his assertion that the introspective and fundamentally private examination of subjective experience can be transformed into an objective science by using experimental methods developed by physiologists to study the senses.

This is why Wundt christened his new science "physiological psychology." Procedurally it differs little from what went on in the physiological laboratory, including controlled introspection. Ever since Bell and François Magendie discovered the functional distinction between sensory and motor nerves, the physiology of movement had progressed more rapidly than the physiology of sensation. It was relatively easy to map motor centers along the neural axes of experimental animals by stimulating certain points and monitoring resultant muscular responses. But animals could not describe the sensation occurring during such procedures. The study of sensation was therefore preoccupied with the physics of the sense organs.[17] In experiments on vision, for example, the physiologist knew the physical properties of light waves and of optics and the anatomical aspects of the eye. But, in order to monitor sensation in physiological terms as an afferent neural process, one had provisionally to describe it in psychological terms as an experience: mixed red and yellow lights *look* orange. Since this introspectively derived fact had to be taken into account, it had to be controlled.

Wundt sought to study the psychological perception, not the physiological sensation, and reasoned that the experimenter could stand the physiologist's approach on its head and procure an experimental psychology. Instead of using the subject's account of alterations in his "immediate experience" to help study the physical aspects of sensation, the psychologist could deliberately and measurably alter the sensory stimulus in order to monitor what was happening in one's consciousness. According to Wundt, what prevented the "armchair" variety of psychological introspection from becoming a genuine science was its incapability of controlling external stimuli and, therefore, of artificially reproducing an identical conscious experience that, though subjective, could be compared with the private experiences of other trained observers. An experiment, we may recall, is simply an observation that can be isolated, repeated, and varied. If psychology could duplicate discrete existential experience, then it was entitled to be called an experimental science. Sufficient comparisons would permit generalizations from which would be extrapolated the laws of mental life.

In order to provide introspection with objective controls, Wundt relied on two basic modes of investigation: the reaction-time experiment based on the physiological procedures of Helmholtz and the psychophysical methods based on the midnineteenth-century mathematical constructions of Gustav Fechner and Ernst Heinrich Weber. Helmholtz had succeeded in measuring the speed of the nervous impulse and hence the time taken for a subject to respond to a simple sensory cue; that is, the time required for the nervous impulse to travel through the central nervous system and then to the motor nerves, provoking muscular reaction. The cues, of course, could be made complex. The experimentalist might, for example, direct the subject to respond not merely to any flash of light but to one of a certain color, intensity, or duration. Or the subject might be required to involve two senses by attempting to determine visually the position of a pendulum when a certain sound occurred. By complicating the sensory stimuli, Wundt hoped to isolate times involved in those mediating processes of association occurring within the central nervous system and then to determine through introspective analysis the nature and role of such conscious phenomena as attention, judgment, memory, and inference. The psychologist would employ such physiological apparatus as audiometers and spectroscopes to control the stimulus and chronoscopic devices to record actual reaction times.

Although one could not measure a thought, one could measure stimuli and, indirectly, sensation. In his 1860 monograph, *Elemente der Psychophysik*,[18] Fechner expressed the mathematical relation between stimulus and sensation. E. H. Weber had earlier concluded that a subject successively lifting a set of objects of gradually increasing weight (o^1, o^2, o^3, . . . o^6 . . .) would fail to perceive the difference between, say, o^1 and o^2. The "just noticeable difference" might arrive only with the hefting of o^6. Weber suggested that the perceived change was proportional to the effect of the prior stimulus; developed a mathematical ratio for expressing this relation; and applied this "law" to auditory, visual, tactile, and thermal discrimination. Fechner developed Weber's findings into a law that stated that the strength of a sensation is proportional to the logarithm of the stimulus and, remarkably, into an idealistic philosophic system that attempted to express the relation of mind to body. The technical achievements and limitations of psychophysics need not concern us here. What mattered was the operational translation of "sensations" into reactions that were susceptible to objective investigation and expressible in precise quantitative terms. Psychophysics and reaction-time experiments took their places alongside introspection in Wundt's laboratory.

The Ambiguity of Wundtian Psychology

Symbolically and substantively, Fechner's law remained essential to experimentalism. It provided the scientific momentum that helped propel the developing enterprise toward disciplinary autonomy. At the same time, however, the methodological specialization that enabled psychophysicians to achieve a measure of independence separated Wundtian endeavor from the broader currents of psychological thought into which Wundt sought to place it. Wundt had tried in his way to use positivistic science to save idealism. It seems ironic, therefore, that a new breed of German psychologists after 1890 should castigate his distinctive approach while overlooking his traditional aims. According to Fritz Ringer, these innovators assumed that experimental psychology

was born in the shadow of the natural science. It was therefore infected with "naturalistic" errors from the very beginning. It took physiology as its model; it made the associationist scheme an epitome of all mental processes; it adopted the theory of parallelism. It tried to "dissolve" the notion of an integral soul, and it favored an atomistic and mechanistic analysis of consciousness in terms of primitive and logically isolated units of sensation. It was Lockean, simple-mindedly empirical, and positivistic.[19]

Wundt could not have accepted this assessment. Regarding psychology as the science of immediate experience *(Erfahrungswissenschaft)* and the method of psychology as introspection *(Selbstbeobachtung)*, Wundt railed against physiological reductionism, calling it

materialistic pseudo-science, which sufficiently reveals its tendency to destroy psychology by claiming that the psychological interpretation of mental life has no relation to mental life itself as found in history and society.[20]

Experimental psychology constituted only a part of what Wundt regarded as the "mental sciences" *(Geisteswissenschaften)*, which included his "folk psychology" *(Völkerpsychologie)*, a sort of historical anthropology of mental life.[21] One must study human nature in the round in order to comprehend mind in its totality. While accentuating experimental psychology's technical distinctiveness, Wundt was unwilling to acknowledge its philosophic isolation. For all the talk about *physiological* psychology, Wundt insisted that psychology was closer to philosophy than to the natural sciences. This stance was partly dictated by prudential considerations involving academic staffing, financing, and examining, as Ringer has duly noted.[22] Nevertheless, Wundt's commitment to voluntarism deeply influenced his alliance with philosophy.[23] He wished to preserve a connection between experimentalism and the broad tradition of empirical psychology that took mind as found outside the laboratory "in history and society"; in other words, in those contexts where the voluntaristic nature of mind was more readily manifest.

As a voluntarist, Wundt insisted, in what he called his theory of actuality, that mind is phenomenal, functional activity, not passive material. Since mind is active, consciousness is a mental process; mental life represents a "stream of consciousness" in ever changing flux. Here, however, theory seemed to contradict practice, for in the laboratory processes were necessarily reduced to static units.[24] Wundt's structural topography of mental elements appeared to many the antithesis of the dynamic analyses of active processes his psychological theory seemed to advocate. The trained introspectionist's exquisitely calibrated mental apparatus failed to resemble the ordinary mind found in history and society. Minute inspection of the connection between stimulus and sensation ignored many of the wider psychological interests in the relation of stimulus to the organism's responses, reactions, and adjustments. Furthermore, since infants, monkeys, and madmen could hardly be trained to introspect, Wundt's program provided little impetus to child, animal, and abnormal psychology, or to those interested in problems of education, biological adaption, or in psychopathology and psychotherapeutics.

While Wundt continually revised his synthetic psychological theory to meet some of these objections, critical attention remained focused on that distinctive aspect of his system which changed less rapidly than the contextual theory surrounding it—the experimental program itself. Laboratory research remained "pure," introspective, predominantly associationist, sensationalistic, atomistic, and structural. Rival formulations stressed the often practical, sometimes objective, antiassociationist, organic, dynamic, and functional nature of psychology. Stressing the novelty of their approaches, psychological reformers overlooked their intellectual debts and minimized the continuities between Wundt's approaches and their own by accentuating the positivistic features of the former. Why this happened in Germany is beyond the scope of this account. The phenomenon, however, was not confined to Germany. The American reformer James Mark Baldwin reminded his listeners at the St. Louis Exposition in 1904 that, although the psychological laboratory was a German innovation, "it is not usually seen that this work does not involve a new point of view."[25] Hall regarded Wundt as "a grand importer of English ideas."[26] It remains a historical irony that Wundt is universally regarded as the founder of the new scientific psychology while his system is seen as a dying gasp of naive, sensationalist Enlightenment empiricism.

In the case of American psychology, this irony has bred a certain historical ambiguity in interpreting Wundt's importance. Accordingly, it might be useful to separate—at least for purposes of discussion—the intellectual and institutional aspects of Wundt's achievement and then to consider which aspects actually attracted students to Leipzig. Wundt had precociously provided a social organization for scientific pursuits: a laboratory, a journal, a research agenda, and an experimental ideology. One can evaluate Wundt's contribution to American psychology by examining which aspects of his scientific and philosophic reputation commended him to Americans, which aspects of his program proved most exportable, and how these imports fared in a new intellectual and cultural marketplace. Most important, one must understand how experimentalism competed with other priorities in the American colleges and universities, specifically in the departments of philosophy where it was initially housed.

CHAPTER 3

Sea Change

I would take all [Wundt's] lectures and work in his laboratory, as if for a degree, and say nothing of my purpose: to see if I could find in psychology either a basis for a science of ethics or a trail through psychology to some other science that might lead on to a scientific ethics. . . .

Ethics! There was no foundation in (experimental) psychology for a science of ethics; not that I could find. There might be some day, when psychology itself is scientific. All I got out of my year of German psychology was a lead into biology on the one hand and into sociology on the other, a curiosity to hear and see what the French thought they knew about such matters, and best of all, a training in the experimental method. . . . Lightly I say this now, but to me, in the spring of 1891, the conflict of ideas and emotions was a crisis that weighed heavily on me. I had lost time. I had lost myself.

—FROM *The Autobiography of Lincoln Steffens* (1931)

I recall very well that I had on one occasion been lecturing enthusiastically on Weber's Law to a class of New York City teachers . . . when I was interrupted by one of my gray-haired auditors with this question: "Professor, will you tell us how we can use this principle to improve our teaching of children?" I remember that question better than I do my answer.

—Charles H. Judd, Ph.D.
(Leipzig, 1896)

Historians who tend to equate the new psychology in America with experimentalism have found in Wundt's laboratory at Leipzig the intellectual epicenter of subsequent developments. Indeed, many Americans had studied there prior to 1900: G. Stanley Hall, James McKeen Cattell, Harry Kirke Wolfe, Edward Aloysius Pace, Edward Wheeler Scripture, Frank Angell, Lightner Witmer, Howard Crosby Warren, Harlow S. Gale, George Thomas White Patrick, George Malcolm Stratton, Charles Hubbard Judd, Guy Allen Tawney, and Wilbur M. Urban. All but Hall, Warren, Gale, and Patrick received their doctorates at Leipzig, "the Mecca," in Edna Heidbreder's words, "of students who wished to study the 'new' psychology." These were the "bold young radicals . . . pioneers on the newest frontier of science."[1] Those less adventuresome, like G. T. Ladd, purportedly admitted that there was only Wundt to light the way. Returning to America from their pilgrimage to Mecca, Wundt's students proceeded to found their own laboratories patterned upon the Leipzig model.

The portrait is too heroic, of course. Few participants in this legendary expedition considered themselves pioneers. Few returned sufficiently inspired by the spirit of pure research to pursue active careers as laboratory scientists for any length of time if at all. While few can justly be called experimentalists, they were all sacramentalists. What they imported was not a fresh set of ideas but rather a new liturgy, prescribed forms within which to express devotion to the increase of knowledge. An experiment may denote inquiry into the unknown or demonstration of the known. Most American laboratories were dedicated not to search but to demonstrate, to celebrate ritualistic reenactments of classic experiments as a form of pedagogical worship, to inculcate scientific values among the student novitiate. Philosophy, once taught by clergymen, required new ministers, and Wundt ordained many candidates for these new academic posts.

Wundt Among Many

Both Germany and America, however, were protestant in matters of science as well as religion. In Germany, for example, there remained the potent empiricist tradition of John Friedrich Herbart who in the early nineteenth century denied the possibility of psychological experimentation and whose conception of an unconscious mind premised a psychology beyond the reach of introspection. Leipzig was the center of Herbartianism when Wundt arrived in the Prussian city.[2] A half-century later, William Preyer attempted to observe patterns of innate reflexes or instincts present in infants at birth and elaborations of more complex behavior in later childhood development. His *Die Seele des Kindes (The Mind of the Child)*, published in 1881, constituted the intellectual cornerstone of the child-study movement in the United States and elsewhere. Preyer promised in Hall's words, "education according to nature," an immensely appealing enunciation of applied scientific naturalism. Preyer's focus presages the central problem of American comparative psychology—the determination of what is innate and what is learned. His study became the prototype upon which J. B. Watson performed his first behavioristic studies on infants. Preyer thus inaugurated a new area of empirical and experimental psychology entirely independent of Wundtian endeavor.[3]

Rudolph Hermann Lotze, who assumed Herbart's chair at Göttingen in 1844, opposed the idea that experimental science could provide clues to the nature of mental processes. Interested in empirical psychopathology, Lotze was widely admired in America, especially by James.[4] A contemporary of Wundt, Franz Brentano also viewed psychology as empirical but not experimental and claimed that physiological psychology was not scientific psychology. In a manner that foreshadowed developments in functional psychology, Brentano insisted that psychology must concentrate, not analytically on contents of mind, but phenomenologically on *acts* not observable through introspection.[5] Carl Stumpf, a close friend of James and Brentano, was another outspoken critic of Wundt's experimentalism, who allegedly carried all the laboratory apparatus he needed under his arm in a cigar box. An "act psychologist," Stumpf decisively influenced Max Meyer, who at the University of Missouri announced his behavior psychology two years before Watson.[6] At Berlin in the late nineteenth century, Hermann Ebbinghaus performed studies in mnemonics that showed little indebtedness to the techniques of physiological psychology.[7] These are only a few of the intellectuals whom Americans encountered in Germany.

In short, students at Leipzig could also be found at Heidelberg, Halle,

Berlin, Prague, Würzburg, Göttingen, Munich, and Vienna. They engaged in no single-minded pilgrimage to one holy spot but in a peripatetic grand tour seldom confined even to Germany. In Europe, they discovered a broader spectrum of psychological views than was available to them in America. Consequently, they found little difficulty seeking out viewpoints compatible with their own intellectual and emotional predispositions. Nevertheless, many Americans did gravitate to Leipzig. And since this is so, it will be useful to consider the early biographies of these putative pioneers, to examine the motives that prompted them to go abroad, and to assess the impact of Wundt on their subsequent careers. William James was the first American to investigate what Wundt had to offer.

James set sail in April 1867, long before Wundt had established his reputation as a psychologist. Ironically, James was fleeing the personally unendurable rigors of the Harvard Medical School's laboratory and his ensuing emotional depression and physical collapse. The Germany that attracted James, comments Ralph Barton Perry, "glowed distantly and enticingly as the home of the great and good things of the spirit and of the new and interesting things in literature, science, and philosophy."[8] James sought recuperative intellectual nourishment from them all, but especially from those Germans interested in applying empirical methods in philosophy. Upon reaching Germany, James purchased Lotze's *Medizinische Psychologie* and thoroughly annotated it during his continental journey. Having attended Wilhelm Griesinger's lectures on psychopathology in Berlin, he purchased the doctor's works in Paris on his return trip. James's interest in the abnormal, stimulated by these works, would eventually draw him to the French school of Jean-Martin Charcot.[9]

At the same time, though, James was beginning to realize that

perhaps the time has come for psychology to begin to be a science—some measurements have already been made in the region lying between the physical changes in the nerves and the appearance of consciousness-at (in the shape of sense perceptions), and more may come of it. I am going on to study what is already known, and perhaps be able to do some work at it. Helmholtz and a man named Wundt at Heidelberg are working at it, and I hope I live through this winter to go to them in the summer.[10]

The traveler from Cambridge was sufficiently acquainted with the German academic calendar to realize that his best chance for work with

Wundt and Helmholtz would have been during the school term. Perhaps he feared his inability to return to research. At any rate, his winter hopes melted in the summer heat of Heidelberg where he caught just a glimpse of his two unavailable heroes. James returned "under the influence of a blue despair" to his continental odyssey.[11]

In succeeding years, Wundt's absence from James's early itinerary had not made the latter's heart grow fonder. In 1875 he grudgingly endorsed Wundt's *Grundzüge* as an encyclopedic compilation of facts. James was already protesting the elementism and sterility of "these new prism, pendulum, and galvonometer philosophers."[12] In 1886 he was helping his German colleague Stumpf "compile a register of Wundt's sins." Stumpf himself was quite sanguine about the prospects of Wundt's intellectual demise. "How often already," he declared, "has not psychology been made 'exact' in this way, only to be led back again into the path—into 'psychological' psychology!"[13] James, however, was less optimistic. He felt that this "Napoleon of the intellectual world . . . will never have a Waterloo, for he is a Napoleon without genius and with no central idea which, if defeated, brings down the whole fabric in ruin." "Cut him up like a worm," James cried, "and each fragment crawls; there is no *noeud vital* in his mental medulla oblongata, so you can't kill him all at once."[14]

In an 1888 letter to James, George Santayana, hoping to obtain his reader's blessing to return to Harvard's philosophy department, elaborated a personal view of contemporary philosophy that he was certain James would find congenial:

First I lost my faith in the kind of [idealistic] philosophy that Professors [George Herbert] Palmer and [Josiah] Royce are interested in; and, then, when I came to Germany, I also lost my faith in psycho-physics, and all the other attempts to discover something very momentus. A German professor like Wundt seems to me a survival of the alchemist. What is the use of patience and ingenuity, when the fundamental aim and intention is hopeless and perverse?[15]

Wundt's systematic *experimental* psychology appeared useless to the metaphysically minded and to the practically predisposed alike. Two years after the *Principles* were published and just one week before the APA's first annual meeting, James declared that Wundt was "turning . . . fast into a humbug," and a "mentally dishonest" one at that. By 1905 he confessed that he had ceased reading him.[16] To the extent that American psychology followed James (and that extent is considerable), it diverged from the psychology of Wundt. In 1896 Charles Judd sent James from Leipzig the published version of his first Wundtian researches, urging James to find therein much in common with his own views. The Harvard philosopher responded in six words: "Would to God it were true."[17]

Ten years after James's halfhearted attempt to study with Wundt, he awarded Harvard philosophy's first Ph.D. to Stanley Hall. This was, it will be recalled, also the first American doctorate granted in the field of psychology. As if to keep his string of "firsts" intact, the recipient immediately embarked for Germany to become in psychological legend Wundt's first American student. Though technically accurate, this designation is misleading. Hall felt that he had learned enough philosophy during his first trip to Germany and enough psychology at Cambridge. In 1878 he sought a competence in physiology and, to that end, arrived at Emil du Bois-Reymond's Berlin institute to study muscular physiology. He attended Helmholtz's lectures in theoretical physics. He observed Paul Flechsig's clinical sessions in neuropathology. He visited the psychopathic wards of Karl Westphal's Charité Clinic. When finally in the fall of 1879 he journeyed to Leipzig, it was the physiological laboratory of Carl Ludwig that attracted him. There he attended lectures on physiology, physics, chemistry, and zoology and listened to the aged Fechner "theorizing how knots can be tied together in endless strings." In addition to all this, Hall spent some time in Wundt's psychological laboratory and listened to his lectures on the history of philosophy. Hall reported to James, "I am on the whole disappointed with Wundt," whose role as his mentor the American denied.[18]

Ironically, Hall's criticisms were the opposite of James's. Where the Harvard sage complained of Wundt's "microscopic psychology," reduced to more exactitude than the subject could profitably bear, Hall, by his own admission "aufgegangen in empiricism," described Wundt "as a man who has done more speculation and less valuable observing than any man I know who has had his career."[19] Historians of the social and behavioral sciences have noted the increasingly positivistic stances of succeeding generations in the developing disciplines.[20] Accordingly, Hall's orientation should come as no surprise. Less often recorded, however, is the common tendency of members of each new cohort to retreat in midcareer from their youthful empirical positions. James is certainly a case in point; and so too is Hall. In fact, the pattern is representative. By the mid-1890s, as we shall later see, Hall had rejected Wundt's physiological psychology in much the same manner as James had done. Meanwhile, he had secured his post at Hopkins, the establishment of which, according to Veysey, "sent many more students to Germany from the United States than might otherwise have gone."[21]

Wissenschaft and Wanderschaft

James McKeen Cattell was one such student. Editor, scientific entrepreneur, and popularizer and promoter of applied psychology, Cattell received his doctorate from Wundt in 1886. Son of one of America's prominent educators, William Cassady Cattell, a Presbyterian clergyman and president of Lafayette College, this future leader of American psychology is regarded as the founder of the mental-testing movement in the United States. He developed psychology at Columbia into the country's strongest department after the turn of the century. Cattell tirelessly campaigned for psychology's "application of systematized knowledge to the control of human nature," acerbically criticized introspective psychology, and faithfully supported behavioristic conceptions within his discipline.[22] When he died, E. G. Boring declared to Cattell's son Jacques: "In my opinion your father did more than William James even to give American Psychology its peculiar slant, to make it different from the German psychology from which [according to Boring] it stemmed."[23] Though Cattell did become Wundt's first assistant and maintained an extremely cordial relationship with him, his own approach to Wundtian psychology may best be described as heuristic.

The young Cattell's initial excursion to Germany in 1880 was essentially a grand European tour "to see the world before setting down to an as yet undetermined profession or business."[24] Interested in literature, Cattell ventured to Göttingen because gentility prescribed that the cultured professional man speak German, and Göttingen's "Hanoverian accent was supposed to be the best."[25] There he chanced upon Lotze, of whom he had never heard, and found in him a philosopher interested in ethics and aesthetics and in bridging the gap between science and religion. Removing to Paris and Geneva, Cattell had decided to return to Lotze for doctoral work, but the celebrated philosopher had died in Berlin in 1881. As a distinctly secondary alternative, Cattell journeyed to Leipzig to study briefly with Wundt, of whom he had also never heard prior to his exposure to Lotze. Significantly, he eschewed work in Wundt's laboratory, developing instead an extended essay on Lotze's philosophy that he successfully submitted to Johns Hopkins University in support of his candidacy for a fellowship.[26] He had decided to become a philosopher.

At Hopkins in 1883 Cattell encountered a philosophy with a difference, but it was still removed from the Wundtian tradition. Stanley Hall was lecturing on pedagogy and on the history of philosophy and, according to Cattell, was preoccupied with "insanity and other pathological aspects of psychology."[27] Cattell wished to remain at Hopkins where he was engaged in a set of experiments measuring mental processes that, in the words of Ross, "would reorient American psychology and set a new standard of experimental competence." But Hall, preferring not to have strong men about him, prevented the renewal of his fellowship. In the absence of a viable American alternative, Cattell returned to Leipzig in 1883.[28]

Most significantly, Cattell carried with him his accumulated data, research design, and plans for apparatus in order to complete his experiments on reaction time begun at Hopkins and soon to be published at Leipzig.[29] Reaction-time experiments were in vogue at Leipzig in the 1880s. Wundt had hoped by means of introspective techniques to calculate temporal constants for elementary associations and perceptions and to use those calculations as a basis for more complex experiments on the "higher thought processes." Cattell's perspective, however, constituted a radical departure from this agenda. Whereas Wundtians would implement subjective controls in an attempt to mitigate subjective biases stemming from such differential factors as attention, fatigue and increased proficiency, Cattell considered such controls tantamount to tampering with the manifest data. Such results, he reasoned, "obtained by the [introspective] psychologist in his laboratory do not give the time which a person really consumes in the process of perception, will, and thought."[30] Cattell was interested in recording rather than suppressing these individual differences. Furthermore, he doubted that introspective controls could adequately compensate for discrete subjective biases, and he therefore eliminated introspection from his procedures. In his unpublished autobiography, Cattell claimed that his first paper broke new ground in three respects: "It measured individual differences; it used paper-and-pencil tests, such as are now applied to determine 'intelligence,' . . . ; the methods and results were entirely independent of introspection."[31] He might have added a fourth innovation: "by bringing the experimental conditions nearer the conditions of real life,"[32] Cattell had supplied the psychological experiment with an exceedingly utilitarian framework. Thus, he exhibited an aspect of science that he had always assumed constituted an essential feature of it. He had assumed this scientific persuasion at Lafayette, assimilated it at Hopkins, and activated it at Leipzig. It was therefore fitting that, in addition to himself, four of the remaining eight subjects of this experiment that manifestly emanated from the Leipzig laboratory were his Hopkins associates, Hall, Dewey, Joseph Jastrow, and E. M. Hartwell. A sixth subject was James Mark Baldwin, who would one day direct the Hopkins psychology department but whose stay in Leipzig was calculated at the time to secure "a distinct advantage in the professional race at home."[33] So accustomed is one to viewing American psychology as a German importation that such examples of American psychology's exportation to Germany have gone unnoticed.

Utilizing a distinction common to the social history of other immigrants, historians of intellectuals might ponder both "push" and "pull" factors influencing patterns of transatlantic migration. Cattell was certainly pushed to Germany the second time around rather than attracted to it. Uprooted from Hopkins and competing domestically in the "professional race," Cattell was discovering what one contemporary calculated four out of five Americans in Germany acknowledged: foreign training provided a second wind down the occupational home stretch.[34]

While Cattell was finishing what would become his last semester at Hopkins in 1883, his father had discovered that Henry Seybert, a wealthy proponent of psychic research, had bequeathed $60,000 to the University of Pennsylvania to endow a chair in philosophy provided that the university would raise an additional sum to appoint a commission to examine the validity of modern spiritualism. The elder Cattell immediately began lobbying with his friend and Pennsylvania's provost, William Pepper, for his son's appointment to the Seybert Chair and urged James McKeen to enhance his credentials through publication. In 1883 there existed no American organ for the dissemination of such research as Cattell was conducting. The shortest route between Baltimore and Philadelphia appeared to pass through Leipzig and Wundt's new journal, *Philosophische Studien*. Several factors stayed Pepper's decision concerning the Seybert Chair until 1886 when the characteristically solicitous William Cattell actually traveled to Leipzig to obtain Wundt's recommendation of his son. He brought back to the provost not only Wundt's favorable report but also reprints of the half-dozen articles Cattell had published in the *Studien* in preparation for his Ph.D. Pepper finally agreed to Cattell's occupancy of the chair. Wundt's endorsement most certainly carried less weight with Pepper than did the elder Cattell's ingratiating insistence that salary was no object. James McKeen Cattell might not have occupied the first chair in psychology in the country, as he later claimed, but quite probably he sat in the poorest. He was enlisted at a salary of $300.[35]

In the meantime, Cattell would travel to Cambridge, England, to establish an unofficial laboratory there and to apply his psychometric techniques to anthropometric studies at Francis Galton's famous laboratory in South Kensington, often described as the birthplace of the mental-testing and eugenics movements. There Cattell's interest in individual differences was refined and solidified. His association with Galton proved so absorbing that he delayed his departure for Philadelphia for nearly a year. After finally accepting his Pennsylvania post in December 1887, Cattell virtually commuted between England and the United States during the succeeding year.[36] In 1891 he moved to a far more lucrative post at Columbia, where he extended his pioneering work in mental testing and attracted to the nascent field of intelligence testing the behavioristic learning theorist Edward Lee Thorndike. In later years, when Cattell would claim that Galton, not Wundt, was "the greatest man whom I have known," he was not only paying a personal tribute but was also asserting an intellectual allegiance. Wundt had merely certified Cattell; Galton had educated him.

Shortly after Cattell arrived at the University of Pennsylvania he would educate another psychologist whom he would send to Wundt for certification. Lightner Witmer had just completed his bachelor's requirements in the Wharton School of Business, entered the University of Pennsylvania Law School, and registered for graduate work in political science under Edmund J. James when he was introduced to Cattell. Needless to say, he had not been considering psychology as a career. But the philosopher George Stuart Fullerton, James's academic archrival at Pennsylvania, weened Witmer away from James by offering him an assistantship under Cattell if he would change his major from political science to experimental psychology. In the spring of 1891, as the philosophy department deliberated over Cattell's replacement, Witmer was offered an enormous salary hike to $1,200, "on condition," said Witmer, "that I would go to Leipzig and remain there for eighteen months."[37] When Witmer later quipped that he had gotten nothing from Germany save his doctoral degree, he overlooked the obvious: he obtained in Germany an American post as Cattell's replacement.

Witmer corroborated Hall's criticism of Wundt's slovenly research methods and James's complaints of his "mental dishonesty." He recalled:

Cattell had put me to work before I left for Europe on a problem on the measurement of the reaction times of all classes of persons. Wundt wouldn't hear of this being a psychological problem and banned it immediately, his idea being that experimental psychology was really based on the conscious reaction of subjects and required concurrent introspection. . . . [H]e made Titchener do over again an investigation on reaction time because the results obtained by Titchener were not such as he, Wundt, had anticipated. Also, he excluded me as subject . . . because in his opinion my sensory reaction to sound and touch was too short to be a true sensory reaction. He advised me to get a cardboard pendulum and practice so as to increase my reaction time and presumably make it truly sensory. I was disgusted at this suggestion.

Understandably Witmer concluded, "I do not consider that I owe much to Wundt."[38] Four years after his return from Leipzig, Witmer, like James, was trenchantly criticizing the obsolescence of "brass instrument psychology" and followed in the practicalist footsteps of Hall and Cattell by founding the world's first psychological clinic. We shall return to Witmer in a later chapter because his career as "clinical psychologist" is especially germane to the question of behaviorism's ascendancy.

Even those students who did feel that they owed something to Wundt often found it difficult to express their indebtedness in the American academic context. Harry Kirke Wolfe received his Ph.D. from Wundt along with Cattell in 1886. Born in Nebraska, he returned to the state's university in the fall of 1889 as professor of philosophy and proceeded to establish a demonstration laboratory for undergraduates the next year. Believing that experimental psychology in America could survive only if based on "general cultivation, pedagogical foundation, and original research,"[39] Wolfe attempted to secure facilities for the latter purpose by promoting the value of psychology to the former two. Finding funds for books and equipment virtually nonexistent, Wolfe proposed in his 1890–91 departmental report that experimental psychology constituted for students a mental discipline "as good . . . as the determination of sugar in a beet or the variation of an electric current."[40] Since Wolfe could not logically maintain that psychology represented a mental discipline *superior to* agricultural science or electrical engineering, his argument was essentially moribund. "Democracy's Colleges," the land grant universities, were striving to illustrate to farmers and mechanics the particular attractions of their curricula.[41] Administrators could find no compelling reason to purchase psychological apparatus for disciplining minds busied with beets and batteries. Existing facilities would do quite as well.[42]

Wolfe tried to redeem his argument by insisting that, in addition to its advantages as mental discipline, "the study of mind is the most universally *applied* of all sciences."[43] He anticipated his department's "practical bearing on methods in the public schools" and predicted psychology's "aid to scientific pedagogy."[44] This, of course, was work for which his austere Wundtian background had hardly prepared him. As for the putative reincarnation in America of the German investigative spirit, Wolfe, who confessed that "the only certain immortality was the immortality of the printed page," never, according to his most noted student, published a piece of research after he left Leipzig.[45]

Wolfe's mortality was institutional as well as literary. The reasons for his dismissal from the University of Nebraska in 1897 are not entirely clear, but certainly his importunate campaigning for laboratory expansion and his lack of training in matters pedagogical contributed to his downfall. This can be inferred from the qualities and applied concerns of the men who superseded him: Albert Ross, Thaddeus Lincoln Bolton, and Ferdinand C. French.[46] Had Wolfe hungered for research facilities after his departure from Nebraska, opportunities were not lacking. He received "numerous offers from other universities" that might have proved more hospitable to his professed calling.[47] Instead he remained in Nebraska, first as superintendent of the South Omaha Public School System, then as principal of Lincoln High School.

The course of events in Nebraska nicely foreshadow the subsequent contours of psychology's academic institutionalization in America.[48] Psychology in general would flourish neither as mental discipline nor as research science but as the intellectual underpinning and scientific legitimator of utilitarian pursuits, especially in the field of education. Undergraduate preparation and research programs would be enriched to the extent that they appeared to assist this primary undertaking.[49] With few exceptions, those Wundtian importations which escaped the scrutiny of inspecting administrators in American colleges' custom-houses quickly passed out of vogue as they failed to sustain the professional needs of academic psychologists. Harry K. Wolfe learned this lesson well. Reschooled in Nebraska's public educational system, he was recalled to the university in 1906 as professor of educational psychology in the Department of Education.

It was in 1906, also, that Edward Wheeler Scripture, having abandoned American psychology three years earlier, received his medical degree from Munich. Scripture never understood, in his words, "why I became interested in psychology . . . and foolishly refused an offer from my father to send me to medical school." For emphasis he added, "Foolishly, I repeat."[50] Twenty-five years after he rectified this mistake, he declared himself unable to read a psychology text without becoming bored. Such sentiments are especially interesting when voiced by the most prolific classical experimentalist in America in the 1890s and the first popularizer of strictly laboratory psychology in the English-speaking world. His disenchantment suggests the fate of the orthodox in America.

After studying with Ebbinghaus at Berlin and Richard Avenarius in pedagogy at Zürich, Scripture moved to Leipzig in 1888, receiving his doctorate from Wundt in 1891. He was a fellow with Hall at Clark until G. T. Ladd called him to Yale in 1892 to direct the psychological laboratory. Scripture immediately created the annual *Studies from the Yale Psychological Laboratory* (1892–1902), most of which represented Scripture's own work, primarily on the sensory aspects of tone. His endeavors apparently attracted few students and provided little grist for Ladd's philosophical mill.[51] Antagonism between the two men, stemming from disputes over who properly should define the scope of psychological investigation at Yale, was compounded in 1895 when Scripture published his first popular work, *Thinking, Feeling, Doing*, a laboratory manual for the layperson. Its author wrote the book "expressly for the people . . . as evidence of the attitude of the science in its desire to serve humanity." Frustrating that desire, according to Scripture, was the armchair speculation of the "new philosophers" such as James and Ladd. Modern philosophy "has contributed nothing but stumbling blocks in the aid of psychology. . . . This new philosophy has no more and no less connection with psychology than with physics, mathematics, and astronomy. . . . Such a philosophy would no more think of claiming a right to meddle in psychology than it would to regulate the manufacture of lathes in a machine shop." Scripture's second popular book, *The New Psychology*, repeated these complaints.[52]

Here at last was an authentic experimentalist prospectus. And it created a furor. Subsequent generations of psychologists would find in Scripture's call for the separation of psychology from philosophy an ideological stance so congenial to their professional aspirations and emotional predispositions that commentators have since tended to identify Scripture's precocious views with the temper of American psychology in the 1890s. Few contemporaries, however, even those sympathetic to Scripture's viewpoint, were willing to equate the new psychology with what went on in the experimental laboratory. Notwithstanding its centrality, the laboratory was simply too flimsy a platform to support an entire profession. James announced his disgust over such "little separate college tin-trumpets" as the *Yale Studies* represented. He regarded Scripture himself as a "barbarian." James's experimentalist-in-residence, Hugo Münsterberg, provided a more penetrating if less livid description of Scripture when he called him an experimentalist but not a psychologist.[53] Ladd became so incensed over his inability to prosecute his own interests in the Yale laboratory that he requested a university committee to investigate his department's state of affairs. The committee's failure to resolve the dilemma contributed to Ladd's forced resignation, Scripture's firing, and the Yale psychology department's virtual though temporary disintegration.[54]

Scripture continued his life's work according to the "specifically German" scientific methods he had learned at Leipzig. Significantly, he found that he could not do so as an American psychologist. In 1912 he founded "a laboratory in speech neurology" at London's West End Hospital for Nervous Diseases. Finally, he became professor of experimental phonetics at Vienna in 1923.[55] But he had at Yale inspired three psychologists: Carl E. Seashore, J. E. Wallace Wallin, and J. Allan Gilbert. They all entered the child-centered field of clinical psychology, where their mentor might have found his niche had he not ostracized himself from the philosophically oriented psychologists who still controlled the discipline in the 1890s. Scripture acknowledged that there were "only two important regions of psychology which had not received contributions from Leipzig": capacity psychology and educational psychology.[56] These were precisely the directions in which American psychology was rapidly expanding. Thus, when he confessed his inability to understand why his work in linguistics was never considered experimental psychology,[57] he unconsciously acknowledged his failure to adapt to the exigencies of the American environment.

Charles Hubbard Judd received his doctorate from Wundt in 1896. He had come to Yale in 1902 as an instructor in psychology and became involved in the Scripture-Ladd dispute. Judd's personal allegiances were unmistakable. He had received Wundt's authorization to translate his *Grundriss der Psychologie* into English. His autobiographical reminiscences and published eulogy of Wundt are among the most flattering memorials to the German master.[58] And his German training no doubt contributed to his impatience with Ladd, who reported that in 1904 Judd "frankly told me that I had not learned anything in Psychology during the last five years."[59] Yet, despite his admiration of Wundt and his support for Scripture, when Judd published his 1907 *Psychology* he declared: "I am quite unable to accept the contentions, or sympathize with the views of the defenders of a structural or purely analytical psychology."[60] Judd was deeply aware that Wundt "felt keenly the dropping away from him of some of his most notable students."[61] An inquiry into the young American's early education reveals the roots of his own apostasy.

Judd had graduated from Wesleyan University in 1894, one year before E. L. Thorndike.[62] There he fell under the influence of the philosopher Andrew C. Armstrong who had, in turn, studied under Princeton's James McCosh, an early absorber of the new psychology. Armstrong, like another McCosh student, James Mark Baldwin (whose views on structuralism will be delineated in chapter 9), had attended Wundt's lectures in the 1880s and had helped build Wesleyan's reputation as a philosophically and scientifically avant-garde institution.[63] Specifically, Armstrong sponsored psychology as the scientific foundation of pedagogy. He used James Sully's *Outlines of Psychology: With Special Reference to the Theory of Education*[64] as a required text and frequently published in Nicholas Murray Butler's *Educational Review*. Reflecting the evolutionary concerns that had stimulated the development of the new psychology in America, the Wesleyan philosopher acquainted his students with James, Spencer, Galton, Lloyd Morgan, and Alexander Bain, as well as with Wundt. The archetypal American psychology—functionalism—emerged, as we shall later see, from an evolutionary genetic psychology devised to underwrite educational and social theory. Judd's first book, *Genetic Psychology for Teachers*, represented an early attempt at this fusion of the theoretical and the practical. His *Psychology* text of 1907 constituted a systematic functionalist synthesis, appearing some months after James R. Angell delivered his presidential address to the APA, "The Province of Functional Psychology."[65] An incipient "functionalism" was gestating at Wesleyan long before Judd's journey to Germany. It is possible that Leipzig's greatest intellectual contribution to American psychology was a negative one of providing a systematic conception of psychology's purpose, method, and scope in opposition to which a native American functionalism could refine and sophisticate its opaque perspective.

Nevertheless, Judd's *Arbeit* was a standard treatment of the perception of spatial distance upon tactile stimulation. He began work in the area of visual space perception at Leipzig and would continue research in this area for a year after his return to Wesleyan in 1896 as instructor in philosophy. At Leipzig, however, Judd's broader interests were already manifest. His interest in social psychology led him to the historian Karl Lamprecht, an avowed evolutionist. He entered Flechsig's course in psychiatry and selected as a minor field the history of pedagogy. It is probable that his interest in education was intensified by his contact with Ernst Meumann, who became Wundt's chief assistant in charge of the laboratory just as Judd arrived at Leipzig. Wundt would subsequently label his assistant a "deserter" for assuming leadership of German educational psychology. Meumann's *Über Oekonomie und Technik des Lernens* appeared in 1903, the same year as Judd's *Genetic Psychology* and Thorndike's *Educational Psychology*. Even Leipzig (let alone Germany) was larger than Wundt.[66]

Judd left Wesleyan in 1898 to accept an appointment in New York University's School of Pedagogy. It was there that Judd perceived the need to make concrete the putative connection between experimental psychology and pedagogy. Judd recalled his

lecturing enthusiastically on Weber's Law to a class of New York City teachers who were seeking increases in their salaries by listening to me, when I was interrupted by one of my gray-haired auditors with this question: "Professor, will you tell us how we can use this principle to improve our teaching of children?"[67]

A similar challenge had two years earlier prompted the University of Pennsylvania's Lightner Witmer to develop the new, practical field of clinical psychology.[68] Challenged to relevance, Judd began immediately "to enlarge the range of [his] experimentation" by studying children's language reactions and motor processes involved in handwriting. (Note how enlarging one's range meant in practice forsaking introspection.) Judd moved to the University of Cincinnati in 1901 as professor of psychology and pedagogy and then, in 1902, to Yale, which seemed to promise more "opportunity for scientific work" along the lines he was pursuing. He was unprepared for the dissension he would find in New Haven. When he left in 1909 for the University of Chicago, the headquarters of American functionalism, he did so because he saw the chance to extend his investigations "into practical fields" and to enlist in these efforts a commodity lacking at Yale—graduate students.[69] Armstrong's interests at Wesleyan were beginning to bear fruit.

Looking back on his German experience in an attempt to reconcile his Leipzig training with his functionalist perspective, Judd accentuated those aspects of Wundtian psychology closest to his subsequent concerns: voluntarism, actuality theory, and historical psychology. Judd insisted that Wundt "recognized the fact that mental life is a process and not a collection of items. His teaching was functional and synthetic, never atomistic and structural." Judd attempted to show that the German's social psychology, his *Völkerpsychologie*, had been overlooked by American psychology. These works, however, had not been available in the 1890s. Moreover, although Wundt labeled sensations and perceptions "mental processes," the fact remains that they were treated in the laboratory "as static bits of consciousness," as Judd himself so treated them while in Germany.[70] At Wesleyan, Judd had read his James, and, in retrospect, he found it easy to overlook "the false elementism" that American psychologists came to associate with Leipzig and that educators found so jejune.

The blending of evolutionary, ethical, and educational concerns that Judd had encountered in Armstrong at Wesleyan and that he had distilled in his genetic experimental pedagogy occurred in a variety of contexts. Edward Aloysius Pace, a Roman Catholic priest and Neo-Scholastic philosopher, had received his theological training in Rome in 1886 at a time when the church was cautiously elaborating a social philosophy sensitive to the needs of an industrial age and the claims of science. Pace remained in Europe to study biology at Louvain, chemistry at Paris, and physiology at Leipzig. He chanced upon a copy of Wundt's *Grundzüge* in a secondhand Parisian bookstore and capped his scientific education with a philosophical dissertation under Wundt on Herbert Spencer's evolutionary theory. In 1891 Pace established a demonstration laboratory in the newly established Department of Experimental Psychology at the Catholic University of America in Washington, D.C. In 1893 he introduced a course called the "Theory of Evolution and Abnormal Study." Soon afterward he involved himself almost entirely in educational concerns and established the Institute of Pedagogy in New York in 1902.[71] His successor, Thomas Verner Moore, a Benedictine monk, had also studied with Wundt, but the German's influence on him was overshadowed by that of Charles E. Spearman, whose factorial analysis promised to resuscitate the idea of "faculty" so compatible with Thomistic philosophy.[72] Moore, who had obtained his medical degree at Hopkins, worked as a psychopathologist and became one of the first American psychologists to accept psychoanalysis. Pace the educationalist and Moore the psychopathologist owed little to Wundt.[73]

Pace's American acquaintance at Leipzig, Frank Angell, likewise received his doctorate from Wundt in 1891. A high school physics teacher, he had intended to study that subject at Würzburg but was distracted at Leipzig by a group of students led by Titchener who were attempting to apply the laws of physics to mental processes. Angell established a laboratory at Cornell before moving to Leland Stanford University in 1892 as assistant professor of psychology. He remained on the Pacific slope the rest of his lifetime, contributing modestly to research on visual imagery and reaction time and battling heroically against the infiltration of applied psychology at Stanford. Angell's orthodoxy was matched by his isolation, which was only partly geographic. From 1892 until the Great War, Stanford granted only two Ph.D.'s in psychology. By that time Angell's replacement at Cornell, Titchener, had directed to completion thirty-seven theses and had concluded that his predecessor had "definitely turned his back upon systematic questions." What Angell had turned toward, in the absence of a vigorous, or even viable, psychological community at Stanford, was intercollegiate sports. He functioned virtually as the university's athletic director for a quarter of a century, and it is perhaps fitting that the university structure that bears his name is not a science building but a football stadium. Titchener alone kept the Wundtian banner flowing over America.[74]

In the 1890s Howard C. Warren, Harlow Gale, and G. W. T. Patrick studied with Wundt but did not take degrees at Leipzig. Warren, in fact, obtained his doctorate only in 1917 when he submitted a portion of his *History of Association Psychology*[75] to Watson at Hopkins in partial fulfillment of requirements. This work illustrates the central influence of Spencer and Bain upon Warren. Nevertheless, at the suggestion of Princeton's A. T. Ormond, Warren sailed to Germany to work with Wundt, of whom he knew nothing save that Leipzig pos-

sessed "the best facilities." Warren admitted that he never "got close
to Wundt" nor to "any of the laboratory crowd." Dissatisfied with
Leipzig, Warren matriculated at Berlin where he worked with Ebbinghaus. He visited Hippolyte Bernheim's clinic at Nancy, France,
and then returned to Germany to study under Stumpf despite the lack
of laboratory facilities at Munich. Warren was recalled to Princeton in
1893 by Baldwin, an archopponent of Wundtian psychology. When
Baldwin left for Hopkins a decade later, Warren assumed direction of
Princeton's laboratory and fought for the inclusion of genetic psychology in the curriculum. Baldwin had inspired Warren's interest in
animal investigations and in child study, activities manifestly at odds
with Wundt's sense of the scope of experimental psychology. These
interests undoubtedly encouraged Warren's sympathy toward Watson's behaviorism. Though Warren remained an eclectic experimentalist, he acknowledged his profound appreciation of the viewpoints of
Jacques Loeb, Max Meyer, and Watson. He admired "the spirit of *ex-
actness* and *thoroughness* in research" that Wundt represented but concluded that Wundt's viewpoint, theories, and findings had been "challenged," "discarded," and "superseded."[76]

Harlow Gale returned from Leipzig in 1894 even less indebted to
Wundt than was Warren. Like Wolfe, Gale was a midwesterner with
cosmopolitan training and local allegiances. Born to a wealthy Minneapolis family, he obtained his A.B. in 1885 at Yale, where he found
Ladd's psychology "a pretense to science"[77] but discovered in the Social Darwinian William Graham Sumner an intellectual hero. After
two years at his hometown University of Minnesota where he studied
economics, Gale returned to New Haven to write his philosophy dissertation on evolutionary ethical theory. In 1890 he began his course
of education in Germany that included work at Flechsig's clinic and
at Leipzig's Anatomical Institute as well as at Wundt's Institute. He
arrived back at Minnesota in 1894 and immediately established a laboratory in the Department of Philosophy.[78]

Although this laboratory reflected his basically physiological training in Germany, Gale, according to David Kuna, "was much too
functionally oriented to neglect the wide range of situations to which
psychology might be applied."[79] As Sumner had resigned his minis-

try, Gale had been deflected from clerical studies by a similar compulsion to find scientific solutions to social problems. He regarded most laboratory experimentation as "petty and trivial peices [sic] of kindergarten busy-work" devised to provide younger experimenters with "subjects on which to demonstrate their grit in climbing the professional ladder."[80] Gale did not climb that ladder. His dismissal from Minnesota stemmed from personal antagonisms and university opposition to his own leftist political persuasions, not from any disparagement of applied psychology. With the exception of a certain alarm expressed over Gale's inclusion of sex education in the psychological curriculum, Minnesota's administration welcomed his pioneering studies in the psychology of advertising and his educational research on children's acquisition of vocabulary. Three years after his departure, the university began building what would become one of the greatest centers of applied psychology in the country.[81]

Like Gale, George Patrick was drawn initially to the ministry, receiving his bachelor of divinity degree at Yale the same year Gale earned his bachelor of arts. Patrick spent the next academic year with Hall at Hopkins, completing his doctoral requirements in 1888, a year after he had assumed the position of professor of philosophy at his alma mater, the University of Iowa. There he immediately established a demonstration laboratory. Patrick was perhaps the only academic professional who did not venture to Leipzig to obtain some sort of certification. He studied with Wundt in 1894, after his career had been decisively fashioned. This fact provides an incidental verification of Gale's thesis on the apprenticeship function of research, for Patrick never published an experimental paper. The placement of individuals such as Patrick, Guy Allen Tawney, and Wilbur M. Urban on the historical roster of Wundt's American students seems designed merely to add numerical weight to the claims for American psychology's indebtedness to the German master.[82] When Urban, for example, was invited to the 1920 Iowa symposium on Wundt's contributions to psychology, he declared himself "not in a position to judge."[83]

George Malcolm Stratton was in a position to judge Wundt's contributions to American psychology, and he did so appreciatively.[84] In 1893 he was an instructor in philosophy at the University of California when his chairman, George H. Howison, solicited James's advice on the feasibility of establishing an experimental laboratory there. James's reply is worth quoting at length:

> Give up the notion of having a laboratory of *original research*. My private impression is that the business is being overstocked in America, and that the results are not appropriate to the money expended. I refer to "exact" work like that of Wundt's laboratory. I fear that in a few years, if nothing more significant in the way of ideas emerges from it all, there may be a reaction which will make trustees repent of their enterprise in founding laboratories.[85]

James understood the motive behind Howison's request. Frank Angell had established his laboratory at Stanford University, the self-styled Johns Hopkins of the West, in 1892. Berkeley, the Pacific Coast's "Harvard," was competing with Palo Alto for students and funds. James, in fact, had a few years earlier been in Howison's position and had adopted the strategy he now counseled against. When Hall created the Department of Psychology at Clark, the threat to Harvard's hegemony had moved from Baltimore to an uncomfortable proximity to Cambridge. Hall and James would exchange verbal blows over the duplication of effort such proximity entailed. In the meantime, however, James initiated a grand fund-raising effort, eventually procuring $4,300 in an attempt to equal and, if possible, to surpass the quality of Clark's experimental facilities. "The situation," as James put the matter frankly, "is this. We are the best university in America, and we must lead in psychology."[86] He penned these words to Münsterberg, whom he would induce to Harvard in 1892 to direct the research laboratory.

And yet two years later, when Howison suggested a similar post at Berkeley for similar reasons, James deprecated the idea. He recommended instead someone "who should be a competent psychologist and exhibitor of classic experiments without having to torture his brain to devise new varieties of insipidity for publication, as he would have to do on the basis lately fashionable." When Howison proposed Stratton for the task, James cautioned against hope that Stratton, "already caught with metaphysical fever," would not forsake the laboratory after a few years in order to write books, as James himself had done. There are "metaphysicians," James said, and there are "tinkers." If Stratton found tinkering absorbing, "two years would be ample to teach him what has been acquired and enable him to teach."[87] And so Stratton, having (as had Witmer) been provided with the promise of professional permanence at his alma mater (A.B., 1888), left in 1894 for two years' work at Leipzig.

To James's, and perhaps to Howison's surprise, Stratton returned to remain both a tinker and a metaphysician. Though Stratton is most often regarded, when he is referred to at all, as a pastoral psychologist,[88] he did continue experimental work—mainly in the field of visual perception and often with an eye (the pun is appropriate) to practical applications.[89] Though Stratton, like many others, was appalled by Wundt's own careless research techniques, he did acknowledge that Americans

who received in those early days the broader currents from Leipzig were thus helped toward an immunity to certain recurrent liabilities. They distrusted any utter subjection of psychology as a whole to physiology, or to animal studies, or to psychopathology.[90]

Stratton's own career[91] illustrates an even broader dispensation, one that obtains in all the cases cited above with the possible exception of Angell. Neither would American psychology solely or even primarily be confined by the experimentalist model.

Patterns

This collective portrait of psychological "pioneers" mirrors the difficulty in extrapolating an absolute relation of German training to American practice. To ask why these inquirers ventured abroad and to ask what it was they obtained there is not to pose the same question, for in many cases purposes were ill-defined and careers undecided. *Wanderschaft* played a more important part in these students' itineraries than did *Wissenschaft*; study abroad often represented a vocational moratorium, a time for decision and discovery. And since the history of intellectuals must always be more than intellectual history, it must not be overlooked that European travel was novel, exciting, expansive, liberating, and cheap. Academic *Wanderjahre*—the easy movement from one German university to the next—embellished youthful adventure with lofty purpose.

At the same time, however, it is obvious that such men as Cattell, Witmer, and Stratton traveled the straight and narrow path of academic careerism directly to Wundt's laboratory door. Ultimately, perhaps, disparate purposes for tarrying at Leipzig became reconciled in the end result. Both the eclectic wayfarer and the coldly calculating careerist realized that German education possessed enormous prestige. Once they had completed their courses of study, all capitalized on their certification in the American market.

The career of J. R. Angell nicely reflects the mixture of vocational and cultural opportunity that German study represented. Undecided in 1891 whether to pursue a career in philosophy or psychology, Angell accepted the advice of John Dewey, under whom he studied at the University of Michigan, to enter Harvard's graduate program in philosophy.[92] At the start of his second semester at Cambridge in February 1892, his father and president of Michigan, James Burrill Angell, informed him that his cousin Frank Angell had just been "called to the Chair of Phys. Psychology in Leland Stanford @ $3000 salary." The elder Angell added prudentially, "The business is looking up."[93] Frank Angell's success in converting his Leipzig credentials into prestigious positions at Cornell and Stanford undoubtedly contributed to the younger Angell's acknowledged eagerness to work with Wundt.[94] The establishment of the APA the month after this encouraging news assured him that the business was indeed prospering. William James, however, wished Angell to remain at Harvard's laboratory as Herbert Nichols's understudy. Angell sought the seasoned advice of his father, who reasoned that "Dewey is proof that one can succeed without going abroad. But I know he wishes he had been able to go when younger." As aware as anyone of the qualities that academic administrators looked for in potential professors, the Michigan president declared that the purpose of foreign study was "for the general culture and broadening of horizon which it gives to our fitter to profit by it [sic]."[95] Fit by any standard, Angell obtained his cousin's letters of introduction and departed for Leipzig.

When Angell discovered at Leipzig that there were no vacancies in Wundt's laboratory, he spent the year instead at Berlin and Halle. He had completed his thesis on Kant under Hans Vaihinger at Halle, but before he had the opportunity to revise it he was called to Minnesota as instructor in philosophy and psychology. Though he realized that "the prospect of a doctor's degree from a German University of high standing was not lightly to be dismissed,"[96] the Minnesota offer coincided with his marital plans, enabling him to end one long-standing engagement by beginning an academic one of briefer duration. Soon after he was summoned by Dewey to Chicago.

Two aspects of this episode are particularly worth noting here. First, contrary to the commonplace assumption that Americans were prompted abroad by "poor opportunities" for research in the United States, Angell would certainly have received better training in experimental psychology had he remained at Harvard, which possessed, as Dewey informed Angell, laboratory facilities superior to any in Germany.[97] Finding no opportunity for such work at Leipzig, Angell declared that he would have gone to Freiberg to study with Münsterberg had not Münsterberg himself just left for Harvard. Cambridge was not the only place Angell might have worked. Münsterberg's arrival at Harvard, after all, represented a tactical aspect of Harvard's competition with the psychology department at Clark. By 1892 the United States possessed more and better-appointed laboratories than could be found in Germany,[98] and yet many Americans continued to choose Leipzig. No doubt they realized that the prestige of the German university and the well-rounded character that European educational travel purportedly enhanced were significant criteria for selecting new academic professionals.

Second, that Angell prospered without his doctorate in psychology suggests that in the early 1890s it was still possible to secure a post without such formal credentials.[99] Ironically, it was precisely this situation that propelled many of the aspirants after Angell into the tenacious grasp of what James called "the Ph.D. octopus." As the career itself became more viable, the tendency to optimize credentials accelerated. German universities—of which Leipzig at the time was the most prominent—were notorious diploma mills where doctorates could be obtained quickly. Since speed was essential in "the professional race at home," transatlantic steamships were preferred to continental railways.

Once embarked on their cisatlantic careers, psychologists exhibited an amazing diversity of interests. Professional lives are individual lives, varied and idiosyncratic despite their circumscription by specific scientific norms, techniques, and objectives. In the case of psychology, diversity itself seems to be the dominant pattern. The broad range of American endeavor suggests that psychologists were exposed to many other influences besides that of Wundt. One thing is certain: the German experience did not convert many Americans to the "religion of research." The career profiles of Americans trained at Leipzig verify Buchner's observation that the psychological laboratory failed to hold its men. But by what authority was it ever supposed to?[100] One should not infer from the fact that students were trained in the laboratory the supposition that they were therefore trained for the laboratory. Their experimental apprenticeships imbued them with the "scientific attitude," and this was sufficient credential to provide them with vocational niches in a growing academic profession. Certainly, they learned specific techniques and studied esoteric bodies of knowledge. Some even retained and refined these acquisitions, continuing to research in the manner in which they were trained. To concentrate on these few, however, is to miss much of what shaped the discipline in America.

"[B]est of all, a training in the experimental method": that was how Lincoln Steffens rationalized his year of study in Leipzig.[101] Journalist, cultural critic, and political activist, Steffens obviously did not employ this method as a vehicle for furthering Wundtian psychology in America. He regarded it as an analytic tool for examining a host of "real-life" problems; as an essential modern mode of knowledge; and even as an inductive approach to a "revolt against formalism" in all areas of social, political, and cultural thought.[102] Instead of viewing the new American psychologists as importers and distributors of physiological psychology, one might well look at them in this more general light as purveyors of a "scientific" outlook on vital philosophic and social questions. Most were not researchers, but all were investigators.

A few months after the APA was founded, the noted biologist and president of Stanford University, David Starr Jordan, announced that

psychology is in the best schools completely detached from metaphysics, and is an experimental science as much as physiology or embryology. By its side ethics and pedagogics are ranging themselves—the scientific study of children, and the study of the laws of right, by the same methods as those we use to test the laws of chemical affinity.[103]

Jordan had gotten the intellectual order of battle right: the philosophic, scientific, and practical contingents of psychology marched along
together. Yet to assume that those interested in ethics on the one side
and those preoccupied with child study on the other side were commanded by that small band of experimentalists in the middle was to
be betrayed by a metaphor. Neither philosophers nor pedagogical scientists in 1892 could possibly have submitted their precious insights
to precise experimental verification like so many chemical elements.
This is not to say that experimental psychology failed to provide scientific legitimation to their endeavors. The conviction that it could do
so was what originally impelled philosophers to enlist it. In the 1870s,
when psychology was—more explicitly than today—both science and
metaphysics, academic philosophers desperately sought to restore scientifically an ethical system intellectually damaged by Darwinism.

CHAPTER 4

Evolution, Science, and the New Philosophy

The metaphysician must enter the physiological field. He must, if he can, conduct researches; he must at least master the ascertained facts. He must not give up the study of the nervous system and brain to those who cannot comprehend anything beyond.

—James McCosh
Christianity and Positivism (1871)

Physical science is becoming so speculative and audacious in its constructions, and at the same time so authoritative, that all doctrines find themselves, willy-nilly, compelled to settle their accounts and make new treaties with it.

—William James
"The Teaching of Philosophy in Our Colleges," *Nation* (1876)

"Darwinism," wrote James Rowland Angell in 1909, "has never been a really vital issue in psychology."[1] Coming from one of the propounders of Chicago functionalism, this statement at first sounds perplexing. Two years earlier he had urged his colleagues to view consciousness—then the focal point of psychology—as a biological adaption to novel environmental situations. In 1909, as if to counsel future historians against interpretive excess, Angell was merely asserting that, long before Darwin had published *On the Origin of Species* (1859), *The*

Descent of Man (1871), and *The Expression of Emotions in Man and Animals* (1872), sense physiology, psychophysics, and neuroanatomy were well-developed fields. But not, of course, in America. To explain the origins of psychology as an academic discipline in the United States, we must appreciate that "psychology" was always an intrinsic part of the American college's philosophic curriculum and that for philosophy evolution was the *key* issue of the 1860s and 1870s. Only when the "old psychology" proved incapable of meeting the philosophic challenges implicit in evolutionary naturalism was the "new psychology" readily admitted into the curriculum. Darwin, as one recent student of American philosophy has indicated, "changed the structure of problems that philosophers tried to solve."[2] As the structure of intellectual problem solving changed, so too did the shape of institutions.

What remained the same was the essential intellectual function of philosophy as mediator between science and religion. The intent of the nineteenth-century liberal arts college, says Stow Persons, "was to organize all knowledge, including knowledge of the cosmos, of man, and of society, into a consistent and intelligible whole."[3] This endeavor, which Persons calls Protestant Scholasticism,[4] attempted to reconcile faith and reason, Christian belief and Enlightenment empiricism. The organization of knowledge thus represented the institutionalization of ideals. Undoubtedly the dissemination and advancement of knowledge (less rare than ordinarily depicted) serviced the practical needs of an emerging industrial nation. We must not, however, allow our own secularity to distort our appraisal of the social vision of those Victorians for whom one of the most practical needs of the age was the inculcation of belief.

Moral science or moral philosophy was the discipline (in both senses of the word) that instructed men in their obligations to civilization. This form of ethical didactics encompassed those subjects which would later emerge as the specialized social sciences. Precursor of the social sciences, moral philosophy was also "successor of theology."[5] Taught to seniors as the culmination of their liberal educations, moral philosophy sought to provide a rational basis for religious and social precept independent of revealed theology. Assuming that Truth is one, academic moralists argued from analogy that the natural and moral worlds were in perfect accord. Thus, one could infer that the natural harmony of the solar system suggested, indeed required, a corresponding harmony in the social system.[6]

Mental science or mental philosophy constituted the psychological linchpin that made plausible arguments from analogy that joined the natural and moral universes. It endeavored to prove that man's non-material mind was capable of comprehending natural and moral laws both intuitively and inductively. This epistemological dualism of sense and intellect maintained the ontological dualism of matter and spirit that every right thinking individual considered essential to belief in God, in an ordered society, and in the evidence of a theologically serviceable natural science. Protestant Scholasticism therefore depended ultimately upon a fundamentally conservative psychology. Should psychology identify mind with matter, it would discredit man's spirituality and undermine the basis of religious belief. Should psychology slip into subjective intuitionism in order to affirm that spirituality, it might condone an ethical individualism incompatible with social order and political authority. In the American colleges, it was the business of the moral philosopher to provide an intellectual defense of these religious and moral values.[7] These academic moralists underwrote their philosophy of science and their ethics with the psychological theories of the Scottish Common Sense Realists.

Common Sense represented an eighteenth-century attempt to restore to philosophy an empirical tradition without the epistemological difficulties that had confronted John Locke.[8] Most important for our purposes, Common Sense underwrote the pursuits of scientists at work in the great laboratory of nature. Scottish philosophy, assuming that sense perception is usually veridical, certified the validity of natural science and assured naturalists of the essential compatibility of their findings with religion. The auspices of the Realists encouraged the development of science within the American college.

The Evolution of Science

Between 1820 and the publication of Charles Darwin's *On the Origin of Species* in 1859 college students in the United States studied proportionally more science than at any time before or since. During this period, says Stanley M. Guralnick, colleges upgraded the level of those sciences already taught, such as mathematics, physics, and astronomy, and added many more, such as chemistry, geology, and biology. Graduate students, who in 1815 could not solve algebraic equations of two unknowns or distinguish between Newton's fluxional notation and fly spots, were by 1840 dealing with ordinary differential equations, all in the course of a single generation. More professors were hired to concentrate on more narrowly defined scientific areas. . . . Scientific apparatus at the average college increased in value from a few hundred dollars in 1825 to many thousands by mid-century, and this was concurrent with the building of laboratories and astronomical observatories to house the new acquisitions.[9]

Robert V. Bruce's statistical study of scientists listed in the *Dictionary of American Biography* between 1846 and 1876 shows that 44.5 percent of the individuals who received income as scientists were supported by educational institutions.[10] Colleges were becoming the appropriate centers of scientific activity in America.

In part, the growth of collegiate science reflected the increasing need of an industrializing nation for technical and scientific personnel.[11] Already by the third decade of the century calls for curricular revision along scientific and technological lines had become sufficiently strident to provoke formalized defenses of the traditional disciplinary purposes of the liberal curriculum, such as the Yale Report of 1828.[12] Significantly, however (and contrary to the usual interpretation), this noted document explicitly and vigorously upheld the cultural and pedagogical values of science.[13] Academic conservatives as well as reformers stressed science as an essential mode of knowledge.

Pedagogically, classical languages had always occupied an unrivaled position in the liberal arts college. The sheer drudgery of conjugating Latin verbs or of Greek "gerund-grinding" purportedly trained the intellect and strengthened the will and hence enhanced the student's ability to master those intellectual tasks he would confront in later life.[14] In the meantime, this formal discipline cultivated the mental faculties by which the undergraduate apprehended those moral truths which it was the college's business to instill. In the second quarter of the nineteenth century, science challenged the prerogatives of classical studies.[15] To their delight, Protestant pedagogues found that chemical formulas and mathematical equations could strain mental muscles as well as any ancient hortatory subjunctive. To the satisfaction of the practically minded, these acquisitions also led to useful knowledge. Elaborated after mid-century by such British university scientists as Thomas Huxley, the argument that science could be both disciplinary and handy had broad appeal in American colleges.[16] Its employment suggests that Americans did not need to depend on the German ideal of *Wissenschaft* to countenance scientific activity within higher education.

Culturally, science supplied vital philosophic and religious benefits to the academic syllabus, benefits even more essential to its ascendancy than the foregoing argument. "Having seen that there are *a priori* truths in mathematics," reasoned James McCosh, "the mind will be better prepared to admit that there are eternal and unchangeable principles lying at the basis of morality and religion, and guaranteeing to us the immutable character of law and of the justice of God."[17] Astronomy attested to the harmony, balance, and order of the heavens, as did political economy closer to home. And if the principles of Newtonian mechanics rendered plausible the Utilitarian philosopher William Paley's unsettling vision of the deity as a celestial clockmaker who constructed his cosmic apparatus but no longer serviced it, the evidences of geology and paleontology indicated that divine interposition occurred subsequent to creation, that God was close at hand.[18] To Americans the greatest scientists appeared also to be the greatest idealists and the most plausible, if not the most ardent, religionists. The president of Amherst College, Edward Hitchcock, recalled in 1863 that "The Title of Professor of Chemistry and Natural History, which I had for twenty years, conveys but an imperfect idea of what I attempted to teach, or rather of the grand object I had in view. That object was to illustrate, by the scientific facts which I taught, the principles of natural theology."[19] Without this essential compatibility of science and religion it is doubtful that the colleges would have invested such huge amounts of money in supporting scientific pursuits.

Science's institutional expansion was a product of ideological commitment. Science provided the quintessential method for uncovering truth. Naturalistic explanations of phenomena were becoming increasingly self-sufficient guides to the way the world worked, and not only scientists but philosophers too disparaged recourse to supernatural explanations. Thus, when Darwin published his *Origin of Species* in 1859, the academic philosophers, committed to empirical methods of argumentation and to scientific modes of thinking, were compelled to await the verdict of scientific specialists on the evolutionary issue. By the 1870s most American scientists had become committed evolutionists.[20] Philosophers were forced to follow.

The Science of Evolution

Though natural theologians and natural scientists allied in finding order in nature, the nature of the order was of crucial concern. In biology the problem of order was particularly troublesome. One plausible argument for the failure to decipher a biological order was that the species were not fixed. Evolutionary theories long antedated 1859 but were never buttressed with the overwhelming documentation that Darwin provided. The *Origin* presented, not simply a theory to be confounded by an alternatively plausible hypothesis, but also a massive empirical compilation of evidence that had to be taken into account.

Darwin's data seemed to support two interrelated principles: fortuitous variation and natural selection. According to the first principle, descendants randomly deviated in form from their progenitors. These fortuitous structural variations were in turn inheritable, thus producing a theoretically infinite diversity of life forms. In order to explain why this proliferation, though abundant, was not inchoate and inundating, Darwin proposed the principle of natural selection. Indebted to Thomas Malthus's demographic explanation of famine, Darwin postulated a struggle for existence between similar varieties of animals for a limited supply of vital necessities. This conception of natural order possessed religiously intolerable implications:

In place of the perfect order and economy of the Newtonian world, Darwin postulated an incredibly wasteful process of random proliferation and ruthless extinction. In place of the benevolent harmony in which all nature conspires to be the happiness of the creation, Darwin presented "nature red in tooth and claw." If indeed order bespeaks an orderer, if like produces like, if natural law is but a mode of divine action, if all effects are intended, what conclusions follow respecting a deity who would design a world on the model of a slaughterhouse where most perished horribly, where the "saving remnant" was saved by chance adaption alone, and where the meek would never live to inherit anything? For those who had made the natural theology the foundation of their reconciliation of religion and science, the Darwinian theory suddenly opened the abyss beneath their feet.[21]

In 1859 Darwin had deliberately excluded *Homo sapiens* from his account. In 1871, when the Darwinians had already carried the day, he published *The Descent of Man*, extending his theory to the development of the species once fixed halfway between beast and angel. Cosmological placement aside, the crucial issue for philosophers now centered on the verification of man's spirituality. The concept of soul had always been identified with man's rational faculties; the distinctive quality that separated man from brute was his possession of conscious mind. Religion could forsake biblical literalism and arguments from design and still survive; it could not, however, afford to deny that man was categorically different from the rest of the animal kingdom.[22] To deny man's soul, to deny his conscious rationality, was to forsake the concepts of free will and of ethical responsibility and hence to undermine the basis of social morality. The fundamental task of philosophy after Darwin was therefore psychological; it had to offer convincing proof for the evolution of consciousness in order to extricate mind from the implications of mechanistic determinism and then to allow ethics to be rewritten in evolutionary style. Thus, when McCosh, a Presbyterian liberal who had accepted evolution, called upon the metaphysician to get himself to the physiological laboratory, the metaphysician knew what it was he was sent there to find.

Psychology and Evolution

"Psychology," the arch-Realist McCosh announced with etymological precision, "is the science of the soul." "Soul" he defined as "that self of which everyone is conscious." Psychology, therefore, is no more and no less than "that science which inquires into the operations of the conscious self with the view of discovering laws."[23] As far as it went, this definition would not have troubled Wundt; as far as the "new" psychology appeared to be going philosophically, Wundt's program did not trouble the Scottish Realist. American academic philosophers came to physiological psychology with less emotional apprehension than the heroic histories of scientific psychology admit.

In fact, until the last quarter of the nineteenth century there was little trepidation in collegiate circles over physiology itself. To Americans the history of neurophysiology—the findings of Pierre Flourens, Magendie, Bell, and Müller—constituted a reassuring documentation of the sequestration of sensorimotor experiments from the analysis of brain as "the organ of the mind."[24] The standard British text from which Americans drew their physiological precepts, William Carpenter's *Principles of Mental Physiology*, viewed the cerebral cortex as "a unitary organ 'superadded' to the sensory-motor centers."[25] As Robert Young has shown, "Between 1822 and 1870 numerous experimental tests provided *no* evidence for localization of functions in the brain or for the production of purposive movements by artificial stimulation of the cerebral cortex, and the interpretation placed on these experiments was that they supported the autonomy of an indivisible mental substance and belief in free will."[26] By the 1870s, however, Gustav Fritsch and Eduard Hitzig had demonstrated cortical excitability by means of electrical stimulation, and David Ferrier had refined, elaborated, and conclusively reinforced their findings.[27] Since evolutionary theory seemed to rule out the miraculous "superaddition" of mind to biological organism, the new physiology of the brain suddenly appeared damaging to philosophic assumptions about freedom and will. Physiological psychology appeared in the 1870s as a safeguard against the eventual elimination by physiologists of consciousness as epiphenomenal.

American academic moralists correctly realized that Wundt's physiological psychology implied not a concession to physiology but an exemption from it. As Stratton maintained, Wundt had rescued psychology from subjection to the science upon which it was styled. At a time when physiologists, according to Ladd, "are denying the reality, unity, and possibility of a permanent existence of the human mind, and are resolving its entire being into a stream of mechanically associated 'epiphenomena,' thrown off from the molecular machinery of the cerebral hemispheres," psychology came to mind's rescue by maintaining "an uncritical, common-sense Dualism."[28] Yale's laboratory director, at odds with Ladd on so many matters, at least agreed with him on this. Scripture asserted that his laboratory training with Wundt had taught him "to treat mental facts as mental facts and not to represent thoughts and emotions as nerve cells tickling one another."[29] To be sure, many proponents of liberal culture would deplore what, in Baldwin's words, they depicted as "the 'soul' confined in a laboratory."[30] But to many this confinement "proved" the existence of mind and soul. Could so many avowed scientists be measuring a mirage? To write metaphysical textbooks affirming the reality of consciousness was one thing; to establish laboratories, to devise sophisticated instrumentation, to publish results in scientific journals was quite another. For those who required the testimony of science in behalf of philosophic and religious belief, the brass instrument was mightier than the pen. Cartesian dualism, elegantly ensconced in the doctrine of psychophysical parallelism, permitted psychologists to appear ontologically agnostic and scientifically respectable. As philosophy mediated between science and religion, psychology mediated between physiology and philosophy in an age of positivism.

Positivism was not without its philosophic consolations. Contrary to their usual depiction as reactionary dogmatists, philosophers, who always considered themselves good scientists, generally applauded the introduction of rigorous scientific methods into psychology. The evolutionary doctrine had broken open a hornet's nest of philosophical hypotheses about the nature of mind and about man's place in nature and society. Positivism implied the suspension of speculation pending lengthy experimental deliberations.[31] James Mark Baldwin expressed the positivistic "tendency of the day in philosophy" in terms of a familiar chemical metaphor:

We are endeavoring, and successfully too[,] to throw all questions capable of such treatment to the bottom, as a precipitate—a psychological precipitate—and are then handing them over to the psychologist for positive treatment. As long as our data remained in a solution of ninety parts water (which, being interpreted, means speculation), it was difficult to handle them scientifically. . . . [W]henever we can secure a sediment, a residuum, a deposit, apart from a speculative solvent, this is so much gain for positive science and to truth.[32]

Such an operation would take time, as James noted in his *Principles of Psychology*. On the same page that he bemoaned the sheer drudgery of experimentalism—"the method of patience, starving out, and harassing to death" of facts—he urged that the sole safeguard against error "is in the final *consensus* of our farther knowledge about the thing in question, later views correcting earlier ones, until at last the harmony of a consistent system is reached."[33] Until their "farther knowledge" was perfected, positivism afforded the philosophically cautious with an ideology for confounding mechanistic and spiritualistic dogmatists alike.

James's colleague at Cambridge's Metaphysical Club, Chauncey Wright, illustrated the usefulness of this ideology when he invoked it against the American academic moralists' most pestiferous wasp, the Englishman Herbert Spencer. The most popular public philosopher in America during the Gilded Age, Spencer constructed a "synthetic philosophy" by fusing a deterministic evolutionary biology to an antireformist sociology with the solder of mechanistic psychology.[34] Wright, an ardent religionist and the man to whom Darwin himself looked to solve the problem of the evolution of self-consciousness, attacked Spencer's deterministic psychological system for its tendency to employ premature scientific generalizations in an attempt to decipher final truths. Such a procedure, Wright argued,

a positivist would regard as correct only on the supposition that the materials of truth have all been collected, and that the research of science is no longer for the enlargement of our experience or for the informing of the mind. Until these conditions be realized, the positivist regards such attempts as Mr. Spencer's as not only faulty, but positively pernicious and misleading.[35]

This was a safer sort of reductionism, this curtailment of the controversial. The roots of the research ideal are many and deep. But in philosophy this ideal might not have blossomed so fruitfully in American soil had it not been fertilized by the need to disparage unsound ponderings.

G. Stanley Hall recognized the widespread appeal of exact and extended research. Master of homespun rhetoric, Hall ingratiatingly declared that although experiment "involves more labor with details and is plainer and humbler" than deductive speculation, it was nevertheless

this method of self-control and subordination [to sound philosophical principles] . . . that has commended the scientific method in psychology to the confidence of conservative administrative boards, and by which its recent remarkable academic extension in the universities and colleges of this country have [sic] been made. It is premature speculative views that these boards justly fear.[36]

Science, like the universities themselves, welcomed new ideas, but cautiously, deliberately and conservatively. Academic philosophers, together with their patrons and sponsors, had witnessed the crumbling of natural theology's seemingly impregnable fortress. They were not about to be misled again. Better a sturdy tentativeness than a fragile complacency.

By defining the science of psychology as the study of consciousness, by insisting that the principal method of psychology was introspection (an ornate version of the Realists' favorite approach), and by adopting the axiom of psychophysical parallelism, the new psychologists had assumed in principle what they feared more radical reductionists would deny in fact. Far from trembling before the materialistic implications of the new psychology, university and college administrators welcomed the novel venture. It was first domesticated at Harvard, where Common Sense philosophy had upheld the values of Unitarianism, "the most intact survival of the Moderate Enlightenment," which, under the influence of Newton and Locke, preached balance, religious compromise, and political conservatism.[37] Harvard's overseers realized in the early 1870s that the "ignoring by philosophers of the physical side of mental phenomena has had the natural effect of exaggerating the importance of materialistic views."[38] They urged the enlargement of psychological courses to right the balance, and James was quick to capitalize on their fears. At a time when physiology was tending toward materialistic explanation, he was able to remind potential patrons of the new psychology that philosophy, including psychology, "means the habit of always seeing the alternative."[39] As the pages of such periodicals as E. L. Youmans's *Popular Science Monthly* brimmed over with accolades to Spencerian psychology, James persuaded Harvard President Charles W. Eliot to allow him to present the new psychology in the classroom by asking rhetorically, "shall the students be left to the magazines [which were] publishing extremely crude and pretentious psychological speculations under the name of 'science'[?]" Or, suggested James, echoing Princeton's President McCosh,

shall the College employ a man whose scientific training fits him fully to realize the force of all the natural history arguments, whilst his concomitant familiarity with writers of a more introspective kind preserves him from certain crudities of reasoning which are extremely common in men of the [physiological] laboratory pure and simple?[40]

James knew Eliot's response to his question before he asked it.

The conditions of physiological psychology's entry into the colleges and universities were similar elsewhere. At Yale, Ladd doubted that one could "pursue psychology as a 'natural science' without the postulate of a soul," which he considered "as a great light at the end of our [scientific] pathway."[41] At Clark, Hall was careful to dismiss any tendency

to balance and foreclose accounts between brain and soul yet. Even to attempt this just now, when from the neural and also from the psychic side both [sic] change, progress and promise are greater than ever before, is worse than waste, it is philosophic and scientific precocity and lack of self-control.[42]

Attending to both "psychic" and "neural" aspects of mind and by proceeding incrementally to add facts to both scales, experimentalism assured the new psychology's patrons that its balance would not suddenly tip to either side. It was this essentially conservative aspect of positivism, as we shall later see, that launched Hall's career at Hopkins, just as it had done at Harvard for James.

It launched other careers too. Hall, for example, had met George Herbert Mead in Germany in 1888 and convinced him to study physiological psychology. Mead's traveling companion and closest friend, William Castle, wrote home about Mead's decision to study the topic as follows:

George thinks he must make a specialty of this branch, because in America where poor bated, unhappy Christianity, trembling for its life, claps the gag into the mouth of Free Thought and says, "Hush, hush, not a word, or nobody will believe in me anymore," he thinks it would be hard for him to get a chance to utter any ultimate philosophical opinions savoring of independence. In Physiological Psychology, on the other hand, he has a harmless territory in which he can work quietly.[43]

Mead realized that experimental psychology involved intellectual control. Scientific thinking was not free and independent thinking; it was ordered, disciplined by the "consensus of farther knowledge." Chroniclers of American psychology's emergence as an independent academic discipline have tended to identify psychology with science and rather complacently to associate science with the liberal spirit of free inquiry.[44] Hence they have found it easy to attribute institutional resistance to psychology's development to the sterile dogmatism of philosophic orthodoxy.[45] In actuality, philosophers and their institutions were more "liberal" and the modalities of science more "conservative" than ordinarily depicted.

Could physiological psychology constitute "harmless territory" and philosophic promise at the same time? What did philosophers hope to gain from it? On one level, the answers are as many as the number of individuals who supplied them. But one general answer is that they hoped to gain a breathing space. The mandates of the "farther knowledge" provided time to refashion the intellectual foundations of the moral and social philosophy once based upon natural theology; time to clothe exposed and cherished beliefs with the garb of evolutionary naturalism. The task of the philosopher remained the same: to articulate the affinities between the natural order, the moral order, and the social order.[46] Since evolution had altered the way in which the natural order had customarily been perceived, the academic philosopher's problem became one of reconciling a new dynamic natural order of evolutionary biology to their traditional conceptions of the moral and social universes in such a way that the latter realms would remain recognizable.[47] Pragmatism, successor and in many respects lineal descendant of Realism in America, provided such an evolutionary philosophical basis for traditional belief.[48] The pragmatic theory of ideas, which conceived of beliefs as evolving responses to the environment, assumed that true ideas were those "that competed well, that survived and worked." Thus, for example, when James reasoned "that religious ideas enabled us to live well—that they were successful—he meant that they were true."[49]

The new psychology that underwrote the pragmatic theory of truth by portraying mind as the organ of adaption was functionalism. In the wake of evolutionary theory, the new psychologists justified their claims to academic recognition by importing a new philosophic method—experimentalism, a method that combined scientific authority and an apparent metaphysical modesty. To this approach they immediately brought the functional perspective, which was essentially a biological metaphor. With this aid—what James Angell called "the biological compass"[50]—the philosopher as psychologist endeavored to cope with the problem of evolution. Philosophy imbued the laboratory with its essential meaning, while experimentalism was expected to bestow upon philosophy the imprimatur of scientific legitimacy. Naturally, when the conservative academic philosopher argued that experimentalism implied the suspension of speculation, he referred to the other fellow's speculation. By expropriating the latest and most scientific approaches to the study of mind, the American academic moralist hoped to disarm philosophic opposition. Identification with the new experimental psychology might lend his own theorizing legitimacy or merely the aura of legitimacy; either way, it conferred an advantage.

CHAPTER 5

Evolution, Society, and the New Psychology

All natural sciences aim at practical prediction and control, and in none of them is this more the case than in psychology to-day. We live surrounded by an enormous body of persons who are most definitely interested in the control of states of mind, and incessantly craving for a sort of psychological science which will teach them how to *act*. What every educator, every jail-warden, every doctor, every clergyman, every asylum-superintendent, asks of psychology is practical rules. Such men care little or nothing about the ultimate philosophic grounds of mental phenomena, but they do care immensely about improving the ideas, dispositions, and conduct of the particular individuals in their charge.

—William James
"A Plea for Psychology as a 'Natural Science,'" *Philosophical Review*
(1892)

Psychology . . . is a . . . branch of natural science. Its theoretical goal is the prediction and control of behavior. . . . If psychology would follow the plan I suggest, the educator, the physician, the jurist and the business man could utilize our data in a practical way. . . . Those who have occasion to apply psychological principles would find no need to complain as they do at the present time. . . . One of the earliest conditions which made me dissatisfied with psychology was the feeling that there was no realm of application for the principles which were being worked out in content terms.

—John Broadus Watson
"Psychology at the Behaviorist Views It,"
Psychological Review (1913)

When innovators spoke of the new psychology, many of them thought of a new philosophy. Envisioning for themselves conventional roles as moral philosophers, they argued that scientific competency rather than theological training should be made the chief criterion for occupancy of such academic niches. The preceding chapter has outlined the intellectual crisis that made such arguments compelling and upon which the new philosophers capitalized. Training in physiological psychology represented the most authoritative badge of scientific certification. Though the evolutionary controversy prompted its implementation within the American college and university, in many respects physiological psychology constituted a simple extension of traditional philosophic inquiry. As epistemologists bound to the assumptions of British empiricism, philosophers had always been preoccupied with problems of sensation and perception. Physiological psychology promised experimental insights into certain fundamental philosophic problems. As such, undoubtedly it would eventually have been assimilated into American academic philosophy without the catalytic challenge of Darwinism, albeit with less urgency and perhaps more caution. As evidenced, however, in the careers of many Americans who studied at Leipzig, the new psychology rapidly expanded beyond the boundaries of both philosophy and Wundtian experimentalism to assume the cultural function of a practical, empirical behavioral science. In other words, the new psychology adopted the cultural function that had most recently belonged to phrenology, the nineteenth-century psychology vehemently opposed to the mental science of the Common Sense Realists that physiological psychology sought to bolster. The enlargement of academic psychology's scope might likewise have occurred without the influence of evolutionary naturalism, but here again Darwin's multifaceted influence on American science and social thought was instrumental. Evolution became the vehicle upon which the social ideology and practical aims of an intellectually indefensible phrenology—the science of individual differences—rode into the academic territory occupied by the science of mind.

Gall and the Phrenological Movement

A century before Watson inaugurated his particular brand of behaviorism, Franz Joseph Gall (1758–1828) embarked upon the first systematic scientific program of behavior research. The Viennese-trained physician and anatomist supported the doctrine of the cerebral localization of mental functions. Deriving his list of faculties or mental powers (innate propensities as categorically variable as self-preservation, duty, love, and imitation) from the Scottish Realist Thomas Reid, he attempted in the first quarter of the nineteenth century to prove that specific regions of the brain were responsible for objectively describable manifestations of human character. While his peculiar assumptions had been largely discredited by the 1870s, Gall and the popular phrenological movement to which his name has become unfairly attached subtly but decisively influenced the new psychology in America.[1]

Four principal propositions dominated Gall's major works: the shape of the skull conformed to the shape of the brain; mind can be analyzed into discrete faculties or functions; these faculties are localized in specific portions, or "separate organs," of the brain; finally, behavioral traits can be explained by reference to the development of brain protrusions and can be predicted by the measurement of corresponding cranial contours, or "bumps."[2] Because each of these propositions proved false, Gall's place within the chronicles of scientific progress lies significantly beneath the range of his vision. Recognized as "one of the most brilliant anatomists of his day" for improving surgical techniques that left discrete convolutions of the brain intact, Gall the biologist is thus recalled for his technical rather than for his theoretical contributions.[3] For correctly surmising that the brain is the organ of mind, Gall the psychologist is merely credited with leaving the science he misdirected "free for all the progress that resulted in physiological psychology."[4] Such a conclusion is more useful for its irony than for its aptness, for the physiology upon which physiological psychology was based proceeded in a direction Gall lived long enough to deplore.

As a morbid anatomist seeking to allocate specific instincts and faculties to specific portions of the cerebral hemispheres, Gall had to contend with the sensorimotor physiologists—particularly with Pierre Flourens—whose findings failed to confirm Gall's doctrine of localized specificity of function. Flourens's improved operative procedures owe a great deal to Gall's own techniques and to his criticism that prevailing methods of vivisection amounted to uncontrolled "mutilation."[5] Gall argued that, before any such physiological experimentation could affirm or deny his hypothesis, it must meet certain criteria. According to Gall, the experimenter must first "be able to limit the entire effect of the lesion to the special region of the brain on which the experiment is made. For if the shock of the operation, the haemorrhage, the inflammation, extend to other parts, what conclusion can be drawn?"[6] Conversely, Gall continued, one must be able "to ascertain whether the animal whose brain is mutilated, an animal agonized by pain and fear, were in a condition to exhibit those propensities, instincts, or faculties connected with the portions of the brain that were left uninjured." Gall the naturalist realized that confinement alone often extinguished instinctual proclivities: "The elephant will not pair in captivity; the nightingale's song ceases."[7] The scalpel and the cage brought the observer into closer contact with the organism that he sought to examine while simultaneously preventing the subject from exhibiting those manifestations of innate proclivities which the scientist sought to explain.

Technical refinements and methodological sophistication would eventually blunt the impact of Gall's exceedingly accurate clinical thrusts.[8] He added, however, a third condition for successful experimentation. Most important, he maintained, "the inquirer should have a clearly defined conception of what he is looking for."[9] In this regard, the physiologists and even the physiological psychologists who came after Gall met his ultimate challenge by abandoning his particular objectives.

Gall admitted that neurophysiology—employing the successful new paradigm of sensorimotor physiology, the Bell-Magendie law—had obtained certain positive results in localizing in the cerebrum and medulla oblongata certain functions relating to "irritability, sensibility, the function of the viscera, voluntary motion, respiration, etc."[10] An avowed antisensationalist, he feared that such successes might tempt the experimenter to forsake the difficult search for the locations of psychological functions that underlie significant patterns of behavior in favor of a reductionist inquiry that claimed to explain mental life by reducing it to mere sensorimotor functions. Unable to comply with Gall's rigorous criteria, experimentalism did precisely that. Robert Young has compellingly argued that cerebral localization had become scientific only by abandoning the goals which Gall had laid down at the beginning of his research: to relate the significant variables in the character and behavior of men and animals to the functioning of the brain. The sensory-motor school was undoubtedly right in rejecting Gall's faculty psychology. However, in being grounded on a secure physiological basis, the sensory-motor tradition cut itself off from the approach to psychology which was the most important aspect of Gall's work. . . . In rejecting Gall's answers, it lost sight of the significance of his questions. Insufficient attention was paid to what the sensory-motor elements should be required to explain.[11]

Physiology substituted small questions that could be answered for large ones that could not.

Physiological psychology emerged from this physiological tradition that had explicitly abandoned Gall's goals. Its scientific elegance likewise stemmed from its ability to eschew the consideration of variables it could not control. Textbook histories that equate experimental psychology with the new psychology in general and that stress patterns of linear cumulative progress thus find in phrenology little more than a defunct progenitor of scientific psychology, a movement that died so that true science might live. However, looking beyond the laboratory to broader coexisting programs of empirical endeavor within psychology, one finds that phrenology invested the new psychology with ample precedent. Phrenology engendered a systematic approach to psychology that was objective in method, functional in approach, practical in scope, and concerned with the assessment of individual differences. As such, it crystallized in certain sectors of American thought a conception of psychology diametrically opposed to physiological psychology's introspective, structural, ascetic science of the generalized human mind.

The objectivism of Gall's comparative empiricism represented a direct challenge to the introspective method of philosophical psychology that Wundt, in the process of refining, would resuscitate. Gall recognized that the introspective study of mind dominated by Common Sense metaphysicians and moral philosophers jeopardized psychology's chances of becoming a biological science. He insisted that "the most sublime intelligence will never be able to find in a closet, what exists only in the vast field of nature."[12] Gall's objectivism had a powerful precursor in Hume and a forceful proponent in Comte. By way of such positivistic psychologists as Cattell, Gall indirectly influenced John Broadus Watson and the behaviorist movement generally.

In his *Treatise of Human Nature* Hume declared:

Moral philosophy has this peculiar disadvantage which is not found in natural [philosophy]. . . . When I am at a loss to know the effects of one body upon another in any situation, I need only put them in that situation and observe the results from it. But should I endeavor to clear up in the same manner any doubts in moral philosophy by placing myself in the same case with that which I consider, 'tis evident this reflection and premeditation would so disturb the operation of my rational principles as must render it impossible to form any just conclusion from the phenomenon. We must, therefore, glean up our experiments in this science from a cautious observation of *human life*, and take them as they appear in the common course of the world, by *men's behaviour* in company, in affairs, and in their pleasures. When experiments of this kind are judiciously collected and compared, we may hope to establish on them a science which will not be inferior in certainty, and will be much superior in utility, to any other of human comprehension.[13]

Comte, who acknowledged his profound debt to Gall, argued in like manner that the "so-called psychological method . . . is in principle invalid. . . . *Internal observation* engenders almost as many divergent opinions as there are individuals to pursue it."[14] Like the physiological method of vivisection, the philosophical method of introspection interfered with the phenomena under observation.

When the phrenological movement arrived in the United States, this aspect of Gall's positivism remained one of its most tenacious features. Brahmin social reformer Samuel Gridley Howe explained to the Boston Phrenological Society in 1836 that

most other metaphysicians . . . hold up consciousness as a mirror before them, and think that they see there an image of man which they attempt to describe; but alas! the mirror is so narrow it will admit but one image at a time, and that the image of him who holds it up. It must be, that, while men judge the mental emotions, dispositions, and characters of others by the consciousness of what passes within themselves, they must ever err.[15]

James McKeen Cattell was decisively influenced by the positivism of Comte. When he declared before the International Congress of Arts and Sciences at the 1904 St. Louis Exposition that "It is usually no more necessary for the subject to be a psychologist than it is for the vivisected frog to be a physiologist," he was elaborating a conception of psychology rivaling the introspection of Wundt.[16] The University of Chicago's J. B. Watson, who claimed that he owed more to Hume than to Dewey, heard Cattell's speech. According to his autobiography, he began that year to complain to his colleagues about the superfluousness of using introspective observers in psychological experiments.[17]

From his home base at the University of Missouri Max Meyer did not have as far to travel to St. Louis as did Watson. Two years before his colleague's manifesto Meyer published his *Fundamental Laws of Behavior* in which he deprecated the "deep rooted habit of describing human behavior as dependent on subjective states, on states of consciousness,—a habit which still largely governs the sciences of human society, preventing them from throwing off the shackles of subjectivity." Meyer scornfully attacked introspection and pleaded for the objective study of human behavior in psychology. "Why," he complained, "do we think of humanity almost exclusively in terms of thought, although our experience contains no other person's thought, but only his behavior?"[18] The Missouri behaviorist called for a "Psychology of the Other One," the title of his 1921 textbook.[19] Three years later in his popular work *Behaviorism*, Watson repeated this call. He announced:

You will soon find that instead of self-observation being the easiest and most natural way of studying psychology, it is an impossible one; you can observe in yourself only the most elementary forms of response. You will find, on the other hand, that when you begin to study what your neighbor is doing, you will rapidly become proficient in giving a reason for his behavior and in setting situations (presenting stimuli) that will make him behave in a predictable manner.[20]

Exactly a century before the publication of *Behaviorism*, Charles Caldwell had announced an identical program in his *Elements of Phrenology*.[21]

Wundt had, of course, supplied introspection with objective controls in an attempt to minimize the complaints of "the positivistic philosophers" who sought to seize psychology from the hands of metaphysicians and moral philosophers. His arguments in behalf of scientific introspection undoubtedly helped persuade those beleaguered academic moralists to incorporate physiological psychology into their intellectual arsenal. But the increasingly vituperous assaults upon introspective methods voiced within academic psychology after 1910 cannot be explained simply in terms of internal anomalies within physiological psychology such as the failure of the Würzburg school to trace "imageless thoughts."[22] It is best explained as the culmination of an entrenched and resilient tradition of objective psychologizing that had attained widespread recognition and forceful expression in the form of nineteenth-century phrenology.[23]

In addition to the objectivist and, therefore, behavioral orientation, phrenology was also overwhelmingly functional. It was, in other words, more interested in activities than in experiences and viewed mind as the organ that accounted for the organism's biological and social adjustments to its environment. Here again Gall had posed a fundamental question that remained a focus of psychological problem solving: To what extent do the prevailing categories of human propensities—amativeness, ambition, aggression, etc.—reflect definite mental functions? Repeated Gall:

Point out to me the fundamental forces of the soul, and then I will undertake to find the organ of each and its position. I found the first problem surrounded by far more difficulties than the second.[24]

In other words, before the vivisectionist could attempt to locate the organs of instinctual behavior, "the inquirer should have a clearly defined conception of what he is looking for." Recall that a century later Titchener had used an analogy drawn from experimental physiology to bolster his argument that the psychologist must attempt "a vivisection which will yield structural, not functional results. He tries to discover, first of all what is there . . . not what it is there for."[25] Gall had argued that before one could determine the organ of a function one must know the function of the organ and that this undertaking could be accomplished only by making a huge comparative analysis of behavior. One must observe man as a social creature, compare human behavioral traits with those of animals, sane individuals with lunatics, children with adults, intelligent people with stupid ones, and so forth. Once a large array of empirical observations had been accumulated, once comparative correlations permitted accurate delineation of discrete instincts or sets of instincts, then the anatomist could begin identifying innate traits with specific cerebral protrusions. These endeavors must, of course, work together; but, contrary to Titchener's argument, the determination of function is logically anterior to the determination of structure.

Although the new psychology discounted phrenology's claim that instinctual traits could be located in divisible bundles of gray cells, it never discarded the comparative empiricism that Gall had invigorated. Particularly among social and animal psychologists, the search to find meaningful categories of instincts represents one of modern psychology's most dominant features.[26] William McDougall, the British social psychologist who taught at Harvard from 1920 to 1927 and who was among the first to define psychology as the science of behavior, was decisively influenced by phrenology, as Bernard Hollander has shown.[27] Watson's first textbook in comparative psychology relied on the doctrine of instincts while attempting to reduce their numbers.[28] His colleague and friend Robert Mearns Yerkes, who claimed that he was more interested in the study of behavior than of consciousness, adopted Gall's arguments about the dangers of vivisection and the extirpation of sensory modalities and preferred ethological observation of animal behavior as a basis for the study of instinct.[29] Yerkes' comparative work with human subjects, like Gall's, took place within psychopathic hospitals. Learning, the central problem of twentieth-century psychology, involved the determination of what is innate and what is acquired. The social and animal psychologists who laid the foundation for a systematic learning theory based their work on the comparative assessments of the relative capabilities of man and animal that Gall had established as one of psychology's basic methods.[30]

Gall's effort to place psychology under the canopy of the biological sciences prompted him to stress the adaption of organism to environment. When James R. Angell formalized the "functional" position in psychology in 1907, he accentuated this same approach. Furthermore, he attacked the sensationalism of Titchnerian psychology in much the same manner as Gall had rebuked the sense physiologists of his day by arguing for the existence "of definite and distinct forms of mental action," or functions, which structural psychology had disregarded. The Chicago functionalist insisted that "even the much-abused faculty psychology is on this point perfectly sane and perfectly lucid." Angell specifically defended this aspect of phrenological thought when he confessed that

mention of this classic target for psychological vituperation recalls the fact that when the critics of functionalism wish to be particularly unpleasant, they refer to it as a bastard offspring of the faculty psychology masquerading in biological plumage.[31]

One of Titchener's foremost students, Karl Dallenbach, made precisely this reference in the most polite and scholarly manner possible. Performing a historical exegesis of extant psychological literature, Dallenback convincingly showed that the psychological usage of the term "function" derived directly from phrenology.[32] When critics of behaviorism came in turn to refer to that program as a bastardization of functionalism,[33] they failed to note that what Watson had done was to combine psychology's functional approach with phrenology's objective procedures.

Objective observation of functional activities furnished an appropriate method for obtaining insights into individual differences, phrenology's central concern. Gall had argued that the tripartite division of faculties (reason, emotion, and will) employed by the Scottish philosophers pursuing a science of mind failed to account for widespread variation of human personality and behavior. The British psychologist Alexander Bain maintained, however, that in addition to a science of mind there was also a science of character. He declared that "the proper view to take of Phrenology is to regard it as a science of Character, accompanied with a theory of external indications."[34] If this general definition of phrenology is accepted, modern psychology cannot be said to have abandoned it.

William James, for example, never surrendered the aesthetic predilection for attempting to correlate psychological and morphological attributes. James considered phrenology "a useful help in the art of reading character" and, according to one of his like-mined students, "believed there was much truth in [it]."[35] The belief was not confined to the nineteenth century. In an uncommonly frank acknowledgment of intellectual lineage, William Sheldon admitted as late as 1940 that his personality theory based upon body typology descended "from a discredited ancestral phrenology."[36]

Ultimately, however, historical analysis of intellectual lineage must be subordinated to an examination of ideological continuity. Viewed in the cold light on scientific verifiability, Gall's confutation was deserved. His tendentious empiricism, disavowal of contrary evidence, and casual reliance on the anecdotal categories of faculty psychology constitute a disregard of scientific method. Yet, seen in terms of scientific goals, the line of descent from phrenology to much of modern psychology is direct. In order to appreciate phrenology's continuing relevance it is necessary to look beyond the internal logic of "successful" scientific achievement to the external appeal of Gall's scientific intent. The phrenologist sought to relate personality, temperament, and intellect to other objectively observable variables in order to establish a basis for the prediction and control of human behavior. Phrenology was objective, functional, behavioral, and concerned with individual differences because above all it sought to be practical. As the new psychology ventured to be useful, it adopted an identical stance.[37] Phrenology's chief popularizer in Britain, George Combe, complained that the Scottish Realists ignored "the obvious fact of different individuals possessing faculties in different degrees of endowment which fit them for different pursuits." Combe's vision of the social purpose of mental science derived from his mentor and Gall's student, John Gaspar Spurzheim, who suggested that "our interest in being acquainted with human nature, increases . . . as we feel the necessity of influencing those we direct."[38] Phrenology sought not only to predict behavior but also to control it.

Phrenological and behavioristic psychology both rose to prominence by offering themselves as sciences of social control. Cattell declared this essential purpose when he claimed that "Control of the physical world is secondary to the control of ourselves and of our fellow men."[39] Hall, who according to his biographer had always leaned toward behavioristic conceptions of his science, offered the new psychology as the answer to "the supreme problem of diagnosing each individual, and steering him toward the fittest place."[40] Max Meyer declared that a science of human control, such as envisioned by Luther Lee Bernard in his *Transition to an Objective Standard of Social Control*, would not arrive until "facts and laws of introspective psychology [had] been correlated with—replaced by—facts of behavior and its laws."[41] And

Watson, of course, followed suit. Child study, eugenics, intelligence testing, psychometrics—in short, the whole range of activities subsumed under the banner of "human engineering" that occupied the majority of psychologists in the early twentieth century—sought to assess individual differences through analyses of human and animal performance.[42]

The Phrenological Legacy

Because Gall's specific theories had been discredited by the time of the new psychology's ascendancy, modern psychology has managed to ignore its phrenological heritage. This policy of benign historical neglect seemed not only intellectually justifiable but professionally expedient, for phrenology had become the apotheosis of nineteenth-century psychological quackery, the province of the peripatetic mountebank and mail-order charlatan.[43] Phrenology involved an assumption that David Bakan regards as crucial to modern psychometric endeavor; namely, "that one can infer the nature of mental functioning on the basis of very little information collected in a very short space of time."[44] The promise of rapid psychological diagnosis drew hordes of believers to the New York City parlors of the firm of Fowler and Wells where "experts" measured vocational aptitude and marital compatibility by reading the skulls of their impressionable customer-clients.[45] The often told story of phrenology in America is a narrative of its vulgarization: of nickel pamphlets and dime charts, of transient lecturers whose credentials were as highly inflated as their claims, of wigs molded to simulate flattering phrenological features like so many cranial codpieces. A serious science had become a popular fad, and a new academic discipline could ill afford to acknowledge its indebtedness to the former without risking identification with the latter.[46]

At the same time, however, phrenology's currency indicated the cultural indispensability of some sort of practical, predictive psychological science. Its promise captivated not only the pervious public and the evangelical reformer but also a more skeptical professional class yearning for a science aimed, in James's words, at "improving the ideas, dispositions, and conduct of the particular individuals in their charge."[47] From among this class came the groups who prompted President Jo-

siah Quincy to invite Spurzheim to Harvard in 1832 and who welcomed him at Yale. Physicians, ministers, public educators, asylum
superintendents, and college professors composed the appreciative audiences that listened to Combe's lectures when he toured the United
States from 1838 to 1840.[48] Sifting through the chaff of bluff, these
groups extracted the kernel of phrenological promise: the conviction
that psychology could and should be removed from the domain of introspective metaphysics to the realm of natural science where mental
phenomena could be observed objectively and explained naturalisti-
cally. This set of assumptions remained intact long after phrenology
was left, in the words of one commentator, "with the dry husks of its
eccentricities—'bumps on the head.' "[49] With or without bumps,
phrenology's theory of human nature and personality recommended
itself to emerging professional groups searching for "positive knowledge" about such matters.[50]

The vogue of phrenology among these groups underscores the centrality of psychological theorizing to a variety of social problems and
to an array of institutional developments in the nineteenth century.[51]
Declining agricultural opportunities and industrial expansion encouraged unprecedented demographic shifts and urban growth. In the cities, America perceived increasing incidences of crime and insanity and
required educational systems responsive to the task of industrial training. In the twilight of American gentility's ascribed cultural hegemony, emergent professional classes achieved status and vocational
identity in the new urban society at least in part by promising to solve
that society's most intractable problems.[52] Many found in phrenology
an etiological explanation of aberrant human behavior; a predictive
technology for assessing character, temperament, and intellect; and a
biological blueprint for social reform. The social engineers of the
twentieth century, together with their patrons and subscribers, would
demand no less of modern experimental behaviorism. When the new
psychology arrived on the American stage, an eager audience anticipated the role it was to play. Gall, Spurzheim, Combe, and their followers had already written the script.

While the new psychology rejected the major aspects of phrenology's defunct framework of explanation, it never escaped the pattern of

expectations that phrenology engendered. E. G. Boring claims that, when America's psychological pilgrims returned from Germany,

with surprisingly little comment on what they were doing and probably but little awareness of it, they changed the pattern of psychological activity from the description of the generalized mind to the assessment of personal capacities in the successful adjustment of the individual to his environment.[53]

What had actually changed was the locus of this supposedly new psychological program. In the 1850s, when railway companies considered employing phrenological scientists to assist the selection of trainmen in order to reduce accidents, the distinction between certifiable expert and enterprising charlatan was already thinly drawn.[54] Seven decades later, when urban electric railway companies, plagued by daily accidents, public indignation, and spiraling indemnity payments, sought similar psychological tests for their motormen, they knew exactly where to turn. Director of perhaps the best-equipped psychological laboratory in the world and distinguished professor in America's most prestigious university, Harvard's Hugo Münsterberg gladly undertook the investigation of their problem.[55] Psychology had not been transformed from the study of consciousness to the science of capacity; rather, utilitarian psychology had been transferred from the phrenological parlor to the psychological laboratory. The essential historical problem therefore involves an examination of how practical objective psychology obtained academic admission, of how this science of individual character, capacity, and conduct managed to coexist with (and eventually to displace) the traditional introspective science of the generalized mind that Wundt had experimentally rehabilitated.[56]

In order to answer this question it is necessary to stage a preliminary inquiry into the American reception of the associationist tradition of British empiricism. While it is generally acknowledged that the new psychology derived its fundamental postulates from an associationism explicitly opposed to the faculty psychology of Gall,[57] what is not sufficiently appreciated is the extent to which British psychology retained an allegiance to the ideological program upheld by phrenology. When Americans looked abroad for a systematic psychology that incorporated mind and character, they followed the well-traveled intellectual trade routes to England, not to Germany, and found in the work of Alexander Bain, not of Wundt, an exemplary expression of the kind of psychology best suited to their needs.

The American Reception of Alexander Bain

In the 1850s Bain established his reputation as Britain's leading psychologist with the publication of his massive two-volume work, *The Senses and the Intellect* (1855) and *The Emotions and the Will* (1859).[58] In these volumes the Aberdeen radical provided associationism with a neurophysiological basis derived from the writings of Müller. Bain formally articulated the doctrine of psychophysical parallelism and tentatively accepted the principles of associationism. Nevertheless, he was a nativist rather than a sensationalist, drew his insights and methods from biology rather than from philosophical psychology, and emphasized the physiological mechanisms that accounted for behavior. Relying on comparative observation of animal and abnormal behavior, he doubted that experimental psychology could isolate significant mental activities, as Gall had distrusted experimental physiology's ability to do the same. His emphasis on habit; his argument that purposeful activity issued from random, spontaneous movements preceding sensation; and his elaboration of the concept of "trial-and-error" learning presaged the work of Thorndike and Watson and of behaviorist psychology generally. Bain held that the aim of psychology was not merely to explicate the laws of consciousness but to diagnose human character. Sublimely oblivious to the work of Fechner, Helmholtz, and Wundt, the founder of the journal *Mind* advocated the use of aptitude tests and the measuring of individual capacities. While Bain's magnum opus is regarded historically as "the culmination of the British philosophical psychology," it was appreciated by contemporaries as the integration of the sciences of mind and character.[59]

The extent to which the new psychology assimilated the program initiated by phrenology is evidenced in the American reception of Bain's classic monograph. In 1868 E. L. Youmans provided the introduction to the one-volume American edition of Bain's condensed work, *Mental Science*. Youmans wrote that

the later advances in Physiology have brought that subject into very close relation with questions of Mind. So important are the data thus contributed,
and so intimate the mutual dependence of these subjects, that it is no longer
possible to study Mind, in the true scientific spirit, without taking into account its material accompaniments. The method hitherto employed of studying mental phenomena by introspection is not superseded, but it has under-
gone an important extension. . . . The old system, which occupied itself with
inquiries concerning mind as an isolated abstraction, threw but little light on
the real psychical mechanism and workings of human nature. . . . But that
the study of mind in its larger aspects, that is, the actual study of man as a
thinking, feeling, and active being, must issue in the noblest applications, is
beyond all rational question. In the whole circle of human interests there is
no need so vital and urgent as for a better understanding of the laws of mind
and character. . . . The acquirement of true ideas concerning human nature,
the springs of its action, the modes of its working, and the conditions and
limits of its improvement, is indispensable for all. Parents need it for the training
of their children; teachers in the instruction of their pupils; employers in their
intercourse with the employed; physicians in treating their patients; clergymen in the management of their congregations; judges and juries. . . . In short,
whoever lives in social relations requires this knowledge for better and higher
guidance in the whole sphere of life. The extension of the subject of Mental
philosophy so as to include the physiological elements and conditions, and help
to a better understanding of the constitution of man, is therefore an important
step in the direction of our greatest needs. Human nature is no longer to be
dealt with by the students in fragments, but as a vital whole. In place of the
abstraction mind, is substituted the living being, compounded of mind and
body, to be contemplated, like any other object of science, as actually presented to our observation and in our experience.[60]

Youmans faithfully represented Bain's psychological agenda. Scientific psychology studies body and mind conjoined. Its subject matter includes personality, motivation, behavior, and adaption. Its orientation is thoroughly functional; its purpose, eminently practical.
Though it would be anachronistic to view this program as a criticism
of Wundt's system, Bain nevertheless had elaborated an alternative to
the tradition upon which the German philosopher built his physiological psychology.

The contrasts between the psychologies of Wundt and Bain illu-
minate the differences between physiological psychology and the new
psychology in general. While the Oxford graduate Titchener, who

studied at Leipzig, hailed Wundt as "the first psychologist," another Oxford product, John Carl Flugel, who was trained entirely in England, calls Bain "the first psychologist."[61] The difference of opinion reflects an important distinction. Wundt merits such recognition because he provided psychology with an experimental research design and a disciplinary organization, important considerations for a scientific group in its initial phases of academic institutionalization. But once those institutional inroads are reasonably assured, a discipline requires a conception of its purposes consistent with the expectations of a society on which it is dependent for support. Bain had delineated the aims and the scope of the kind of scientific psychology that ultimately prevailed. Youmans's accurate précis of Bain's practical program, as prescriptive as it is descriptive, represents a virtual blueprint of the disciplinary agenda pursued in America until Watson decisively excised Bain's equivocal considerations of the metaphysical problems and introspective methods that comprised so much of the psychological thinking of the mid-nineteenth century. Philosophical questions aside, Wundt's contribution rests in his ability to mobilize a scientific endeavor by prosecuting certain well-tested psychophysical and physiological techniques. He succeeded by industrializing in an intellectually credible fashion what psychology could actually accomplish. Bain, on the other hand, articulated a vision of what psychology should attempt to accomplish. As the discipline pursued Bain's practical functionalist goals, it departed the ascetic sanctuary of physiological psychology's laboratory.

Bain's work represents a critical link between the "forward-looking" behavioristic aspects of psychology and its roots in the phrenological tradition. Its functionalism, distrust of introspective methods, moving of psychology from its philosophical context to a biological one, physiological orientation, and utilitarian stance all stem from Bain's early and amply documented commitment to phrenology.[62] Even though Bain elaborated a sensorimotor view commonly considered in opposition to faculty psychology, his conception of the scope of psychology, derived from his adherence to phrenology, remained intact. Just as Wundt kept alive the introspective programs of philosophers concerned with insulating the study of mind from the assaults of experimental physiology, Bain sustained the interest in underlying physiological mechanisms of behavior and in objective analysis of mental phenomena following the denigration of phrenological notions of cerebral localization. However, he did not do so without the aid of a concept conspicuously absent from his system, the concept of evolution.

Evolution and the Revival of Phrenological Concerns

When Bain discarded his phrenological theories based upon the concept of mental faculties for a sophisticated sensorimotor theory grounded upon the principles of association, he had sacrificed what Angell would later regard as one of phrenology's most compelling features: the postulate "of definite and distinct forms of mental action." In place of innate faculties, Bain substituted the idea of spontaneous random movements that precede sensation and, through habitual repetition, produce voluntary action and terminate in purposeful behavior.[63] The establishment of laws of connection between random, voluntary, and purposeful activity would await the refinement of experimental procedures in comparative psychology in the late 1890s. In the meantime, Bain's reductionist hypothesis seemed to offer small gains to educators, alienists, and other professionals accustomed to viewing mind as a congeries of phrenological faculties and requiring greater emphasis on hereditarian modes of explanation than Bain's theory of random motion seemed to supply. Evolutionary theory provided these groups with exactly what they needed.

Herbert Spencer had adopted Bain's emphasis on learning as a fundamental problem of psychology. In his *Principles of Psychology* he invoked the idea of the inheritance of acquired characteristics in his argument that an organism's learned responses modify its nervous constitution and that those structural modifications become hereditarily transmissible. Combining association with evolution, Spencer replaced the Lockean tabula rasa of the individual with that of the race,[64] thus explaining how random movements become stabilized as instincts in the collective history of the species. By extending the principles of associationism from the experience of the individual to the experience of the tribe, the former proponent of phrenology[65] in effect converted phrenological faculties into hereditary instincts and provided an evolutionary conception of mind and behavior that retained the familiar notion of interaction between heredity and environment.

Spencer's notions appealed to the same groups that had flocked to the preachings of phrenology, and for many of the same reasons. Additionally, evolution commanded attention because it promised to explain change, "a sense of which," notes Stow Persons, "was so pervasive in the late nineteenth century."[66] Within educational theory, psychiatry, criminology, and social policy concerning "the race problem," evolutionary psychological theories were advanced as plausible explanations to pressing social problems. As phrenology's credibility sank under the weight of neurophysiological counterevidence and popular vulgarization, evolution provided a convenient theoretical framework for prosecuting the same kinds of empirical investigations once countenanced by phrenology. Education was one such concern.

The development of universal public education as democratic means of furnishing basic training for industrial society's children was accompanied by a search for a coherent pedagogical theory. The child-centered curriculum supported in the 1840s by the phrenological views of Horace Mann found new authoritative backing in the late nineteenth century in evolutionary naturalism. Recapitulation, a synthesis of evolution and embryology that hypothesized that the mental growth of the child repeated the phylogenetic development of the race, suggested to educationists that pedagogy be reformed to coincide with the child's natural sequence of growth.[67] G. Stanley Hall's child-study movement, informed by this new genetic paradigm, represented an exhaustive empirical compilation of children's behavioral traits such as Gall had envisioned. Its approach shifted slightly from generalized descriptions of static mental, moral, and physical traits to descriptions of the dynamic development of those traits. The essential purpose remained the same: to establish a composite portrait of mind while simultaneously eliciting patterns of hereditarily explicable individual differences.

The study of individual differences was also conspicuously manifest in the criminal anthropology of Cesare Lombroso. His *L'uomo Delinquente (Criminal Man)*, published in 1876, reinvigorated pre-Darwinian notions of hereditary degeneration by using anthropometric results to reinforce the conclusion that the criminal mind represented an atavistic throwback to the delinquent's racial past.[68] While the eugenics movement, which attempted to explain—among other things—the hereditary roots of criminal abnormality, is often seen as a consequence of evolutionists' concern with variation and, more specifically, with the investigations of Darwin's cousin, Galton, the overriding connection between phrenology and eugenics has been well documented.[69]

Social perception of increasing criminality complemented that of increasing insanity. The acknowledged failure of alienists to cure insanity by means of "moral treatment" paved the way for the introduction of neurological concepts of "mental illness."[70] Contemporary neurological thought, decisively influenced by John Hughlings Jackson and, through Jackson, by Spencer, assumed that the nervous system evolved in complexity and that this evolution represented a biological adaption to an increasingly complex civilization. Hughlings Jackson had maintained the doctrine of psychophysical parallelism: the nervous system of strictly sensorimotor processes was paralleled by ideas of sensation and movement. Thus, neurological thought left room for psychological as well as physiological investigation. Insanity was thought to result from disruption of this finely tuned and sensitive nervous structure through physical disease, through hereditary degeneracy, or through the impact of faulty ideas or traumatic emotional experiences. In the 1870s and 1880s, therefore, psychiatric thought was pursued by most neurologists in what Nathan Hale has called "the somatic style" and somewhat later in the hands of Freud along strictly psychological lines.[71] In a way, physiological psychology would mediate between these two extremes.

Statistical findings reinforced social perceptions in finding alarming correlations between insanity, crime, and immigration. The influx of southeastern Europeans and the migration of southern blacks elicited most apprehension in the major seaboard cities of the eastern United States, the centers of the new psychology in America.[72] The evolutionary theories of Spencer and his disciples, including the American John Fiske, and the eugenical investigations of Galton, conspired to make the assumption of immigrants' inferiority a problem for racial psychology.[73] Since mind was seen as the organ of adaption to the environment, immigrants' sudden change from relatively primitive cultural contexts to more civilized ones presented them with adaptive problems for which their inherited acquisitions had not prepared them. This exact formulation had already attained widespread recognition through the phrenological preachings of Charles Caldwell and George Combe.[74] In brief, the most glaring ills of American society seemed to form an interrelated cluster of problems significantly explicable in psychological terms, initially in terms of phrenological categories of explanation and finally in terms of evolutionary theory. Psychology as a diffuse (one might say "undisciplined") body of thought provided the groundwork for more than academic philosophy.

The Academic Institutionalization of Practical Psychology

Thus far, we have endeavored to show that, while Wundt refined the introspective study of the generalized human mind into the pure experimental psychology that came to be called structuralism, there remained throughout the nineteenth century a resilient tradition of objective, comparative, functional, practical psychology rooted in the phrenology of Gall and refurbished with the evolutionism of Spencer. Such a reminder constitutes an essential antidote to conventional portrayals of modern psychology evolving from structuralism to functionalism to behaviorism, and to the ubiquitous assumption of disciplinary endeavor moving "from philosophical psychology to experimental psychology and then on to applied psychology."[75] As virtually every contemporary description of the new psychology in American indicates, what was novel about the movement was the admixture of academic concern with both consciousness *and* character, with both mind *and* behavior, with both philosophy *and* social science.[76] The importation of Wundtian psychology was an important ingredient in the new psychology's scientific advancement, but the overwhelming cultural vision of the new psychology, the organization of its knowledge, and the very texture of its undertakings reflected the legacy bequeathed by Gall, endorsed by Bain, and restored by Spencer. Awareness of the fact that the new psychology represented an alliance of these two traditions constitutes an essential presupposition for fruitful discussion of the origins of behaviorism.

There remains, however, a fundamental question posed earlier as to how such inquiries into the mentality of madmen and murderers, of slow learners and rapidly proliferating immigrants became assimilated into the syllabus of academic philosophy. To be sure, the nineteenth-century moral philosopher was vitally concerned with such social issues as temperance, public schooling, and prison and asylum reform.[77] Still, there remains an obvious distinction between proselytizing for abstinence from alcoholic beverages and investigating the effects upon perception of intoxication, between urging humanitarian reform in the asylums and monitoring psychotic episodes, between elaborating the democratic benefits of public education and studying how children learn. The transition from ethics to practical psychology would depend ultimately upon the social and emotional predispositions of psychologists who found the treatment of such problems compelling and upon the dictates of a society on which psychologists were dependent for support. Such matters are the concern of subsequent chapters. Presently it suffices to show how certain aspects of the evolutionary controversy in philosophy and the Darwinian revolution in science facilitated this transition.

The compatibility between Wundtian psychology and the philosophic inclinations of the collegiate Realists has already been described. Academic philosophers had, however, always been wary of practical psychology because of its tendency toward materialistic explanations of mental phenomena. Especially in the form of phrenology, practical psychology, eschewing epistemology, metaphysics, and introspection, represented Common Sense Realism's ideological antithesis. Practical psychology leaned toward positivism that, many feared, was a stepping-stone to the spiritual quicksand of materialism. But just as the threat of evolution prompted philosophers to confront materialism on its own grounds by importing the positivistic physiological psychology of Wundt, the popularity of Spencer's mechanistic psychology encouraged the academic moralists to provide alternative hypotheses to Spencerian notions of the way the world worked.[78] As had no other psychologist since Gall, the metaphysically agnostic Spencer pleaded that the proof of his theories rested on their ability to provide plausible explanations for society's most urgent problems. To counter Spencer meant to encounter these problems more directly than the abstracted traditions of moral philosophy had previously permitted.

Ironically, when the new psychologists looked about for a countervailing framework of explanation of such problems, they found in Darwinian biology an approach that provided immeasurable philosophic consolation. Any apprehension that the substantive claims of evolutionary biology presaged analyses of mind solely in terms of physical or physiological laws was balanced by scientific comprehension of the fact that Darwin's own methods were far removed from any such reductionism. Attempting to solve a single problem of how species originated, Darwin had gathered his data from paleontology, geology, archeology, zoology, breeders' studies, demography, comparative anatomy, anthropology, botany, and a host of other natural historical sources. Such methodological eclecticism, argues Brian Mackenzie, served "to stimulate the assumption that a wide variety of kinds of evidence could legitimately be applied to the study of fundamental problems about living organisms. . . . The influence was determinative for both biology and psychology." Mackenzie's point merits quoting at length:

Regarding the units of scientific inquiry, Darwin made a wide-ranging scientific study, encompassing both animals and man, that owed little or nothing either to the reduction-laden concepts of physics or to the theology-laden concepts of most biology. He demonstrated that it was possible to make a major study which was wholly naturalistic and which would, after some dispute, be accepted as scientific, which had such variables as population pressures, adaption, reproduction, and variation among its fundamental units of explanation and description. Thereby, he showed that qualities other than physiochemical or even physiological ones could gainfully be employed and claimed to have causal significance in a naturalistic and scientific theory. The reducibility of these units to physiochemical ones was never an issue because . . . the evident fertility of such units, in their own field of applicability, made their reduction anything but a pressing issue. The success of evolutionary theory in biology thus made the reduction of biological—and by extension psychological—events to physiochemical ones a problem for future detailed explication rather than, as it had previously been, an impediment to the development of a theory which was scientific, but not based on physics.[79]

Within American academic psychology it is a demonstrable fact that from the very beginnings of institutionalization the new psychologists employed statistical methods for correlating individual differences and anthropometric techniques for measuring them; questionnaire methods for compiling data on child development; clinical studies of behavioral abnormalities; and, somewhat later, naturalistic observations of animals. The new psychologists engaged in mnemonics and hypnotism; they analyzed dreams; most of their interests took them beyond the laboratory door.[80] Surely such studies would and did develop within the respective fields to which they were germane. Educators would amass statistics; doctors would record cases of neurasthenia; and poets would interpret the meanings of dreams. But the example of Darwin's catholic approach encouraged the new psychologists to claim that, on the one hand, they were staunch traditionalists mapping the province of the old psychology—the normal adult human mind—and that, on the other hand, they were surveying this territory by using novel methods of empirical triangulation. They could approach the normal through the abnormal, the adult through the child, man through the animals, and consciousness through behavior. Darwinism reinvigorated the comparative empiricism of Franz Joseph Gall.

While the scientific promise of this eclectic approach for a unified conception of mental life remained to be seen, the professional advantages were immediately apparent. The new psychologists could portray themselves as custodians of continuity and purveyors of change simultaneously. Their claim to academic recognition did not hinge precariously on precocious calls for redefinition of psychology's purpose and scope. Rather, it seemed to rest modestly and reasonably on their insistence that they possessed new methods that represented a considerable improvement over "the armchair and the lamp." However mundane and naively empirical many of these methods (such as the questionnaire) proved to be, they possessed in the hands of the psychologist a prestige associated with the laboratory. Conversely, psychologists were able to argue convincingly that their accumulation of data from a wide variety of sources insured that "psychology will not have to wait till its greater laws [derived from the laboratory] shall be wholly established before she becomes of practical influence in common affairs."[81] Such assurances were particularly welcome, since the new psychology arrived precisely at the time when the reform presidents of the major universities were accentuating the practical aspects of academic endeavor.

These eclectic approaches to the study of mind encouraged the opening of lines of communication between academic psychologists and such nonacademic institutions as the clinic, the asylum, and the class-room. The repositories of their data were the arenas of social policy debate. This not to say that the new psychologists immediately par-layed their academic certification into practical roles as experts, for such competency as that term suggests remained to be justified. Rather, it is to suggest that the institutional linkages between academic psychol-ogy and the social agencies upon which such roles would eventually be grafted existed from the very beginnings of psychology's academic institutionalization and that justification for conducting certain types of research could readily be translated into utilitarian terms. The very ambiguity of what it was that psychology was about broadened its ap-peal, not only to its patrons, but to those drawn to psychology as a career, and facilitated its remarkable institutional success. This expan-sive catholicity, this sanguine expectation that a science of mind would emerge from the combined approaches of disparate investigations, this actual contact with social problems *was* the new psychology.

In the year of the APA's founding, when prospects of psychology's academic growth seemed secure, and when there were finally suffi-cient psychologists to listen, James predicted that if

the hard alternative were to arise of a choice between "theories" and "facts" in psychology, between a merely rational and a merely practical science of the mind, I do not see how any man could hesitate in his decision. The kind of psychology which could cure a case of melancholy, or charm a chronic insane delusion away, ought certainly to be preferred to the most seraphic insight into the nature of the soul.[82]

Twenty years later, Watson's declaration that psychology should be defined exclusively as the study of behavior mirrored the extent to which that hard alternative had been forced upon the profession. The next half of this work is devoted to elucidating the pressures that shaped that choice. It begins with the expectations and experiences of James, Ladd, and Hall, whose careers reflected the tensions implicit in the new psychology's manifold vision.

CHAPTER 6

The Search for Authority: William James and George T. Ladd

Shall I get me a little nook in the country and communicate with my living kind . . . or shall I follow some commoner method—learn science and bring myself into man's respect, that I may better speak to him?

—Henry James, Sr. to Ralph Waldo Emerson [1842?]

It is more than doubtful whether Fechner's "psychophysic law" . . . is of any great *psychological* importance, and we strongly suspect that Helmholtz's "unconscious inferences" are not the last word of wisdom in the study of perception; but because these things are very difficult and very "scientific," people who do not understand them will remain persuaded that they are of portentous moment, and will distrust all teachers who have not swallowed and assimilated them.

—William James
"The Teaching of Philosophy in Our Colleges," *Nation* (1876)

"Physical science," wrote William James in 1876, "is becoming so speculative and audacious in its constructions, and at the same time so authoritative, that all doctrines find themselves, willy-nilly, compelled to settle their accounts and make new treaties with it."[1] We saw in

chapter 2 how the metaphysical speculations of the German physiological reductionists prompted Wundt to devise physiological psychology, a rather inflated intellectual currency minted to save idealism
from scientific bankruptcy. And it was suggested in chapter 4 that the
religious audacity of Darwin's biological theories encouraged American academic philosophers to initiate diplomatic relations with Leipzig. Thus, when James declared that "one must have gone through
a thorough physiological training" in order to challenge recent developments in science and philosophy,[2] his argument appeared both intellectually logical and emotionally resonant. It was also professionally
expedient; which is to say that it possessed a social and institutional
logic too.

James was implicitly insisting that instead of the traditionally prescribed theological schooling his own scientific training represented the
best criterion for occupying a philosophic chair. Ultimately, the fulfillment of his professorial ambition depended upon the compatibility
of his scientific inclinations with certain organizational imperatives
within American higher education generally and at Harvard specifically. Science had become the ideal representation of intellectual authority, and postbellum academics in virtually every area of scholarship were attempting to heighten their social status and to enhance
their cultural and intellectual influence by calling their pursuits scientific.[3]

Harvard, the Culture of Science
and the Culture of Professionalism

This intimate connection between social strategies of professional uplift
and intellectual adherence to the methods and viewpoints of science is
readily discernible at Harvard. A half-century before James began his
teaching career in 1872, when Harvard was merely one of several New
England colleges serving the socioeconomic elite, college professors
constituted a much-abused group. Pedagogues rather than scholars
whose parietal functions outweighed their commitments to specific
bodies of knowledge, Harvard academicians were an undistinguished
lot, patronized by the Brahmin mercantile class and often ridiculed by
students. In general, they tended to have little training in their nom-

inal fields of interest and to have been selected for their academic roles more on the basis of character than of intellect. Themselves graduates of the college, they were bound to their alma mater by chains of intense provincial loyalty. Usually they were Unitarians. Many regarded collegiate teaching as a vocational moratorium, a brief interlude before settling down to a "real" career. Those who fashioned a permanent life within the confines of Harvard Yard were considered deficient in ambition. Seen in retrospect, they might well be regarded as amateurs.[4]

By mid-century, however, the academic community was beginning to cohere into a recognizably modern "professional" form. The professorate was becoming more cosmopolitan in its religious, socioeconomic, and educational background; increasingly committed to research and publication rather than to teaching primarily; and more concerned with gaining the esteem of disciplinary colleagues at other institutions than with enhancing local reputations. The new academicians regarded Harvard, in Robert McCaughey's apt phrase, as a "professional perch." They tended to possess certifiable credentials in their specialties, to spend a longer time obtaining such credentials, and to regard academic employment as a permanent career. These two portraits of "amateur" and "professional" academicians are, of course, ideal sociological types; most of the faculty fell somewhere between these extremes. Still, the steady aggregate movement from the former condition to the latter between 1821 and 1892 has been statistically documented. A Harvard professorship was becoming an increasingly valuable commodity.[5]

Many reasons have been advanced to explain this shift. What may have begun as a reaction to Jacksonian anti-intellectualism and a reflection of the anxieties of a waning genteel class, the urge to make academic life respectable, to raise the occupational status of scholarship, was aided positively by the example of German scholarship and negatively by religious declension.[6] For whatever reasons, the professionalization of academic life, as Thomas Haskell has argued, was more than a self-interested occupational tactic; it was "a major cultural *reform*," a way to establish intellectual and cultural authority in a manner conducive to the pursuit of truth, the growth of knowledge, and the perpetuation of a "community of the competent." Professionalization involved "efforts to build an institutional framework that would identify individual competence, cultivate it, and confer authority upon the individuals who possessed it."[7] Seeking to construct such a framework, scholars emulated the most successful of the nineteenth-century academic architects—the scientists.

The professionalization of science preceded that of other areas of scholarship in part because it meshed with the nation's urgent social, economic, and political needs. Westward expansion and rapid industrialization facilitated the development of physical and geological science. The need to keep a growing urban population healthy in the face of epidemic disease and well fed in the face of declining soil fertility assisted the growth of the medical and agricultural sciences.[8] Colleges and universities would remain the appropriate settings for the preservation, transmission, and development of scientific knowledge; these institutions would continue to house the vast majority of scientific laborers.[9] But the needs of government and industry prompted the gradual disengagement of science from general education and the initiation of organizational attempts to identify and to encourage scientific competence. These developments assisted the rise of a national scientific estate.

During the 1840s—the decade in which James, Ladd, and Hall were born—the term "scientist" came into parlance to distinguish the professionally trained and established expert from the gentlemanly amateur "man of science."[10] This shift was institutionally symbolized by the creation of the American Association for the Advancement of Science in 1847, the year of the founding of the Lawrence Scientific School at Harvard. Intensely involved in the creation of the AAAS were two of Lawrence's most outstanding faculty members: Louis Agassiz, who would become James's scientific exemplar, and Benjamin Peirce, father of James's close friend and fellow philosopher Charles S. Peirce. In the 1860s Agassiz and Peirce began vociferously campaigning for the application of professional criteria for academic appointments of scientists at Harvard. Their most celebrated victory came in 1863 when they persuaded Harvard President Thomas Hill to confer the prestigious Rumford Professorship on the Application of Science to the Useful Arts to Wolcott Gibbs, a New Yorker, a Columbia graduate, a German-trained student of Justis Liebig, and a nationally known research scientist. His competitor was a Bostonian, a Harvard graduate, and an assistant professor of chemistry at Lawrence. Though he lacked European training and a reputation for research, he boasted credentials that in another era or in a contemporary nonscientific arena would have guaranteed him the post. His father was a Harvard alumnus, a former mayor of Boston, and a onetime member of the Harvard Corporation. It was clearly a contest between a professional "outsider" and an amateur "insider," and when Gibbs accepted the Rumford Chair, Charles W. Eliot was informed by the man whom six years later he would replace as president that his contract had been terminated.[11] As we shall see, the moral attached to this episode was not lost on James, who transferred out of chemistry in the year of his teacher's disappointment into Agassiz's "department" of zoology. Eliot's eclipse may help explain why James liked to stress that he was "a stranger to Harvard College."[12] Despite his "local ties" and "cat-like dread of venturing away from Harvard"[13]—almost despite himself—James sought in the ensuing decade to cultivate the image of the professional, the scientist, the outsider. Harvard scientists were lighting the way to professional autonomy and cultural authority, and James was determined to follow.

William James

Born in 1842 into a family of considerable means and gentle eccentricities, William James was the older brother of the novelist Henry James and the first son of the nonconformist theologian and public philosopher, Henry James, Sr. Regarding proper education as the transcendence of all forms of orthodoxy, the elder James acquainted his sons with a "pluralistic universe" of high culture and cosmopolitan society; of European travel, languages, manners, and literature. The resultant intellectual and temperamental liberality that marked William James's thought and character as a mature scholar and that continues to be celebrated as his most precious asset provided small benefits to a young man searching for a vocation. Plagued by the dubious habit "of always seeing the alternative" and enabled by economic circumstance to avoid forcing a career choice, James simply could not decide what he should become.[14]

After studying painting in America and Europe, James surrendered his ambition to become an artist and entered the Lawrence Scientific School in 1861, as others of his generation marched off to war. Historian George Fredrickson has detected during this period "a change in the attitude of the gentleman-intellectual toward society and the active life." Partly as a result of the bloody sectional conflict, the genteel man of letters "was prepared to be a 'practical man,' working in an institutional setting. He was ready to make an heroic effort to find his place in the America that was coming into being."[15] Perhaps the most heroic aspect of this attitudinal shift were efforts to adapt new roles to individual personalities bound to older ideals and conventions.

At Lawrence he first learned chemistry from Eliot until the latter was obliged to resign. Finding laboratory work irksome and tedious, the would-be scientist thereupon became Jeffries Wyman's pupil in comparative anatomy and physiology. In Wyman, an evolutionary theorist as well as a biologist, James found a man with broader scientific and philosophic interests than Eliot had possessed. In 1863 he entered the Harvard Medical School where Wyman was Hersey Professor of Anatomy. Through his teacher the twenty-one-year-old medical student became acquainted with a remarkable scientific intelligentsia that included Agassiz, Peirce, Gibbs, and Asa Gray. Here was a community of men whose scientific breadth matched the literary cosmopolitanism of Cambridge and Boston and whose prestige—due in large part to the cultural significance of the evolutionary debate—overshadowed the celebrity of the literati. In some respects, Agassiz became James's intellectual ideal—one who aimed "at no less than an acquaintance with the whole of animated Nature."[16] At the end of March 1865, James interrupted his medical studies to join Agassiz on a nine-month zoological expedition to Brazil.

Resuming his medical studies the next year, James began flirting with philosophy. Unsure of his career and prompted by an illness that would probably have been diagnosed by contemporaries as neurasthenia, he again broke off his studies in April 1867 and journeyed to Europe, his physical sanatorium and vocational moratorium. Undoubtedly, this peripatetic procrastinator had learned from the example of Agassiz and from the Eliot-Gibbs incident that Europe represented the professional training ground for the academically ambitious. Attending Wilhelm Griesinger's lectures on psychopathology in Berlin, he announced his intention "to stick to the study of the nervous system and psychology." Both studies met at the nexus of his emotional difficulties and career aspirations.[17]

In the spring of 1868 James described his dilemma to his friend Oliver Wendell Holmes, Jr., whose father in the 1840s had been in the vanguard of the movement to reform Harvard's medical faculty along the lines of scientific professionalization.[18] James reported:

> I had hoped to get working at physiology, not that I have any special interest in its details, but that there is work there for somebody to do, and I have a (perhaps erroneous) suspicion that psychology is not *à l'ordre du jour* until some as yet unforeseen steps are made in the physiology of the nervous system; and if I were able by assiduous pottering to define a few physiological facts, however humble, I should feel that I have not lived entirely in vain. But now I see that I can never do laboratory work, and so am obliged to fall back on something else. . . . I shall continue to study, or rather *begin* to, in a general psychological direction, hoping that I may get into a particular channel. Perhaps a practical application may present itself sometime—the only thing I can now think of is a professorship of "moral philosophy" in some western academy, but I have no idea how such things are attainable, nor if they are attainable at all to men of a non-spiritualistic mold.[19]

Philosophy appealed to James because it considered nothing less than those "universal questions" of spiritual and cultural significance. Science attracted him because it appeared capable of grounding answers to such questions in bedrock certainty. No doubt thinking of Agassiz, James confessed envy of the biologist whose "concrete facts form a fixed basis from which to aspire as much as he pleases to the mastery of the universal questions when the gallant mood is on him."[20] Accordingly, he found it impossible "to break off connection with biological science."[21]

Yet neither was James capable of immersing himself in it. The problem with science was that it required such "assiduous pottering." James coveted the scientist's prestige but not his everyday routine. Shortly before he returned from Europe, he declared that "my only ideal of life is a scientific life"; yet he realized that he was "about as little fitted by nature to be a worker in science of any sort as anyone can be. . . . I should feel as if all value had departed from my life if convinced of *absolute* scientific impotence."[22] James simply could not "settle down to some one occupation for the rest of his days, and atone for the narrowness of his scope by the thoroughness of his treatment of it."[23] His mind begged to be challenged by broader concerns. Returning to Boston in November 1868, he began to chart a professional course that would allow him to compensate for his incorrigible philosophic drift with the compass of scientific mastery. In the process, he brought German scientific psychology to the attention of the American academic world.

In October 1871 the Harvard board of overseers complained that

Psychological studies cannot be said to rank very high among us. They are neither taught by as many teachers nor studied by as many students as they might be;—nor do they seem to excite the interest among those engaged in them which should be felt in questions concerning every generation of educated men.[24]

This announcement may have prompted James's renewed interest in physiological studies. That fall James's friend Henry Pickering Bowditch had inaugurated experimental physiology at the Medical School, and James frequently visited Bowditch's private laboratory in Boston. The following spring James accepted an offer from Harvard to teach comparative anatomy, and was appointed instructor of physiology in August 1872. His successful teaching debut coincided with the initiation of his famous philosophical correspondence with Charles Renouvier, out of which sprang James's celebrated conclusion that he could engage in science without accepting a deterministic world view.[25] At the end of his first teaching term, James confided to his diary:

I decide today to stick to biology for a profession in case I am not called to a chair in philosophy. . . . Philosophy I will nevertheless regard as my vocation and never let slip a chance to do a stroke at it.

Despite occasional doubts about his capacity for philosophic endeavor, James continued to work in physiology keeping his focus upon "mental science"—the field with which the overseers continued to express their disenchantment. At the end of the 1873 academic year, they complained that "neither the number nor the spirit of those who take electives in philosophy is what it ought to be."[26]

In 1875 James was able to move closer to his professional goal by offering a graduate course entitled "The Relations between Physiology and Psychology." That year also he established a demonstration laboratory—the first of its kind—in Lawrence Hall. The overseers applauded James's course with the previously cited remark that by ignoring physiological studies philosophers inadvertently exaggerated the importance of materialistic views. President Charles Eliot immediately proposed that James bring the force of this moral to bear upon the undergraduate mind. James would meet materialism head-on by introducing "Physiological Psychology—Herbert Spencer's Principles of Psychology" in the college. James viewed this opportunity as a springboard into philosophy. In 1877 he taught "Physiological Psychology" under the auspices of the philosophy department and informed Eliot that he wished to be considered "a candidate for the first philosophical vacancy that should occur." Three years later he was inducted into philosophy as an assistant professor.[27]

The thirty-eight-year-old physiologist's access to this coveted niche owned much to the measured appeal of his arguments to Eliot, who sanctioned James's innovation, not because he sensed its intellectual inevitability, but because he realized its institutional expedience. Intellectually, as we have seen, philosophy required the new psychology; professionally, James—whose Swedenborgian background deprived him of proper theological credentials—required it to gain entry into Harvard philosophy; and institutionally, as we shall see, Harvard in its bid for academic supremacy demanded it. Nurtured by these three streams, the new psychology took root at Harvard.

Eliot, James, and the Professionalization of Harvard Philosophy

Returning from two desultory years of study in Europe where he observed the German educational system and made a lukewarm and belated attempt at enhancing his scientific credentials, Eliot returned to Boston in 1865 to an appointment in chemistry at the (Massachusetts) Institute of Technology.[28] In 1869 he published an extensive and timely two-part article in the *Atlantic Monthly* entitled "The New Education," which captured the attention of Harvard's overseers as they convened to elect a new president.[29] Higher education, wrote Eliot, suffered from "clerical administration." Divinity schooling and pastoral training were no longer compelling prerequisites for the management of "large educational establishments" responsive to scientific culture, to trustees drawn increasingly from the business world, and to visions of institutional expansion involving the enrollment of a national clientele and therefore the rejection of sectarian affiliation or identification. "Fortunately for the country, education is getting to be a profession itself."[30] The modern university required the services of a "captain of erudition" compatible with the captains of industry who supported it, an academic broker-politician who had studied educational systems abroad—someone, in short, like Eliot.

In the eyes of the overseers, Eliot's arguments for the professionalization of educational leadership balanced nicely with his reputation as a loyal "insider," an innovative teacher, and an astute organizer. In his inaugural address, Harvard's twenty-first president outlined an executive course that he pursued for forty years. For all his scientific background and technical school experience, Eliot held firmly to traditional collegiate ideals. Harvard would continue to produce men of broad cultural sympathies and insight by providing "an accurate general knowledge of all the main subjects of human interest." Yet, sensitive to the needs of industrial society, Eliot intended Harvard to provide in addition "a minute and thorough knowledge of the one subject which each may select as his principal occupation in life."[31] Eliot recognized that the division of labor in society must be matched by "the division of intellectual labor." In Eliot's view, the specialization of intellectual work implied a psychology of individual differences. A general liberal education alone was insufficient; it was premised on a conception of mind as "a globe, to be expanded symmetrically outward. . . . A cutting-tool, a drill, or auger would be a juster symbol of the mind."[32] The new education must recognize the "natural bent and peculiar quality of every boy's mind" and the complementary need of industrial society for trained specialists in a multitude of fields. Harvard intended to provide its graduates with marketable careers in a society increasingly structured according to standards of function rather than class. Yet it also sought "to broaden, deepen and invigorate . . . all branches of learning" in order to insure that the specialized expert need not remain a cultural troglodyte.[33] Eliot's ability to provide this combination of assurances to wealthy patrons and potential clients helped him build Harvard into the nation's leading institution of learning.

Eliot's ambitions demanded curricular revisions that struck at the heart of the philosophic syllabus. A university democratically designed to meet all demands must recruit a large and diversified faculty. In order to entice an adequate complement of professors, the president saw the need to raise salaries during the initial years of his incumbency. By 1878 the instructional staff had doubled. Eliot intended to subsidize faculty expansion with the tuition recovered from increased enrollments. It was therefore absolutely essential that enrollment increases keep pace with faculty growth, and Eliot realized that in order to attract the largest possible student clientele it was necessary to dissociate Harvard from the last traces of sectarian affiliation.[34] "A university," insisted Eliot in his inaugural address, "is built, not by a sect, but by a nation."[35] Philosophy at Harvard, personified by Francis Bowen, embattled defender of the Unitarian faith, presented Eliot with an annoying reminder, while not of Harvard's vestigial denominational foundations, at least of its currently flimsy sectarian supports. Eliot was especially open to philosophical innovations capable of offsetting Bowen's orthodoxy; James did not disappoint.

Eliot had made his intentions known to Bowen from the start. "Philosophical subjects," advised the newly inaugurated president, "should never be taught with authority . . .; they are full of disputed matters, open questions, and bottomless speculations."[36] Eliot's call for the exposition rather than the imposition of philosophical opinion was rooted in his own liberal temperament and scientific prejudices, but it was prompted by the need to make Harvard philosophy sufficiently eclectic to attract—or at least not to repel—a heterodox student body. In 1877, when Eliot permitted James to offer his course on the connection between physiology and psychology within the philosophic curriculum over Bowen's protest, prudential considerations dictated his action. That year—for the first time since the Civil War—Harvard's expenditures exceeded income because enrollment had not kept up with faculty increases.[37] Eliot's famed elective system had come to grief at least in the areas of philosophy and psychology, as the overseers' almost annual complaints indicated. Students were plainly bored.[38] James had emerged as a popular teacher at Harvard in the early 1870s;[39]

placing his course on philosophy's roster might stimulate the revival of philosophic study. It certainly revived James's hopes for a philosophic position.

Inadvertently and with little sensitivity to the consequences of his educational policies, Eliot had converted Harvard into an arena of intense academic competition conducive to innovations such as James's. Ironically, Eliot was initially no advocate of professionally based appointments criteria; he handed four of his first six appointments to old friends, only one of whom had previous teaching experience. However, his determination to increase the salaries (and therefore the loyalty) of trusted friends at the top, when combined with the need to expand the faculty, forced him to do most of his hiring at the bottom where salaries were lower. By creating a large pool of aspirants at the lowest end of the occupational ladder, Eliot accelerated the tendency among the junior faculty competing with one another to accrue professional credentials in order to reach the top.[40]

In reality, there were not one but several ladders. The elective system that permitted students to specialize in particular interests required a similar specialization among instructors whose decisions to ascend a particular ladder were significantly conditioned by their predictive assessments of vacancies at the top. The received wisdom that interprets James's vocational vacillation exclusively in terms of very real philosophical and psychological ambivalences ignores the determining force of institutional exigencies. By 1871 Henry Bowditch, who received his M.D. degree the year before James, had preempted physiology at Harvard.[41] He was thirty-one years old; Bowen was sixty, and quaintly redundant. James knew where he might anticipate an opening that would lead to a chair.

Thus, while Eliot regarded James's undergraduate offering mainly as a fillip to philosophy's declining popularity, James did not miss his chance to apprise his former teacher of the greater significance of his new course. James declared that

the principal claim I should make for it is the intrinsic importance at the present day, when at every side naturalists and physiologists are publishing extremely crude and pretentious psychological speculations under the name "science"; and when professors whose educations have been exclusively literary or philosophical, are too apt to show a real inaptitude for estimating the force and bearing of physiological arguments when used to help define the nature of man. A real science of man is now being built up out of the theory of evolution and the facts of archeology, the nervous system and the senses. It has already a vast material extent, the papers and magazines are full of essays and articles having more or less to do with it. The question is shall the students be left to the magazines, on the one hand, and to what languid attention professors educated in the exclusively literary way can pay the subject? Or shall the College employ a man whose scientific training fits him fully to realize the force of all the natural history arguments, whilst his concomitant familiarity with writers of a more introspective kind preserves him from certain crudities of reasoning which are extremely common in men of the laboratory pure and simple?

Apart from all reference to myself, it is my firm belief that the College cannot possibly have psychology taught as a living science by anyone who has not a first-hand acquaintance with the facts of nervous physiology. On the other hand, no mere physiologist can adequately realize the subtlety and difficulty of the psychologic portion of his own subject until he has tried to teach, or at least to study, psychology in its entirety. A union of the two "disciplines" in one man seems the most natural thing in the world, if not the most traditional. But if tradition be required, Göttingen with Lotze, and Heidelberg and Zürich with Wundt would serve as most honorable precedents for Harvard College.[42]

In one stroke James had struck several of Eliot's responsive chords.

First, by suggesting that his course focused upon the themes daily displayed in the public press, James was assuring Eliot that it would provoke a popular response among students. Second, James's condescending references to the "inaptitude" of philosophers "educated in the exclusively literary way" and to the necessity of "scientific training" were guaranteed to appeal to the president whose inaugural address contained references to philosophy's "bottomless speculations" and to the need for acquainting all students with "what is meant by scientific observation, reasoning and proof."[43] James was assuring Eliot that there was a biological bottom to philosophic speculation. Third, despite Eliot's respect for scientific values, James's allusion to the intellectual "crudities" of laboratory men was certain to appeal. Eliot himself had little taste for research, had lost his post at Lawrence to a research chemist, and was disinclined to bring the research ideal to Harvard. "What the country needs," insisted Eliot, "is a steady supply of men well trained in recognized principles of science and art . . . who thoroughly understand what is already known."[44] James's demonstration laboratory was precisely what Eliot required: a place, as he said in his inaugural, that "would have science taught in a rational way, objects and instruments in hand—not from books merely, not through memory chiefly, but by the seeing eye and the informing fingers."[45]

Finally, James's call for a union of the two "disciplines" of psychology and physiology in one man must be seen in terms of its institutional as well as its intellectual logic. Viewed in the context of career realities at Harvard, his advocacy was also an argument for one man changing ladders halfway up the rungs. James's justifications for the feasibility of that step into philosophy were so compatible with Eliot's plans that one might be tempted to call them opportunistic; but, in fact, James ingenuously subscribed to his president's educational ideals.[46] He would be, in his own words of advice to Howison on Stratton, "a competent psychologist and exhibiter [sic] of classic experiments" and not the tortured tinkerer. James would master psychology to criticize it, not to advance it. "In short," he declared, "philosophy . . . claims her own where she finds it. She finds much of it today in physics and natural history, and must and will educate herself accordingly." Such a training would "enable [the psychologist] to teach, and show his pupils the physiology of brain, senses, and psychophysic methods in general." James admitted: "*I* always enjoyed that much of psychology." Novel scientific discoveries may or may not be important, said James, but "the fact that they involve a change in the method and *personnel* of philosophic study is unshaken"—as unshaken as the subsequent philosophical career James built for himself upon that self-fulfilling fact.[47]

And so what came to be called the new psychology—or at least a portion of it—made its way into the American philosophic curriculum. It arrived unheralded by enthusiasts for the research ideal or by advocates of its application to any problems other than philosophic ones. Almost immediately, however, Eliot's conception of the true purposes of the university was drastically altered by the creation of Johns Hopkins University in Baltimore. When James's foremost student, G. Stanley Hall, secured a permanent professorship there in 1883, he encountered a new set of institutional mandates that prompted him to move psychology into the realms of both laboratory research and practical application. When Hall moved on to Clark University in 1889 to establish a separate Department of Psychology, Harvard was forced to follow Clark's competitive example, for reasons that will be explained in the next chapter. Just as Bowen finally retired and Eliot offered James the Alford Professorship he had coveted for more than a decade, James suggested instead the creation of a separate professorship for himself in psychology, arguing that such an innovation was necessary to keep Harvard "in the foremost files of time."[48] Soon afterward Harvard's new professor of psychology inaugurated a brisk fund-raising campaign to acquire the equipment needed to convert his demonstration facility into an active research center. He also provided the new laboratory with a director—Hugo Münsterberg, an ardent experimentalist who would soon become America's leader of applied psychology. Then, having performed his "greatest stroke for Harvard," having sent his *Principles of Psychology* to his publisher, and tiring of the "nasty little subject," James demanded to be reappointed professor of philosophy.[49] He had performed a service in advancing psychology; the converse of this statement is equally true.

George Trumbell Ladd

While James was "scribbling a 'Psychology' toward completion" in 1888, he was surprised to receive in early April a copy of Ladd's *Elements of Physiological Psychology*. "I had no idea," he wrote its author, "that you were interested in any such thorough way in that side of psychology." James called Ladd's book "an honor to American scholarship."[50] "Coming, as it did, from a professor of philosophy at Yale who had been a Congregational minister," wrote Titchener at Ladd's death, "*[Elements of Physiological Psychology]* gave the young science an air of respectability (I can think of no better word) which was of high advantage in its struggle for life."[51] The highly orthodox source of this massive compendium of German experimentalism partly explains James's astonishment and suggests that the new psychology could germinate in diverse intellectual and institutional climes.

Eight days younger than James, Ladd was born in less congenial intellectual surroundings in Ohio's Western Reserve. Frontier frugality, however, did not imply lack of educational opportunity. Ladd followed the route to a scholarly career prescribed to Congregationalist sons whose families had small financial resources. In 1866 he departed for Andover Theological Seminary.[52] The Andover curriculum of classical languages and theological study aimed at providing congregations with a "learned ministry" capable of meeting the challenges of modern biblical scholarship, of mediating between science and religion. Not only would an enlightened clergy inspire a parish by means of exemplary piety; it would also uplift it intellectually.[53]

In 1876, as James and Hall were campaigning in the *Nation* for the application of scientific method to philosophy, Ladd, then a Milwaukee minister, published in the journal of conservative Yale Congregationalism, the *New Englander*, his "New Theology." Stressing the need for empirical scholarship, Ladd criticized the tendency of theologians possessed of "time and brains for scientific study" to engage in idle speculation. "This wrestling," he continued, "of nature, the Bible, history, and consciousness, in the interests of a polemical theology, must give way before the more patient and exhaustive study of all these sources by means of the improved helps which have recently been furnished."[54] In Milwaukee, Ladd continued meanwhile to call his sermons lectures, but realizing that "he could not convert the church into a college,"[55] he began publishing frequently in eastern journals in an attempt to convert a pastorate into a professorship. In 1879 he won an appointment as Southworth Lecturer on Congregationalism at Andover. Almost immediately upon his appointment he accepted a professorship of philosophy at Bowdoin College in Maine.[56]

The articles that had helped recommend the aspiring scholar to this small New England college resembled the sort of natural theology he had condemned in his 1876 manifesto. His essays sprinkled au courant allusions to Darwin, A. W. Volkmann, du Bois-Reymond, and Helmholtz, all of whom were enlisted to support the a priori conclusion that nature exhibits final purpose.[57] Ladd's call to Bowdoin to establish a separate department of mental and moral philosophy suggests that, while collegiate philosophizing still retained a theological orientation, it was at least doctrinally liberal and scientifically sophisticated. His simultaneous assumption of the Andover lectureship coincided with the celebrated takeover of that bastion of Congregational orthodoxy by a contingent of liberal theologians.[58] The historian George Peterson has called this institutional transformation one of the "seminal points of reform" of American higher education as a whole. Andover teachers and graduates stocked the presidencies and faculties of New England colleges throughout the remainder of the century.[59] Ladd nearly numbered himself among them in 1881 when Bowdoin offered him its presidency. Ladd declined in favor of a philosophic post at Yale.[60]

In 1880 Ladd had occasionally visited New Haven to discuss with Noah Porter, Yale's philosopher-president, the reorganization of philosophy at Bowdoin. Porter had been Yale's professor of moral philosophy and metaphysics for thirty-four years and its president for a decade. His *Human Intellect*, published in 1868, and *Elements of Intellectual Science*, published in 1871, had become the most popular college textbooks in psychology, or mental philosophy, before James McCosh's *Psychology* (1886) and James's *Principles* (1890). Porter's preeminence stemmed from the broad range of his erudition. He had overcome many of the handicaps of Scottish Realism and was totally familiar with the most modern of British empiricists—Spencer and Bain. In addition, he had studied in Berlin, where he assimilated German idealism—especially the critical philosophy of Friedrich Adolf Trendelenberg, who appreciated the philosophic usefulness of scientific methodology.[61] The theological keystone of Porter's psychological enterprise was the teleological demonstration of the existence of "an uncreated thinker" or final purpose.[62] According to Herbert Schneider, his appeal lay in his ability to give his theological psychology "the appearance of scientific objectivity."[63] Ladd found in Porter an exemplar for his self-ordained role as intellectual mediator between the old and the new. Seventy years old and approaching retirement, Porter saw Ladd as a protégé who conceived it his duty to examine psychological and physiological science in order "to know all that modern materialism has to offer" metaphysics.[64] In 1881, therefore, Porter offered Ladd a professorship in mental and moral philosophy, and Ladd had to choose between the institutional authority of the Bowdoin presidency and the intellectual authority of a Yale professorship. As the chairman of Bowdoin's board of trustees acknowledged, "the offer from Yale was such as came to exceedingly few young men, and to them only once in a lifetime."[65]

For the next six years at Yale, Ladd, by his own reckoning, spent "as many as twenty-five or thirty hours a week" mastering physiological and psychological treatises while preparing his *Elements*. He possessed "no laboratory for experimental research, and only a very meagre equipment of apparatus for illustrating the results of the research of others."[66] His familiarity with experimentation derived from the solicitude of Yale physiologist J. K. Thatcher. In his preface to *Elements*, Ladd stated the overwhelming purpose of his monumental labors:

Some writers have certainly indulged in extravagant claims as to the past triumphs of so-called Physiological Psychology, and in equally extravagant expectations as to its future discoveries. On the other hand, a larger number, perhaps, have been inclined either to fear or to depreciate every attempt to mingle the methods, laws, and speculations of the physical sciences with the study of the human soul. . . .

As a result of some years of study of the general subject, I express with considerable confidence the opinion that there is no ground for extravagant claims or expectations, and still less ground for any fear of consequences.[67]

Concluding that physiological psychology did not jeopardize the autonomy of the soul, Ladd felt confident that he had made modern materialism safe for metaphysics. In the process, he made available to a nascent academic discipline an experimental encyclopedia.

Like James and Hall, Ladd had come to psychology in an attempt to reconcile the claims of positivism and idealism. Unlike his contemporaries, he failed to expand his vision of psychology's purposes beyond that single aim and thus sacrificed whatever hopes he may have entertained of assuming disciplinary leadership. Porter was his mentor, an educational conservative who held firm to the idea of collegiate labor as mental discipline, denounced the transformation of Yale from college to university as "an outgrowth of materialistic tendencies," blocked faculty efforts to initiate the elective system, and refused to offer assistance to the Hopkins trustees seeking advice about university-building.[68] "The manners & customs of the Yale faculty," smirked Eliot in 1880, "are those of a porcupine on the defensive. The other colleges were astonished at first, but now they just laugh."[69] Ladd was a quintessential porcupine with little enthusiasm for research and no desire to promote psychology as an autonomous discipline. But his success in gaining a prestigious philosophical post shows that the new psychology could grow in a variety of institutional settings. James would never have been an acceptable candidate to Porter; he carried as much metaphysical baggage as Ladd, but he carried it less conspicuously. Eliot would have rejected the theologically minded Ladd out of hand. Nevertheless, Ladd's endeavor was not *ab origine* so very different from James's. Different institutional exigencies would largely dictate the scope of their activities. One institutional development, however, served to force psychology at both Harvard and Yale into a similar pattern of activity: the founding of Johns Hopkins University. By the mid-1890s, G. Stanley Hall and the "Hopkins idea" had become American psychology's guiding light.

CHAPTER 7

The Search for Authority: G. Stanley Hall

I may have no influence at all, but I do believe I have some things in my head and note-books to say which are so true to *me* that it will be the supremest intellectual luxury to work and hunt around till I can get them said somehow.

—G. Stanley Hall to William James,
15 February [1880]

[A] summons is issued to the forces of the soul to rally, to marshal themselves, to submit to discipline, to do in a definite and purposeful way a certain piece of work.

—George T. Ladd
Psychology: Descriptive and Explanatory (1894)

From the tiny rural village of Ashfield, Massachusetts, few roads emerged for the intellectually ambitious. Born in modest circumstances in 1844 to a farming family, Stanley Hall was raised in the stern traditions of conservative Congregationalism. Ashfield's rocky fields provided fitting soil for the stony austerity of Hall's puritan upbringing. A principal legacy that Hall's childhood milieu bequeathed to him was a desire to escape it. The trail that led beyond the young man's confines started at the schoolhouse door.[1]

In 1863, after a year's preparation at a local academy, Hall entered

Williams College. Thirty miles from Ashfield, Williams was the first step of a long journey toward a scholarly career. At Williams, Hall initially cultivated literary and artistic tastes but soon turned toward philosophy under the inspiration of Mark Hopkins, Williams's president and professor of moral philosophy and rhetoric. Hopkins's textbook, *Lectures on Moral Science*, appeared the year before Hall's arrival. An educator rather than a scholar, Hopkins attempted a synthesis of moral and natural philosophy that duly attended to the physiological aspects of mental science.[2] Hopkins was the exemplar of the oldtime president-philosopher. But in 1871 when James A. Garfield defined college education as "Mark Hopkins on one end of a log and a student on the other,"[3] the ideal embodied in that famous statement had already become nostalgic. Hall "knew the German universities were the goal of aspiring scholars" but, lacking adequate funds, realized that "the clerical profession was still the chief path open to a young man of philosophical interests."[4] Upon graduating from Williams in 1867, Hall enrolled at Union Theological Seminary in New York City.

Union only whetted the young divinity student's appetite for Germany. Its curriculum exposed him to liberal Protestantism, and its metropolitan context provided him with a social education he found "irresistible."[5] Compared with Ashfield, New York City appeared exotic and uninhibited; compared with Williams, Union seemed an intellectual vanguard. Moreover, the Union faculty encouraged students to study philosophy in Germany. One such student, George Sylvester Morris, had just returned from Germany and would fashion a philosophic career at major American universities without the passport of a divinity degree. Morris would later become Hall's chief competitor for a post at Johns Hopkins University, but at the time Hall "looked up to him as fulfilling my very highest ideal—a man who had been abroad and knew philosophy."[6] Determined by Morris's example to pursue philosophy as a vocation, Hall secured patronage, interrupted his studies, and sailed for Europe in June 1869.

In Germany, Hall came under the influence of Adolf Trendelenberg, Morris's mentor, who acquainted Hall with the need to approach philosophic problems empirically. Empty pockets frustrated Hall's attempt to remain in Germany to obtain his Ph.D. Less than a year and a half after his arrival, he was forced to return to the United

States, complete his studies at Union, and use his divinity degree—along with an exaggerated report of his "three years" abroad—as certification for a college teaching post in philosophy. While searching for such a position, Hall spent two years in New York City as tutor to the children of a wealthy Jewish banker. There he entered into a circle of Comtean positivists and "free thinkers" who turned his philosophical thinking into the channels of naturalism. Finally, in the summer of 1872, at the age of twenty-eight, Hall obtained a position at Antioch College in Ohio. Upon the resignation of Antioch's president-philosopher George W. Hosmer in the following year, he became Bellows Professor of Mental Philosophy and English Literature.[7]

Hall's position was nevertheless temporary. Knowing that his chair would devolve to the next president, Hall nearly exhausted himself in an unavailing attempt to become Antioch's indispensable man. His impermanence, however, was underlined by the panic of 1873 and by declining enrollments. By 1875 he was again seeking an appointment elsewhere and searching about for a safe philosophical stance that would avoid the "seductive extremes" of idealism and materialism and thus commend him to conservative trustees. Before he left Antioch, he had familiarized himself with Wundt's *Grundzüge* and began to see in "the application of scientific methods in psychology" a safe route into a permanent philosophical position. Hall was not prepared to return to Germany to secure more specialized training in the methods of physiological psychology until he had exhausted his search for an appointment elsewhere. Hoping for an offer from the newly established Johns Hopkins, he returned east in 1876 and settled in Cambridge.[8]

While waiting, Hall decided to enroll as a graduate student in philosophy under James. No sooner had he arrived in Cambridge when an article bearing his initials appeared in the *Nation*. It was calculated to show Eliot that the writer's view of "College Instruction in Philosophy" was identical to the Harvard president's.[9] That the typical pattern of philosophical instruction, complained Hall, is based upon "theological considerations . . . is largely responsible for the supposed unpopularity of the studies." In phrases reminiscent of Eliot's inaugural address, Hall claimed that philosophy "is generally given into the hands of one of the older and 'safer' members of the faculty, under the erroneous belief that it should be the aim of this department to indoctrinate rather than to instruct—to tell *what* to think, than to teach *how* to think." Hall implied that the "application of scientific methods in psychology" made possible "the application of philosophical systems to history, politics, law and education." Philosophy could become practical only if its methods became scientific. Accordingly, "methods of instruction need to be remodelled."[10] Hall had orchestrated his indictment to appear alongside James's note on "The Teaching of Philosophy in Our Colleges," which tempered Hall's rough assessment with the assurance that "the unfortunate condition of things which 'G. S. H.' and we alike regret is already on the eve of changing."[11] James, however, had more cause for patience; he himself stood to gain from those changes at Harvard which appeared imminent elsewhere only at Hopkins. In April 1877 Hall informed James of the possibility of a philosophical opening in Baltimore, and James, seeking leverage to promote his aspirations with Eliot at Harvard, immediately initiated negotiations with Daniel Coit Gilman, Hopkins's president.[12] Hall was hoping to capitalize on James's formula for vocational salvation either at Hopkins or at Harvard should James opt for the former. In order to increase his chances, he completed his doctoral dissertation, "The Muscular Perception of Space," in 1878 and departed once more for Germany in quest of a more thorough scientific training that would recommend him to the new Hopkins president.[13]

Hall, Gilman, and the Professionalization of Psychology

There seemed little reason to doubt that the formula James had used to gain entry into philosophy at Harvard would work at Hopkins, for Gilman's views of higher education initially seemed very similar to Eliot's. At the very end of 1874 Gilman had been selected president of Hopkins by a group of astute businessmen-trustees remarkably free to shape the university as they saw fit. When the Baltimore financier Johns Hopkins died a year earlier, he had bequeathed half of his $7 million estate for the building of a new university and the other half for a new hospital.[14] Gilman had all the right credentials to guide the former. He had taught at Yale's Sheffield Scientific School, had investigated European educational systems, and had received some scholarly training in Germany. Attentive to America's industrial expansion, he had been in the vanguard of attempts to establish specialized scientific educational systems. Previously president of the University of California and an adept administrator, Gilman was a religious liberal, an avowed antisectarian in educational policy, and in curricular matters a middle-of-the-road reconciler of classic liberal education and utilitarian training.[15] In all these respects he resembled Charles W. Eliot, who wholeheartedly recommended him for the post. And, like Eliot, he conceived of philosophy as moral education; not "as a research subject but as edification."[16] Faced, however, with certain political, religious, and administrative requirements, Gilman changed his view of philosophy's role at Hopkins.

The predetermining cause for Gilman's turnabout was his decision to build his university into a national center for scientifically oriented scholarly research and graduate education patterned largely after the model of the German university. In what Hugh Hawkins calls "perhaps the worst prediction of educational history," Eliot cautioned against this course. Graduate schools, warned Eliot, had to be built upon a firm collegiate foundation in order to insure community support and to provide a sufficient pool of students for postgraduate work.[17] Eliot had underestimated both the national need for such an indigenous institution and the increased professionalism of his own faculty, many of whom found the Baltimore experiment extremely attractive. Gilman's decision to disregard Eliot's advice and to concentrate on graduate studies was partly dictated by considerations of faculty procurement. Starting from scratch, Gilman faced a different hiring problem from the one Eliot had encountered six years earlier. He could not select a professorate on the basis of traditional loyalty; nor could he gradually acquire one by the slow and safe process of replacement and supplement. What he could do was to monitor academic discontent elsewhere and advertise an antidote at Hopkins, to mold inchoate and often frustrated tendencies toward professionalism into a purposeful university policy. Hopkins would provide light teaching loads, support for independent investigation, research assistants, departmental autonomy—in short, the institutional paraphernalia of a growing disciplinary self-consciousness. When Gilman began inviting Harvard notables, Eliot felt the competitive "presence of this new and very se-lective buyer in the academic marketplace."[18]

Gilman's strategy not only threatened to deprive Harvard of its most precious national advertisement—world-renowned scholars—but it also severely weakened Harvard's graduate programs. Harvard had 58 graduate students in 1876 and only 41 in 1880. By that latter year, Hopkins—which scandalized Eliot by offering what he considered bribes in the form of graduate fellowships—had over 100 candidates for the Ph.D degree. This situation was even worse elsewhere. Between these same years the graduate enrollments at Yale and Cornell—two of the handful of major psychological research centers in the 1890s—dropped from 67 and 23 to 29 and 7, respectively.[19] When in the late 1870s and 1880s undergraduate enrollment began to expand nationally be-cause of the enlargement of public secondary schooling, the value of graduate students as underpaid undergraduate instructors correspond-ingly increased. At the end of Hopkins's first academic year, Eliot—seeking to keep his faculty from glancing longingly toward Balti-more—attempted to relieve professors "of such routine work as can be equally well done by persons whose time is less valuable."[20] In short, Gilman's innovation, combined with undergraduate expansion, forced other university presidents to compete with Hopkins for faculty and students by refurbishing their graduate programs.[21] With no special commitment to the investigative ideal, these reluctant reformers thus established the precondition for the American development of psy-chology as a research science and as an academic profession.

This institutional precondition, though, did not constitute a suffi-cient cause for such a development. Like Eliot, Gilman initially viewed philosophy in traditional terms, "thinking of psychology as a minor item to be cared for by the department of philosophy." But by 1884 he was "speaking of the 'group of philosophical studies' under one Professor of Psychology."[22] The reasons for Gilman's reconsideration had to do with the commanding position of the biological sciences at Hopkins and the adverse public reaction that followed their introduc-tion.

Anticipating the construction of the hospital that Hopkins had en-dowed, the university authorities had decided that their institution would house the largest and best department of biology in the country. "I do not suppose," reminisced Gilman, "that anyone connected with the university had thought of the popular hostility toward biology."[23] Eliot's warning about the implementation of postgraduate schooling at Hopkins had at least been grounded in realistic apprehensions. Baltimorians had already become predisposed to suspect Gilman's educational aims when it became apparent that their local community stood to gain few immediate benefits from Hopkins's largesse if the university attended primarily to scientific research. When Thomas Henry Huxley, an acknowledged aetheist and exponent of Darwinism, arrived in Baltimore in 1876, the animosity that had been channeled by local politicos into charges of elitism was readily transformed into warnings from the pulpit of godless materialism. That same year at conservative Princeton, James McCosh informed the trustees of his school, "We cannot keep our students from reading the works of such men as Herbert Spencer [,] Darwin [,] Huxley and Tyndall."[24] It was one thing to acknowledge the impossibility of censoring Huxley's works in American universities; another to invite him to give the key address at Hopkins's opening ceremonies. Gilman had hoped by inducing Huxley to give that address to advertise Hopkins to the American and European scientific communities from which he sought to procure his faculty.

Unfortunately, he had also raised Hopkins's agnostic colors to conservative religionists. The opening exercises, wrote one New York reporter, opened and closed without prayer or benediction. He continued:

Honor, here, was refused to the Almighty. The gentlemen at the head of the University were well aware of this. But if the neglect was due to the unchristian or materialistic sentiments of the authorities, then we can only say, God help them, and keep students away from the precincts of the young institution.[25]

One minister complained that it was "bad enough to invite Huxley. It were better to have asked God to be present. It would have been absurd to ask them both."[26] He nevertheless confessed that it was still possible for the university to surmount its unfortunate beginnings. "It was several years," confessed Gilman, "before the black eye gained its natural colour."[27] The trustees prescribed that the blemish be treated with the salving compress of philosophic orthodoxy. To that end Gilman initiated a cautious policy of inviting a number of philosophers to deliver series of lectures before deciding on a permanent appointment.

Meanwhile Hall, recently arrived in Germany, published in *Mind* a scathing review of the condition of "Philosophy in the United States," in which he continued his criticism of religiously dominated instruction. Complaining that James's offering at Harvard represented "the only course in the country where students can be made familiar with the methods and results of recent German researches in physiological psychology," Hall expressed hope "that the new University of Baltimore will soon establish a chair in physiological psychology and another in the history of philosophy."[28] Hall had incessantly advised Gilman since 1876 that he was eminently qualified to occupy either chair.[29]

In the wake of the Huxley affair, religiosity constituted an especially relevant aspect of one's philosophic qualifications. Hall had to assure Gilman that he, the history of philosophy, and physiological psychology were similarly safe. Hall wrote to Gilman:

As to my religious sentiments, I am a graduate in divinity . . . am in the habit of church-going and indeed am still a nominal church member I believe. I do not think it is possible for any one to become deeply interested in philosophy without devout respect growing more profound at every step.

The history of philosophy, he reported, avoided "all the *odium theologicum* . . . from whatever quarter" because the historical method allowed the teacher to introduce unorthodox ideas without having to sponsor such ideas himself. As for his psychological views, Hall declared, "I am as far as *possible* from materialism in every form." His physiological studies had led him to conclude "that materialism is simply want of education."[30]

Undoubtedly sincere, Hall also knew that materialism meant want of employment. In 1876 he was not particularly proselytizing for the advancement of the science of psychology; he was merely campaigning for his own philosophic future. Either field—history of philosophy or physiological psychology—would do. By 1879, however, his philosophic prospects seemed bound to the fortunes of psychology because his former hero, G. S. Morris, who had introduced Hall to the former field, had just been appointed as a Hopkins lecturer on the history of philosophy. Hall abruptly ceased pleading his versatility, informing Gilman that his work had been "entirely physiological for the last three years, with daily laboratory work, latterly with Wundt & Helmholtz—this entirely in the same line as James."[31] The comparison was appropriate, for, as Hall knew, James had just declined Gilman's invitation for a lectureship in psychology, recommending Hall in his place.[32] Because James's decision to remain at Harvard obviated Hall's chances of teaching psychology there, because Harvard discountenanced the historical approach to philosophy,[33] and because he feared that his diatribe on the state of American philosophy had ostracized him from a university position elsewhere, Hall's professional hopes hinged on psychology. Hall had become committed to a single specialty.

A characteristic aspect of professionalism, however, is that once bound to a nonexpanding field specialists become extremely adept at enlarging the range of interests to which that field may be applied. Praying that circumstances "will not send him west again," and fearing that "neither psychology nor philosophy would ever make bread,"[34] Hall began while in Germany to pursue psychological studies along nonphilosophical lines. Considering a career in medicine, he extended his interest to psychopathology, but, sensing the groundswell of enthusiasm in the United States for educational reform, he reasoned that "the most promising line of work would be to study the applications of psychology to education."[35] When Hall finally did get his chance to lecture at Hopkins in 1881, his cultivation of both of these interests dictated Gilman's provision of a temporary appointment.

Returning from Germany, Hall immediately secured something of a national reputation in the new and popular field of pedagogy by lecturing educators on the need to apply the principles of psychological science to their classroom pursuits. In 1881 at Harvard, Eliot had provided him with an opportunity to give public talks on pedagogy as a university lecturer. The success of Hall's lectures impressed Gilman, who was anxious to show the Baltimore community that his university—criticized for its esoteric scientific elitism—was sensitive to practical public issues. When Hall finally received a permanent post at

Hopkins in 1884, it was as professor of psychology and pedagogics. Hall's triumph was also aided by his and James's ability to persuade Gilman that his training provided a crucial "connecting link between your medical and your philosophical departments."[36] Child psychology and abnormal psychology were hardly pursuits Gilman had initially envisioned for philosophy at Hopkins, but they became endeavors he warmly welcomed. Applied concerns informed psychological research in America from its very beginnings at Hopkins.

When Hall arrived at Hopkins in 1881, two other part-time lecturers were in residence and on trial. Many accounts of Hall's ascendancy over Charles Sanders Peirce and Morris have interpreted his victory as a testimony to the rising authority of science. More precisely, however, the establishment of psychology at Hopkins was conditioned not by biological science's cultural power but by its vulnerability. The overwhelming presence of science at Hopkins exacerbated fears of materialism there. Hopkins, many felt, was the most secular university in America and, therefore, was the most critical arena for attempts to find, in Charles Peirce's words, "*a modus vivendi* . . . between philosophy, science, and religion."[37] Hall seemed perfectly suited to this task. Here was the country's first doctorate in psychology, a man who had been abroad once as a philosopher and once as a scientist, a dissector of brains, an understudy of the reductionist Helmholtz, an intellectual on the advancing edge of "the actual condition of thought" in what he himself called "the psychological age"; and he could authoritatively conclude that "materialism is simply want of education." Thus, to a university reeling under charges of "modern paganism," Hall conveyed "the healing word almost from the side of biology itself."[38] In 1885, during the university's annual commemoration day ceremonies devoted to official recognition of the institution's relationship with the local community, Gilman approvingly cited Hall's assurance that the "new psychology, which brings simply a new method and a new standpoint to philosophy, is I believe Christian to its root and centre." The Bible, said Hall, "is being slowly re-revealed as man's great text-book in psychology."[39] Hall's psychology promised to soften the edge of biological science as it cut into Christian culture.

Once Hall had established himself at Hopkins, it seemed that the best thing the new psychology could do for religion was to ignore it.

Appropriately, Hall chose to publish his introductory lecture, "The New Psychology," in the liberal theological journal, the *Andover Review*.[40] Yet, despite perfunctory religious reassurances, nothing of theological or metaphysical substance graced his program of psychological studies. "All who have absorbed themselves in [psychophysics]," claimed Hall, "have seen the logical impossibility of every purely materialistic theory of knowledge." Brain physiology seemed to offer at present "a justification of an idealistic view of the world."[41] Thus acquitted, psychology could go its separate way. Hall's prospectus seemed to indicate that it was heading toward practical objectivism.

In his inaugural lecture, Hall divided the "New Psychology" into three parts: comparative, experimental, and historical psychology. The first field owed its inspiration to the broad evolutionary outlook of Darwinian biology and to Darwin's expositor at Hopkins, William Keith Brooks, biologist and former classmate of Hall at Williams.[42] Evolution, according to Hall, had bequeathed two problems to psychology: that of defining instinct (was it phylogenetically organized "reflexes" or "lapsed or fallen intelligence"?); and that of determining "what is *a priori* and innate in man." Both questions possessed immense "practical value" to educational and psychiatric science.[43] Moreover, evolutionists had contributed to psychology an important procedural refinement involving the realization that questions "once thought accessible only by introspective or speculative methods" could now be "treated objectively and with great methodological refinement." Hall doubted that animal psychology could become rigorously experimental but insisted that it was "no less scientific" for that.[44] The comparative empiricism and objective observation of behavior urged by Gall had come to Hall, as to the new psychology generally, by way of evolutionary biology.

Even in the field of experimental psychology, there was little Wundtian introspection at Hopkins. Peirce had actually engaged in experimentation before Hall's arrival and, as a good positivist, had concluded that there was "no reason for supposing a power of introspection and consequently the only way of investigation in psychological questions is by inference from external facts."[45] Peirce had elsewhere provided scientific professionalization with an epistemological rationale by arguing that science was a social response to uncertainty.

Science justified its claims to social autonomy and to cultural authority by selecting problems capable of objective verification. The truth of any matter was what the consensus of opinion of the best minds declared it to be. "Every science, before it was a real science," Peirce explained to Gilman, "was a theatre for empty talk and metaphysical nonsense. Psychology has just left this stage" and was beginning to congeal into an ongoing community of the competent by avoiding introspective speculation.[46] In his "New Psychology" address Hall signaled his subscription to this viewpoint. "Self-examination," he intoned, "reduced [philosophers] to the condition of primitive thinkers with no consensus."[47] Hall had earlier acknowledged that, while "self knowledge was highly spoken of . . . in a purely religious or ethical sense," he never escaped the feeling that it was "unpractical and paralyzing."[48] In the years to come, he would become an archfoe of introspection and of consciousness as the method and focus of psychological study, respectively.

"More central, and reduced to far more exact methods" than comparative psychology was the field of experimentalism. Hall briefly described the scope, methods, and development of sense physiology, psychophysics, and neuroanatomy. His exposition illustrated the decisive influence of Bain and of British physiology on his thinking. Hall conceived of the brain "as a complex reflex center of many mediations between the senses and the muscles" and viewed the experimenter's task one of measuring "the strength, duration, freedom, accuracy, and many-sidedness of our reactions on the various stimuli which reach us." Hall bemoaned the fact that physiological psychology had been "thus far chiefly applied to the study of elements fundamental to consciousness rather than to its more complex processes." Like Bain, Hall preferred to concentrate on movement rather than on sensations, and to view the entire body as the subject of psychological investigation. Hall planned to explore "memory, association, and volition under the action of attention, toxic agents, fatigue, practice, age, etc." He would use the methods of physiological psychology, with which Wundt sought to decipher the general laws of normal consciousness, to fashion a differential psychology.[49]

Finally, Hall sketched the dimensions of historical psychology that he viewed as a humanistic discipline tailored to the undergraduate curriculum. Patterned after Wundt's *Völkerpsychologie* and informed by Hall's own cosmic evolutionary perspective, it incorporated genetic psychology, anthropology, philology, literature, and even the history of philosophy. In short, historical psychology endeavored "to go back of all finished systems [of thought] to their roots, and explore many sources to discover the fresh, primary thoughts and sensations and feelings of mankind." It aimed at nothing less than an evolutionary psychohistory of culture. Hall's disavowal of personal allegiance to the notion "that psychology is all there is of philosophy" was unconvincing. At Hopkins, philosophy would be subsumed under psychology administratively and intellectually.[50]

Research, Utility, and Liberal Culture

Laurence Veysey has deciphered three competing academic persuasions vying for supremacy in the modern university: research, utility, and liberal culture.[51] Hall and the new psychology generally paid homage to all three. In the undergraduate curriculum, psychology continued to function much like the mental and moral sciences in the "oldtime" college as a liberal area of study. Additionally, it was seen as an appropriately safe discipline within which to acquaint beginning students with the methods and discipline of science. The "self-control" of psychological science made it a fitting introduction to philosophic studies. Science meant more than organized empirical knowledge; it connoted, Hawkins observed, "a much-admired way of living and thinking." As David Hollinger has perceptively put it,

Science, everyone knew, was quintessentially open-minded and expansive, as opposed to being dogmatic and sterile; to be identified with science was, potentially, to be identified with a liberal willingness to entertain new ideas. Yet this touted open-mindedness was not anarchic; science was disciplined and cautious, and it had a sense of community. Hence the practice of science seemed an attractive model for the practice of life: one could change and grow, but steadily and surely.[52]

Academic philosophy, its pedagogical business being to provide such models, found psychology compatible with its purposes. The majority of laboratories created in the 1890s and beyond were demonstration facilities that owed their existence not simply to the need to exposit "classic experiments" but more fundamentally to indoctrinate students into the culture of science.[53] Concentrating on innovations—such as support for scientific research—which distinguished the "new university" from the "oldtime" college, histories of higher education have often tended to undervalue the resilience of collegiate ideals. Much of the support and enthusiasm for the new psychology had little direct connection with the advancement of scientific knowledge.[54] Hall echoed James's complaint that experimentalism suffered from the lack of "philosophizing." Psychologists, he pointed out,

sleep on balances with apparatus that records the slightest change of pulse . . . ; they test themselves with mild doses of narcotics . . . ; they multiply or reduce air pressure over the entire dermal surface; they select a square inch of skin, and with every known test educate it for months; they fatigue definite muscle groups. . . . Fruitful and important as all this is, it by no means covers the ground of the old college philosophy. It has little ethical power in it, and for the average student it is not, perhaps, always idealizing.[55]

When James addressed the celebrants of Princeton's sesquicentennial in 1896, he requested that Baldwin refrain from introducing him as a psychologist. "Moralist" or "man of letters" would do nicely.[56] George Ladd, who more than either of his two contemporaries sought to harmonize science with liberal culture, acknowledged that it was "the scientific spirit to which the university education primarily appeals" but found it "difficult to understand how any man can attain the genuine scholar's *liberal* mind, who takes no interest in the process and laws of his own mental and moral life, and [those] of other men." Ladd saw psychology as "an indispensable auxiliary to the entire group of liberalizing pursuits" and as a useful "mental discipline."[57]

Indirectly, of course, the "scientific spirit" that invaded the undergraduate curriculum encouraged the development of the research laboratory—again—not as the workshop of scientific progress but as the seminary of pedagogical certification. No philosopher, insisted James, could *teach* psychology without a thorough physiological training. One of Hall's favorite lines of critical attack in his usually trenchant reviews of psychological literature involved undermining a book's authority by referring to the author's lack of laboratory training. Responding to one such attack on his *Elements*, Ladd reminded Hall that he had at least "read and observed physiology" thoroughly. What mattered, he insisted, was his success "in sending out a great many pupils who are in no danger of jumping naked and raw into the very slough of materialism."[58] The demand for demonstration laboratories in which students could be schooled implied the need for research laboratories in which the demonstrators themselves would be trained.[59]

What inspiration for research James, Hall, and Ladd may have instilled in others certainly did not derive from personal example. The only evidence of Hall's experimental work rests with four unpublished preliminary researches performed by his Hopkins understudies that he coauthored. Just one published experiment owed its inspiration to Hall. "Harvard men speak of James's experiment as if he performed only one," reminisced Carl Seashore, who at Yale undertook the single experiment that Ladd claimed "by proxy. . . . The hypothesis was wrong, the technique inadequate, and the conclusion was unwarranted."[60] The activity itself counted for more than the results. It is not enough to explain the lukewarm commitment to research by James, Hall, and Ladd by portraying them—however accurately—as "transitional figures" torn between traditional ideals of liberal culture and the modern spirit of science. Though "harder" conceptions of psychology would demand an increasingly intense allegiance, there were many "transitional generations" to follow. Of the six Americans who received Ph.D. degrees under Hall at Hopkins, only Edmund Clark Sanford became an experimentalist.[61] Until the end of the nineteenth century the laboratory continued to function partly as a training ground where would-be philosopher-psychologists learned by doing and—often on a onetime basis—certified their competency by publishing experimental findings.[62]

For some, research became an emotionally and professionally fulfilling end in itself. Someone, after all, had to expand the frontiers of knowledge from which philosophy would extrapolate its data. As the prospect of growth for research laboratories increased, the idea of creative investigation gained more adherents, the laboratory became more closely identified with scientific advance, and the image of the research scientists as austere seeker after truth became elevated to the level of an ideal. The central ideology that developed around the theory of science for science's sake involved two related assertions: (1) new knowledge should be evaluated solely in terms of its significance for existing theory, and (2) scientists should be appraised on the exclusive basis of their contributions to that body of knowledge. Most university-based sciences in the 1880s widely advertised these values as products of altruistic inspiration and selfless solicitude for a transcending cause. Applied science was regarded as a distinctly minor and even dangerous endeavor, for the imposition of extraneous, utilitarian considerations upon the scientist's work might not only deflect his attention from major theoretical questions but also bias his interpretation of experimental results.[63]

Like the commitment to liberal culture, however, the research ideal represented only a portion of the new psychology's professional ideology. When philosopher-psychologists paid rhetorical allegiance to the investigative spirit, they had no intention of encouraging the hiving off from philosophy of an independent scientific discipline. As truth came more and more to be seen as the product of inductively acquired knowledge, research became an increasingly essential intellectual ingredient of philosophizing. Even Cattell, no zealot for philosophy's claims upon psychology, realized that to "allot to science those subjects concerning which we have knowledge, and to reserve for philosophy those questions concerning which we know nothing, is evidently subversive to philosophy."[64] Still, there was no intellectually valid reason why philosophy departments needed to provide institutional support for research when they could readily extrapolate their findings from allied scientific fields, as Ladd had done at Yale. Coldly considered, professional necessity dictated the philosopher-psychologist's support for research.

Philosophy was an ideologically sensitive field in which candidates were still subject to scrutiny by academic administrators and trustees. By advancing a concept of psychological science withdrawn from worldly concerns and therefore esoteric to outsiders, Hall and his followers were able to convince an academic leadership, which rarely embraced the idea of pure research enthusiastically, that they alone were qualified to determine ground rules for recruitment, training, and control of disciplinary peers as well as the legitimate scope, methods, and priorities of psychology. Previously, said James, the academic philosopher owed "his position to general excellence of character." Hall longed for "the supremest intellectual luxury" of working and writing without a conservative administrator looking over his shoulder. The canons of research implied that intellectual work was impersonal and that only the specialized community of the competent could control access and award merit. The ideal of pure science evolved in part as justification for departmental autonomy. The cult of publication would displace the cult of personality.[65]

Advocated as an instrument by which the innovative career patterns James and Hall had successfully but fortuitously fashioned might be institutionally stabilized, research became its own raison d'être. Having advanced its fortunes by announcing its compatibility with sound religious principles, the new psychology needed to maintain that the compatibility was entirely coincidental and that metaphysical postulates did not dictate the course of scientific investigation. Such insistence engendered an intellectual division of labor. By the early 1890s the scientific impulse became embodied in a single individual, the laboratory director, who purportedly represented the objective, disinterested, emotionally detached aspects of psychological science; his departmental superior, a philosopher-psychologist, made credible the philosophic implications of laboratory work. Occasionally, as with Münsterberg at Harvard, the laboratory director himself pursued philosophical objectives. Often at smaller universities where funding was a problem the departmental head perforce served as laboratory director.[66] But generally the bifurcation of function became the standard institutional pattern, especially after Hall surrendered the Clark laboratory to Sanford in 1889.[67] By the mid-1890s this division of labor resulted in a conflict of interest as certain researchers came to resent the unwelcomed intrusion of philosophic concerns into the laboratory.

Yet even among those committed to research as a career, the idea of pure science was rarely more than a rhetorical convention. The motto of Johns Hopkins University was indeed "Veritas vos liberabit," but the truth was never intended—to paraphrase Carl Becker—to free one to sit around and contemplate the truth. While president of the University of California, Gilman had endeavored to give "precedence only to those [branches of learning] which sound judgment indicates as most useful in our day."[68] His tribulations with California's agricultural interests, however, had taught him that making preferential decisions to support departments of learning on the basis of their predicted or proven ability embroiled higher education in interminable political controversy damaging to the university's autonomy.[69] At Hopkins, Gilman found the ideology of science for science's sake a convenient device for obviating political and financial interference in university affairs by interested supporters. Such an ideology was tolerable only when based upon the premise of science's *ultimate* utility. Scientific generalizations, Gilman assured university patrons, are "scarcely conceived . . . before the practical world has made there from the most serviceable deductions."[70]

Realizing that his petition for a post at Hopkins had succeeded largely on the basis of his potential usefulness to the fields of medicine and education, Hall made certain that the experimental laboratory he formally founded in 1884 would not become the refuge of ascetic science. The researcher, he once exclaimed, was the "knight of the Holy Spirit of truth." Yet, taught by his own experience that psychology "should not try to be too pure," Hall proceeded to serve both God and Mammon.[71] With respect to medical psychology, Hall announced that experimentation, by attempting to localize centers of psychological functions, could contribute to psychiatric explanations

of the mental state of individual lunatics . . . or extended comparative studies of a single delirium . . . ; the complex psycho-physics of epilepsy . . . ; or again the special psychology of each crime class . . . the blind, deaf, pauper types and other defectives.[72]

Like Gall before him, Hall would conduct his students on tours of local insane asylums and pauper institutions in order to sensitize them to particular psychological problems and to systematize clinical records according to workable categories of abnormal psychology. Psychiatry, ventured Hall, would "reanimate several quite atrophied departments of mental science."[73]

Conversely, Hall hoped that psychology would revitalize neglected aspects of medical science. "The time was," complained Hall, "when the doctor . . . studied to control the mind and heart and imagination of his patient." But that was "before the power to take the *whole* man into account had been lost in easier micrologic medical specialities." By "widening its sphere to include the physical, emotional, and volitional as well as the intellectual nature of man," experimental psychology would appraise medical students of the wider implications of their professional roles while providing a scientific foundation for psychiatric studies.[74] The relationship between psychology and biology at Hopkins was congenial and intimate—so much so that one historian of psychology there found it impossible to determine student's departmental affiliations by simply studying their course transcripts.[75]

James had obviously stimulated his foremost student's interest in psychopathology, but Hall's emphasis on psychiatrics at Hopkins at the expense of attention to pedagogics, for which his title implied his responsibility, was probably conditioned by the medical profession's relatively higher status. In 1885, when the medical departments began administratively organizing in preparation for the opening of the medical school, Hall requested of Harvard's Bowditch an honorary M.D. degree to facilitate his interaction with the new Hopkins contingent.[76] Nevertheless, he did not refrain from directing potential educators to their source of "serviceable deductions." "Those who devote themselves to the work of education as a profession," announced Hall, "are strongly recommended to give their chief time and labor to grounding themselves in Psychology and Philosophy, which constitute the scientific basis of their profession. Pedagogy is a field of applied Psychology, and if the latter is known the application is not hard to make."[77] Science, after all, was science; it would proceed down its own path unencumbered. But while the "Knights" of the research laboratory were embarked on their "Sacred Quest" for truth, the chivalric code bade them do good deeds along the way.

CHAPTER 8

The Crisis of Experimentalism

[Psychology is] a *science* already existing, and, indeed, like all the other principal sciences, some centuries old. We of to-day have entered into the inheritance of past ages; and it is becoming for us to do so with generous acknowledgment of what the past has done for us.

—George Trumbell Ladd
"President's Address Before the New York Meeting of the American Psychological Association" (1894)

And what about philosophy, the science of sciences? Alas! philosophy is still in the Middle Ages. One by one the other sciences have freed themselves; the lingering clutch of philosophy on psychology is a last hope of respectability.

—Edward Wheeler Scripture
Thinking, Feeling, Doing (1895)

We promise a science of conscious life. . . . But we shall be false to all our promises and we shall turn the confidence and sympathy which has endowed chairs and built laboratories, into derision and rejection if we confine our science to a little round of testing in the laboratory.

—William Lowe Bryan
"A Plea For Special Child Study" (1893)

Research, utility, and liberal culture: in the 1880s these categories remained aspects of a coherent, if not completely unified, disciplinary vision held together by the scientific humanism of James, Hall, and

Ladd.[1] By the mid-1890s, however, they had already come to represent rival conceptions of psychology's scope. In order to understand this rapid change it is useful to consider research, utility, and humanistic study not only as intellectual ideals but also as designations for client-centered services that psychology provided in order to earn its academic livelihood. As we have seen in Hall's representative prospectus, the laboratory trained three classes of students. First, it educated the future philosopher by providing him an opportunity, in Harvard philosopher Ralph Barton Perry's words, "to cultivate his scientific side." Psychology thus provided an academic service to a venerable humanistic discipline and, once removed, to a general undergraduate audience.[2] Second, the laboratory perpetuated its kind, training the research scientist whose reference group consisted primarily of his disciplinary peers and secondarily of biological scientists seeking insights into psychophysiological problems. Finally, the laboratory schooled professionals interested in the practical applications of psychology to both education and medicine. The laboratory was producing three groups whose intellectual aims and professional ambitions were, if not always incompatible, fundamentally distinct.

In an institutional sense, this multiplicity of function proved initially fortuitous. Psychology grew rapidly as an academic discipline because of its pluralistic appeal as philosophy, biology, and social science. Intellectually, however, this protean development caused psychology growing pains. Popularity aside, psychology's basic legitimacy as a field of knowledge rested on its claim as experimental science, and the imported program of physiological psychology that made credible that claim proved incapable of serving three masters. The introspective analysis of the ideal-typical conscious mind that proved so hospitable to philosophers' epistemological and metaphysical problem solving provided little sustenance to proponents of utility anxious to find psychological explanations why certain individuals—whether in the clinic, the classroom, or the factory—performed differently than other individuals. Between these forces, which were gradually aligning themselves into antagonistic camps, stood the laboratory directors. Jealous of their scientific reputation, some researchers resented philosophic alliances as detrimental to their self-image and attempted to adopt a natural science program, which the sponsors of utility favored. At the same time, however, they realized that discarding consciousness as subject matter left them with little to distinguish their science from physiology. When Titchener attempted to cut the Gordian knot by elaborating a purist view of experimentalism that eschewed both philosophic and practical implications, he found his system under attack by both warring factions. Ultimately, experimental psychology was forced to make a choice.

In the 1890s, allegiances—with the exception of the stance of Cornell psychology—were seldom as clear-cut as the foregoing categorization implies. Choices seldom came in the form of epiphany, and most of the spokesmen for the new discipline—realizing that psychology's vitality depended upon its multiple investment in the concepts of research, utility, and humanistic study—tried to reconcile disparate purposes. But the effort entailed bitter debate. Throughout the 1890s, recalled James R. Angell, "there was a considerable controversy abroad about the true objectives of psychology." Boring called the period "a furious decade" in American psychology. Walter Bowers Pillsbury compared the relationships among the community of the psychologistically competent to a "meeting of paranoiacs in a hospital ward."[3] Scores of specific intellectual debates were exacerbated by personal animosities and institutional rivalries. Generally, though, amid the multitude of disagreements two fundamental issues stood out: whether psychology could or should become an exact natural science, and whether it was to be devoted primarily to theoretical or to practical problem solving. The first problem principally involved the relation of philosophy to experimental psychology; the second, the determination of the distance between the laboratory and society. Both issues were intimately related and were settled not by debate but by the intellectual and institutional pressures that necessitated the debate in the first place.

Psychology as a Natural Science

In the early 1890s, Alexander Bain sent Mark Baldwin his celebrated two-volume psychological treatise, which arrived at Princeton taxed with a 25 percent duty. "I protested the duty," recalled Baldwin, "citing the law according to which scientific books were admitted free,

and pointed out the appropriate features of the two books. Back came
the reply from Washington, 'Our experts report that these books are
in no sense scientific.' "[4] The problem was confined neither to the importation of texts nor to the 1890s. As late as 1910, a group of prominent biologists privately polled concluded that psychology was a subdiscipline of either philosophy or physiology. Few considered it an
independent science.[5] The question of definition of boundaries constituted the central intellectual and professional issue in American psychology from the early 1890s to the United States entry into World
War I. Fittingly, the task of defining the discipline's scope—of cutting
out its own exclusive intellectual terrain—first fell to its reigning
triumvarate: James, Hall, and Ladd.

In 1890 James published his *Principles of Psychology*. The ensuing
criticism of his massive work by Hall and Ladd shows that in many
ways the tensions and ambiguities within the *Principles* mirrored
American psychology's central dilemma. On the one hand, the philosophically minded and religiously committed Ladd felt that James was
imposing too narrow a scientific limitation upon psychology.[6] On the
other hand, Hall, the preeminent advocate of dismissing philosophical
questions from psychology, criticized James for his "strange neglect of
fundamental biological principles." He called the author "an impres-
sionist in psychology" and labeled his book "a portfolio containing
sketches old and new, ethical, literary, scientific and metaphysical."
Hall was perplexed that "Dr. James's psychology does not drop the
soul" and that states of consciousness ("the warp and woof of all") were
used by James as explanatory dei ex machina. Nothing was so seriously wrong with James's work, he characteristically concluded, that
could not be cured "in a radically revised edition."[7]

Ladd would have called for revision on different grounds. To him,
James's belief that consciousness could be scientifically explained in
terms of cerebral physiology represented "an extremely contracted
conception of psychology as a natural science." By his own admission
a "pronounced spiritualist in psychology," Ladd preferred to equivo-
cate on the natural science issue:

But may we pursue psychology as a "natural science" without postulate of a
soul, and without any metaphysical implicate or postulate whatsoever? Possibly: I am not prepared to say that we cannot; but the way is straight and
narrow and there are few, if any, who succeed in finding it.[8]

Continuing his argument elsewhere, Ladd declared that "if I thought that our somewhat like a score of psychological laboratories in this country were founded to serve such a method of advancing the so-called science, I would most willingly see them all perish in a single night."[9] Responding to Ladd's criticisms (and implicitly to Hall's), James attempted to correct the impression that he had claimed

that psychology as it stands to-day, *is* a natural science, or in an exact way a science at all. Psychology, indeed is today hardly more than what physics was before Galileo, what chemistry was before Lavoisier. It is a mass of phenomenal description, gossip and myth.

James insisted that he wanted his *Principles*, first to render faithfully the contemporary state of the discipline, and then "by treating Psychology *like* a natural science to help her become one."[10] In order to accomplish this second aim, James elaborated the doctrine of empirical parallelism. Psychologists, said James in his chapter entitled "The Mind-Stuff Theory," must ask

whether, after all, the ascertainment of a blank unmediated correspondence, term for term, of the succession of states of consciousness with the succession of total brain-processes, be not the simplest psycho-physic formula, and the last word of a psychology which contents itself with verifiable laws, and seeks only to be clear, and to avoid unsafe hypotheses.[11]

James denied that he had claimed "that psychology as a natural science must aim at an account of brain states exclusively." While mental states are "correlated *immediately* with brain states," argued James in a passage that strikingly foreshadowed behavioristic procedures, they are also "correlated with many other physical events, peripheral nerve currents for example, and the physical stimuli which occasion these."[12] There were only two paths open to the opponent of cerebralism:

He ought either to reject it in principle and entirely, but then be willing to throw over, for example, such results as the entire modern doctrine of aphasia—a very hard thing to do; or else he ought to accept it in principle, but then cordially admit that, in spite of present shortcomings, we have here an immense opening upon which a stable phenomenal science must some day appear.

James would not pretend that such a science was extant; but he could at least "cheer those on who are working for its future and clear metaphysical entanglements from their path."[13]

Ladd would select the first course. He sardonically admitted his readiness to hail "the expected 'Lavoisier' with his grand generalization that shall lift our knowledge of mental behavior to the level with that certainty which the behavior of planets has for the mind that knows the law of gravitation; *if only* this grand reformer of psychology ever arrive. But in this region he is not expected."[14] No doubt thinking of James's reference to the neurological doctrine of aphasia, Ladd predicted "that some of the most widely accepted of these formulas are destined to be thoroughly shaken up, in the not far away future." To assume that psychology must postpone its claim to the name of science until the discovery of "some law, like that of gravitation in physics or of chemical equivalency in chemistry, has been discovered . . . is itself, at least premature and unscientific." Psychology is "a *science* already existing and, indeed, like all of the other principal sciences, some centuries old."[15] It was for Ladd the science of the metaphysical implications of the mind-body relationship.

Ultimately, it was Ladd, not James, who was constricting the definition of psychology. James had not disagreed with Ladd's definition of psychology as "the description and explanation of states of consciousness as such."[16] He had, in fact, cited Ladd's definition in the first sentence of his 1892 abridgment of his *Principles*. In his larger work he had insisted that introspection "is what we have to rely on first and foremost. . . . I regard this belief as the most fundamental of all the postulates of Psychology." Preserving introspective method implied acknowledgment of consciousness and, hence, of the soul itself. "Many of the staunchest believers in the soul," declared James, "admit that we know it only as an inference from experiencing its *states*." Parallelism ("the wisest course") insured that "our psychology will remain positivistic and non-metaphysical."[17]

By hypothesizing "a blank unmediated correspondence" between mental and physical states, James countenanced a division of labor within psychology. Psychologists interested in "the biological study of human nature' could pursue a separate course of investigation that could in no way conflict with the more metaphysical aspects of psychological endeavor because they were simply examining the same phenomena from a different standpoint. The studies were convergent. Ultimately, the scientist's results could be handed "over to those specialists in philosophy, where the metaphysical aspects of physics are already allowed to belong."[18] In the meantime, psychologists might no longer be required to pay customs duties on their posted treatises.

Ladd feared that parallelism would inevitably lead to psychological reductionism that would subvert the "reality, unity, and possibility of a permanent existence of the human mind" into a mere "stream of mechanically associated 'epiphenomena' thrown off from the molecular machinery of the cerebral hemispheres." Accordingly, he sponsored "an uncritical, common-sense Dualism" as an alternative to parallelism. "Psychology," claimed Ladd, "assumes that 'things' are and 'minds' are; and that, within certain limits determined by the so-called 'nature' of both they act causally upon each other." In other words, psychology must subscribe to Wundt's views and assume that physical and psychic phenomena are not only distinct but fundamentally different from one another. Since they interact causally, an objective investigation of mental states by means of analysis of physical phenomena was an impossibility. The two "series" of phenomena were "utterly incomparable."[19]

In effect, dualism constituted a strategy for keeping laboratory experimentation subordinate to philosophic objectives. "The piling up of experimental results," claimed Ladd, "the enlarging of collections of statistics, the anthropological and other 'objective' data, all assist the science of psychology only in so far as they help the more extensively, accurately, and profoundly to analyze this representative self consciousness." Whenever the psychologist, "through fear of being considered too subjective or too metaphysical, neglects to cultivate or depreciates and denounces the analytic of a trained introspective observer, he is in a fair way soon to be found offering for sale his own peculiar birthright." While he can collect data from other minds, he must always come back to his own consciousness to interpret the meaning of these signs, for "no interpretation of consciousness is possible in any terms whatever without self-consciousness."[20]

James appreciated the value to psychology of introspection and the value to philosophy of psychology; he insisted: "I yield to no man in my expectation of what general philosophy will some day do in helping us to rational conceptions of the world."[21] But, while Ladd continued his campaign for dualism throughout the 1890s in order to keep psychology propaedeutic to philosophy, James's plea for a parallelism that would free psychology to become a natural science derived from his desire to promote psychology's more practical applications.

"What is natural science, to begin with?" asked James: "It is a mere fragment of truth broken out from the whole mass of it for the sake of practical effectiveness exclusively. *Divide et impera.*" While Ladd envisioned such a division of labor obviating philosophic rule, James logically maintained that mental events "lie certainly in large part in the physical world' and therefore merit attention by the physical sciences.[22] James was no mere booster of specialization for its own sake; he saw in the development of certain portions of psychological investigation the promise of useful results. Psychological "events," said James, are "of such tremendous practical moment to us that the control of these conditions on a large scale would be an achievement compared with which the control of the rest of physical nature would appear comparatively insignificant."[23] It was in this debate with Ladd that James pleaded for a psychology of "practical prediction and control" and cited the professional groups "incessantly craving for a sort of psychological science" that would provide "practical rules" for controlling (James said "improving") the "conduct of the particular individuals in their charge."[24]

In nearly behavioristic terms, James argued that certain conceptions of psychology provided such practical guidelines: "The brain-path theory based on reflex action, the conception of the human individual as an organized mass of tendencies to react mentally and muscularly on his environment in ways which may be either preservative or destructive" have already provided a theoretical framework for the diagnosis and cure of maladjusted individuals. Considering such tentative but hopeful advances by psychologists allied with "the physiologists and naturalists . . . the biologists, doctors, and physical researchers," James argued that "their impulse to constitute the science in their own way as a branch of biology, were an unsafe one to thwart." He contended that Ladd's insistence that psychology's subject matter must remain the "real being" whose mental life unfolds "sui generis, according to laws of its own," frustrated that impulse. James concluded that "the real being is for practical purposes, an entire superfluity which a *practical* psychology can perfectly well do without."[25] Twenty years later Watson would say precisely the same thing about consciousness itself.

Of course, James was arguing not for the denial of philosophical considerations altogether but merely for the bifurcation of psychological inquiry. His plea was couched in terms of professional self-interest. A nascent discipline seeking to justify its activities to society in order to secure support could ill afford to lose the confidence of educators, alientists, clergy, and penal superintendents searching for scientific insights into their peculiar problems. Both the "pure-blooded philosopher" and "the practical man" had "legitimate business to transact with psychology." If the former persisted "in forcing the consideration of the more metaphysical aspects of human consciousness" upon "the men who care nothing for ultimate rationality," psychology would become culturally isolated and professionally moribund. Biologists and neurologists would devise a practical psychological science "whether we help them or not." And if society had to choose "between a merely rational and a merely practical science of mind," James left little doubt which one it would support.[26] In order to prosper, the discipline had not only to cultivate its philosophic garden but also to sell fruit from the tree of psychological knowledge.

Psychology Pure and Applied

Most psychologists realized the economic dangers of selling unripe fruit. Reluctant to promise more than their fledgling pursuit might reasonably deliver, they found in the ideology of pure science a convenient rationale for circumventing utilitarian pressures. Yet they also realized that only those sciences which had proven their worth were in a position to make the most unqualified affirmation of the idea of science for science's sake.[27] The intellectual and financial supporters of "pure" science could tolerate the scientist's withdrawal from the concerns of the larger society about him because they were confident that serviceable science would remain available when needed.

The proponents of pure psychology found it necessary to justify in ethical terms their withdrawal from worldly concerns. Accordingly, they claimed that they had not renounced the moral codes of their era but had merely transferred them from the arena of political and social activity into the realm of academic investigation.[28] Ladd, for example, who called for a "virtual aristocratic government" to put an end to political corruption, believed that "the practical welfare of mankind" depended on "the classes that have leisure, social standing and wealth" rather than upon "the character of the so-called common people."[29] Only the altruistic reformer without desire for personal gain could be sufficiently disinterested to effect impartial, equitable social restructuring. Characteristically, Ladd sought to equate the motives of the patrician reformer in society with those of the pure researcher in science. He argued that "the truly great men in science" had always been "benefactors of mankind" because

while they have been more unwilling than ordinary men to swerve a hair's breadth consciously from the strictest truth . . . they have also recognized that the highest and truest truth which is given us men to know, somehow seeks and finds an embodiment in conduct and character.[30]

Ladd sketched a portrait of the scientific Mugwump: a disinterested seeker after truth whose cultivated honesty not only raised him above "ordinary men" but enabled him to unravel the laws of conscious life that would form the basis of the moral uplift of humanity. His scientific knowledge would elevate "the life of conduct" and facilitate "the development of character."[31]

Most often, psychologists tried to justify a policy of cultural laissez-faire with analogies drawn from the established sciences, not from politics. "Science," said Cattell, "has its beginnings in common knowledge of daily life collected for practical ends." But only when it becomes pure science—such as physics—do most practical applications ensue. Astronomy, remarked Ladd, was "originally devised in the interests of humanity as astrology, and then becoming truly scientific has returned far more than all its costs as navigation, meteorology, . . . etc." And astronomy, reasoned Cattell, does not aim "to produce changes in the course of Nature." It "can not alter the orbits of the planets. . . . But material science, while searching for truth, has not failed to contribute to the practical needs of society."[32]

The staunchest advocates of ascetic science had never been reluctant to make promises. Virtually every intraprofessional speech and popular article maintained that psychology would benefit general medicine, psychiatry and neurology, pedagogy, the industrial arts, sociology, anthropology, criminology, and jurisprudence. Ladd portrayed psychology as the handmaiden of all the sciences, and Cattell claimed that psychological science would eventually preside over "the distribution of labor, wealth, and power." Despite the controversies over method and scope, Ladd admitted that psychologists could at least agree on one thing: psychology would contribute to "the practical welfare of the people."[33] Such a consensus, however, represented a hollow unanimity, for it begged the question of imminence. Even Titchener, who as late as 1909 denounced the use of psychology as "a cure for sick souls," admitted that his science would ultimately prove useful; but he calculated that it might take at least a century.[34] Ladd envisioned an applied psychology following upon the eventual discovery of the laws of consciousness but did not expect the explication of those laws in the near future. Pure science required not only total honesty but also self-denying patience.

Most psychologists realized that their patrons might not be blessed with the same confident perseverance. Seeking both the professional autonomy that the notion of pure science seemed to provide and the institutional and popular support that seemed to follow upon their ability to justify psychology as a useful science, the spokesmen for the new psychology stretched the logic of their appeals to the point of contradiction. Hugo Münsterberg, for example, insisted that "psychology does not work for a social premium and cannot be determined in its course by social anxieties. But the psychologist as a member of the social organism, has to adapt his endeavors to the needs of society."[35]

Seeking the prestige and cultural status of the physical scientist, psychologists of the early 1890s assured potential patrons that, in Scripture's words, "we can do as much for education and mental life in general as physics does for railroads, bridges, and electrical engineering."[36] Throughout the decade, however, as we shall soon see, many of the psychologists who were talking like physicists were working like engineers. By the end of the century rhetoric had caught up with reality. In 1904 Cattell proclaimed that, if he did not believe that psychology could be applied in useful ways, he would regard his occupation "as nearer to that of the professional chess-player or sword swallower than to that of the engineer or scientific physician."[37] Cattell's choice of vocational titles was indicative of his and his colleagues' changing attitude toward science; a decade earlier he might have substituted for "engineer' the title "physicist" and for "physician" the term "medical researcher." Just as Ladd's patrician reformer had given way in reality to progressivism's social efficiency expert, psychology witnessed the arrival of the "mental engineer."[38] By the turn of the century, application had become the standard. Clinging to the role of pure researcher would have seemed to most as professionally unpalatable as devouring daggers.

In 1893 William Lowe Bryan was already reminding his colleagues of the professional dangers of pursuing science for its own sake. "We promise a science of conscious life," he cautioned:

But we shall be false to all our promises and we shall turn the confidence and sympathy which has endowed chairs and built laboratories, into derision and rejection if we confine our science to a little round of testing in the laboratory.[39]

In the following year, Cattell was reeducating his associates to the practical wisdom of Benjamin Franklin, who had proclaimed that scientific discoveries were important only because they "extend the power of man over matter, avert or diminish the evils he is subjected to, or augment the number of his enjoyments." Though Cattell discreetly condemned Franklin's "materialistic" point of view, he nevertheless warned his co-workers that "science for the sake of science is in turn in danger of dillitanteism [sic]." Science does not, he insisted contrary to his earlier expression, find "an adequate end in the satisfaction of intellectual curiosity." In 1899 the University of Michigan's Alfred H. Lloyd, who had studied under James, declared: "Knowledge as mere knowledge, science solely for science's sake, objective, special science, is indeed blind to reality, but knowledge identified with will, applied science, is even reality itself." As Dewey said a year later, "Unless our laboratory results are to give us artificialities, mere scientific curiosities, they must be subjected to interpretation by gradual reapproximation to the conditions of life." The urgent calls throughout the decade for an applied science of psychology indicate the presence of a powerful ideological persuasion. Beneath its rhetoric lay institutional realities that explain its emergence, tenacity, and eventual ascendancy.[40]

The Institutional Contours of
Academic Psychology

Generally speaking, the ideology of immediate utility arose in response to a problem that the advocates of pure science had left unanswered: What were the actual mechanisms that enabled interested groups to extrapolate useful results from a distinterested science? How could psychologists insure that their investigations did not yield "mere scientific curiosities"? Who but the actual experimenters—ideally oblivious—could be expert enough to know? Dewey's demand that psychological experimentation be subjected to "interpretation by gradual reapproximation to the conditions of life" implied that psychology become problem-oriented. As we shall see, institutional pressures made it easy for a large portion of the psychological community to adapt to that demand.

A useful starting point for an analysis of these pressures is the careers of G. Stanley Hall and his students. This is not an unrepresentative focus. Hall obtained the country's first doctoral degree in psychology; established the first American research laboratory at Hopkins; created and controlled the first American journal for experimental publication; founded the first autonomous department of psychology at Clark; and was the first president of the American Psychological Association, which he founded in his own home. Excluding his own degree, he awarded every American Ph.D. degree in psychology before 1893, and eleven of the first fourteen. By 1898, fifty-four students had received American doctorates, thirty of them from Hall. Until about 1894, Hall was the unrivaled leader of American psychology.[41]

At Hopkins, it will be recalled, Hall was enormously interested in a practical psychology and in a speculative genetic psychological theory. As Ross has shown, however, he saw the need to project the austere image "of a rigorously scientific discipline, centered on the experimental laboratory."[42] On the one hand, Hall's stance was dictated by his solicitude for the advancement of psychology as a scientific discipline and was reflected in the highly empirical contents of his *American Journal of Psychology*.[43] On the other hand, by constricting psychology's scope to coincide with the areas of his own acknowledged supremacy, Hall hoped to secure professional leadership. In a barb certainly directed at Hall, Ladd claimed that he had come to realize "that not a few who cry most loudly in the name of 'science' show quite plainly that it is chiefly for their own sakes." James resented Hall's attempt to make "all men believe that the way to save their souls psychologically lies through the infinite assimilation of jawbreaking German laboratory articles."[44] James and Ladd feared that Hall was eliminating philosophical considerations from his conception of psychology. Certainly part of the incentive to create rival facilities at Harvard and Yale was the desire—not entirely successful—to produce psychologists attuned to the laboratory's broader relevance.

To Hall's chagrin, his rigid empirical stance received less support at Hopkins than he had anticipated. The university uncharacteristically refused to subsidize Hall's journal, and Gilman even declined to acknowledge publicly the laboratory's existence.[45] The university's "black eye" was still smarting. Unable to compete with the established sciences at Baltimore, Hall accepted in 1888 an offer by the trustees of Clark University in Worcester, Massachusetts, to become its president and head of a separate department of psychology.[46] Hall took with him his staff, laboratory, and journal, thus completely dismantling psychology at Hopkins. For a few short years Clark was the Elysium of pure science and the center of American psychology. Clark's quick collapse and the subsequent rehabilitation of its psychology department as a clearinghouse for practical studies signaled the direction of the discipline in the 1890s.

Hall had managed to convince Jonas Clark, the university's founder and sole benefactor, that the new institution should devote itself exclusively to graduate study. No attempts would be made at comprehensiveness; psychology and biology would predominate. Almost immediately, however, local hostility toward pure science—such as had plagued Johns Hopkins University—caused Jonas Clark to waver in his commitment to Hall's plan. He had originally intended to found in Worcester a college for poor children of the local community, and when, in 1892, the trustees voted against the establishment of an undergraduate institution, Clark withdrew his dwindling financial support altogether. The crippling of Hall's "Worcester plan," according to Veysey, "revealed how the conception of abstract research had failed to gain firm-minded acceptance . . . in the American of that day."[47] The coup de grace was administered in March when William Rainey Harper, president of the newly founded University of Chicago, "raided" Clark and lured away over half of its scientific faculty.[48]

The collapse of Hall's vision to build a science of psychology upon a local foundation convinced him of the need to secure a broader institutional base independent of community pressure, personal patronage, and tentative university support. Psychology required a larger organizational umbrella. In 1891, as Jonas Clark was gradually withdrawing his support from his university, Hall attempted to cement an alliance between that institution, its psychology department, and the National Education Association. He founded the *Pedagogical Seminary*, a journal devoted to child study, and announced before an enthusiastic audience at the 1891 NEA meeting in Toronto the need for a scientific pedagogy. In July of the next year, he sponsored at Worcester a two-week summer school on the subject attended by school superintendents, teachers, and normal school principals. The enthusiastic response prompted Hall to continue these sessions annually until 1903. Child study was becoming an integral part of the normal school curriculum, and Hall had convinced the reforming segments of the NEA that the new psychology constituted the scientific basis of that study.[49]

Seeking to regularize relations between the NEA and psychology, Hall realized the need to establish a formal professional organization of psychologists. Therefore, on July 8, 1892, at least a dozen scholars convened in Worcester at Hall's invitation to form the American Psychological Association.[50] Hall's intent was not limited to his plans for affiliation with the educational profession. Within his own discipline, his status had been damaged by his narrowly empirical stance. When his design to preside over a preeminent but localized scientific community at Clark was dashed by Jonas Clark and William R. Harper in March, he turned his sights toward a broader-based professional leadership of a national scientific community. Such an organization, Hall realized, had to be based upon an inclusive membership policy in order to attract a representative national constituency, thus providing for psychology a semblance of unity. His choice of professional associates proved much more representative of contemporary psychology's scope than the selection of material that he deemed suitable for his *Journal*. In all, twenty-six recipients of invitations to join in the undertaking accepted membership. At the preliminary meeting, the charter members present elected five additional men. Although fourteen of the twenty-five original members excluding Hall were either his former students or present members of his department at Clark, he included several prominent philosopher-psychologists—including James, Ladd, and Josiah Royce—the heads of prominent laboratories, and two alienists from the McLean Hospital in Somerville, Massachusetts: Edward Cowles and William Noyes, Jr. The object of the association, as described in its constitution, was simply "the advancement of Psychology as a science. Those are eligible for membership who are engaged in this work."[51] Since no two members could have agreed on a precise definition of psychological science, the object of the APA was implicitly controversial. Yet Hall had at least created a forum for ensuing debate while providing to other professional organizations and potential patrons the appearance of a unified scientific community dedicated to common goals. According to plan, Hall was elected the association's first president and delivered the keynote speech at the first annual meeting held at the University of Pennsylvania on December 27.

Over half the association's members appeared in Philadelphia over the Christmas holidays. The dozen papers they read to each other presents a telling indicator of the actual contours of psychological research at that time.[52] Following Hall's opening address on the history of psychology in America, his former student Cattell proceeded to demolish one of the cornerstones of traditional physiological psychology, psychophysics. Drawing on the procedures of experimental physics and mathematical probability theory, he argued that the "just noticeable difference" of the intensity of any stimulus had little to do with the actual increment in the intensity of sensation but rather with perceptual error. The so-called j.n.d. was actually an "error of observation." It was therefore impossible to measure the relation of sensation to perception. Implicit in his attack was his familiar contention that psychology dealt not with the laws of consciousness but with the assessment of individual differences in response.[53]

Cattell's former student, Lightner Witmer of the University of Pennsylvania, made this contention explicit in his discussion of chronoscopically measured reaction times "on all classes of observers." His conclusions suggested that "the effect of continued practice" explained the variations between different series of experiments with untrained subjects and between the results of these groups and those of "skilled observers." Witmer too was interested in individual differences "from an anthropometrical standpoint."[54] He was subjecting traditional psychophysical techniques to what Dewey called "interpretation by . . . reapproximation to the conditions of life."

Another Hall student, Joseph Jastrow, followed Witmer's presentation with an account of experimental psychology at the Chicago World's Fair. Jastrow had set up at the Columbian Exposition a laboratory "designed for the collection of tests of sense and motor capacity." He had also devised an exhibit showing "the results of statistical research in the school-room." Again, the focus of interest was upon individual differences; the display was housed in the general exhibit of anthropometry within the Department of Ethnology.[55] The psychologists at Philadelphia were showing an acute interest in the untrained observer. Harvard's Hebert Nichols, who had studied with Hall, reported his experiments on four hospital patients in a routine physiological investigation of pain. Another of Hall's students, Indiana's W. L. Bryan, reviewed his work on psychological tests of schoolchildren. Hall's experimentalist, Sanford, abstracted some of the investigations of Clark's "skilled observers," but the topic ranged from routine physiological reaction-time studies to statistical analysis of dreams and assessment of diurnal patterns of mental efficiency.[56] The last speaker was Hugo Münsterberg, who proceeded to castigate the entire program that preceded him.

Recently arrived from Freiburg, Harvard's new laboratory director expressed his dissatisfaction "at what has thus far been accomplished in experimental psychology." The sampling of papers at the APA's first meeting served to reinforce his view that psychology "is rich in decimals but poor in ideas." The chief problem, said Münsterberg, was that psychology had neglected introspective analysis by trained observers:

It is indeed a misleading ideal of psychology to make more measurements its goal. . . . Experiment must not take the place of self-observation, but only offer more exact conditions for self-observation. . . . To be sure the boundaries between psychology and philosophy are not to be destroyed and philosophy ought never to pass over into mere psychology, but it is also necessary that the choice of psychological questions should recognize the needs of philosophy in a higher degree.[57]

Münsterberg thus delineated what might be called the classic conception of the new psychology, a conception that never received much of a hearing in America. He exhorted his colleagues to "push the centre of interest in experimental work from the half-physiological questions to the higher psychological problems." He complained that the range of laboratory investigation—problems of sensation, perception, and reaction times—was not only constricted but redundant, since such problems "can be solved just as well in physiological laboratories." "If psychology," he warned, "unites with physiology in order to cut loose from philosophy, it must lose more than it can gain."[58]

Psychology's central problem in the 1890s was defining its boundaries between philosophy and physiology. "Once and again," observed Robert S. Woodworth, who had received his doctorate at Columbia in 1899, "I have heard it predicted that psychology would pass away in proportion as physiology developed. . . . Psychology, it seemed, had no ultimates of its own, and could be completely resolved into either physiology or thin air."[59] George Stuart Fullerton, who had hosted the Philadelphia meeting, declared in 1896 that he rued the day when psychology, as a branch of philosophy, was "served in a sauce of epistemological speculation," but warned that "the living question is that of the relation of psychology to physiology and of the line of demarkation between them."[60] Münsterberg's rival, Yale's E. W. Scripture, agreed with his Harvard foe when in 1891 he contradicted the "widely-spread opinion that the only science of mental phenomena which can be of value must be the science of their relations to accompanying nervous changes." Agreeing also with Ladd, he declared that psychophysical experimentation was an aid to psychology, not psychology itself, and he therefore protested "the unjustified subordina-

tion of psychology to physiology."[61] "To prevent misunderstand-
ings," explained Cattell two years later, "it may be worth while to notice
what is not done in laboratories of psychology. They are not intended
for the study of physiology."[62] Intentions are often distinct from realities; psychologists were protesting too much. Münsterberg, in fact,
viewed Scripture and Cattell as representations of precisely the tendencies they depreciated.[63] He fully intended that psychology occupy
its own orbit in the scientific universe, but he insisted that philosophy
must continue to exert its influence to keep psychology from falling
into the gravitational field of physiology. Technically, this could be
accomplished by means of introspection into the so-called higher mental processes. Theoretically, a coalition between philosophers and introspectionists would provide psychology with its only hope of elaborating "ultimates of its own"—theories that were not dependent upon
physiological hypotheses and laws.

Despite the efforts of those who attempted to keep psychology within
the philosophical saucepan in order to prevent its falling into the
physiological fire, Münsterberg's 1892 description of the actual contours of experimental investigation was more accurate than his exhor-
tations were effective. Laboratory work continued to concern itself with
rudimentary studies of sensation and reaction times and continued to
utilize untrained observers. Instead of introspective analyses of the
higher mental processes, experimentation busied itself, in Jastrow's
words, with "the collection of tests of sense and motor capacity, and
the simpler mental processes."[64] And it increasingly distanced itself
from philosophy. Three principal factors explain this state of affairs:
intradepartmental specialization; the pattern of graduate training and
placement; and the overwhelming pressures toward application.

The Education of Psychologists

Almost immediately, the split between philosophers and experimentalists was widened by the divisive wedge of specialization. "The Laboratory," remarked R. B. Perry, "requires a different set of aptitudes
from those which commonly prevail among philosophers."[65] James's
distinction between metaphysician and tinker was hardly absolute, but
it soon received institutional sanction. Two developments encouraged

the formulation of discrete academic requirements for the psychological Ph.D. degree: the growth of special scientific knowledge and the
technical exigencies that required the researcher to spend his after hours
in the laboratory as mechanician devising apparatus rather than in the
armchair as metaphysician rounding out his empiricism in philosophic
thoroughness.

Differing attitudes followed from differing aptitudes, thus contributing to the schism. In the 1890s the experimental psychologist was
a valuable and fast-selling commodity in the philosophic marketplace.
Students competing for laboratory positions selected graduate departments that provided undivided opportunities to enhance their specialized credentials. Departments competing in turn for students tended
to conform to their demands. In places like Berkeley, where Howison
continued to enforce philosophic prerequisites, students went elsewhere for certification, and his psychological program—"unproduc-
tive" by one account[66]—languished. Once hired, psychologists resented the condescension—often expressed in financial terms—of
departmental heads. When J. Allan Gilbert could no longer tolerate
Patrick's patronizing attitude at Iowa, he quit the profession, informing his replacement, "you are going to hell."[67] Even in more hospitable climes, the bifurcation had set in. While a graduate student at
Harvard, Knight Dunlap informed Münsterberg that he could not
comprehend the philosophical basis of the latter's psychological system. The laboratory director replied that no one did and that, furthermore, it did not matter. What counted was scientific accomplishment.[68]

Carl Seashore sensitively recounted an episode that reflected the attitudinal differences between philosophers and psychologists. A graduate student of Ladd when Scripture arrived at Yale, Seashore was
torn between philosophy and experimentation. While searching for a
dissertation topic, he suggested to Ladd that he might like to work on
the problem of inhibition. The philosopher thereupon sent Seashore
to study the account of the topic that he had published in his own
Elements of Physiological Psychology. "I found the statement very lucid
and comprehensive," said Seashore, "and that put a damper on my
enthusiasm for experimentation." Approaching Scripture with the same
problem, the student encountered a fraternal slap on the shoulder and

an enthusiastic counsel to proceed experimentally from scratch. Recalled Seashore:

This had a magnetic effect; although then ignorant of what it implied, I date the birth of my scientific attitude from that moment. For the first time I sensed a feeling of companionship in a creative approach to psychology and felt that the laboratory was going to give me satisfaction which could well compare with the deep satisfaction I had felt in the learned and all-comprehensive textbooks.

To Seashore this experience served as an example of the distinction between the viewpoints of the "sponsors" and the "founders" of psychological experimentation.[69]

While Seashore could choose between philosophic and experimental "satisfactions," the generation he and his cohorts trained—the first generation of twentieth-century doctorates—was largely deprived of alternatives. Their curricula were more specialized; their backgrounds, more diverse. As the decade progressed, students were increasingly attracted to psychology from education rather than from philosophy—for reasons we shall soon encounter.[70] As their educations became more technical and practical, they lost the ability—and even the patience—to comprehend their philosophic sponsors. Dunlap, who received his Harvard Ph.D. in 1903 and had attended Josiah Royce's lectures, confessed:

I didn't know what Royce was talking about, and didn't much care. I had the same experience later with John Dewey, whom I heard first at Harvard. . . . I found these philosophers sounded well, until one began to inquire what their phrases meant, when translated into terms of everyday life. I decided that if what these philosophers were preaching was important, then I was going in for unimportant things.[71]

Despite his original interest in philosophy, J. B. Watson, who received his doctorate from Chicago in the same year, experienced a similar disappointment with Dewey: "I never knew what he was talking about then, and unfortunately for me, I still don't know."[72] Psychologists were not disposed to follow those whom they could not understand. Philosophers could continue to extrapolate from psychological research, but they were incapable of directing it. The most concrete manifestation of that inability was the decline of introspective studies and the proliferation of those "half-physiological" researchers that Münsterberg deplored.

Psychology's dependence upon physiology was an inadvertent result of the kind of training that the introductory student received. Regardless of intent, the novice who came to the psychological laboratory confronted the overwhelming ambience of physiological design. The American student interested, for example, in auditory problems would be introduced to the reigning paradigm of the physiologist Helmholtz. He might learn the rudiments of anatomical and physiological knowledge about hearing from Ladd's *Elements*. The student would examine the available anatomical and physiological models of the ear, which even the poorest laboratories provided. He would then be set to work at the physicist's tuning fork and the physiologist's sound pendulum or tonometer. Throughout the 1880s and 1890s psychological facilities were furnished by French and German manufacturers of physiological instrumentation that were not constructed with the psychologist's needs in mind.[73] These brass instruments were designed to control stimuli and to help measure sensation. The psychologist who sought to analyze perception was supposed to rely on a less precise— or, at least to the novice, less impressive—instrument: his introspecting mind. To those taught to identify science with accuracy and precision, introspection seemed like an untidy procedure.[74] Robert Woodworth once resorted to introspection during an investigation and confessed to "feeling half ashamed of myself for doing so."[75] Physiology's manifest progress and growing prestige adversely affected the psychological apprentice's attitude toward his own discipline. For him, the disciplinary spokesmen's insistence that psychology constituted an autonomous field appeared more wishful than descriptive; their contention that the psychological laboratories did not concern themselves with physiological investigations sounded disingenuous. Many shared the opinion that advances in psychology perforce awaited prior advances in physiology.[76] Such attitudes inhibited the sort of confident creativity and self-assured inventiveness that leads to theoretical innovation. As a result, according to Münsterberg, psychology "has really advanced scarcely a step."[77]

Psychological experimentation seemed to be treading the same ground in part because it had to meet two distinct needs: demonstration and

research. Experimental psychology in America drew many of its ap-
prentices from undergraduate philosophy courses. American students
were not necessarily bereft of scientific background, but they were ordinarily deprived of prior physiological orientation. The basics of
physiological experimentation in the American university were available almost exclusively within medical schools in advanced courses in
anatomy, morphology, histology, and so forth. The first duty of the
laboratory director in the United States, therefore, was to write his
own training manual, which began with the demonstration of the most
rudimentary psychophysical experiments.[78] Harvey Carr, for example, recalled that his collegiate training in experimental psychology
amounted to "nothing but a series of stunts wholly devoid of psychological significance."[79]

Interestingly, graduate students were finding that their stunts were
readily publishable.[80] At the level at which laboratory deans expected
experimental investigation eventually to be conducted, psychology
promised to become an enormously complex pursuit. Yet, at the level
on which most students confronted it, psychology was proving to be
a very simple undertaking. For example, Edward Chace Tolman arrived at Harvard undecided upon a career in philosophy or psychology. One summer school session served to convince him "then and
there that I did not have brains enough to become a philosopher . . .
but that psychology was nearer my capacities."[81] Baldwin confessed
that one of the prime reasons for psychology's rapid growth was "because the actual state of the subject is such that research is a matter of
comparatively less difficulty than in the older scientific branches."[82]
The quickness with which raw novices could become published scholars of elementary researches in a virgin field encouraged their complacency in dealing with "half-physiological" questions and exacerbated
Münsterberg's apprehensions that psychology would "degenerate into
a superficial scholastic sport."[83]

Psychologists of Education

Shorn of philosophic control and largely nonintrospective in design,
experimental psychology avoided the image of scholasticism by culti-
vating its reputation for service—as Münsterberg's later work would

exemplify. In part, the movement toward nonphilosophical, objective, quantitative studies of simple mental processes had been encouraged by those aspects of specialization, bifurcation, and training already discussed. Unquestionably, however, the single aspect of psychological endeavor that crystallized these disparate tendencies into a recognizable pattern was the widespread efforts by psychologists to make experimental contributions capable of direct application to life outside the laboratory, especially in the field of education. At Hopkins, Hall's appointment as professor of psychology and pedagogics represented a titular expression of a central and mutually beneficial institutional relationship during the 1890s and beyond. This intimate connection manifested itself in the careers of Hall's Hopkins students. William H. Burnham followed Hall to Clark where he became professor of pedagogy and hygiene. Cattell immediately applied his capacity psychology to the "mental measurement" of students at the University of Pennsylvania before moving to Columbia in 1891. There, in cooperation with Livingston Farrand and the anthropologist Franz Boas, formerly of Hall's Department of Psycholology at Clark, he constructed a series of tests correlating anthropometric measurements to physical and mental development. Establishing relations with Teachers College, Cattell helped transform Columbia into the center of educational psychology in the next century, a center prestigious enough by 1904 to lure John Dewey there from Chicago.[84]

Primarily a philosopher, Dewey nevertheless evinced an early interest in the theoretical aspects of educational psychology that derived from his Hopkins experience. In 1889 he collaborated on an *Applied Psychology* devoted to the practical aspects of educational theory and taught a course in educational psychology at Michigan. In 1894 he moved to the University of Chicago to preside over the departments of philosophy and pedagogy. When J. R. Angell arrived shortly afterward to direct Chicago's laboratory, psychology became the intellectual link between the two departments.[85] Much of the laboratory's equipment came from Jastrow's World's Fair exhibit. Like Dewey, Jastrow was not primarily an experimentalist; like Cattell, however, he did exhibit an interest in the educational implications of "mental anthropometry." Professor of psychology at the University of Wisconsin since 1888, Jastrow brought psychology in the guise of psychometrics to the public's attention at the fair. At Madison, with his student William Chandler Bagley, he continued his interests in the statistical study of individual differences in mental development.[86] Another of Hall's Hopkins students, George Patrick, encouraged the application of psychology to education. Appointed professor of mental and moral science and didactics at the University of Iowa in 1887, he established a demonstration laboratory there in 1890. When he procured funds to convert his workshop into a research facility five years later, he hired as laboratory director J. A. Gilbert, who under Scripture's direction at Yale had devised a program of tests on the muscular sensibility of schoolchildren. Two years later, when Gilbert left Iowa to become a psychiatrist, he was replaced by Carl Seashore, who received his degree from Yale in the same year as Gilbert and who had participated in the same testing program there.[87]

The educational impulse was not confined to the first crop of psychologists that Hall had produced. Those returning from Leipzig—Scripture, Wolfe, Pace, Witmer, Gale, Judd—all were exhibiting an interest in pedagogical science. The dramatic increase in public financial support of education in the United States between 1880 and 1900 surely helped psychologists focus their professional and intellectual attentions.[88] In 1894 the NEA organized a Committee on Psychological Inquiry and established its child study department, as child study congresses sprang up throughout the country.[89] "We may be glad," Cattell announced to his colleagues the following year, "that experimental psychology has practical applications in spite of quasi-official dicta to the contrary. In the United States more than one hundred and fifty million dollars, collected by enforced taxation, is spent annually on public schools in the attempt to 'change human natures.' "[90] Several months after Cattell's remarks, his former student Witmer created the world's first psychological clinic at the University of Pennsylvania and urged before the APA the "Organization of Practical Work in Psychology." Such work would involve "the direct application . . . of psychological principles to therapeutics and to education."[91] Witmer's program aimed at the "restoration" of "retarded" schoolchildren and utilized psychometric tests as indicators of performance that could be administered before and after various pedagogical, hygienic, and medical attempts at the remediation of what we would nowadays label

"learning disabilities." Such tests would then provide a scientific verification of the effectiveness of various attempts at "cure."[92]

Psychologists' professional entry into the institutions of education
were not limited to the narrow door of the clinical laboratory, which
did not widen until the next decade.[93] State boards of education were
supporting new educational departments within colleges and universities and the establishment of normal schools for the training of
teachers. Psychologists were finding occupational niches in these
growing departments and schools as teachers of teachers. Moreover,
psychology departments themselves were reorienting the direction of
laboratory research in order to certify this new generation of educational psychologists. Departments of psychology were also profiting
by the increase of students fashioning careers for themselves as educators.[94] This influx proved a godsend to financially embattled Clark,
and to its psychology department in particular. One-quarter of all the
advanced students at Clark were enrolled in the field of pedagogy. In
psychology specifically, Hall granted twenty-seven doctorates in the
1890s; nearly three-quarters of these recipients found positions in
teachers colleges, training schools, or child-study departments. Others, even though nominally appointed to departments of philosophy,
continued to cultivate their educational concerns.[95]

In a decade of intense social turmoil, Americans were putting their
faith in "the imperfect panacea" of education to solve social, economic, and political problems.[96] There is little reason to believe that
the protective armor of pure research was sufficient to shield the psychologist from this aspect of his cultural milieu. But even if psychologists had not been disposed to apply their science to the solutions of
practical problems, certain demographic pressures within their discipline were forcing them away from the sort of abstract research that
Münsterberg had deemed necessary for the development of psychology as an autonomous science. Throughout the 1890s no laboratory
produced more than two Ph.D.'s annually until 1898, when Cornell
produced three.[97] Psychologists, therefore, could hardly justify more
than one research scientist per department. The career fortunes of future researchers depended on the continuing expansion of laboratories. This expansion in fact did not occur as rapidly as the prolifera-

tion of doctorates obtained by Americans in both the United States and Germany, as Table 8.1 illustrates.

As is apparent in a comparison of the figures in the two right columns, by 1895 there existed more doctorates in America than laboratories. In light of this fact, James's 1894 counsel to Howison at Berkeley that he abandon plans for a research laboratory because "that business is being overstocked in America" was timely advice. In 1895

TABLE 8.1

Numerical Comparison of Doctorates and Laboratories

Year	American Ph.D.'s	German Ph.D.'s	Running Total Combined Ph.D.'s	Running Total Laboratories
1884–92	9	8	17	19
1893	5	—	22	22
1894	4	—	26	27
1895	8	1	35	29
1896	5	6	46	30
1897	7	1	54	31
1898	16	2	72	33
1899	18	—	90	33

Source: Information for this table has been extrapolated from Robert S. Harper, "Tables of American Doctorates in Psychology," *AJP*, 62 (1949): 579–87 and C. R. Garvey, "List of American Psychological Laboratories," *PB*, 26 (1929): 652–60. In the final column, the Hopkins laboratory has been abstracted after 1892 and the McLean Hospital facility throughout. Information regarding American recipients of foreign doctorates was derived from [anon.], "Origin and Development of American Psychological Departments," p. 52; Haslerud Papers, Archives of the History of American Psychology, University of Akron, Akron, Ohio.

Seashore had to wait two years as a Yale postdoctoral student for his colleague Gilbert to quit the field before he could step in. Prudentially, he bided his time as lecturer in education. The following year, Walter Bowers Pillsbury—whom Cattell called one of the four best psychologists of his generation—was delayed an extra year at Cornell before finding an assistant professorship at Michigan. The Ann Arbor post became available only because the incumbent, Edgar Pierce, was forced by his father-in-law's death to abandon psychology in order to run the family business.[98] Laboratories were increasing arithmetically while doctorates were growing geometrically. By the end of the century there were nearly three Ph.D.'s for every laboratory, a fact that helps to explain the pronounced increase then in calls for a practical psychology. Even allowing for attrition and apostasy, one might expect—given this Malthusian specter—an occupational famine.

With the research business overstocked, students could be expected to risk the capital investment of years only if assured that alternative forms of employment were available. Vying for students, laboratory directors saw to it that such professional platforms were constructed. Learning from his own experience at Yale, Seashore quickly established relations with Iowa's Department of Education and with the nearby Child Welfare Research Station.[99] This pattern of events was similar elsewhere, fortified by a variety of motives: by the desire to diminish philosophical control over the psychological curriculum; by the need to share in funds made available by state departments of education and social welfare; and often by straightforward psychological imperialism.[100] By the time Harvey Carr entered graduate school at Chicago in 1902, he had to make a choice between two curricula: philosophy-psychology or psychology-education.[101] It is ironic that such a choice had to be made at the one university where attempts to unite intellectually the philosophic and the practical were insistent. But the split reflected an institutional reality: each course of study was designed to equip the student for different tasks and careers. The division of labor that James had called for a decade earlier had been formalized.

The tasks of the psychologist interested in educational applications did not extend beyond the "half-physiological" problems Münsterberg had deprecated. Child study was the center of concern for educationists searching for a scientific pedagogy. It involved a massive empirical compilation of the results of mental tests, questionnaires, and reports from teachers and parents aimed at producing a statistical composite of the cognitive and emotional development of the normal child. Upon this basis, pedagogy would be reformed to coincide with the developmental sequence of the child's mental growth. The most rigorously empirical aspect of this movement was the particular province of the experimentally trained psychologist who could devise and administer tests to determine such motor and "mental" skills as sensual acuity, muscular strength and coordination, speed of reaction, perception of movement and time, and simple memory. These results would be correlated to the subject's age, genealogy, class rank, and so forth in hopes that a consistent developmental portrait would emerge. Psychologists converted such experimental apparatus as the chronoscope, kymograph, ergograph, and plethysmograph—all originally intended to assist the introspective act—into devices to record and measure children's skills. This psychological program eliminated introspection, investigation of the higher thought processes, and philosophic perspectives: the essential ingredients of classic experimental psychology.[102]

The vogue of popular psychologism promised social support of the discipline. Accordingly, most psychologists were inclined to agree with the sentiments that informed Joseph Jastrow's presidential address to the APA in 1900: "Psychology and life are closely related; and we do not fill our whole function if we leave uninterpreted for practical and public benefit the mental power of man."[103] Psychologists had so exuberantly advertised their serviceability in the 1890s that the public began taking them at their word. Scripture claimed that his interest in testing began in the early part of the decade when he was asked by a publishing firm whether psychologists could determine the qualities that would make a good typesetter. In 1896 W. L. Bryan was commissioned by the Union & Wabash Railway to study the habit formation involved in telegraphy. Witmer testifies that his clinic began the day a Philadelphia teacher introduced him to a "chronic bad speller" and to her challenging assumption that if psychology was worth anything it could diagnose the boy's problem. Seashore reported that a similar challenge prompted the development of the Iowa Psychological Clinic.[104] Psychologists readily recalled such episodes as evidences that, as Madison Bentley believed, "the pressure to extend psychology toward the practical arts came chiefly from those arts themselves."[105] Psychologists were not, however, hiding their light under a basket.

Regardless of source, the pressures toward application were reflected in the psychological literature. In 1898, one-quarter of all the experimental articles in the United States were explicitly concerned with the application of psychological principles to practical concerns; one-quarter of all experimental subjects were children or adolescents; one-quarter of all published investigations were physiological in orientation. The sponsors of experimentalism who defined psychology as the introspective analysis of the normal adult mind had cause for alarm. Less than half the experiments used normal adult human subjects. Only a quarter of the published experiments dealt with the higher mental processes, and only *two and one-third percent* involved introspective analysis.[106] A new psychology was replacing the new psychology.

In his 1894 presidential address before the APA, Cattell proclaimed: "This Association demonstrates the organic unity of psychology, while the wide range of our individual interests proves our adjustment to a complex environment."[107] In reality, psychology's eclecticism was jeopardizing psychology's unity. Its philosophic sponsors demanded the continuation of introspectionist programs in order to keep consciousness psychology's subject matter, yet the version of Wundtian psychology that Titchener upheld provided little philosophical grist.[108] Meanwhile, practitioners interested in applying psychophysical principles to educational problems were shaping experimentation to their own ends. The instrumentation, quantitative precision, and accumulation of objective data intended to augment self-examination were being transplanted into nonintrospective settings to serve newer patrons. In these contexts, psychology resembled physiology, and the similarity seemed to threaten psychology's claim to disciplinary autonomy. What was needed to insure psychology's "organic unity" was not mere organizational identity, as Cattell stated, but theoretical consistency. Divided on aims, psychology began to split into rival theoretical schools. Searching for a viewpoint that would reconcile the philosopher's requirements for philosophic and social theory with the practical needs of education and child study and that would provide a theoretical framework for experimentation that did not encroach upon physiological explanation, psychology began to discard the physicalist model in favor of the genetic viewpoint.

CHAPTER 9

Turning Point: Geneticism, Functionalism, and Animal Psychology

[A]s soon as I first heard it in my youth I think I must have been almost hypnotized by the word "evolution," which was music to my ear and seemed to fit my mouth better than any other.

—G. Stanley Hall
Life and Confessions of a Psychologist (1923)

Darwinism has never been a really vital issue in psychology.

—James Rowland Angell
"The Influence of Darwin on Psychology" (1909)

Damn Darwin.

—John Broadus Watson to
Robert M. Yerkes, October 29, 1909

When Boring declared that American psychology "had inherited its physical body from German experimentalism, but had got its mind from Darwin," he was testifying to the presence of two distinct traditions: the physicalist and the genetic.[1] The former, as we have seen, involved the analytical attempt to reduce mental phenomena to their simpler elements by means of introspection. This tradition descended from Wundt and is often mistakenly represented as coextensive with the new psychology. It maintained, as J. R. Angell observed, a "transverse view of life phenomena."[2] This was the psychology of content.

Genetic psychology constituted an alternative approach to mind by viewing it "longitudinally" or historically. It was based on the paradigm of evolutionary biology rather than of physics. Genetic psychology was developmental in that it included analysis of the ontological changes of individual organisms from embryonic life to maturity. It was comparative in that it investigated the relation of mental processes and of responsive activity among different species and, phylogenetically, among organisms of the same species. Based on the tradition of naturalistic observation extending back to Gall, Lamarck, Haeckel, Spencer, and Darwin—indeed, one may as well include Aristotle— this psychology was necessarily concerned with the behavioral manifestations of mental life. Introspection formed no part of its approach. Indebted to embryology, zoology, and Lamarckian biology and relying on the theory of recapitulation, this science provided biological analogies for ethology, ethnology, ethics, and the social sciences generally. Informed by phrenology and even by faculty psychology, it sought ultimately to understand the psychological roots of conduct and character.[3] This was the psychology of act.

Boring is correct to remark that in the nineteenth century the difference between the psychologies of act and content was the difference between arguing and experimenting.[4] Genetic psychology was indeed speculative, a fact that did little to impede its acceptance. Geneticism was a compelling conception. First, it promised to provide an explanatory framework for the essentially descriptive studies of the experimental laboratory. Second, its evolutionary biological perspective served to consolidate nonintrospective endeavors within American psychology. Most of the early modern developments in applied psychology—including the study of individual differences, testing, child study, clinical psychology, and eugenics—occurred within the genetic context. Finally, this same perspective seemed to supply philosophers and social theorists with a psychological key to the paramount problem of the bearing of biological evolution on conceptions of human nature.

This broad appeal of genetic psychology led to efforts to make it more empirical. Many psychologists in the late 1890s entertained the hope that, if the genetic viewpoint could be brought into the laboratory and somehow fused with the laboratory's physicalist perspective, psychology as a discipline might possess a unified theory capable of consolidating the philosophic, scientific, and practical programs essential to psychology's professional growth. Formal attempts to elaborate a genetic viewpoint and to use it to inform experimental endeavor began with Hall at Clark, found forceful expression in the writings of Baldwin at Princeton, and attained refined experimental articulation in the functionalism of Dewey and Angell at Chicago. Most important for our purposes, genetic psychology encouraged the introduction of animal psychology into the American laboratories and thus set the stage for Watson and his behavioristic agenda.

Genetic Psychology at Clark

The tripartite program of comparative, experimental, and historical psychology that Hall had envisioned in his 1885 inaugural lecture at Hopkins found no concrete expression until a decade later at Clark. Experimentalism, "reduced to far more exact methods" than either comparative or historical psychology, provided the image of scientific rigor Hall deemed essential to the discipline's success.[5] By the mid-1890s, however, that image had been tarnished by the controversies surrounding introspective psychology's sterility, on the one hand, and applied experimentalism's proximity to physiology, on the other. In particular, this image had been shattered at Clark when it failed to support the practical work that Hall felt was increasingly essential to psychology's public support. When in 1894 Hall turned wholeheartedly in the direction of child study, those genetic concerns which he had always managed to subordinate to the experimental image emerged full-blown.[6]

Drawing on the works of the biologist Henry Drummond and of the comparative psychologist George John Romanes, Hall saw in evolutionary analogies to biological recapitulation a paradigm for the genetic study of mental faculties.[7] In 1895 Hall undiplomatically editorialized that the child-study movement based upon genetic psychology would soon surpass in importance the experimental psychology he had fought so long to establish. The next year he predicted that "the old adult psychology"—which is to say the purportedly central aspect of the once "new psychology"—would be completely assimilated "into a new genetic psychology."[8] This prophecy entailed a reworking of Hall's original plan for psychology outlined a decade earlier. Hall's new 1899 agenda signified the increasingly central role of comparative psychology at Clark.

The decennial celebration of Clark University provided the heads of each department with the occasion to review one decade's progress of research and to plan the next. Speaking for psychology, Hall now arranged psychology into three new categories: comparative psychology, individual psychology, and the study of mental attitudes.[9] This last category, which Hall also called the "psychology of the permanent apperceptive groups," was admittedly the furthest removed from the laboratory. It was to be a dynamic investigation "which does not stop at demonstrating the fact of mental habit, but goes on to investigate the effect of one sort of habit upon the rest." Cited as examples were the effects upon character of such diverse occurrences as disease and paternity and the acquisition of religiosity, "all of which promise much and should have an important place in the psychological department as a counterweight to the laboratory."[10]

Individual psychology was similarly practical in its aims and likewise divorced from the laboratory:

What underlies temperament? What are the laws of the growth of character? Why do some pupils do well with some teachers and not with others? What is the best treatment for reform school boys? How shall one deal with exceptional and peculiar children in the family?

Naturally, proponents of scientific experimentation objected to Hall's program at Clark. Hall himself recognized "that many of these questions extend far beyond the possibilities of the laboratory."[11] Previous research at Clark attempting to shed scientific light on such practical issues by means of the theoretical beacon of genetic psychology made this confession painfully apparent.[12]

Although Clark provided unsurpassed facilities for experimental research, the cumulative "counterweight to the laboratory" of Hall's disparate enthusiasms had so tipped the balance against experimentalism that his department's scientific reputation diminished. Furthermore, as a result of professional quarrels surrounding Hall's control of the *American Journal of Psychology*, Titchener became co-editor in 1895 and proceeded to fashion the publication into the mouthpiece of the Cornell laboratory.[13] This situation further freed Hall of the need to encourage his laboratory's productivity along traditional experimental lines. While the academic values of *Lehrfreiheit* and *Lernfreiheit* were upheld at Clark as nowhere else in America, the investigative freedom that often conduced to what one student called "unalloyed enthusiasm" also contributed to intellectual laxity. Arriving at Clark in 1903, Lewis Terman encountered a "lunatic fringe" of students "educated beyond [their] intelligence."[14] Clark mathematician Henry Taber reported that the "standards for the doctors [sic] degree maintained by President Hall in his *own* department (Gentic Phychology [sic]) . . . have been occasions of grave scandal at Clark."[15] Obvious to Hall was the need to devise an empirical anchor to prevent what he himself called his "crazes" from pulling his department out of the mainstream of scientific psychology.[16] While Hall depreciated "the old adult psychology," he never abandoned the realization that the laboratorry still provided psychology with the badge of scientific authenticity. He therefore sought to introduce genetic psychology into the laboratory as comparative psychology, the central division of his new program.

Involving investigation into the relation of instinct to "mental attitudes" and individual differences, comparative psychology would, in Hall's view, unite both the "fundamental" (i.e., the experimental) and "practical" fields. Hall complained of the lack of "accurate knowledge of mental life of even the commonest animals; there are many anecdotes, but not many reliable observations, and very few experiments." Uncertain of the extent to which animal psychology could be reduced to experimental techniques, he nevertheless recognized that the comparative method had "broadened and enriched other sciences in which it has been applied." He therefore called for its "full introduction into psychology."[17]

In general, comparative psychology was introduced at Clark as a supplement to an embattled form of experimentalism within the discipline at large. More particularly, it was implemented in order to provide scientific substantiation, methodological refinement, and symbolic authentication of a genetic psychology that furnished practical insights into education, mental and moral hygiene, and child study. Hall's child-study movement attempted both to determine "the content of children's minds" at various ages and to discover which behaviors were the results of adaptive learning and which were products of their "original natures."[18] The object of the first portion of this program was to bring educational methods and materials into conformity with the child's natural sequence of mental development. The object of the second pursuit was to determine which aspects of the child's behavioral repertoire could be changed by means of alterations of his or her environment. Two fundamental techniques were used to accomplish these objectives: the questionnaire method that Hall had pioneered and the anthropometric techniques employed by the anthropologist Franz Boas, a docent in psychology at Clark. The first method was roundly attacked by the generation of psychologists Hall had helped to train in rigorous experimental procedures.[19] Sensitive about their scientific reputation, many psychologists disavowed the identification with scientific psychology of naive empirical collections of observations by untrained contributors. The second method, involving the unfortunate loosening of children's garments, created a public furor in Boston in 1891.[20] Hall enlisted animal studies in the cause of genetic psychology in order to obviate both kinds of objections.

The methods of animal psychology seemed capable of contributing to child study's two main objectives and of providing alternatives—or at least supplements—to both of its approaches. In addition to an unverifiable composite of normal development obtained by the questionnaire method, animal psychology permitted a careful field observation of a single species. Psychology justified its withdrawal from direct focus on the child in the name of increased objectivity, whereas recapitulation theory, which assumed parallel development between species, legitimated comparative psychology's ultimate utility.[21] In addition to naturalistic observation, animal psychology allowed comparisons between the animal's instinctual behavior and its responsive activity when aspects of its environment had been deliberately modified. Thus, it augmented the second central feature of child study: the determination of what is innate and what is acquired. In 1894 the renowned British comparative psychologist C. Lloyd Morgan published his *Introduction to Comparative Psychology* in which he reported results using both procedures. Morgan's work represented an important step away from the anthropomorphic tendencies of earlier comparative studies and stimulated hopes that animal psychology would provide an exact program of experiment needed to restore scientific respectability to the categories of genetic psychology.[22]

Comparative psychology quickly captured the attention of researchers at Clark. In 1898 Willard S. Small began experimental research on "The Mental Processes of the Rat" and published in 1901 the first animal studies in which the maze technique was formally employed. In 1899 Linus W. Kline published his "Suggestions toward a Laboratory Course in Comparative Psychology." The next year Andrew J. Kinnamon began a series of experiments on discrimination and intelligence in monkeys. In the first decade of the twentieth century, James P. Porter and Herbert Burnham Davis would continue studies in animal learning. Simultaneously, students such as Edgar J. Swift, Louise Ellison, and Charles E. Brown were applying insights drawn from these studies to childhood learning and to adult intellection. An inspection of the Clark doctoral dissertations awarded in experimental psychology in that decade reveals a decided move toward objectivism.[23]

The need to find an experimental basis for an educational psychology underwritten by the genetic viewpoint led paradoxically to an abandonment of that viewpoint. Aided by biological objections to the theory of recapitulation and by psychologists' disenchantment with Hall's unscientific procedures of using analogous records of parallel development to account for mental growth in humans,[24] animal psychology increasingly came to focus on the second aspect of child study: the determination of how organisms learn. "Recapitulation," remarks Dorothy Ross, "seemed most plausible for those aspects of child behavior most far removed from the central learning experiences of children."[25] Likewise, it was unaccountable to the canons of experimental exactitude psychologists considered essential legitimation for psychological science as well as for a practical educational psychology.[26] The connection between education and animal psychology can be read in the careers of the early comparative researchers at Clark: Kline, Kinnamon, and Davis shortly became heads of normal schools, and Small entered the field of comparative hygiene. Only Porter remained in the comparative field, heading that subdiscipline at Clark and publishing only two small studies on imitation before becoming dean of Clark College. Once made editor of Hall's *Journal of Applied Psychology*, he too entered the field of educational psychology. Comparative psychology at Clark constituted a scientific stepping-stone to vocational perches in educational fields. But what they left behind in the animal laboratory was not recapitulation theory but a gestating learning theory—the focal point of twentieth-century behaviorism.

Edward Lee Thorndike

The career of E. L. Thorndike indicates that the roots of animal psychology in educational theory and child study were not confined to Clark. As an undergraduate at Wesleyan, Thorndike came under the influence of A. C. Armstrong, a philosopher who taught psychology as the scientific basis of pedagogy, using as a required text James Sully's educational psychology.[27] At Wesleyan, Thorndike's introduction to James's *Principles* served as a magnet to draw him to Harvard for graduate work in 1896. In Münsterberg's absence, Edmund Burke Delabarre directed the Harvard laboratory and permitted Thorndike to carry out his first experiment on children. Then the Harvard authorities, fearing a repetition of the unfortunate episode of Franz Boas and the Boston schoolchildren, forced him to discontinue his research. Deprived of children, Thorndike turned to chickens and suggested experiments that might discriminate instinctive from intelligent behavior. In order to continue these studies financially unencumbered, he applied for a year's fellowship at Columbia where, upon his acceptance, Cattell informed him that his animal work would suffice as his thesis topic.[28]

Thorndike confessed that his chief motive for engaging in animal work was to satisfy his degree requirements and to secure his scientific reputation. He acknowledged "no special interest in animals," an apathy prudentially engendered by the dearth of jobs in the field. Nevertheless, in 1898 he completed one of the modern classics in comparative psychology, "Animal intelligence." His effort earned him two offers: one as professor of psychology at the normal school at

Oshkosh, Wisconsin; the other as instructor of education at the Case Western Reserve's College for Women. After one year at the latter institution, he returned to New York as instructor in genetic psychology at Teachers College. Despite offers from Columbia, he remained there the rest of his career. As Thorndike's biographer has noted, Sully's *Outlines of Psychology*, which Thorndike read at Wesleyan, accentuated the importance to educational psychology of the genetic approach, the study of individual differences, and the "stamping-in" of learned responses—essential elements of Thorndike's comparative and educational psychology.[29] Thorndike had based his educational career as well as his educational theories on his animal researches, as had his contemporaries at Clark. As with them, his early interest in child study and his genetic approach evolved into an interest in learning per se, an interest he prosecuted so consistently that he was regarded—at least by Ivan Pavlov and the Russian "reflexologists"—as the founder of behaviorism.[30]

James Mark Baldwin

In 1895 as Hall was struggling to formulate a psychology around genetic conceptions of mental development, Mark Baldwin published one: *Mental Development in the Child and the Race*.[31] Baldwin's career typifies the vocational pattern of the generation of psychologists educated in the 1880s, enhancing their academic portfolios by identifying with German scholarship and laboratory techniques, and yet subordinating experimentation to fundamentally philosophic objectives. Like many of his contemporaries, Baldwin can still be regarded by historians of psychology as a scientist encumbered by philosophical baggage and by intellectual historians as a social theorist seeking to make philosophy instrumentally relevant to American culture by allying it with evolutionary science.[32] His career shows that interest in child study and genetic psychology could stem from philosophical as well as from pedagogical objectives.

Educated at Princeton and repelled by the restrictive atmosphere there, Baldwin journeyed to Berlin and Leipzig in 1884 in order to become acquainted with the new psychology. Returning to his alma mater for doctoral work under James McCosh in 1887 while studying theology and instructing in modern languages, he found that the "fetish" of German scholarship alone was insufficient to gain a post. Fearing that Baldwin "may have been contaminated while abroad," McCosh directed his student to "refute materialism" in his dissertation. The refutation, coupled with his theological training, secured for him his first position as professor of philosophy at Lake Forest University in Illinois, which Baldwin described as "a small institution exploiting a large name . . . devoted to the education of candidates for the Presbyterian ministry and specializing in missionaries to China." Finding this experience excruciating, he managed to obtain the chair of metaphysics and logic at the University of Toronto in 1889 and there fulfilled the second requirement for professional advancement by establishing an experimental laboratory in 1890. While at Toronto he published his *Handbook of Psychology*, which secured his reputation and earned him the Stuart Chair in Psychology at Princeton, where he founded his second laboratory.[33]

At last securely established, Baldwin immediately proceeded to attack the reigning conceptions within American experimental psychology. In a report prepared for the 1893 Columbian Exposition at Chicago, Baldwin protested against what he called "a 'ready-made' view of consciousness" that retained the old faculty psychology's grammar of memory, thought, and will as somehow "distinct from one another . . . one of which may be held in reserve while the other is acting."[34] In contrast to this viewpoint, Baldwin proposed a new syntax, insisting that psychology must be concerned with "mental functions" rather than with "mental faculties" and must regard these functions as "genetic" rather than "intuitive," as "growing" instead of "ready-made." He continued:

The new functional conception asks how the mind as a whole acts, and how this one form of activity adapts itself to the different elements of material which it finds available. . . . The particular way in which this one function shows itself is a matter of adaption to the changing conditions under which the activity is brought about. . . . The mind is looked upon as having grown to be what it is, both as respects the growth of man from the child, and as respects the place of man in the scale of conscious existence.[35]

Returning to Princeton from Chicago, Baldwin absorbed himself in a vigorous program of laboratory research in order to prove his point experimentally. In 1895 in the *Psychological Review*, which he had founded the year before, he attacked the "ready-made" view of consciousness upheld by Titchener. Baldwin claimed that observations of trained introspectionists offered no insights into the normal mind. In a series of experiments on the "type theory of reaction," Baldwin showed—as Cattell and Witmer had previously suggested—that the introspectionist's increased practice and proficiency in interpreting acts of consciousness biased his experiments.[36] The ensuing controversy between Baldwin and Titchener served to articulate a fundamental schism within psychology: some researchers were studying mind; others were concerned with minds and their adaptability.[37] As other psychologists, particularly those at the University of Chicago, took up Baldwin's cudgel against Titchener, the distinction became more manifest, and the experimental schools of structuralism and functionalism began to form.[38]

The immediate effect upon Baldwin of his encounter with Titchener, however, was his "lessening of interest" in experimental work. Baldwin reminisced:

Already at Princeton, the new interest in genetic psychology and general biology had become absorbing, and the meagerness of the results of the psychological laboratories (apart from direct work on sensation and movement) was becoming evident everywhere. I began to feel that there was truth in what James was already proclaiming as to the barrenness of the tables and curves coming from many laboratories.[39]

James stated in 1896 that "results that come from all this laboratory work seem to me to grow more and more disappointing and trivial. What is needed is new ideas."[40] A year earlier Baldwin himself had concluded his engagement with introspective psychology with the challenge to his colleagues to provide "theories, theories, always theories! Let every man who has a theory pronounce his theory!"[41]

And Baldwin pronounced his theory. He had castigated experimental psychology—Titchenerian psychology in particular—because of its inability to supply insights into social philosophy and ethics. To Baldwin the introspective analysis of the individual mind and its "ready-made" contents deflected attention from the central fact of man as a social creature responding to social pressures. Baldwin's mission was to rescue free will from the ravages of a mechanistic evolutionary psychology that Spencer had used to support antireformist concepts of historical individualism. Baldwin enlisted Darwin in support of his aim to free consciousness from the biological order of cause and effect. In a theory called organic selection, Baldwin argued that variation, not natural selection, was the key ingredient explaining evolutionary change. He assumed that "plasticity"—the ability to learn and adapt—was itself a biologically transmissible trait of use to the individual in the struggle for survival. Those most likely to survive were individuals who were most social because those individuals possessed the ability to draw upon the experiences of others. Hence, "gregariousness" was another useful trait. Plasticity and gregariousness would evolve together into an ever expanding force capable of freeing man from the deterministic control of natural selection. Mankind could *artificially* select and mold its environment.[42]

Baldwin's theory was similar to his friend C. Lloyd Morgan's conception of "emergent evolution," and Baldwin was alive to the possibility that comparative psychology with its genetic and functional viewpoints could be used to prove his points.[43] "Habit" and "accommodation"—prime foci of the animal psychologist—were, as R. Jackson Wilson notes, "thinly veiled biological analogies to tradition and progress in society"—the foci of the social philosopher.[44] Imitation was another process central to Baldwin's doctrine of organic selection, and animal studies were becoming attentive to the question of the role that imitation played in the process of learning. Additionally, comparative methods constituted the only feasible approach to the problem of the transmission of learning across generations. Like Hall, Baldwin would introduce animal psychology into the psychological laboratory in order to find substantiation for his particular theories.

In 1903 Baldwin was called to Johns Hopkins University to revive the laboratory that Hall had literally dismantled by 1889. Overcoming loyalties to Princeton, Baldwin regarded the move as an opportunity for "founding and developing a new center . . . to forward philosophic studies generally in America."[45] In 1905 he recognized that genetic psychology had "done most service hitherto negatively, in its antagonism to a psychology exclusively associational, on the one hand, and to one exclusively structural, on the other hand."[46] By 1908, however, he secured funds to make a positive contribution to genetic psychology by creating an animal laboratory sufficiently lavish to lure J. B. Watson from Chicago. A few weeks after Watson's arrival, Baldwin entered his associate's office, informed him of his abrupt resignation, declared his startled colleague the *Psychological Review*'s new editor, and disappeared behind a "cloud of scandal" into Mexico.[47] Thus freed from any possible philosophic pressure on the nature of his work, the man whom Mortimer Adler called the Billy Sunday of psychology now commanded the pulpit from which to disseminate his new gospel. This, however, is getting ahead of the story, for Watson had come to Hopkins from Chicago, where a decade earlier the functionalist program Baldwin initially announced had been enacted.

Chicago Functionalism

While Baldwin and Hall had both adopted James's disposition to view mind as the mechanism of adaptation to environment, James himself hailed John Dewey as the philosopher most likely to bring his own genetic conceptions to empirical fruition—to combine, as it were, Hall's practical goals with Baldwin's theoretical ones. In 1904 James declared:

Professor Dewey, and at least ten of his disciples, have collectively put into the world a statement, homogeneous in spite of so many cooperating minds, of a view of the world, both theoretical and practical, which is so simple, massive, and positive that . . . it deserves the title of a new system of philosophy.[48]

The Harvard philosopher was, of course, referring to the "Chicago pragmatists" and to functionalism, the psychology that underwrote the philosophic school.[49]

The efforts to rescue religious belief, to appropriate science for idealism, and to provide a scientific basis for ethics and education characterize the intellectual circle that gathered about Dewey.[50] Taking its cue from insights, derived from Trendelenberg and Bain and given American expression in the pragmatism of Peirce and James, that conscious thought is a response to a living problem encountered by an organism seeking to adjust itself to its environment, Chicago philosophy perforce came to concentrate on psychology, which Dewey referred to as a "natural history of psychic events."[51] Beliefs about reality were true if they allowed the believer to function successfully. Analysis of such ideas in terms of their results would allow philosophers to formulate a logic that could then be applied to education, ethics, and aesthetics. But there was a more basic component to such a philosophy, namely the assumption that beliefs about reality become catalysts to activity that changes the environment itself. Consciousness, being instrumental, was therefore real. Beliefs about reality were reality. Chicago psychology directed its attention not to mental contents but to mental activities.

An early expression of this orientation came in 1896 when Angell and Addison W. Moore published an experimental statement of this theoretical position in "Reaction-Time: A Study in Attention and Habit."[52] Angell and Moore attempted to settle the controversy between Baldwin and Titchener. The orthodox explanation of differences in reaction time held that reactions were more rapid when the subject attended to the (manual) movement to be executed rather than to the (auditory) stimulus to be applied. Baldwin had argued that the differences were explicable in terms of practice. Angell and Moore showed that the subject attends to whatever juncture of the coordination seems to require the most supervision in the interests of the most efficient response.[53] Both the "type theory" and the "practice theory" were correct as far as they went, but neither was comprehensible without the experimenter's willingness to look at the total coordination viewed as the problem-solving activity of a subject who reacts with both ear and hand simultaneously. "The hand therefore," Angell and Moore concluded, "is stimulus as well as response to the ear, and the latter is response as well as stimulus to the hand."[54] The "type theory" of reaction, by looking at stimulus and response as two distinct elements *within* the act, could not explain the act itself. The sound did not constitute an "external stimulus" or "cause" of the act but was part of the act. One could not account for different reaction "types" unless one considered the purpose or function of the total activity.

Dewey quickly elaborated Angell's and Moore's theme in his famous "Reflex Arc Concept in Psychology."[55] The tripartite division of reflex arc into its distinct and successive sensory, ideational, and motor components, argued Dewey, was an abstraction, a reflection of the atomistic thinking against which Baldwin had railed. In real life, they are but ongoing functions of a continuous, coordinated, adaptive activity. A "whole" act, consisting of both stimulus and response, may itself constitute a stimulus to a subsequent act. For example, a child's seeing a bright object may result in his grasping the object, and the act of seeing-reaching-grasping may lead in turn to some other activity. In such a simple successfully coordinated adjustment, the distinction between stimulus and response is clear-cut; if repeated often enough, the act becomes nonreflective and habitual. Certain successful acts become even automatic and reflexive. Consciousness enters into activity only when the coordination is unsuccessful; that is, when the organism fails to adjust to the environment. The bright object before the child might be a candle's flame, so that the child's grasping response results in a painful burn. The reflex arc concept enables the experimenter to ask only one question of this situation: Given a stimulus, what is the response? But the problem for the child who has been both entertained and pained by bright objects is not immediately one of determining the proper response; rather, it is one of determining the nature of the stimulus. His attention is thereafter directed toward the sensory aspect of the coordination, toward better visual discrimination of the problematic object. Seeing—once part of the "stimulus phase" of a successful act—becomes in problematic encounters part of the response. The reflex arc concept could not account for the labile character of experience; and, therefore, neither could dualism.

Dewey's "reflex arc" thesis became the rallying point of Chicago pragmatism and Chicago functionalism as self-conscious movements in philosophy and psychology, respectively. To the functionalist, consciousness was no longer considered a phenomenological manifestation of mind; it became a functional phase of the biological organism's adjustment to its environment. Instead of focusing on mental contents, functional psychology would examine mental activity defined as the acquisition, retention, organization, and evaluation of experiences that, in turn, were viewed as guides to adaptive behavior.[56] Since mental activities cannot be apprehended apart from consideration of the conditions that give rise to them and the consequences that follow from them, psychology promises to become a thoroughly practical predictive science.[57]

The Chicago formulation was a corporate manufacture,[58] and it was sufficiently compelling to provoke a reaction from E. B. Titchener, probably the only psychologist in the country that thought of his department as representing a "school" of thought. While the Chicago camp employed biological analogies to legitimate the study of mental functions, Titchener utilized analogies drawn from the *history* of biological science as counterarguments. The Cornell psychologist warned of the danger that,

if function is studied before structure has been fully elucidated, the student may fall into that acceptance of teleological explanation which is fatal to scientific adavance: witness if witness be necessary, the recrudescence of vitalism in physiology. Psychology might put herself for the second time, and no less surely though by different means, under the dominion of philosophy. In a word, the historical conditions of psychology rendered it inevitable that, when the time came for the transformation from philosophy to science, problems should be formulated, explicitly and implicitly, as static rather than dynamic, structural rather than functional.[59]

Prior to the formation of the Chicago school, Titchener's warnings about the dangers of philosophical usurpation would have served as a powerful sanction. James, as we have seen, argued that psychology must for the sake of its professional survival provide both a philosophical and a theoretical science of mind, on the one hand, and a practical science of conduct and character, on the other hand. The basic premise of Chicago functionalism suggested the fusion of both programs. The same pragmatic theorem that held that true ideas were those which permitted successful adjustments between the organism and its environment demanded a similar functional test of pragmatism itself. A philosophical system could be proven true or false according to its ability to underwrite successfully practical endeavors. Chicago's city and its university were seedbeds of educational and social reform, and Dewey pushed his theories into every area, especially into education. In 1902 he became director of the university's School of Education and proceeded to work out his progressive educational theories in terms of a genetic functional psychology.[60] Pragmatism was not only the philosophy of action; it was philosophy in action. Functionalism, which was so pervasive that Boring called it the American psychology,[61] rose to prominence because it promised to unify philosophy, experimental science, and social science.

That functionalism intended to achieve this unification was the implicit message of Angell's 1906 presidential address to the APA, "The Province of Functional Psychology." Diplomatically declaring at the outset that functionalism was merely "a point of view," he succeeded by the conclusion of his message in presenting a convincing demonstration that it was a well-nigh universal one. Functionalism, Angell argued, could be seen as the convergence of three psychological conceptions. The first conception involved the disposition to examine mental operations rather than mental contents. Functionalism proposed "to get at mental process as it *is* under the conditions of actual experience rather than as it *appears* to a merely postmortem analysis."[62] Angell here attempted to enlist the support of those psychologists who were concerned with individual differences and mental testing by suggesting that they had already subscribed to this proposal:

> As a matter of fact many modern investigations of an experimental kind largely dispense with the usual direct form of introspection and concern themselves in a distinctly functionalistic spirit with a determination of what work is accomplished and what the conditions are under which it is achieved.[63]

Conversely, Angell attempted to steal support from Titchener by arguing that his analogy between psychological and physiological structures was misleading. Angell pointed out "that mental contents are evanescent and fleeting" and bore no relationship to "the relatively permanent elements of anatomy." Rather than being more scientific than analysis of function, structuralism was less so because its proponents, despite their "flourish of scientific rectitude," had not been able to show that the contents of mind could ever be replicated. "Functions, on the other hand, persist as well in mental as in physical life."[64]

The second pervasive conception of functional psychology was similar to the first: the view of mind "as primarily engaged in mediating between the environment and the needs of the organism." No doubt thinking of Hall's program at Clark, Angell suggested that if those in-

terested in genetic psychology would adhere to the experimental program enacted at Chicago, geneticism would no longer occupy "the position of an innocuous truism or at best a jejune postulate" but would
possess "a problem requiring, or permitting, serious scientific treatment." Angell realized that psychological theory "has been vitalized
and broadened by the results of the genetic methods thus far elaborated," but he insisted that genetic psychology's "great desideratum"
should be the elaboration "of adequate methods." "Moreover," he reminded the advocates of utility,

not a few practical consequences of value may be expected to flow from this
attempt, if it achieves even a measureable degree of success. Pedagogy and
mental hygiene both await the quickening and guiding counsel which can only
come from a psychology of this stripe. For their purposes a strictly structural
psychology is as sterile in theory as teachers and psychiatrists have found it
in practice.[65]

Angell was aware of the hostility existing between philosophers and
the proponents of applied psychology. Anticipating opposition to his
previous proposal from the former group, he admitted that it was

not perhaps unnatural that the frequent disposition of the functional psychologist to sigh after the flesh-pots of biology should kindle the fire of those con-
secrated to the cause of a pure psychology and philosophy freed from the con-
taminating influence of natural science. As a matter of fact, alarms have been
repeatedly sounded and the faithful called to subdue the mutiny. But the purpose of the functional psychologists has never been, so far as I am aware, to
scuttle the psychological craft for the benefit of biology. Quite the contrary.
Psychology is still for a time at least to steer her own untroubled course. She
is at most borrowing a well-tested compass which biology is willing to lend
and she hopes by its aid to make her ports more speedily and more surely. If
in use it prove treacherous and unreliable, it will of course go overboard.[66]

Persuasively and reassuringly, Angell implied that psychology was
destined for philosophic harbors. Biologists, he asserted, "treat consciousness as substantially synonymous with adaptive reactions to novel
situations." And "every philosophy save that of outright ontological
materialism" holds that mind plays a paramount role in the evolutionary process. Angell suggested:

If one takes the position now held by all psychologists of repute . . . that
consciousness is constantly at work building up habits out of coordinations

imperfectly under control; and that as speedily as control is gained the mental direction tends to subside and give way to a condition approximating physiological automatism, it is only a step to carry the inference forward that consciousness immanently considered is *per se* accommodation to the novel.[67]

The viewpoint that consciousness supervened in an otherwise determined cause-effect chain of experience salvaged idealism and free will from reductionist science and became a central tenet of American functionalism.[68]

Functional psychology surely dominated a large province. It claimed relevance to philosophic and practical aims, promised to provide genetic conceptions with experimental verification, and intimated that it improved psychology's relations with the biological sciences. More broadly still, it adhered to optimistic doctrines of progressive evolutionism, as did pragmatism, the philosophic movement with which Angell explicitly identified it. Functionalism confirmed man as a willing being whose active consciousness constituted "an instrument for more effective living."[69] Within psychology specifically, functionalism infused experimentalism with a sense of organized purpose and even mission. More specifically, its laboratory agenda was, unlike Hall's, conciliatory; it required, not the abandonment of the techniques, methods, and findings of physiological psychology, but merely their subscription to a new viewpoint. But functionalism did seem to require a supplement. Whether introspection focused on mental elements or mental activities, it still failed to satisfy the scientific demand for independent verification. Functionalism had made its stand as the experimental refinement of genetic psychology's viewpoint. Animal psychology would provide Chicago functionalism with the most precise expression of methodological refinement.

Animal Psychology

Angell regarded comparative psychology, as did Hall and Baldwin, as "a concrete example of the transfer of attention from the more general phases of consciousness as accommodatory activity to the particularistic features." Animal psychology, he claimed, "is surely among the most pregnant [movements] with which we meet in our own generation." In a sense, animal psychology legitimated the more general and still tentative functional program because "the frontier upon which it is pushing forward its explorations is a region of definite, concrete fact." Furthermore, it authenticated functionalism's claim that it possessed a scientific "biological compass." Since comparative psychology's theoretical categories were designated "by such terms as selection, adaption, variation, accommodation, heredity, etc.," the inclusion of animal psychology in the Chicago laboratory served to maintain and to advertise functionalism's concentration upon genetic conceptions. Angell pointed out that all such categories were primarily functional because they apply primarily to behavior. "Indeed," he claimed, "behavior may be said to be itself the most inclusive of these categories."[70]

Six years later, his former student Watson would announce that psychology studied nothing but behavior, that consciousness was epiphenomenal, that functionalism was a vestige of outworn philosophic speculation, and that its primary approach—introspection—should be outlawed from the psychologist's working vocabulary.[71] Watson claimed that he learned very little from Chicago functionalism. Obviously, he had not learned to be conciliatory. And yet, paradoxically, by the 1920s most psychologists were calling themselves behaviorists. Before examining why "behaviorism" in some form or another became an acceptable paradigm, we must examine why Watson considered it an essential one.

CHAPTER 10

Of Mice and Men

It has always been a feature of our plan for the use of the chimpanzee as an experimental animal to shape it intelligently to specification instead of trying to preserve its natural characteristics. We have believed it important to convert the animal into as nearly ideal a subject for biological research as is practicable. And with this intent has been associated the hope that eventual success might serve as an effective demonstration of the possibility of re-creating man himself in the image of a generally acceptable ideal.

—Robert Mearns Yerkes
*Chimpanzees: A Laboratory
Colony* (1943)

Behaviorism ought to be a science that prepares men and women for understanding the principles of their own behavior. It ought to make men and women eager to rearrange their own lives. . . . I am trying to dangle a stimulus in front of you, a verbal stimulus which, if acted upon will gradually change this universe. For the universe will change if you bring up your children, not in the freedom of the libertine, but in behavioristic freedom—a freedom which we cannot even picture in words, so little do we know of it.

—John Broadus Watson
Behaviorism (1924)

Long before Arthur Koestler christened behaviorism "the philosophy of ratomorphism,"[1] commentators had recognized the obvious connection between animal psychology and Watsonianism. One pair of observers has labeled Watson's animal experimentation "the chief causal agent in the birth of behaviorism." Edna Heidbreder has concluded that behaviorism fundamentally represents the extension "of the methods and point of view of animal psychology into human psychology." Watson himself had described his efforts in similar terms: "Behaviorism, as I tried to develop it in my lectures at Columbia in 1912 and in my earliest writings, was an attempt to do one thing—to apply to the experimental study of man the same kind of procedure and the same language of description that many research men had found useful for so many years in the study of animals lower than man." He acknowledged a "deep bias on these questions" stemming from "nearly twelve years of experimentation on animals" and concluded his manifesto by remarking on the natural disposition of the scientist to "drift into a theoretical position which is in harmony with his experimental work."[2]

Experimental animal psychology had grown sophisticated in the decade between the publication in 1894 of C. Lloyd Morgan's *Introducing to Comparative Psychology* and Watson's 1903 dissertation entitled *Animal Education.*[3] According to traditional interpretations, this blossoming continued throughout the following decade, so that "in 1913, when behaviorism was officially inaugurated, animal psychology had attained a position that commanded respect."[4] Such a view contrasts sharply with Harvey Carr's complaint that, at precisely the time of animal psychology's reputedly rising prestige, his Chicago students "expressed an aversion to choosing a thesis topic in this field for fear that they would become known as comparative psychologists, and that this label would be detrimental to their professional placement and advancement."[5] In anticipating shifts in the direction of vocational wind currents, graduate students are particularly weatherwise. And in this instance they were characteristically prescient. By 1908, the year Watson left Chicago and Carr arrived, animal psychology had become more rigorously empirical, had prescribed more objective methodologies, and had significantly expanded its research horizons by elaborating a host of problems susceptible to experimental and statistical verification. In short, it had reached reached what sociologists of science call the take-off stage of growth. Simultaneously, however, it increasingly became the object of attack by philosophers, introspectionists, physiologists, and—perhaps worst of all—college administrators. Such depreciation jeopardized comparative psychology's perpetuation and growth. Professional stature failed to correspond to scientific promise. The history of any science containing logical anomalies should at least recognize a few such sociological ironies.

One scientist devised a strategy called behaviorism in an attempt to mitigate the effects within comparative psychology of the crisis this chapter attempts to outline. Before considering Watson's career, it might be useful to delineate the essential feature of that crisis: comparative psychology's relative isolation from the mainstream of disciplinary activity in the first two decades of the twentieth century. To be sure, later-day proponents of psychology's cumulative scientific progress could look back and recognize that animal psychology's nonintrospective methods, objective vocabulary, and primary focus on behavior as a biological surrogate of consciousness represented the clearest example of inchoate but growing trends within early-twentieth-century human psychology. Such correlation, however, does not justify the supposition that animal psychology tutored human psychology during that period.

In mere numerical terms, such tutoring would have seemed arduous. Reviewing "Psychological Progress" in the United States for the year 1908, Edward Franklin Buchner noted that animal psychology was "growing by leaps and bounds."[6] Buchner was then a departmental colleague of Watson, who at that time was the only full professor of animal psychology in the country. The reviewer, therefore, might be excused for imagining a verdant forest beyond the ripe tree immediately before him. In fact, in that year only six animal experiments were published, representing 4.1 percent of the total output of American laboratories and a mere six-tenths of 1 percent increase over the previous decade.[7] When Watson suggested to Yerkes in 1909 that those interested in animal behavior dine together at the forthcoming APA meeting, he knew he need not reserve a banquet hall. Besides himself, Yerkes, and two biologists, Watson named only five psychologists.[8] By 1910 the Association contained 218 members, 187 of whom Cattell listed in that year's edition of *American Men of Science* as having contributed to psychology. While 19 entries listed comparative concerns, only six were actively engaged in animal research.[9]

Numerical strength is no exclusive measure of intellectual impact, but several other factors indicate that comparative psychology's slow institutional growth was the result of firm opposition. Part of the resistance was intellectual. Those who defined psychology as the introspective study of mind felt, as Titchener did, that comparative psychologists lacked "a psychological standard." Titchener felt that the animal researcher merely adopted a physiological associationism of "the crudest sort" as a framework and then disguised that fact "by a washing over of the scaffolding with biological fluid by the adoption of biological analogies and points of view."[10] Those, like Münsterberg, who eschewed "half-physiological" experiments on humans realized that comparative psychology routinely traversed more than half the distance from philosophy to physiology. At different stages in their careers, both Watson and Yerkes—the two major comparative psychologists of the period—called themselves physiologists.[11] To a discipline attempting to portray itself as an independent science, animal psychology's uncomfortable proximity to that neighboring science represented an annoying reminder of psychology's intellectual dependencies. Introspective method allowed the discipline as a whole to avoid such identification; psychology studied conscious experience. Comparative psychology perforce studied behavior of nonintrospecting subjects. Titchener and others grudgingly held that animal psychology was of some small worth but only if behavioral data were cautiously translated into terms of animal consciousness.[12] Since doing so would involve reasoning by anthropomorphic analogy, orthodox psychologists concluded that "animal psychology was at best an indirect and relatively unimportant part of our science."[13] As long as general psychology was defined as the study of consciousness, animal studies remained a peripheral endeavor. Faced with only token support, comparative researchers seeking to improve their professional lot could employ two strategies: they could argue that animal psychology, too, was a part of the study of consciousness; or they could insist that general psychology actually was the study of behavior. Psychologists in other specialties such as "experimental pedagogy" could and would make the latter claim, but comparative psychologists—owing to their particular plight—were the ones who most urgently forced that conception on their colleagues.

Ideological as well as intellectual resistances helped to suppress animal psychology's professional growth. The new field owed its existence to the genetic psychologists, Hall and Baldwin, who had enlisted comparative psychology in their battle against traditional forms of experimentalism. There were still sufficient numbers of traditionalists at large in 1910 to suspect animal psychology's intentions. Ironically, genetic psychologists themselves soon felt betrayed by animal psychology's avoidance of the broad, philosophically pregnant problems of heredity and evolution.[14] In the unsettled climate of fin de siècle biological opinion, comparative researchers were sensing the wisdom of the very last sentence of James's authoritative *Principles of Psychology:* "And the more sincerely one seeks to trace the actual course of *psychogenesis*, the steps by which as a race we may have come by the peculiar mental attributes which we possess, the more clearly one perceives 'the slowly gathering twilight close in utter night.' "[15] When James presented this caveat, biologists were already questioning the validity of the assumption that acquired characteristics were inherited. In the late 1880s August Weissmann proposed the theory that the "germ cells" that determined heredity in offspring were distinct from "body cells" and hence not susceptible to environmental influence. Weissmann's findings touched off a tumultuous debate in biological circles between proponents of his view who called themselves neo-Darwinians and advocates of the idea of inheritance of acquired characters, the neo-Lamarckians. The "rediscovery" of Gregor Mendel's laws of heredity in 1900 further complicated the debate. "Mendelians" in biology turned to breeding experiments in order to find simple ratios of dominant or recessive heredity traits; their opponents, the "biometricians," employed statistical techniques.[16] Experimental psychologists extricated themselves from the debate. As Watson exclaimed in 1909, "Damn Darwin. The Neo Darwinians and Neo Lamarckians, etc. are in a worse hole than psychologists."[17]

Comparative psychologists often voiced opinions—obiter dicta—about the implications of evolution and heredity, but their own experimental work usually eschewed such considerations. Basically, they attempted to determine what native congenital equipment their subjects exhibited at birth and then to establish situations that would permit the experimenter to observe how "instinctive" behavior becomes modified.[18] In other words, they avoided questions of inheritance and concentrated instead on how organisms learn. Animal researchers thus ignored the philosophic purposes of genetic psychology while supplying to the educators drawn to genetic psychology a potentially useful science. "I am pretty sure," said Watson in 1912, "that any careful investigator in experimental education will have to be an animal psychologist. . . . We will just have to give executives and educationalists time for this to soak in."[19] Faced with lack of support for their activities, animal psychologists could really not afford to "give time" and instead began supplying arguments in behalf of their unrecognized potential.

A chief reason that this potential went unrecognized is that after 1910 psychologists who sought social and educational applications of psychological findings had largely turned their attention to the intelligence tests of Alfred Binet.[20] Compared with the promise of testing, animal psychology seemed to possess little immediate usefulness. In 1910, for example, Yerkes chided Cattell for his failure to cultivate animal research, a neglect that Yerkes claimed was especially regrettable in view of Columbia's proximity to the Bronx Zoo. Cattell replied that the zoological garden did not compare with the "opportunities offered for work in pathological, social and ethnic psychology" by the city itself.[21]

All this is not to say that all psychologists firmly deprecated animal psychology but simply to stress that most members of the discipline felt that insights into the human mind or human behavior could be best accomplished by investigations of humans. If intellectual doubts were the sole consideration, most departments would have sponsored a program in comparative research. Animal psychology did, after all, give currency to the claim that psychology itself was an exact natural science—a claim highly valued in some circles. Despite some philosophical suspicions of reductionist tendencies within animal research, most psychologists were sufficiently broad-minded to allow animal psychology's results to speak for themselves—provided, of course, that their funding matched their liberality.

In fact, comparative psychology competed with the traditionally furnished laboratory at a disadvantage. Cats, unlike chronoscopes, had to be fed. University authorities resented requests for the completely new kinds of apparatus required for animal experimentation.[22] Psychologists accustomed to work on problems of visual and auditory perception were not used to the olfactory sensations that accompanied comparative psychology's rush to scientific maturity. Animal researchers were often relegated to attics with their odoriferous subjects. Physical isolation only reinforced their sense of disciplinary marginality. Most important, comparative research was ill-suited to university economies. The general laboratory served the functions of both demonstration and research. To undergraduates it taught the discipline of science—a service that helped fund graduate research. The comparative laboratory provided no such dual purpose. Indeed, the need to control the animal subject's environment demanded a dispensation from pedagogical requirements. Department heads and university administrators, especially in the wake of the panic of 1907, frequently had choices to make. When one adds to these impediments complaints from local humane organizations and antivivisectionist societies,[23] the amazing aspect of comparative psychology was not that it grew so slowly but rather that it grew at all. It was this situation— given here in the barest outline—that Watson tried to alter by announcing his behaviorist agenda in 1912.

John B. Watson and Chicago

The often noted belligerence of Watson's psychological rebellion is largely explicable in terms of his social and educational background.[24] Watson was born in 1878 to a large family in a painfully poor rural area near Greenville, South Carolina. Dominated politically by Jacksonian democratic sentiments and religiously by Baptist fundamentalism, the Carolina Piedmont faced agricultural decline, industrial expansion, and population growth in a postbellum era marked by economic panic and fierce racial strife. Watson's father had earned a local reputation as an incorrigible brawler and heavy drinker whose chief service to the community was his long and frequent absences from it. Watson's mother, Emma, found emotional consolation in revivalism and raised her children in her rigid faith. Watson himself was baptized in a millpond—a "vaccination," he remarked in later years, that "didn't take."[25]

Seeking to break the chain of poverty, Emma Watson sold the family farm in 1890 and moved to Greenville, the provincial center of a rising middle class. There educational opportunities for her children might provide the catalyst for her family's social mobility. John Watson found it hard to adjust to his new urban and educational environment. He admitted "few pleasant memories of these years." Self-described as "lazy," "insubordinate," and academically inferior, Watson was the constant butt of jokes and pranks. He was arrested once for firing a revolver within the city limits and once for " 'nigger' fighting," an outlet for his repressed hostility which he described as one of his "favorite going-home activities."[26]

Since South Carolina possessed no public high schools in the nineteenth century, the sixteen-year-old Watson entered Furman University for further training. Though "rife with Baptist polemics," Furman was nevertheless, as Buckley has shown, "a college in transition in the 1890s."[27] A growing business community and an increasingly secular middle-class constituency provided the impetus for Furman's "more materialistic allegiances." Watson described his college years as "bitter"; he was a lackadaisical student who "was unsocial and had few close friends." Nevertheless, his college experience expanded his vocational horizons. Graduating from Furman in 1899, he spent a year as principal of Batesburg Institute, a private academy near Columbia, South Carolina. At the end of one year, he had grown weary of his parietal responsibilities and realized that continued vertical mobility required additional training.[28]

Writing to William R. Harper, president of the University of Chicago, Watson pleaded for a graduate fellowship by explaining that he would "never amount to anything in the educational world" without the training and credentials that a "real university" could supply.[29] Considerations other than Chicago's nominally Baptist origins prompted Watson's application. At Furman, Watson had at least excelled in philosophy and psychology. In 1897 his philosophy professor, Gordon B. Moore, had spent a sabbatical year at Chicago studying "physiological psychology" and returned to Furman during Watson's senior year to introduce the subject in an inhospitable locale. Stanley Hall may have won a place for psychology at Hopkins by professing the subject's "subordination" to sound religious principles, but to Watson psychology and philosophy as taught by Moore seemed characterized by an iconoclasm congenial to Watson's rebellious temperament. Moore's own heterodox views on biblical literalism led eventually to his dismissal from Furman. Perhaps it was the mutual recognition of temperamental affinity that led to a test of wills between teacher and student in 1898. Moore had announced that he would fail anyone who "ever handed in a paper backwards." Although, according to Watson's own account, he had been an "honor student the whole year," Watson took the dare and was duly flunked. The episode cost Watson an extra year at Furman and offers a preview of the distaste for conventional restrictions that would manifest itself in Watson's later scientific life.[30]

Arriving at Chicago in 1900 with fifty dollars in his pocket, Watson supported himself during his three years of graduate study by doing a variety of menial tasks that included cleaning the rat cages of the neurologist Henry Herbert Donaldson. In the following year Watson formalized his program of study: he would "major" in experimental psychology with Angell; take a first minor in philosophy with Dewey, Tufts, and A. W. Moore; and take a second minor in neurology with Donaldson. To augment his neurological training he took courses with the famous physiologist Jacques Loeb. Like his baptismal "vaccination," his first minor, philosophy, "wouldn't take hold." "With animals," however, Watson felt "at home," and chose for a dissertation topic research correlating the growth of the central nervous system medullation with the complexity of behavior in the white rat. Angell, as we have seen, was interested in the light animal psychology shed on the problem of consciousness as the mechanism of adaption. It was Donaldson, however, by whom Watson "was guided at every moment" of his work.[31]

Donaldson had received his doctoral degree under the biologist H. N. Martin in 1885 at Hopkins, where he also worked with Stanley Hall. Following a sojourn in Europe at Hall's suggestion, he returned to Hopkins for a year and then joined the Clark faculty as assistant professor of neurology. In 1890 and 1891 he performed minute anatomical study of the brain of Laura Bridgman, the Helen Keller of her generation and the subject of an earlier psychological study by Hall. From this classic anatomical work came Donaldson's lifetime focus on the quantitative study of the growth of the brain and nervous system. In 1892 he was recruited by Harper during the period of Clark's financial embarrassment and left Worcester for Chicago, where he introduced the white rat as the ideal subject for such studies.[32]

Hall had sensitized Donaldson to the connection between psychological function and anatomical structure at Hopkins and had provided an institutional base for such investigations at Clark, where Small had introduced the maze technique for the study of the mental processes of animals. Donaldson renewed his alliances with psychology at Chicago. Thus, when Watson arrived there at the turn of the century, he had at his disposal Angell's interest in genetic growth of function, Donaldson's experimental subjects, and Small's design for psychological experiments with animals. But the interdepartmentalism that facilitated Watson's researches also underscored his marginality. He found himself between two disciplines, a situation evidenced by Donaldson's offer to him of an assistantship in neurology in 1903.[33]

Watson's borderline status was reinforced by his association with Loeb, who allied himself intellectually with the nineteenth-century German physiological school of mechanistic reductionists. A philosophical monist and a staunch materialist, Loeb denounced the Darwinian school of comparative psychology that provided Chicago functionalism with a source of its inspiration. Genetic psychology, in Loeb's rigorous view, did not lend itself to experimental demonstration. The concepts of instinct and habit seemed hopelessly anthropomorphic. Drawing on the ideology of Rudolph Virchow and the medical materialists who attacked Haeckel's romantic gospel of recapitulation and on the work of plant physiologist Julius Sachs, Loeb attempted to reduce explanation of the behavior of higher organisms to physicochemical tropisms that accounted for the movements of plants. To Loeb there was no psychology other than physiology.[34]

Though Angell lived next door to the German physiologist at Chicago, they were in no sense philosophical neighbors. When Watson approached Loeb in 1901 about the possibility of experimenting on the associative processes in dogs affected with brain lesions, Angell discouraged the idea by warning Watson that Loeb was " 'not a safe man' for a youngster to work with."[35] Nevertheless, Loeb's ideas informed Watson's work. His thesis focused on the animals' kinesthetic reactions as much as on their neurological development. Watson found that his subjects' successes in running the maze depended largely on muscular "sense"—a more molar form, in Watson's view, of Loeb's tropisms. Elaborating on Thorndike's "trial-and-error" methods, Watson also found that his subjects' successes were dictated largely by the experimenter's control of the animals' nutritional and sexual needs.[36]

The immediate effect upon Watson of his association with Donaldson and Loeb was his realization of the gap between his own work and the researches conducted in the psychological laboratory proper. In part, his rejection of introspection stemmed from his aversion to formal conventions: "I never wanted to use human subjects. I hated to serve as a subject. I didn't like the stuffy, artificial instructions given to subjects. I always was uncomfortable and acted unnaturally."[37] Watson's depreciation of introspection also stemmed from the methodological positivism he had assimilated from his biological mentors. He regarded the "mental gymnastics" of introspective analysis as essays in scientific inaccuracy. It was futile, he would say in 1912, to assume

that I can immediately lay hold of a state of consciousness and say, "this, as a whole, consists of gray sensation number 350, of such and such an extent, occurring in conjunction with the sensation of cold of a certain intensity; one of pressure of a certain intensity and extent," and so on *ad infinitum*.[38]

After completing his dissertation, Watson was asked to remain at Chicago as assistant to Angell. It was then, according to his account, that he began asking his associates, "Can't I find out by watching their behavior everything that the other students are finding out by using O's [introspective observers]?" He reports that he "received little encouragement."[39]

In 1904, however, he must have imbibed some hope that he was not alone when he heard Cattell's St. Louis speech in which the celebrated psychologist called for an objective psychology. Cattell had quipped that it is "no more necessary for the subject to be a psychologist than it is for the viviscted frog to be a physiologist."[40] That year Watson took Cattell's message literally and journeyed to Johns Hopkins University Hospital to learn vivisectional techniques. He returned to Chicago to employ these methods in his researches upon kinesthetic and organic sensations of maze-running rats. Watson proceeded to extirpate various sensory modalities and thus to determine which functions or combination of functions aided the subject's total adjustment to its environment.[41] By 1905 Watson was attempting to find an objectivist terminology that could remove some of the more obviously anthropomorphic language used in psychological parlance.[42] And already by that time he was discovering that his inquiries were not commanding departmental support.

"I am very hampered in my research at present," he wrote to Robert Yerkes in August 1904: "We have absolutely no place to keep animals and no funds to run the 'menagerie' if we had the place."[43] By June of the next year support had so dwindled that Watson felt he had to solicit outside funding in order to continue his work.[44] In March 1906 he reported that lack of space necessitated the implementation of round-the-clock shift schedules for his researchers.[45] Not surprisingly, he seriously attended Baldwin's offer in the fall of the following year of an associate professorship at Hopkins.

Baldwin, as we have seen, had his own plans for animal psychology at Hopkins. Angell was apparently unwilling to frustrate them by withholding Watson from him. After six years of work at Chicago, Watson had just been appointed to the rank of instructor. He hesitated in accepting Baldwin's offer in order to pressure Angell into making better provision for himself and his facilities. Baldwin thereupon offered him a full professorship and another $1,000 raise in salary. Watson was reluctant to leave the laboratory he had spent years building with his own hands and later recounted that he would have stayed had Chicago promised "even an associate professorship."[46] But apparently Watson's services were not considered commensurate with that rank. More than title and pay entered into Watson's decision. He knew that the East Coast was the center of his professional world and had, as early as 1906, expressed a desire to be situated there. He considered himself, Yerkes, and Herbert Spencer Jennings the "big three" in animal work and longed to eliminate the "space barriers" between them. Jennings was a biologist at Hopkins, and by 1909 Yerkes had journeyed to Hopkins to begin a long collaboration with Watson.[47]

Furthermore, Watson felt that animal research was not receiving sufficient attention in the psychological journals. Only months after Baldwin's offer, Watson had expressed to Yerkes his intention of controlling journal reviews in order to "keep the comparative interest forced upon the human psychologist."[48] Baldwin was the editor of the *Psychological Review;* within weeks of his arrival, Watson had replaced him.

And so Watson became professor of experimental and comparative psychology and director of the psychological laboratory at Hopkins in 1908 at the age of thirty. At Chicago he had complained of the requirement of having to teach so many courses in human psychology.[49] The move to Baltimore was a tangible expression of hope for the support of animal work he felt he had not obtained at Chicago. It seems peculiar, therefore, that in his very last letter to Yerkes from Chicago, Watson expressed apprehension that the Hopkins post would require him to work exclusively with animals: "As you told me in your letter I shall have to get busy on the human side as well as the animal. . . . You will see that my comparative work will not be very much in evidence during the first year of my stay in Hopkins."[50] Why would Yerkes, who had fought tooth-and-nail at Harvard as Watson had done at Chicago for the right to specialize in animal work, offer such advice in 1908? And why would Watson seem inclined to accept it? Some of the answers lay in the plight of animal psychology at Harvard and in the apprehensions among comparative researchers that the turn of events in Cambridge presaged.

Robert Mearns Yerkes and Harvard

In 1899 Harvard's philosophy department announced the introduction of animal psychology into its experimental program.[51] The announcement represented less a program than a promise made feasible by the arrival of Yerkes. Two years older than Watson, Yerkes was born and raised in the bucolic outskirts of Philadelphia "inhabited by intelligent, self-respecting, law-abiding, prosperous folk." The "comfort" and "prosperity" of the surroundings that Yerkes remembered "as nearly ideal" contrasted sharply with Watson's childhood environment and nurtured a personality less prone than Watson's to perceive social and scientific conventions as restrictive. Graduating from Ursinus College in 1897 and tentatively envisioning a medical career, Yerkes was provisionally accepted at Harvard in that same year and, upon successful demonstration of academic aptitude, was admitted for graduate work in zoology. Finding himself "keenly interested in zoology and also in psychology," he was persuaded by Royce—who realized that the nearby competitor, Clark University, had just inaugurated a similar program—to combine these interests as comparative psychology.[52] Transferring into the philosophy department in 1899, Yerkes received a letter from Thorndike who expressed his pleasure in finding "someone awake to the importance of animal psychology." Thorndike, however, was not sanguine about Yerkes' ability to prosecute that interest at Harvard; he suggested that Yerkes obtain a fellowship in zoology at the University of Pennsylvania.[53]

Thorndike's reservations stemmed from personal experience and proved well founded. When he began his studies on chickens in 1896, his boardinghouse constituted his laboratory, and other students regarded his interest as "bizarre." His landlady evicted his subjects, and when he attempted to board them in the psychological laboratory, the department proved just as inhospitable. William James himself compensated for his inability to procure space in the Agassiz Museum by offering his own cellar as an experimental refuge. Thorndike later praised Cattell's efficiency for providing space at Columbia for his "most educated chickens," but Cattell's commitment was not long-lasting. After a few short years of animal work, Thorndike followed the professional path of least resistance by turning to educational psychology.[54] Zoology, he suggested to Yerkes, was the field in which those interested in animal research would find adequate support.

Yerkes' first published work emanated from Harvard's laboratory of comparative zoology in 1899. Working with Charles B. Davenport, he began his researches on the tropistic responses of invertebrates and gradually moved into the field of nerve physiology. Once situated in the philosophy department, Yerkes began investigating the more "molar" problems of the connection between instinctual response and habit formation in amphibians. "Always," he maintained, "my research has been more nearly physiological than psychological, for I have dealt with problems of behavior, not with experience."[55] Such a description involved a damaging confession; the department inhabited by the philosophical giants of the age was being infiltrated by crabs and crayfish. Though catholic, the situation seemed incongruous to administrators. Accordingly, upon completing his dissertation in 1902, Yerkes was offered a teaching fellowship for the following year instead of the instructorship he had anticipated. He asked Münsterberg to inquire of the president if there had not been some mistake, and Eliot responded by questioning whether such work "corresponded . . . to the intentions of the Corporation." Yerkes' research represented "a new sidebranch," Münsterberg explained. Eliot reluctantly provided Yerkes with his instructorship, but it was a title the comparative psychologist retained for the next six years.[56]

By 1905 Yerkes was openly expressing his dissatisfaction with his situation at Harvard. His sense of isolation and marginality was increased the following year when he found himself uninvited to departmental meetings.[57] In May he had Royce plead his case for promotion to assistant professor. "As a student of the problems of current philosophical discussion," implored Royce,

I feel that the new Comparative Psychology is no "frill," no ornament, no merely external affair to be added to our department work, but is a very central and significant branch of investigation. I confess that, to me personally, the results reached along a good many lines of research in experimental psychology have proved to be disappointing; but *this* branch . . . must grow increasingly valuable. . . . It is not "animal" psychology merely that is in question. Comparative human psychology, race psychology, social psychology, educational psychology, must all make use of the means that the work followed by Dr. Yerkes is now developing. If we want to keep in the modern movement at all, we need this work to go on, and to grow. . . . I believe thoroughly in the work of the philosopher; but it is well for the philosophers to have a naturalist among them. Yerkes is a great prize for us to possess.[58]

Royce concluded by hoping for Yerkes' promotion and permanency. Despite his insistence that animal psychology was no "frill," his arguments nevertheless implied that Yerkes was the philosopher's token "naturalist." Royce's plea was unavailing.

Yerkes disappointment turned to anger in 1908 when he was again passed over for promotion in favor of James Houghton Woods. An independently wealthy Harvard alumnus and member of a prominent Boston family, Woods had been an instructor in philosophy since 1903.

An insider and an amateur, he had been appointed without pay; the prestige of identity with Harvard philosophy sufficed to legitimize a career of public lecturing and foreign travel. He did little teaching at Harvard and no research.[59] When Eliot promoted him to assistant professor, Yerkes considered it a personal humiliation, justly doubted his department's commitment to scientific research, and demanded a similar promotion.[60] Once again, Münsterberg wrote to Eliot on Yerkes' behalf, seeking to disabuse the president of the notion that Yerkes was engaged in "strictly animal work"—a notion that Eliot was logically entitled to maintain. Said Münsterberg disingenuously:

I wish to point to the fact that he is not an instructor in animal psychology, but in Comparative Psychology. The term Comparative Psychology means today, and is understood by Dr. Yerkes to mean, both the ontogenetic development of the mind and the phylogenetic development. His specialty is thus child psychology as well as animal psychology. It is true that his research has put more emphasis on the animal side simply because for practical reasons I always objected to the bringing of children into the laboratory rooms. . . . [I]t is evident that such topics can hardly be separated from the problems of educational psychology. Educational psychology, on the other hand, is evidently not a new specialty and certainly one which is demanded today practically from every college. I suppose that Dr. Yerkes would not object at all if the Corporation was to promote him with the distinct understanding that his lecture courses were to emphasize the more educational aspects of psychology.

Eliot curtly responded that the letter "has served its purpose."[61] Obviously, Münsterberg had communicated to Yerkes the "distinct understanding" he had reached with the corporation, for it was during this episode that Yerkes wrote to Watson of the need "to get busy on the human side."

Yerkes avoided heeding his own advice as long as possible, but the tacit agreement that had secured his promotion was not dissolved when Eliot resigned in 1909. Abbot Lawrence Lowell, soon after assuming the presidency, informed Yerkes "that educational psychology offered a broader and more direct path to a professorship and to increased usefulness than did . . . comparative psychology, and that [he] might well consider effecting a change."[62] When Yerkes insisted that he continue the work he considered himself "pre-eminently suited for" in disregard of the university's considerations of his "academic usefulness," Münsterberg's support collapsed. In 1911 he complained to Yerkes that animal psychology was interfering with human psychology and keeping students from introspective training. Not that exclusive work in "the study of the behavior of animals" is unimportant, Münsterberg claimed: "I insist only that it is no longer psychology." The laboratory director reproached Yerkes for his separatist tendencies, regretted that animal psychology "has so far not opened any wide perspective of knowledge," and claimed that the department's original philosophic opposition to the inclusion of animal work "indeed seems to have been practically justified." In case Yerkes failed to grasp Münsterberg's message, he bluntly expressed doubts about awarding the Ph.D. degree to students whose research was exclusively comparative and threatened as a last resort simply to abolish the program.[63] Within the year, Yerkes had accepted a position at the Boston Psychopathic Hospital where in March 1913 he began working in earnest on "the human side," thus exhibiting the breadth of comparative psychology that his former supporters had advanced as the field's sole claim to institutional support.[64]

The Push Toward the Practical.

In February 1913 Watson congratulated Yerkes on his decision to work at Boston Psychopathic. "Far from suspecting that you had any such longings," teased Watson, "I think I remember some 2 or 3 years ago your saying that you had little interest in this type of work. . . . I thought that you, Titchener and Holt were rather against [it]. However, I think you are headed in the right direction."[65] It was the direction in which comparative psychologists as a group were being pushed—toward the practical and the human. Lawrence Wooster Cole, for example, received his master's degree under Yerkes in 1904 and returned as full professor to his alma mater, the University of Oklahoma, where he had instructed since 1900. For four years he researched exclusively upon raccoons. Then for reasons of retrenchment he was abruptly fired. Unable to procure an offer elsewhere in comparative psychology, he returned to Harvard to receive his doctorate in 1910 and thereupon obtained an instructorship in experimental psychology at the University of Colorado. His academic credentials, in other words, were improving while his academic status was declining. In 1911 he reported to Yerkes his efforts to switch into human psychology; by 1912 he confessed that for the past two years he had been emphasizing educational psychology. That year he became full professor and head of the Colorado department.[66]

Melvin E. Haggerty received his doctorate under Yerkes in the same year as Cole and returned to Indiana University where he had taught since 1909. This was the year in which he began complaining that the lack of funding was crippling his research and in which another Indiana psychologist, Ernest H. Lindley, observed that psychology's salvation there depended upon the support of educational and medical interests. The following year Haggerty's assistant professorship was expanded to include educational psychology. He began working in the School of Education's new "orthogenic" clinic, modeled upon Witmer's innovation. Two years later he found it necessary to expand his interests even further and, with Lindley, initiated a course in applied psychology. By 1913 his animal work had come to an end; in 1915 he became professor of educational psychology at the University of Minnesota.[67]

In terms of the movement of personnel from one field to another, comparative psychology was being forced by institutional and economic pressure into the "human side" of psychology. As we have seen, no student who received a doctoral degree in comparative psychology at Clark escaped the pull of education's gravitational field. The situation was similar at Harvard. Every student Yerkes cited in his reminiscence, "Early Days of Comparative Psychology," published in 1943, had—if they found jobs within the profession at all—moved into the fields of education, educational psychology, or vocational guidance within a few years of their departure from Cambridge.[68] Comparative psychologists were departments' most expendable men and, in periods of retrenchment, were often the first to be sacrificed, as Eliot P. Frost (Ph.D., Harvard, 1908) found out at Yale in 1912.[69] Most often, animal researchers were, as Yerkes put it, "tactfully advised" to move into the more practical and—in terms of university economies—more self-sustaining fields of human psychology. G. V. Hamilton, who had studied under Yerkes along with Frost, spoke for most of his beleaguered colleagues a few months before Watson's manifesto when he declared: "I find myself gradually accepting as inevitable a development toward the applied and practical rather than the more dearly beloved academic side of things."[70]

Eventually the exodus of experimenters from animal psychology to educational and vocational psychology created an audience sympathetic to comparative psychology's claims to practical relevance. Immediately, however, this withdrawal served to drain talent from the kinds of investigation needed to substantiate such assertions. Professionally, it simply deprived the field of the numerical strength that might have helped it assert its prerogatives within the APA. At Hopkins, Watson felt this pressure keenly. While Baldwin had viewed his mission at Hopkins as the revival of philosophic studies, the university had planned for him to inaugurate a program in education. In 1904 Baldwin called G. M. Stratton from Berkeley to Baltimore as professor of psychology, and in 1906 Stratton in turn invited his former student Knight Dunlap, who had received his doctorate from Münsterberg, as instructor. In 1908 Stratton returned to California, leaving Dunlap stranded in a psychological wasteland. Between Hall's departure and 1912 the department granted only one doctorate in psychology, and that to Trigant Burrow who became a psychoanalyst. After Dunlap declined Baldwin's suggestion that he turn to educational psychology, the chairman invited E. F. Buchner to Hopkins in 1908 as full professor of education and philosophy. Soon after Watson's arrival, the university initiated, in Dunlap's words, "its disastrous series of steps to cater to 'local needs,' which began with the institution of courses for local teachers."[71] Buchner was the department's center of attraction.

In 1910 Buchner announced: "In an age saturated with the development of a pragmatic theory of life . . . it becomes a matter of serious doubt whether the one field of science which has been father to the movement can possibly stem this tide toward the practical and continue undisturbed in its devotion to its ideals of a pure science."[72] Dunlap and Watson viewed Buchner as a local embodiment of that disturbance which was depriving their research of vital support and recognition. A few months after Buchner's announcement, Watson petulantly labeled his colleague "a high class janitor—he was got here to coax these hayseed teachers to eat out of the University's hand, nothing more."[73] A year after his arrival, Watson regretted that he had moved to a university community "which practically never heard of psychology." As Yerkes had begun at precisely the same time, Watson started searching for a conception of psychology that would serve "its local purpose."[74] Since their institutional locations were different, their strategies varied. At Hopkins, President Ira Remsen adhered, in Watson's grateful words, to a "policy of leaving a man alone."[75] With Baldwin gone and Jennings present, Watson encountered little philosophic opposition to his radical formulations of psychology's scope. At Harvard the situation demanded more diplomacy and compromise.

In view of his private battles with Lowell and Münsterberg, Yerkes' public profession of orthodox psychological faith seems comprehensible and even transparent. Writing (appropriately) in the *Journal of Philosophy, Psychology, and Scientific Method* on "Psychology in Its Relations to Biology," Yerkes began:

There was a time when I agreed heartily with those who say, "What difference whether psychology be considered a part of biology or an independent science, should we not in either case work as we are working?" But recently an examination of my experience as teacher has convinced me of the incorrectness of this view. . . . I have almost completely changed the materials of my course in the subject. What formerly I accepted as subject-matter of psychology and presented as such to my students, I now consider matter of neurology and general physiology; and, conversely, what I now deem the proper and important materials of psychology, I then either relegated to some branch of philosophy or ignored.[76]

Yerkes affirmed his belief in psychology as the study of conscious experience and in the existence of psychic causality.[77] Then he proceeded to argue for the role that behavior work might play in such a study. With Münsterberg looking over his shoulder, Yerkes wisely used other scientists to make his points.

Having asked twenty eminent biologists to express their opinions on the scientific status of psychology, Yerkes reported that their responses fell into three categories. Approximately half of his respondents held that there existed no science of psychology, only the physiology of the nervous system. This group denied the ontological reality of consciousness altogether. A somewhat smaller group affirmed the existence of consciousness and therefore the possibility of "a study of the nature and properties of consciousness independent of the nervous mechanisms," but insisted that the methods of science could extend only to the treatment of the nervous system. One morphologist perfectly described psychology's central dilemma when he stated, "I have always supposed that, when considered from the standpoint of introspection, it (psychology) is a part of metaphysics, but when treated experimentally it is a branch of physiology." A far smaller number of biologists felt that there existed a "science of consciousness whose methods are essentially the same as those employed by the physical and the biological sciences."[78]

Having elicited these opinions, Yerkes proceeded to make the first two conceptions emblematic of attitudes that jeopardized psychology's "right to the name science." Insisting that "few, if any, sciences are in worse plight than psychology," he urged "whole-hearted" subscription to the third conception voiced by biologists as psychology's "working basis." "We lack enthusiasm," exhorted Yerkes, "we are divided; we waver in our aims; we mistrust our methods as well as our assumptions; we question the value of every step forward, and, as an inevitable result, our subject lags at the very threshold to the kingdom of the sciences." Not surprisingly, he advanced comparative psychology as the field capable of providing criteria for the objective scientific verifiability necessary to imbue the whole discipline with sustaining faith.[79]

Yerkes was attempting to reorient his discipline to the objective methodological approaches that informed experimental researches in animal behavior in order to make his own specialty more secure. He would get into the "human side" by means of the same tactic Watson would use; that is, by urging his associates to get into the animal side as a way of resolving a disciplinary "crisis." Yerkes, however, had begged an important question: animal experimentation was objective because it studied *behavior*, not consciousness—or at least so it seemed to his colleagues.[80] After calling for objective measurements and "quantitatively accurate descriptions" of "psychological objects," he merely assumed that he was examining "psychical phenomena," the description of which would eventually lead to explanatory laws expressed in terms of psychical causation.[81] Publicly he continued to praise the value of introspection while personally he eschewed it in his work and privately deprecated it in his correspondence.[82] Precariously perched at Harvard, he met the reigning conceptions of Münsterberg halfway. "Comparative psychologists especially," he declared, "need to realize that they are not compelled to turn to physiology for explanations of their phenomena."[83] The incorrigible Watson would not have known where else to turn.

The Birth of Watsonian Behaviorism

"Am I a physiologist?" Watson asked Yerkes in 1909.[84] As early as 1907 he seemed entitled to the designation when he chided Jennings for inferring consciousness from the behavior of lower organisms. As he told Yerkes simultaneously, "it is not up to the behavior man to say anything about consciousness." Again in 1908 he deplored the uselessness of expressing animal activity in mentalistic terms.[85] He had asked Yerkes about his status in 1909 because he had just begun writing his first book and found himself at an intellectual crossroads. He desperately wanted to make a contribution to the science of animal behavior but found himself at a loss to do so from a psychological standpoint. He wrote Yerkes:

I am terribly at sea as to finding a proper place and scope for psychology. What are our simple presuppositions and what is our scope and what are we good for? . . . I have come out with this—one chapter will be—Behavior a biological problem—the scientific determination of modes of behavior and the modus operandi of behavior. . . . The Second [chapter] the psychological implications in modes of behavior. My interests are all in the first where an objective standard of determination is possible and where interpretation takes the line of the *importance of the observed* facts . . . without mentioning consciousness or deviating from a (wide) biological point of view. What is there left? Am I a physiologist? Or am I just a mongrel?[86]

Three months later Watson answered his own question: "I am a physiologist." Having made that confession, he realized that he could maintain his identity in the profession in which he had established himself only if he could "remodel psychology as we now have it (human) and reconstruct our attitude with reference to the whole matter of consciousness." He professed:

I don't believe the psychologist is studying consciousness any more than we are. . . . All of our sensory work, memory work, attention, etc. are parts of definite modes of behavior. I have thought of writing . . . just what I think of the work being done in human experimental psychology. It lacks an all embracing scheme. . . . It has no big problems. . . . This might be changed if we would take a simpler, behavior view of life and make adjustment the key note. But I fear to do it now because my place here is not ready for it. My thesis developed as I long to develop it would certainly separate me from the psychologists—Titchener would cast me off and I fear Angell would do likewise.[87]

Watson had once mildly boasted that with the backing of Angell and Titchener he would be able to get any manuscript accepted. As a leader, if not *the* leader, among comparative psychologists, he realized that he could ill afford to jeopardize his field's tenuous relationship with general psychology by risking ostracism. He therefore withheld his iconoclastic critique until he had secured his institutional and professional base.[88]

By 1912 Watson had attained such security. The previous year he had begun politicking within the APA for greater participation in the process of nominating members for positions on the council and for the presidency. As a result of his machinations, he became a member of the nominating committee in 1912. At the end of the following year he surrendered his position to Princeton's Howard Warren, who had just been elected president. A former student of Baldwin, Warren was interested in genetic psychology, sympathetic to Watson's views, and owned the *Psychological Review* in which he urged Watson to publish his famous manifesto. He chaired the 1914 nominating committee— composed of Watson's former teacher, Angell, and the former comparative psychologist, Thorndike—that elected Watson the APA's president for the following year. By December 1912, when Watson broached his behavioristic proclamation at Columbia, he had become a force within the councils of his professional organization.[89]

In 1912 also he had cemented new alliances at Hopkins. On May 21 he obtained permission to separate psychology from philosophy and to make it an independent department with himself as head. He had thereby freed himself from any possible philosophic sanctions such as he had worked under at Chicago and under which Yerkes was still laboring at Cambridge.[90] Seeking new sources of potential support, he had obtained a week earlier a place for animal psychology within the medical school curriculum under the auspices of Adolf Meyer, who had come to Hopkins to direct the Phipps Psychiatric Clinic.[91] Meyer had been a docent in psychiatry in Hall's Department of Psychology at Clark since 1896. Soon to become the leader of non-Freudian psychiatry in America, Meyer was an early proponent of the need to base psychiatry on the findings of experimental biology and psychology. He believed that "mental symptoms" of psychopathological disorders stemmed from biological dysfunction and, as early as 1897, was stressing psychiatry's need to view all life as "reaction, either to stimuli of the outside world or of the various parts of the organism." By 1907 he was hailing animal psychology as a superb means by which the psychiatrist could observe reactions: "we study these for what they do," he claimed, "for the conditions under which they arise and for the ways in which we can modify them."[92]

Meyer's 1912 overture to Watson that his animal researches would be a welcomed addition to the Phipps Clinic, which opened the following year, constituted the comparative psychologist's saving grace. In 1912 Ernest Southard, the director of the Boston Psychopathic, had enlisted Yerkes in the hope that he "would become more interested in studying the behavior and experience of men than of mice."[93] In other words, he was hoping that Yerkes would abandon his own field and transport his methods and point of view into the arena of human psychology. That year Watson obtained a similar offer from Thorndike "to go over into experimental pedagogy." "He too seems to think that I belong there," said Watson. These were the kinds of temptations that engendered apostasy among those committed to animal research. "In my point of view," insisted Watson, "I am already doing the scientific side of experimental pedagogy [with rats]."[94] Yerkes would attempt to justify the usefulness of the comparative approach to psychiatry,[95] but his hopes for support of animal research rested with the Department of Philosophy at Harvard. On the other hand, Meyer's well-endowed university-based clinic welcomed not only Watson's viewpoint but his subjects as well. While he declined Meyer's immediate offer, Watson nevertheless realized that he held a trump card should his gestating theory adversely affect his fortunes within his own academic discipline.[96]

By 1912 Watson had significantly strengthened his position at Hopkins and within his profession. He had also obtained an appropriate forum for the dissemination of his views. In the winter of 1912–13 he would give a series of eight public lectures at Columbia, the American center of applied psychology and the headquarters of Cattell, who had inspired Watson's objectivism; of Thorndike, who had declared for the science of human behavior at Teachers College; and of Woodworth, who two years earlier had likewise labeled himself a physiologist. Watson never thought that the signs were particularly auspicious for his announcement, but, given the situation of comparative psychology, he doubted that they would improve.[97]

In the winter of 1912 Watson announced that psychology should become an objective experimental science of the prediction and control of behavior. His subsequent career as polemicist and extravagant popularizer, coupled with seven decades of whiggish textbook historicism, have served to invest Watson's manifesto with an importance overlooked by his immediate contemporaries and have obscured Watson's original purpose, which was to make his own field of investigation more secure as a branch of academic psychology.[98] "It has been maintained by its followers generally," Watson began, "that psychology is a study of the science of the phenomena of consciousness. . . . On this assumption, behavior data (including under this term everything which goes under the name of comparative psychology) has no value *per se*." As a result, Watson found embarrassing the question "what is the bearing of animal work upon human psychology?" and frankly admitted that his investigations "contributed little to human psychology." He confessed that the disciplinary requirement that animal researchers amend their findings by analogical interpretation led the comparative psychologist into an experimental cul-de-sac in which he was forced to go beyond his data to make contributions to the science of consciousness.[99]

Functionalism had established overriding criteria for comparative research: the business of the animal psychologist was to devise experiments that would enable the investigator to determine which responses were "positively conscious" and which were "purely 'physiological.' " Watson complained that in the process of framing such investigations the animal researcher was uncovering a wealth of important and verifiable facts that orthodox psychology discarded as tangential. He insisted that "one can assume the presence or the absence of consciousness anywhere in the phylogenetic scale without affecting the problems of behavior by one jot or one tittle; and without influencing in any way the mode of experimental attack upon them." To make consciousness the ultimate focal point of research involved for the animal researchers working "under false pretenses," and Watson preferred "to give up the province altogether and admit frankly that the study of the behavior of animals has no justification, than to admit that our search is of such a 'will o' the wisp' character." The threat was, of course, rhetorical. Watson sought justification for behavioral research *as* psychology and therefore insisted that "some kind of compromise" must be reached: "either psychology must change its viewpoint so as to take in facts of behavior, whether or not they have bearings upon the problems of 'consciousness'; or else behavior must stand alone as a wholly separate and independent science." Watson realized the institutional improbability of his second alternative.[100]

He also understood why his colleagues would discountenance his first proposal. Prior to publishing his manifesto, Watson had heard at the December meeting of the APA in Cleveland the reservations voiced by Angell on the matter of "Behavior as a Category of Psychology." The admission that mental life could be expressed in terms of objective behavior, Angell warned,

would involve trespassing rather freely on the preserves of biology, physiology, and neurology on the one side and upon those of the social sciences on the other. But such trespass is perfectly legitimate provided the trespasser is willing to face the chance that he may find himself annexed, appropriated, and in general swallowed up by the owner of the territory which he invades. When she abandons the stronghold of consciousness as her peculiar institution, psychology is moderately certain to find that as an autonomous government she has ceased to exist and has become a mere dependency of biology or some other overlord.[101]

This fear constituted the central aspect of disciplinary resistance to Watson's program.[102] The "compromise" that Watson urged seemed

tantamount to mere capitulation to physiology. Accordingly, the behaviorist sought to construct a framework for psychology that, though
baldly biological, elaborated a set of problems distinct from those upon
which the physiologist routinely centered his attentions.

The scientific focus of the behaviorist's investigation was the reflex,
a concept by no means new to either biology or psychology. As early
as 1888, William James had declared:

The only conception at the same time renovating and fundamental with which
biology has enriched psychology, the only *essential* point in which "the new
psychology" is an advance upon the old, is, it seems to me, the very general,
and by this time very familiar notion, that all our activity belongs at bottom
to the type of reflex action, and that all our consciousness accompanies a chain
of events of which the first was an incoming current in some sensory nerve,
and of which the last will be a discharge into some muscle, blood-vessel or
gland. . . . Viewed in this light the thinking and feeling portions of our life
seem little more than half-way houses toward behavior; and recent Psychology accordingly tends to treat consciousness more and more as if it existed
only for the sake of conduct which it seems to introduce, and tries to explain
its peculiarities (so far as they can be explained at all) by their practical utility.[103]

In the Darwinian tradition, animal psychologists had always assumed
that reflex action was organized into two modes: habits and instincts.
But between the time of James's remarks and Watson's declaration,
animal physiologists had repudiated these categories as useless. Seeking to reduce reflex action to neuromechanistic responses analyzable
in terms of physicochemical laws, the mechanistic school led by Loeb,
Albrecht Bethe, Thomas Beer, and Jacob Johann Von Uexküll declared itself "an enemy to the death of all comparative psychology."[104]
Animal psychologists could either lay down their claim to science and
begin probing the consciousnesses of ducks and mice, or they could
continue their objective programs as physiologists. Privately, Watson
believed that instinct and habit "are ultimately analyzable into the simple
reflexes, or tropism."[105] His behaviorist program, however, contemplated no such reductionism. In their quest for mechanistic explanations of reflexive behaviors, of leg twitches and salivary responses,
physiologists had left open to the psychologist the whole field "of habit
formation, habit integration and the like." Watson claimed for the
psychologist the holistic examination of "all of the processes of adjust-

ment which the animal as a whole employs, and in finding out how these various responses are associated, and how they will fall apart, thus working out a systematic scheme for the prediction and control of behavior." The business of the experimental psychologist, as Watson had hinted at as early as 1907, was to reassemble the complex of movements that the physiologist individually identified and to show how these sets of *movements* produced predictable *acts*. This could be done, according to Watson, by isolating and identifying internal and external stimuli and observing the connections between stimulus and response. Such relations could be explained largely in terms of learning theory, performed in part upon humans as well as other animals, and accomplished entirely without resort to introspection.[106]

Watson realized that his theoretical formulation "is weak enough at present and can be attacked from many standpoints."[107] Therefore, he directed his appeal toward, and sought to cement an alliance with, those groups within the discipline furthest removed from psychology's manifest vital center, the laboratory of adult, human, introspective experimentation. He admitted:

What gives me hope that the behaviorist's position is a defensible one is the fact that those branches of psychology which have already partially withdrawn from the parent, experimental psychology, and which are consequently less dependent upon introspection are today in a most flourishing condition. Experimental pedagogy, the psychology of drugs, the psychology of advertising, legal psychology, the psychology of tests, and psychopathology are all vigorous growths.[108]

Watson was claiming that his tentative program offered applied psychology an overriding legitimating conception of psychological science's proper scope:

If the psychologist would follow the plan I suggest, the educator, the physician, the jurist and the business man could utilize our data in a practical way. . . . One of the earliest conditions which made me disenchanted with psychology was the feeling that there was no realm of application for the principles which were being worked out in content terms.[109]

Virtually every page of Watson's manifesto contained either illustration or inference that psychological endeavors aimed at practical application could find experimental support in animal research.[110] If

Watson could obtain a consensus on the issue of psychology as the science of the prediction and control of behavior, his particular field would become not only secure but central. Twenty years earlier James had anticipated a biologically oriented psychological science for the "practical man." He might not have predicted that it would begin in his basement.

The Reception of Watsonian Behaviorism

The extent to which Watson succeeded in his self-ordained mission is problematic. On the one hand, there are so many "anticipations" of Watson's individual postulates, so many psychologists who had criticized introspection or had defined psychology as the science of behavior, that Watson was forced to ask if he had "put up a straw man and have been fighting that."[111] On the other hand, between 1913 and 1917, it was apparent that the "straw man" was fighting back.[112] By the 1920s Watson retained only a handful of followers, and yet it was in the 1920s that Boring declared that "it seemed as if all America had gone behaviorist."[113] In 1913 G. V. Hamilton, who considered Watson "hasty," "careless," and "confused," observed, "Everybody seems to be a behaviorist, of a kind, nowadays." After eight pages of criticism of Watson's naive theories, Yerkes concluded, "Nevertheless I must insist that I am still a behaviorist."[114] Obviously, contemporaries perceived a distinction between Watsonianism and behaviorism. Yet retrospectively there is near unanimous agreement that Watson is the founder of behaviorism.

Commentators who have analyzed as scientific antecedents the individual postulates that entered into Watson's formulations and have concluded there was nothing new in behaviorism have, as Burnham notes, missed the point that Watson synthesized these elements into a new whole.[115] But those who have concluded that this synthesis "crystallized" psychological thinking have missed another point, for very few psychologists accepted Watson's formulation.[116] Fred Lyman Wells, a noted clinical psychologist at the McLean Hospital, wrote in 1913 that Watson's manifesto was well received, "due not so much to either its source or content as to a changed attitude in those who read its words."[117] Wells's career location suggests that the origins of behaviorism lay not in Watson's formulation but in a professional ideology engendered by practical enterprise. Watson secured a consensus but not a constituency. Those who accepted behaviorism united not around his specific scientific ideas but around his general conceptualization of psychology's purpose and scope. These investigators were most often not the elite "old guard" leaders and their faithful followers who possessed easy access to journals for purposes of combating Watson's polemics.[118] They were Watson's silent majority. The origins of behaviorism reside in the patterns of their professional activities, in the institutional exigencies that shaped those patterns, and in the shifting intellectual allegiances that these patterns called forth.

CHAPTER 11

The Silent Majority:
1900–1920

For students of objective behavior to regard themselves as martyrs, heroes or prophets is now unnecessary.

—E. L. Thorndike
Review of Watson's *Behavior: An Introduction to Comparative Psychology*
(1915)

During the academic year 1912–13 in which Watson was lecturing at Columbia, the psychology department there was hosting another visitor. Professor of psychology at Wundt's Leipzig Institut, Felix Emil Krueger had come to the United States as an exchange professor. Reviewing the American psychological scene, Krueger concluded that the most valuable contributions to the field were occurring "in animal and social psychology, in psychological pedagogy and in some other lines of applied psychology," the fields Watson was attempting to unite. The German scientist voiced no apprehension over psychology's possible encroachment upon biological and physiological terrain. On the contrary, he cited approvingly Poincaré's remark that "all sciences are growing, particularly in their boundary provinces." What mattered was that psychology seemed to be producing substantive scientific results. The lesson Krueger claimed he had learned during his American year was that the objective applied psychology of individuals could be rigorously experimental.[1]

Krueger noted that as psychology turned toward applied investigation it abandoned introspection and began to justify its expansion into
biological fields in terms of its "humanistic" value as social science.[2]
Such justification is readily apparent in the pre-Watsonian calls for a
science of behavior. In 1908, for example, William McDougall insisted that

psychologists must cease to be content with the sterile and narrow conception
of their science as the science of consciousness, and must boldly assert its claim
to be the positive science of the mind in all its aspects and modes of functioning, or, as I would prefer to say, the positive science of conduct and behavior.
Psychology must not regard the introspective description of the stream of
consciousness as its whole task, but only as a preliminary part of its work.
Such introspective description, such "pure psychology," can never constitute
a science, or at least can never rise to the level of an explanatory science; and
it can never in itself be of any great value to the social sciences. The basis
required by all of them is a comparative and physiological psychology relying
largely on objective methods, the observation of the behavior of men and animals of all varieties under all possible conditions of health and disease.[3]

McDougall argued that as psychology began to assert its claims as an
independent science it was forced to demarcate its boundaries safely
beyond the spheres of social science and "was thus led to accept a too
narrow view of its scope and methods and applications."[4]

For two decades psychology had been slowly expanding its scope
and applications and converting to objective methods. Watson correctly noted "certain signs of disaffection and mutiny among the ranks
of the faithful"[5] and sought to unite them into a new school. What
they held in common was an interest in practical application; what they
overwhelmingly lacked was a unified theoretical framework for their
endeavors. As long as their specialized activities remained fragmented
and disorganized, the definition of psychology's purpose and goals would
be dictated by an unrepresentative quorum, a ruling minority who
possessed a systematized conception and program. And as long as
psychology remained defined as the introspective study of consciousness, animal psychology would remain peripheral. Attempting to unite
the discipline around the definition of psychology as the science of the
prediction and control of behavior, Watson sought to impugn the ideology of ascetic science: "For a 'pure' psychologist to say that he is not

interested in the questions raised in these divisions of science because they relate indirectly to the application of psychology shows, in the first place, that he fails to understand the scientific aims in such problems, and secondly, that he is not interested in a psychology which concerns itself with human life."[6]

America's premier "pure" psychologist, E. B. Titchener, understood the aims of such studies and claimed convincingly that they represented neither psychology nor science. Titchener maintained that Watson's goal of prediction and control of behavior bore "the stamp of technology." As he argued,

science goes its way without regard to human interests and without aiming at any practical goal; science is a transcription of the world of experience from a particular standpoint, deliberately adopted and deliberately maintained; the pursuit of a practical end is the earmark of technology. . . . Watson is asking us, in effect, to exchange a science for a technology; and that exchange is impossible; for a technology draws not upon one but upon many sciences, and draws upon many other sources than science.[7]

Science, according to Titchener, was uninterested in the practical outcomes of its investigations. Behaviorism purported to be the science that investigated outcomes—defined as behavioral responses. Therefore, behaviorism did not merely assist applied psychology, as Watson had argued; it was applied psychology.

Watson's examples of behavioristic work gave credence to Titchener's arguments. An experiment in "the psychology of drugs," Watson suggested, might attempt to assess the effect of caffeine upon the speed and accuracy of work.[8] An investigator seeking to control the variables in such an experiment would need to know something about pharmacology and physiology, the subject's diurnal efficiency, and the work environment. Nothing in the canons of traditional physiological psychology invested such an experiment with precedent. Only one aspect of such studies was psychological: the investigators who claimed competence over such tests were certified as psychologists. The legitimacy of their claims inhered in their adoption of the social function of the practical commonsense psychologizer of the phrenological age. Their scientific legitimacy rested not on the fact that they were experimental psychologists but on the fact that they were experimentalists.

Like any clever campaigner, Watson's reference to "psychophar-macology" was an appeal to a local constituency. In his audience sat Columbia's Harry Levi Hollingworth, an early proponent of applied psychology, who earlier, in 1912, had published the results of pre-cisely this type of investigation.[9] Two years earlier, as we shall see, Hollingworth had declared for "a psychology of behavior." Through-out the discipline less prominent psychologists at work on a variety of practical problems were coming to similar conclusions. By 1910 over 50 percent of all the psychologists listed in *American Men of Science* ac-knowledged activity in the several fields of applied psychology. Wat-son may have been asking psychologists to exchange a science for a technology, but he also realized that for many the trade had already been made.

The Promise of Applied Psychology

"All life is of one living," Jastrow announced in 1916; "the psycholo-gist, far less than the devotee of other specialties can afford to diagram or artificialize his *Fach*. He should be in the world and of it, . . . for his is the duty of directing and safeguarding the precious mechanisms upon which all living proceeds."[10] By the second decade of the twen-tieth century, Jastrow's cliché rhetoric embodied a truism of which few psychologists needed to be reminded. The ideology of progressiv-ism supplied psychologists with a persuasive rationale for practical relevance. Just as the successful application of science to technology and industry had resulted in a new era of prosperity, science would now be enlisted to solve the problems of social maladjustments that rapid technological innovation and industrial expansion had caused.[11] The twin articles of faith underlying the era's confidence in social re-structuring were the beliefs that "science was the mainspring of inev-itable progress" and that "man could make and remake his own world."[12] Psychologists readily subscribed to both points of view.

In an age permeated with the values of "mastery" as opposed to "drift," of scientific management and social efficiency, the ideology of pure science lost much of its vitality.[13] Paradoxically, scientists had so convincingly portrayed their labors as completely honest and austere, disinterested and objective, that inadvertently or otherwise they had persuaded reformers and reformers' wide audiences that a scientific approach to social problems was the best guarantee of impartial, effective treatment of those problems.[14] In this altered ideological environment, orthodox psychology, according to Dewey, was "daily becoming more incredible and more irrelevant to our present intellectual and social situation." Dewey sympathized with Watson's complaint of the "discrepancy between the researches actually carried on by experimentalists and the language in which alone it is supposed to be proper to formulate them."[15] Critical of introspection, Dewey claimed that the reconsideration of mind as a set of acquired attitudes possessed startling consequences "for the struggle to gain control of the forces forming society." To Dewey, the "introduction of the experimental method is all one with interest in control—in modification of the future." Of course, he said, social control was as old as life itself:

But the need of that control at the present time is tremendously accentuated by the enormous lack of balance between existing methods of physical and social direction. The utilization of physical energies made possible by the advance of physics and chemistry has enormously complicated the industrial and political problem. . . . We are overwhelmed by the consequences of the very sciences into which have gone our best thought and energy for these past few hundred years. We apparently do not control them; they control us and wreak their vengeance upon us. . . . The recourse of a courageous humanity is to press forward . . . until we have control of human nature comparable to our control of physical nature.

Dewey disclaimed the idea that psychologists should become "boasters or sentimentalists regarding the possibilities of our science," but he maintained that "we are entitled in our daily work to be sustained by the conviction that we are not working in indifference to or at cross purposes with the practical strivings of a common humanity."[16] The best cure for science was more science.

In the next number of that year's *Psychological Review*, Watson wrote:

Psychology is the division of science which deals with the functions underlying human activity and conduct. It attempts to formulate through systematic observation and experimentation a series of principles or laws which will enable it to tell with some degree of accuracy how an individual or group of individuals will adjust themselves to the daily situations of life as well as to the uncommon and unusual situations which may confront them. It is equally a part of the function of psychology to establish laws or *principles for the control of human action* so that it can aid organized society in its endeavors to prevent failures in such adjustments. It should be able to guide society as to the ways in which the environment may be modified to suit the group or individual's way of acting; or when the environment cannot be modified, to show how the individual may be molded (forced to put on new habits) to fit the environment.[17]

Watson's claim that he never understood Dewey does not diminish the striking ideological affinities between their thought. As the progressive intellectual J. Allen Smith declared, "We were all Deweyites before we read Dewey."[18] And, as F. L. Wells had suggested, many psychologists were behaviorists before they read Watson. Their intellectual allegiances stemmed in part from professional and institutional requirements and opportunities as well as from the ideology of progressivism that gave to their applied activities compelling altruistic justification.

Undoubtedly, the greatest single institutional factor that provided momentum for applied psychology's growth was the expansion of state universities in the Midwest. Veysey has distinguished three institutional patterns in American higher education after the turn of the century: the small, homogeneous New England college; the large private eastern university; and the growing public universities of the West.[19] Despite the overgeneralization involved, it might be useful to view these types as respective settings for the three academic services psychology provided: undergraduate philosophic and scientific instruction, research, and application. In the eastern colleges, where psychology was ordinarily taught under the auspices of philosophy, little friction occurred between philosophers and psychologists. This was not because philosophers had capitulated to psychology's demand for autonomy but rather because, in the words of one observer, "the type of psychology taught . . . is the philosophical, non-empirical, generalizing variety current before 1880."[20] In the larger heterogeneous eastern universities, intradepartmental animosities were more intense, reflecting rival conceptions of psychology's scope. Across the Appalachians, the major universities were also heterogeneous, but, according to Veysey, contained less discord and offered fewer internal contrasts because their constituency was itself less diverse than the society surrounding the eastern schools.[21] By 1910 the Big Ten rivaled the Ivy League in the

competitive institutional hierarchy of higher education. State-con-
trolled and dependent upon public funds for support, the western
universities gave their curricula a distinctly practical cast. Their presidents tended almost universally to subordinate the academic value of
research to the politically progressive yardsticks of efficiency, expertise, and service.[22] By the end of the first decade of the twentieth century, roughly one-third of the country's psychologists were employed
by these universities. Their numbers were growing, and so were the
pressures toward the practical they experienced.

"Since you left I have heard further concerning the general situation
at the University of Missouri where you are going," wrote Stanley Hall
to Max Meyer in 1900. Trained under Stumpf and the physicist Max
Planck at Berlin, Meyer briefly held an unpaid appointment at Clark
before assuming his frontier professorship. Hall warned Meyer of the
western prejudice against German-trained scholars and told him that
he would "find conditions so different from those here and in Germany" that he should particularly heed the following advice:

You may be called upon to address teachers, and in all State Universities as
distinct from private endowments it is really necessary, in some way, to make
the influence of a new Chair felt outside the University, lest some irrespon-
sible, sensational man or party criticize it in the Legislature. . . .

The ideal there is for Professors to make themselves useful in the development of a department . . . that shall become popular . . . ; that standards
be not too high or work too hard, and that interest be cultivated and given a
practical turn whenever possible. . . .

Next to this you can, no doubt, strengthen yourself most there if you give
some attention to education and thereby make your Chair a power in the state.[23]

Meyer overcame his German training and acquitted himself well,
contributing principally to the field of the psychology of music until
1911, when he published *The Fundamental Laws of Behavior*, which, according to W. B. Pillsbury, "propounded all of the essentials of the
doctrine [of behaviorism] a year or more before Watson adopted his
position." Meyer devoted his second decade at Missouri almost exclusively to educational psychology. In the 1920s he turned to investigations of the psychological effects of drugs. At the end of that decade
his popularity turned to notoriety when he included some empirically
gathered questionnaire material about illicit sexual relations in his course

in social psychology. The incident resulted in his dismissal in 1930.[24]

Meyer's lasting contribution at Missouri was his elaboration of a theoretical behavioral framework for the practical subdisciplines of psychology. Had he been an American working in a more prominent eastern institution and capable of communicating his notions in the evangelical language of a southern Baptist, the name John B. Watson might be less prominent today. Nevertheless, around 1913, Missouri was regarded as the center of behavioristic studies. This reputation did not derive only from the work emanating from Meyer's laboratory, the entrance to which bore the message "No metaphysicians or dogs allowed."[25] In 1912 the Missouri sociologist and cultural radical Maurice Parmelee published *The Science of Human Behavior*,[26] a remarkable volume that digested the work of animal physiologists, anthropologists, comparative psychologists, biologists, and neurologists and that attempted to supply social scientists with a psychobiological basis for their investigations.

In three decades at Missouri, Meyer produced only one Ph.D.: Albert Paul Weiss, another German immigrant who began his contributions to psychology in the field of educational measurement and who by 1917 had become Watson's most vocal defender. Weiss condemned the functionalist's preoccupation with consciousness as a deflection from the psychologist's social concerns. He claimed that he was less interested in upholding the doctrine of special creation than in promoting the general welfare of society.[27] The department in which Weiss spent his entire professional career supported his enthusiasms. Psychology at Ohio State University was headed since 1912 by George F. Arps, a native of Indiana and a proponent of objective practical psychology. By the early 1920s he had collected at Columbus one of the most prominent groups of applied psychologists in the country.[28]

Throughout the Midwest the practical motive provided psychology with its institutional raison d'être. Another of Hall's associates, Joseph Jastrow, encountered at Wisconsin a situation similar to Meyer's at Missouri. Hall had written Meyer that he would be "handicapped by no tradition" but that he would be blessed with "no apparatus [and] no laboratory" either. Students, said Hall, will look "a little askance at a new department at first." When Jastrow arrived at Wisconsin a dozen years earlier, he had to resign himself to having his new laboratory "looked upon as a sort of dime museum until the notion becomes domesticated." By the turn of the century he had come to realize that dime museums could be profitable and that "popularization of psychology was essential to its public appreciation and official support." He was employed, after all, by an institution whose president, Charles K. Adams, had conceded that the university was a child of the state and "has no individuality and rights apart from the will of the parent." The university, Adams declared, belonged to "the people."[29]

In 1902 Charles R. Van Hise replaced Adams as president and restored a measure of autonomy to the university by rephrasing the democratic notion of public service into the vocabulary of reform-oriented expertise. The child would educate the parent in the proper conduct of social and governmental affairs.[30] In an environment of activist social science, Jastrow discovered that applied psychology was "the pay-vein that supports the mine." Embracing the fields of education and mental hygiene, Jastrow converted psychology at Wisconsin into an advertising agency of applied endeavor.[31]

"Conversion" may be a more appropriate term for describing the reorientation of the region's psychologists who were born and trained in the East rather than for depicting midwestern psychology itself. Western universities and colleges had always been citadels of practicality. Just as Missouri had been the locus of phrenological activism in the mid-nineteenth century, traditions at the University of Wisconsin had prepared the way for men like Jastrow. The political economist and philosopher John Bascom, who served as Wisconsin's president from 1874 to 1886, had published a popularization of psychology in 1881 entitled *Science of the Mind* and two years earlier had produced a pioneering work called *Comparative Psychology: Growth and Grades of Intelligence*. It was Bascom who had imbued Jastrow's teacher, Hall, with his scientific ideals at Williams College. The wheel had come full circle. Significantly, when Jastrow recalled psychology's "twentieth century achievement," he spoke of its rebirth, not of its originality. Utility, in his opinion, had sparked the "American renaissance of psychology." To speak of that rebirth "without explicit recognition of the practical motive would be a glaring omission; for that renaissance found its momentum in the appeal to psychology for the regulation of human affairs." Understandably, Jastrow declared, "I must be a behaviorist."[32]

At the University of Iowa, Carl Seashore depreciated the "attitude of laboratory psychologists . . . of displaying a halo of pure science unadulterated and uncontaminated by any interests of usefulness." Like Meyer, Weiss, and Jastrow, Seashore was a foreign émigré. Born in Sweden in 1866, he was nevertheless from the age of three a child of the Iowa farmlands. In his mind the similarity between his "pioneering experience of life on the challenging prairie" and his "pioneering in psychology" on "a virgin mental frontier" represented more than an analogy.[33] In 1897, as we have seen, George Patrick, who later endorsed behaviorism, invited Seashore to the University of Iowa. There he came to exemplify to American psychologists Krueger's claim that problem-directed or "mission-oriented" research could contribute to theoretical advance. Seashore's dominant interests remained in the field of audition, but his practical orientation assured him "that to specialize very intensively invariably means an extraordinary spread of interests."[34] In the first two decades of the twentieth century, Seashore established relations between his department (and even his special interests) and the departments of physics, otology, speech, music, physiology, and physical education. He secured working alliances with Iowa's College of Education, School of Religion, Medical School, and its psychiatric hospital, as well as with the state's institute of mental health and the Child Welfare Research Station. In 1908 he organized the Iowa Psychological Clinic. Seashore devised the university's admission tests and was one of the country's first psychologists to convert his laboratory into a service station for industrial concerns. In 1910 he chaired the committee of the American Psychological Association that recommended psychology be taught as the science of behavior rather than of consciousness. In his presidential address before the APA the following year he predicted that historians would come to "characterize the period upon which we are now entering as the period of the rise of the applied psychological sciences." The success of his institutional strategy for promoting applied psychological research is evidenced in the rise of his department's stature. In a decade, it had moved by the 1920s from fourteenth to third place in the production of Ph.D.'s. And Chicago and Columbia lost their superior positions to Iowa in the following years.[35]

The vitality during these decades of Columbia, with its alliance with Teachers College and its concentration on educational psychology and testing, shows that applied psychology was certainly not confined to the western United States. But the strength of Columbia's graduate program in psychology depended largely on its ability to attract students eastward, as Leipzig had done for an older generation. Psychology at Minnesota, for example, was rebuilt upon the Columbia model by returning midwesterners. Minnesota's graduate program had become defunct following the dismissal of its early applied psychologist Harlow Gale. It was reestablished when James Burt Miner, a Wisconsin native and a Columbia Ph.D., arrived in 1908 to inaugurate a program of educational and vocational testing. The following year Herbert Woodrow, born in Oklahoma and trained at Columbia, arrived to establish educational psychology there. And in 1915 Indianian John Frederick Dashiell arrived with an interest in educational psychology. Dashiell received his Ph.D. soon after Watson's Columbia lectureship and by the 1920s had begun investigations in comparative psychology at the University of North Carolina, where he wrote his behavioristic textbook, *Fundamentals of Objective Psychology*. By World War I, applied interests had grown so steadily at Minnesota that separate departments of educational psychology and child welfare had been established. It is no surprise that many of the leading behaviorists and learning theorists, including G. M. Guthrie, Joseph Peterson, J. R. Kantor, Karl Lashley, and B. F. Skinner, spent portions of their careers at Minnesota.[36]

Applied psychology was simultaneously expanding steadily in the Great Northeast where most psychologists continued to be located. But there it competed with other priorities, and evidences of its growth were often camouflaged by the foliage of philosophical and theoretical concerns. Across the Appalachians, practicality represented psychology's principal justification. When, for example, Yale's Richard M. Elliott was considering a post at Minnesota, he expressed doubts about his adaptability. Despite his "strong behavioristic learnings" and belief that "America's educational future lies with the state universities," he was a theorist rather than a practicalist. At Yale, theoretical work, he admitted, "insures me respect and some measure of commendation. Can I be sure that the same work at Minnesota will not be judged either redundant or that of an armchair dilletante?"[37] In 1903 Edwin D. Starbuck, a student of both James and Hall, was looking for a job in his midwestern homeland. Starbuck had done his dissertation at Clark on the psychology of religious conversion. No western department, he moaned to James, would support his work in the psychology of religion; and if he were to prosecute his allied interest in the genetic psychology he had assimilated at Clark, it would perforce be within departments of education. In 1906 he discovered that his major field of work had, after all, a practical pedagogical side: moral training. He reached a compromise with Seashore and became director of Iowa's Research Station in Character Education.[38] Just prior to his dismissal from Nebraska in the late 1890s, Leipzig-trained H. K. Wolfe had sent his last student, Madison Bentley, to the structuralist stronghold, Cornell. After he was rehired in 1906, however, as professor of educational psychology, he encouraged his first student, H. L. Hollingworth, to enter Columbia.[39] Reentering his discipline in the twentieth century as an applied psychologist, Wolfe was carried forward by the main currents of professional activity not only in the Midwest but at large.

Within the discipline generally, applied concerns were taking hold for reasons that had little to do with psychology's regional characteristics. Foremost among these was the crucial problem of obtaining research funding. In 1903 James McKeen Cattell, psychology's entrepreneurial spokesman, regretted the fact that only eight members of the APA were not engaged in teaching, an occupation subversive "to the cultivation of a spirit of scholarship and research."[40] Psychology's emergence from philosophy and continued administrative subordination to it adversely affected its scientific progress. Academic administrators had come to view it primarily as a teaching rather than a research profession. In 1912 a comparison of departments of psychology in thirty representative institutions with those of education, zoology, political economy, physics, and philosophy showed that psychology ranked lowest in terms of annual appropriations. Funding for laboratory research was not forthcoming, and the vast majority of department heads polled felt that the discipline's affiliation with philosophy was responsible. Most favored identification with the biological sciences as a remedy for chronic exiguousness.[41]

At the APA's twenty-fifth anniversary meeting in 1916, Cattell proposed additional remedies. He had received responses from 215 of the association's members to the question: "How much time do you devote to research?" He discovered that only 16 psychologists devoted more than half of their time; 50 spent between one-quarter and one-half of their time; 43, less than a quarter; and 106, no research whatsoever. "A man," complained Cattell, "must be regarded as an amateur in work to which he does not devote more than half his time." According to Cattell's criteria, the discipline contained few professionals. In order to improve psychology's professional and scientific image, Cattell suggested four ways to promote research: (1) have universities pay professors for research as well as teaching; (2) promote the establishment of endowed research institutions; (3) have the federal, state, and local governments finance investigations; and (4) conduct research on "an economic basis" by selling psychological services to interested clients.[42] The last two methods, especially, entailed applied work, but in 1916 experimentalists were no longer inclined to consider such work reprehensible.

In 1903 Cattell had condescendingly labeled applied psychology as an endeavor "into which those who prove inept for research can overflow." A decade later one diagnostician of psychology's professional health—and a Titchenerian at that—observed that institutional support of psychology was greatest in those departments that favored applied work. In 1916 Cattell warmly advocated consulting psychology and perceived that the discipline's principal tendencies were "to investigate behavior and conduct rather than mind and consciousness; to study individual and group differences; to make practical applications and develop a profession of applied psychology."[43] Viewed as professional strategy, these movements constituted a single trend, each component supporting the other.

Cattell's four formulas met with varying degrees of success. In 1909 Titchener became the country's first research professor, and the only one in psychology before the war. Such appointments were not popular with university administrators. The development of research institutions, such as Yale's Institute of Human Relations, was also a postwar phenomenon, as were organized ventures into psychological sales and services, such as Cattell's own Psychological Corporation.[44] Individual ad hoc efforts at psychological consultation were sporadic but prophetic. Again, it was in the midwestern universities, less bound by the strictures of the "pure science" ethos, that such patterns began. Indiana's Bryan, as we have seen, had undertaken an investigation in the late 1890s for the Union & Wabash Railway. In 1901 a publishing firm approached Münsterberg and Thorndike about the feasibility of employing psychology in advertising, but the two East Coast psychologists spurned its advances. Walter Dill Scott of Northwestern University avidly accepted the challenge and thereby initiated a new applied field. At Iowa, Seashore experimented for Bell Telephone and received income for his patented apparatus. But in the East, when it was discovered that Hollingworth had accepted remuneration from the Coca-Cola Company for his caffeine experiments, a minor scandal erupted. Slander served as no sanction, however; the midwesterner could find in his files for the years 1907 to 1916 copies of over forty private investigations undertaken at industry's expense.[45]

The dominant pattern of application in the prewar period involved alliances with state-sponsored, child-oriented service institutions. Henry Herbert Goddard, a product of Clark and leader of the eugenics movement, was perhaps the first psychologist in the country to achieve a full-time nonacademic post when he became director of psychological research at the Vineland Training School in New Jersey in 1906. The more common pattern was exemplified in Witmer's university-based and state-subsidized psychological clinic. While efforts of this type began in the East, they proliferated in the West in population centers commonly deprived of psychiatric services. Such institutional arrangements were not always conducive to experimental research, but they hastened the development of applied psychology, insulated it with the justification of altruistic reform, and generated a host of problems eventually susceptible to experimental investigation. Indirectly, they helped to subsidize research and directly supplemented psychologists' academic earnings.

It is difficult to separate psychologists' pleas for research funding from complaints of personal impecuniousness. Prior to the growth of applied psychology, the solution to the financial problems of impoverished teachers was more teaching. Angell acknowledged:

Teaching has in the United States many drawbacks. Indeed, throughout almost all of my career at Chicago, I was obliged to add to my normal salary by every available means—by teaching in the summer, by teaching university extension courses, by lecturing before clubs, and by teaching in local institutions in the late afternoons, at night, or on Saturdays. All this took a heavy toll of time and energy and left me with too little resiliency for my research and writing.[46]

The attitude of many psychologists toward teaching is admirably summed up in an account by Walter Bingham. While working alongside Thorndike at Columbia, Bingham recounts that Thorndike glanced at a clock and declared: "I must give a lecture in five minutes. It would be fifty per cent better if I spent this time in preparation. But let's compute another coefficient of correlation."[47] Thorndike was one of America's premier psychologists and commanded a princely salary; his career was available to very few. Angell parleyed his family name into university administrative work, leaving the profession after the war to become head of the Carnegie Corporation and, later, president of Yale. Psychological researchers less blessed by genius or birth were discovering that applied psychology provided the means by which to escape the vicious circle of teaching in order to research; to advance science; and, in the process, to advance their own careers.

Many psychologists considered instructional duties detrimental to their professional advancement. After a brilliant doctoral apprenticeship in Germany, for example, Raymond Dodge won an appointment in 1896 at Ursinus where he was required to teach—in addition to psychology—logic, history of philosophy, ethics, aesthetics, pedagogy, and the history of English literature. "Don't laugh!" commented Dodge: "It was tragedy." This productive contributor to applied psychology during the war spoke bitterly about "the crime of burying youthful research enthusiasm and scientific interest under heavy loads of teaching during the most productive years." Understandably, Dodge was "easily persuaded to abandon undergraduate and other academic responsibilities" after the war in order to pursue a career in applied psychology.[48] Before the war, however, applied endeavor constituted supplementary work for the academician. Often personal insolvency provided an impetus for such encounters.

Swelled with pride over his professorship at Wisconsin, Jastrow had purchased a pretentious residence in Madison that confirmed his own idea of his status but that did not match his small salary. In the fall of 1894 he suffered a nervous collapse engendered by overwork and anxiety about his financial situation. In December 1898 he published an article in the *Educational Review* entitled "The Status of the American Professor" in which he complained bitterly about insufficient salaries. Two months later in the same journal he published "Practical Aspects of Psychology," which effectively constituted an outline for the resolution of his dilemma. The following year his first of many popular works on psychology and its applications appeared. His own career, he realized, was

a far cry from the academic "purity" of the experimental laboratory at its inception. Despite the tendency for the pressure of application to overshadow the patient investigation of principles, no one regrets the impetus to psychological pursuits fostered by the rewards of profitable, if at times hasty, application.

Jastrow had fewer regrets than most.[49]

Psychologists did not need to overextend themselves financially to feel the debilitating effects of academic indigence. At Columbia, Hollingworth's greatest problem "was in making intellectual activity contribute directly toward the relief of physical hunger as well as to that of spiritual thirst." As he put it more plainly, "How could a man on a salary of $81.66 to $100.00 monthly meet minimum living costs of $155 and still devote himself, as he desired and as was expected of him, to a life of research and scholarly endeavor?" He taught at Columbia, at Teachers College, at Barnard at every possible opportunity. Every examination day he proctored at fifty cents an hour. "But the real solution" he confessed in 1940,

was hit upon when I turned applied psychologist. I might as well say once and for all, to the undoubted amazement of my colleagues and professional associates, that I never had any genuine interest in applied psychology, in which field I have come to be known as one of the pioneers. It has been my sad fate to have established early in my career a reputation for interests that with me were only superficial. . . . My activity in the field of applied psychology was mere pot boiling activity, and now that it is over there is no reason why the truth should not be revealed. . . . I became an applied psychologist in order to earn a living.[50]

As we shall see, he adopted behaviorism in order to become an applied psychologist.

In 1916 George Sarton wrote to Jacques Loeb of a scientific "vulgarization of a higher type" by those "who prefer to call it 'humanization' to avoid confessing [it] is mercenary. Most American scientists study science as a dentist studies dentistry . . . their attention being exclusively given to positive immediate results." Loeb replied by indicting Münsterberg as a prime representation of "the greatest degeneracy a scientist can reach, namely that of terminating as a journalistic money-making hack."[51] This former proponent of pure psychology turned "gradiloquent humbug" had become by 1914 the most prolific propagandizer for applied psychology in the country. From 1905 until his death in 1916 he criticized introspection; castigated psychologists who were unwilling to "link theoretical psychology with the practical needs of the community"; and published volumes on educational, legal, industrial, medical, and cultural psychology. In all these works, he had contradicted his earlier stance. Münsterberg was one of the giants of American psychology, and when he endorsed behaviorism in 1914 as a promising vehicle for applied psychology his opinion carried immense weight.[52]

Münsterberg's enthusiastic espousal of applied psychology provided Yerkes with a solution to his dilemma at Harvard. Prior to his acceptance of the post at Boston Psychopathic, Yerkes had found it necessary to teach at Radcliffe, the university extension department in Boston, and Harvard's summer school. His applied position not only proved to Münsterberg that he was at work on the "human side" of psychology but also freed his time for research. Just as the war broke out, he was anticipating an appointment as the state's official psychologist, an offer that would double his salary and that prompted Harvard to offer him a half-time teaching schedule at full pay. Finally, Yerkes found "it possible to continue his work at Cambridge to great advantage."[53]

Knight Dunlap found Münsterberg "in full glory" when he arrived at Harvard in 1900. Despite the German's philosophic impenetrability, the California-born Dunlap felt that he "profoundly altered the course of American psychology, even if not into the exact course he would have chosen." Dunlap meant that Münsterberg had failed to impose his philosophic system on psychology but that he had provided an intellectual and emotional rationale for the pursuit of applied psychology.[54] It was at Hopkins, when educational concerns began crowding out Dunlap's research program and when he found himself "in dire poverty" that he decided "that psychology was, after all, a practical subject, which could be aligned with 'common sense,' and the natural sciences; and I was beginning to cast about for ways in which it could be based on the methods of general science."[55] Simultaneously, his new colleague, Watson, had set about writing his first textbook (which included his manifesto) "largely for money." "I need it," wrote Watson, "as no man has ever needed it before. I am in debt and I've got to get out." He began writing popular articles. He was, according to Dunlap, desperately "looking for some simplifications of attitude which would align his work with human psychology." And according to his own account, which Watson subsequently verified, Dunlap greatly assisted him in refining his conceptions. "The seeds planted by Münsterberg," suggested Dunlap, "were sprouting."[56] They were watered with hopes of financial solvency.

Psychologists, of course, were not the only academics who considered their salaries exiguous or who experienced tensions between their functions as teachers and as researchers. The endemic—almost existential—nature of their dilemma, however, does not diminish the impact of economic considerations on the development of professional styles of activity. Applied psychology came to be seen in professional terms as a legitimate way of securing essential support for scientific research and, in personal terms, as a preferable occupational alternative to supplementary teaching. In those sectors of the discipline where psychology was a public as well as an academic pursuit, the conception of psychology as a science of behavior received enthusiastic support.[57]

The Promise of Behaviorism

Throughout the entire period with which we have been dealing, applied psychology referred primarily to pedagogy. Well over one-third of the whole psychological profession expressed an interest in educational problems by 1910. Three-quarters of those psychologists who cultivated applied concerns did so in the field of educational psychology.[58] To those interested in learning, behaviorism constituted an apt designation for psychological science, for behaviorism *was* learning theory.

In 1911 Thorndike published a revised and expanded version of his doctoral thesis, "Animal Intelligence." Soon afterward he completed his three-volume *Educational Psychology*. Together, these works represent a distillation of a decade of research. Thorndike's theory expressed in these works has been labeled "connectionism." It was a "stimulus-response"—or more exactly, a "situation-response" psychology. Indebted to Bain, Lloyd Morgan, and British associationism generally, Thorndike viewed learning as the establishment of a bond between a particular stimulus and a resulting activity.[59] "Mind" he regarded as merely "the sum total of connections between situations which life offers and the responses which the man makes."[60]

In his classic animal researches, Thorndike concluded that learning is subject to the two laws of "Exercise" and "Effect." The first law stated a familiar principle of associationism: the more frequently a response occurs, the greater the tendency to repeat it. Of greater importance to Thorndike was the law of effect, which stated that responses that result in pleasurable outcomes "stamp in" those responses and favor the likelihood of their occurrence. Conversely, responses that result in "punishment" are likely to be dropped from the animal's repertoire. Take a typical puzzle-box experiment as an example. A well-fed cat placed in a box latched from the inside might inadvertently trip the latch and secure its own release. Replaced, the animal would duplicate many of the same useless movements before repeating its liberating feat. Mere repetition—the law of exercise—does not produce efficient learning. But place a hungry feline inside the same box within view of food beyond its reach, allow it to feast upon escape, and its subsequent latch-opening learning would become much more efficient. In successive trials, the cat would significantly reduce the number of random movements and proceed with more directness to the successful outcome. How this "stamping-in" occurred might be a neurological problem; for Thorndike, the psychologist's task was to control the animal's environment in order to determine by quantitatively measuring efficiency of response which incentives were most powerful and which schedules of reinforcement were most productive. The researcher could use the same techniques to measure "transfer of training," or the effect that mastery of one sort of task has upon the learning of other tasks. The psychologist need not infer subjects' consciousness, ratiocination, intelligence, or powers of memory; he or she had only to monitor behavioral performance and express quantitatively the results of objective observations.

When psychologists first left the field of introspection in order to examine the child, they focused on objective psychometric measurements of motor capacity; that is, on how and how quickly a subject responded to a specific sensation. Education, however, demanded not merely the ascertainment of individual or group differences in capacity or even of generalized capacity but also the determination of the extent to which general or particular capacities could be improved. Under the influence of functionalism, by the turn of the century psychologists began to take a more "molar" view of stimulus as a total situation in which the responding organism operates. Animal psychologists particularly were finding that variation in response to specific stimuli could be obtained by manipulating contingent stimuli. By altering the subject's environment, in other words, they could obtain measures of performance as well as of capacity. The object was to investigate what sorts of "rewards" or "punishments" enhanced or inhibited efficient performance. The promise of such investigation for pedagogy was obvious.

The applicability of Thorndike's theories to human educational psychology encouraged the tendency to define psychology as the science of behavior. In 1910 Hollingworth concluded that "the minute study of sensation yielded little that could be utilized by the teacher." Likewise, the investigation of motor response possessed "little that had concrete value" to education. "It was only when," said Hollingworth, "as in the last few years, the whole circuit of appeal and response, sensation and movement, has come to be considered as a unit, when psychology went beyond the doctrines of sensory element and of motor mechanism, to become a psychology of behavior, that advances in application came rapidly."[61] In 1913, before Watson published his manifesto, Robert M. Ogden declared:

Dealing as [educators] do with adjustments of various sorts; emphasizing as they must the learning-process, and individual traits and tendencies; they are prone to adopt a psychological system which is usually biological in its general outline. A science of behavior is what they need.[62]

Certainly a science of behavior is what they got. Thorndike's experimental pedagogy won such rapid acceptance that conceptions of learning that were not based on the idea of stimulus-response reinforcement were, as Arthur Powell puts it, "largely ignored for a generation."[63]

Behavioristic educational psychology predominated among psychologists and educators for professional as well as for scientific reasons. Between 1890 and 1918 there was slightly more than one public high school built each day of the calendar year. Enrollments increased 700 percent. Between 1902 and 1913 public expenditure for education more than doubled; between 1913 and 1922 it tripled. More public funds were invested in education during these decades than in national defense and public welfare combined. By 1920 only four groups of wage earners were larger than the pool of public educators.[64] In the first decades of the century, schools of education were expanding to meet these growing demands and opportunties. As the public school system itself became more complex and bureaucratized, educational leaders found in learning theory an educational psychology that did not seem threatening to institutional structures. Rival conceptions such as the functionalist Charles Judd's that attempted to base educational psychology upon a broad social-psychological viewpoint or that stressed genetic developmental models of child learning seemed to imply the possibility or necessity of altering the school system or classroom protocol.[65] Learning theory, on the other hand, provided a model that proposed to raise the pupil's performance to meet preestablished norms. Simultaneously, within university departments of education, tendencies toward specialization and the heightening of professional credentials created an environment in which the highly specialized and rigorously scientific experimental psychologist might thrive.

Within departments of psychology complementary forces were at work. By 1910 there was a strong feeling that the educational psychology that both informed and emerged from the child-study movement was infested with charlatanism and pseudo-science.[66] In professional terms such complaints often reflected psychologists' embarrassment over being unseated from the movement's leadership by educators. Child study was a science easily mastered. A behavioral connectionist learning theory that was at once rigorously experimental and highly quantitative provided a foil for an outmoded, democratized empiricism and perhaps would supply psychologists with the scepter of educational supremacy. On the one hand, adoption of "harder" conceptions of educational science represented an intraprofessional strategy: thanks to child study, educational psychologists were déclassé; their turn toward the laboratory represented a flight from marginality. On the other hand, experimental pedagogy embodied an attempt to retain disciplinary control of pedagogical science and to insure that a due portion of the immense public revenues that flowed into universities in support of education reached psychology's coffers.

This was no trivial consideration. In nineteen representative eastern institutions, psychology courses occupied more annual instructor hours than education courses (3,661 versus 2,259 hours). In the same number of midwestern schools—in the area of greatest institutional expansion—the situation was quite the reverse. Psychology rendered 2,791 hours of instruction compared with 8,584 hours of educational teaching.[67] When psychology was taught within departments of education either by educators or by certified psychologists, these departments reaped state funds. When psychologists obtained positions within these rapidly growing departments, they often found themselves isolated from disciplinary colleagues. Advocacy of experimental pedagogy, laboratory-based learning research, contained the implicit argument that psychologists possessed a program at once highly esoteric and obviously germane to educators.[68] The creation in 1910 of the experimentally and statistically oriented *Journal of Educational Psychology* as an alternative to Hall's *Pedagogical Seminary* signaled the transformation of educational psychology into a science of behavior.

The large number of former comparative researchers employed as educational psychologists measurably paved the way for the acceptance of this shift. When, for example, the comparative psychologist M. E. Haggerty found himself forced into applied psychology at Indiana, he sought to frame his disparate activities with a unifying conception and concluded in 1912 that psychology's chief purpose should be the discovery of "the fundamental laws of learning."[69] Yet, even among those educational psychologists not primarily involved with learning theory, behavioristic conceptions proved compatible with their preoccupations. The majority of educational psychologists concerned themselves with the elaboration of various educational tests and scales. Few psychologists thought that intelligence tests measured intelligence. By defining "mind" as the sum total of connections between one's environment and one's responses, Thorndike had provided a behavioristic rationale for testing. A standardized test provided the opportunity to observe a statistically representative subset of connections of a predetermined sort. Such a sample was an indicator of present performance and, ideally, a predictor of future performance. It told the tester nothing about his subject's consciousness; nor did the construction of scales. Thorndike had promoted the inclusion of scales of performance in the teacher's arsenal of pedagogical methods. A teacher desiring to measure student progress in handwriting, for example, could employ a rank-ordered series of handwriting samples compiled by experts in the field. Such a scale provided the teacher with a graduated, quantitatively expressible measure against which to plot pupil progress. The establishment of precise criteria for every schoolroom activity represented the best way to monitor the child's learning and the teacher's effectiveness. To be an educational psychologist after 1910 involved with either learning theory or tests and measurements and to define psychology as the introspective study of consciousness was to create a certain cognitive dissonance that Watson sought to alleviate.

Historian Robert Church has asked why psychologists interested in education after 1905 seemed to forsake the social meliorism that characterized educational reformers and other social scientists during the Progressive era and to adopt the rather detached canons of learning theory.[70] While he has supplied insightful answers to his own question, Church has overlooked a group of activist educational psychologists who went by a different name. Clinical psychology meant something different in prewar America than it does today. It was a form of diagnostic "special" education for the intellectually "retarded" or the emotionally disturbed or "problem" child. Its progenitor, Lightner Witmer, required a theoretical canopy for his pioneering work and, accordingly, subscribed to behaviorism.[71]

In 1896 when Margaret Maguire, a teacher in the Philadelphia Public School System, brought to the University of Pennsylvania's psychological laboratory for diagnosis a "chronic bad speller," Lightner Witmer's interest in individual differences took a very practical turn. The laboratory director's ability to solve his first case involved no appreciable scientific breakthrough; the "mental deficiency" retarding the pupil's progress was remediated through optometrical prescription. In short, eyeglasses seemed to improve intellect. The ramifications of what might otherwise be recalled as a cute pedagogical success story were not lost upon Witmer. Within months he published an article proposing the establishment both of a practical laboratory capable of examining the physical and mental conditions of schoolchildren and also of a training school for the remedial treatment of those psychologically or physiologically diagnosed as deviates or defectives. In 1897 Witmer conducted a summer school for the treatment of "backward children," and the success of this program prompted university officials in 1907 to enlarge the clinic. Monies were procured to inaugurate publication of a specialized journal, the *Psychological Clinic*, partly patterned after Hall's *Pedagogical Seminary*. In 1909 the university allocated to the clinic an enlarged budget and increased physical plant, and designated it a distinct administrative unit directly responsible to the trustees.[72]

The clinic's purpose is revealed in its operational format. Children would be referred to the clinic through the school system. Following medical diagnosis, subjects would undergo anthropometric, psychometric, and optometric examinations. Complementing psychologist and physician, the social worker would prepare a case study of the child's background. Clinical records would be compiled with the threefold purpose of correlating case histories in order to produce generalizations, of standardizing tests, and of establishing new diagnostic techniques. Testing completed, attempts at remedial treatment would proceed.[73]

Witmer's standard clinical procedure involved using both psychometric measurements of a child's powers of memory, visual discrimination, and muscular coordination and also paper-and-pencil "intelligence" tests as before-and-after indices of performance. Often following surgical removal of sources of physical discomfort such as impacted teeth or swollen adenoids, the restoration of impaired vision, the resolution of a domestic crisis, or the improvement of the subject's environment by means of proper hygienic and dietary care, the subject would be retested in various psychological examinations and would show marked improvement. The discovery of wide-ranging test scores administered before and after medical, hygienic, or pedagogical treatment convinced Witmer that intelligence tests were merely indicators of performance and that eugenicist explanations of the hereditary roots of feeblemindedness needed refining in light of environmental explanations of capacity and performance. Witmer subscribed to the environmentalism implicit in Thorndike's theory of learning and, later, to Watson's formulations. "All the behavior of a lifetime," wrote Witmer, "may be considered as an operation, i.e., a sequence' of adaption to environment." Psychology, he claimed, is "correctly defined as a science of behavior."[74]

According to one of his associates, Witmer was "perfectly aware that scientific research is not in his line," but he knew "how to manage his business and forge ahead."[75] When Titchener remarked that technology partakes of many sciences and of many helps besides science, he might have had Witmer's clinic in mind. Once psychologists entered the fields of remediation, experimental scientific controls were often suspended. The clinician confronted children in pedagogical disarray, not chickens in puzzle boxes. He had neither the time nor the right to relegate some subjects to control groups for purposes of comparative analysis. The ethical element implicit in such work required the psychologist to admit nonpsychological sources of assistance. This catholicity fostered behavioristic conceptions in two ways. First and most simply, the engagement with educationists, sociologists, social workers, and medical personnel encouraged the clinician to employ a psychological vocabulary and a scientific syntax comprehensible to his coworkers. Second, as social workers and teachers supplied Witmer with personal histories of his subjects, he began to stress the usefulness of such environmental records in his diagnoses. Persuaded by current biological opinion to discard the neo-Lamarckianism that informed genetic psychology, Witmer was compelled to adopt environmental explanations of psychological problems in order to resolve them.[76] Claimed Witmer:

Feeblemindedness, insanity, moral degeneracy, these are doubtless in a certain proportion of cases the direct result of an inherited factor. Nevertheless, mental and moral degeneracy are just as frequently the result of the environment. In the absence of the most painstaking investigation, accompanied by a determined effort at remedial treatment, it is usually impossible to decide, when confronted by an individual case, whether heredity or environment has played the chief role. Who can improve a man's inheritance? And what man's environment can not be bettered? In the place of the hopeless fatalism of those who constantly emphasize our impotence in the presence of the hereditary factor, we prefer a hopeful optimism of those who point out the destructive activity of the environment. To ascribe a condition to the environment, is a challenge to do something for its amelioration; to ascribe it to heredity too often means that we fold our hands and do nothing.[77]

By 1914 nineteen psychological clinics were doing something; at least fifteen of them were modeled upon Witmer's creation. An additional fifty universities, colleges and normal schools provided courses in clinical work.[78] Clinicians' roles inevitably expanded beyond the pedagogical to the areas of crime, delinquency, and emotional disturbance. A few psychologists by 1912 had found professional niches in criminal reform institutions as laboratory directors, an occupational area that grew out of clinical endeavor. Having repudiated much of genetic psychology, clinicians adopted a rough-hewn conception of learning theory, or habit formation, in its place. "In this country," complained Witmer in 1911, "the treatment of the criminal is still conducted with a view only to punish or segregate, scarcely ever to educate or cure."[79] Attempting to convince the public that reeducation was possible implied the expansion of psychology into new occupational pastures. Nebraska-born Jean Weidensall (Ph.D., Chicago, 1910), formerly psychologist at the New York State Reformatory for Women and at the time director of the psychology department at Cincinnati's Bureau of Social Hygiene Research, reviewed Watson's manifesto in the *Psychological Bulletin*. She found that "it was outlining the psychology we shall find most useful."[80]

At exactly the same time, psychiatrists were finding behavioristic psychology somewhat promising. Nathan Hale has shown that psychotherapy's "crisis of the somatic style" was at its peak between 1904 and 1909.[81] Just as clinical psychologists were repudiating deterministic models of mental retardation, psychiatrists were becoming extremely dissatisfied with the therapeutic uselessness of the neurological paradigm of psychopathology that attempted to explain mental disease in terms of discrete brain lesions and thus to develop a theory of cerebral localization of psychological functions. In 1909 G. Stanley Hall invited Sigmund Freud to the famed Clark University Conference where some of the nation's most prominent psychologists and psychiatrists were introduced to a psychoanalytic theory that discarded somatic etiologies.[82] Psychotherapists were torn between the "hard" experimental style of neurological thinking and what many regarded as the unscientific metaphysics of Freud. Whereas Watsonianism was viewed within the psychological community as a left-wing movement, it was seen in psychiatric circles as a possible middle-of-the-road reconciliation that preserved the experimental rigor of laboratory science while simultaneously assigning etiological significance to nonconstitutional environmental variables.[83]

As early as 1910, Gilbert Van Tassel Hamilton, a California psychiatrist who had studied with Yerkes between 1905 and 1908, became an early supporter of the notion that "the psychopathology of the future [will] owe much to comparative psychology." In those early years Hamilton had established at the McLean Hospital's psychological laboratory apparatus for studying unusual reaction types in canines. By 1914 he was procuring frustration reactions in animals whom he deprived of expected rewards following their successful completion of learned routines. He found that their reactions mirrored neurotic manifestations in humans and thereafter based his "psychotherapeutics on a science of behavior which has the advantages of a wide scope and an unhurried pursuit of principles by critically developed methods."[84]

Yerkes had begun a similar program at the Boston Psychopathic in 1912, and the following year Adolf Meyer at the Phipps Clinic had established a psychobiological perspective favorable to Watson's pursuits at Hopkins. In 1916 Watson was rephrasing Freudian categories into biological terminology, stressing formation of habit syndromes. In 1918 Horace W. Frink followed Watson's behavioristic suit in his popular introduction to psychoanalysis, *Morbid Fears and Compulsions*.[85]

Few psychologists by 1913 centered their attention on psychotherapy, and few psychiatrists paid much heed to behaviorism. Indirectly, however, behaviorism found favor within psychology among both traditional experimentalists and the new breed of clinicians because of its confrontation with psychoanalysis. In the first place, psychologists realized with Hall that if Freudianism was verified, "it [would play] havoc with many of the systems . . . of laboratory psychology."[86] Freud had premised an unconscious mind beyond the reach of introspection and objective experimentation alike. Academic psychologists generally responded caustically and furiously to psychoanalysis.[87] By converting Freudian concepts into behavioristic terms, Watson provided the most direct alternative to psychoanalytic categorizations that were experimentally undemonstrable. Behaviorism came to laboratory psychology's rescue, even to those pursuits it had no intention of saving. In the second place, psychiatrists were castigating clinical psychology's encroachments into medical areas. Jealously guarding their traditional hegemony in matters therapeutic, they insisted that clinicians confine their activities to the mere administration of tests.[88] By supporting behavioristic experimentation's contributions to psychiatric investigation, clinical psychologists could legitimately "wonder what innate qualities physicians possess, or what special observation powers they have, or the kinds of instruction they receive" to validate their claims to exclusive competency in the field of psychotherapy.[89]

Unlike clinical psychologists, applied psychologists in the field of advertising had no professional competitors. In 1911 Hollingworth set the terms of discourse for subsequent practitioners in the field:

The statistical study of judgments has too long been confined to the comparison of simple sensory stimuli. A psychology which aims to be an account of behavior cannot go far without making a careful study of more complex judgments such as those of appeal and interest. Such a psychology is more interested in performance than in capacity. . . . Especially will this be true of a psychology which aspires to be concretely serviceable. Such a psychology will find little use for the introspective method. It will be interested, not in the momentary content of a conscious moment; nor in the descriptive character of the sensory fragment which may at the moment be the bearer of meaning; nor in the instrument, criterion or vehicle of an act of apprehension, a comparison, a feeling or a choice. It will be most of all interested in the outcome of this moment in form of behavior, an act, a choice, a judgment, and in the character, reliability, constancy and significance which the outcome of a mental operation bears.[90]

That year Hollingworth's first doctoral student, Edward Kellogg Strong, completed his dissertation, "The Relative Merit of Advertisements," which was concerned with "the factors which operate to influence response to stimuli."[91] The entire field of business psychology, concerned with the selection of employees, the optimization of efficiency, and consumer research, found in behaviorism a hardheaded, commonsense practicality that Watson himself exhibited after the war. Leaving Hopkins following a scandal surrounding his divorce, Watson left academic life for Madison Avenue; found employment in an advertising company; and, in his words, "began to learn that it can be just as thrilling to watch the growth of a sales curve of a new product as to watch the learning curve of animals or men."[92]

The story of applied psychology's professional growth has been charted elsewhere; it suffices merely to indicate its foundations.[93] Nearly every facet of applied work originally derived from educational psychology's interest in the child. Psychologists' first encounters with nonacademic service institutions represented outgrowths of applied work in education.[94] As they moved into the public and industrial sectors, they brought with them what intellectual baggage they could conveniently transport. Learning theory became an overriding paradigm for much of this work. The term "behaviorism" was widely employed not only by those handfuls of experimentalists in the laboratories of comparative psychology or by a few Neo-Realist philosophers or by an occasional theorist who sought to provide the social sciences with a psychobiological foundation; rather, behaviorism became the insignia of the practicalist. For reasons we have shown, he was entering "the real world" and required a calling card that would prevent educational, medical, or industrial leaders from confusing his wares with the brand of psychology they might have encountered in their college days twenty years earlier.

The Balance of Power

Of course, many of their former teachers were still active. In his 1913 presidential address to the APA, H. C. Warren suggested that psychology should include accounts of both the "inner and the outer aspects of experience." Psychology, said Warren, "is the science of the relations between the individual and his environment. These relations may be studied either objectively as behavior, or introspectively as events of consciousness."[95] The intradisciplinary politics of psychological science demanded such a compromise in 1913. Approximately half the profession registered no applied interests whatever.

Pillsbury had reflected this balance of power in his 1911 *Essentials of Psychology*. Psychology, said one of Titchener's foremost students, studies not mind but evidences of mind. Since the most manifest evidence is behavior, psychology "may be most satisfactorily defined as the science of behavior."[96] As Watson complained in his manifesto, however, Pillsbury quickly returned to subjectivist explanations of experience. When one of Pillsbury's students commented to him that his text could be read either as a structuralist account or as a behavioristic tract, Pillsbury commented with satisfaction, "That is just the way I want to leave it." Titchener received his former student's text in the following spirit: "Pillsbury, I suspect, is hard up, and has deliberately aimed (of course, preserving his scientific conscience) to write a book that will strike current interests—and pay."[97] But for every writer who stuck his neck out of his conservative scientific collar in order to look out and survey the current contours of his discipline, there was another, like Dunlap, who "leaned over backwards," for fear that his textbook, *A System of Psychology*, "would be useless as a text if . . . too radical."[98] Centripetal political and economic pressures produced a climate of opinion in which few were prepared, as Warren supposed, to hail Watson "as a second Moses."[99] It was the war—not Watson—that showed psychologists the promised land.

"The war has given applied psychology a tremendous impulse," observed G. Stanley Hall, who had recently created the *Journal of Applied Psychology:* "This will, on the whole, do good, for psychology, which is the largest and last of the sciences, must not try to be too pure."[100] Proponents of pure research in the 1920s felt that few psychologists were trying.[101] Mobilization had invigorated the social ideals of service and efficiency and had stimulated the postwar demand for what was precipitately called psychotechnology. The Englishman, Frederick Charles Bartlett, spoke for psychologists in every belligerent country when he recognized the awesome responsibility of his wartime mission, "in which whatever psychology I knew must be harnessed to the solution of some very practical problems." Psychologists' military sabbatical quickly resolved itself into collective epiphany. Lewis

Terman's remark that the war opened to him "a new world of experiences" mirrored the impressions of nearly all his co-workers.[102]

Viewing the discipline as a whole, these new experiences represented not a transformation but a quickening of impulses toward applied psychology already under way before the conflict. The organization of psychological work during the war and the institutional and professional consequences of that work afterward have received fairly comprehensive treatment.[103] Psychology's military exploits had advertised its potential to business and industry in a way otherwise impossible. But a major factor contributing to the rise of applied psychology after the war was itself psychological. One cannot read the reminiscences of participating psychologists without sensing that their military experiences represented the high points of their professional careers.

They had gone to war, but not quite. Trench warfare, poison gas, deadly disease were theoretical problems to them. They made genuine contributions without suffering grisly casualties, and in the process, as Cattell later remarked, they put psychology "on the map and on the front page." The war had provided psychologists with an exciting if momentary relief from the everyday labors that Cattell described as "scarcely more stimulating than the routine of the factory or of the farm." Angell admitted that he found it "rather exciting to be connected . . . with the nation's war machine." Not even "pacifist principles" and "doubts about the war" could keep the Quaker-bred Edward Tolman from seeking a commission in the psychological testing service. Dodge considered his navy commissioning "one of the great moments of my life" and became enveloped in a "shadow of sorrow" as the war came to an end. Incredibly, Yerkes regretted that the war did not last longer.[104] When it did end, academic life, by contrast, scarcely seemed compatible with excitement. The newly discovered ability for some to see their research rapidly translated into practical action provided many psychologists with a sense of satisfaction and accomplishment that their university experiences could not have furnished. However intellectually satisfying pure research might have been, applied science proved to be an emotionally fulfilling endeavor, one that these veteran psychologists were reluctant to surrender in peacetime. Perhaps Yerkes had this in mind when he predicted that "It will be long . . . before our profession entirely . . . forgets that almost incredibly extensive and precious gift of professional service."[105]

Applied psychology had become a military obligation, and in the immediate postwar depression years it became a self-interested one. In the 1921 edition of *American Men of Science* over three-quarters of the 353 psychologists listed applied interests. Among the 149 entries who had previously appeared in the 1910 edition, one-third of them added new categories of application to their listings. Only one dropped an applied interest. In 1919 the APA's Committee on the Academic Status of Psychology informed the membership "that Applied Psychology may be provisionally defined as the science of the control of human behavior." Such a definition would seem to imply that a major portion of "pure" psychology should be concerned with human behavior's prediction.[106]

The Origins of Behaviorism

Donald Napoli has suggested that applied psychologists were "the first occupational group to start the journey to professionalism directly from the university. They recognized no nineteenth-century progenitors and thus never experienced the shift from volunteer work or apprenticeships to formal training."[107] Napoli advances this observation as an explanation of the bitter conflict between applied psychologists and their "pure" academic counterparts who felt that practicality compromised the discipline's scientific status. While this interpretation helps to explain a perennial tension within psychology, it typifies the tendency among historians of psychology to overlook the essentially symbiotic relationship that had always existed between various subgroups within the discipline and between the discipline as a whole and the society that supported it. The "pure" psychology imported from Leipzig in the 1880s and early 1890s had had its applications. It was considered propaedeutic to philosophy, and philosophers were its patrons. Yet psychology had secured support by attracting other subscribers—from the proponents of spiritualism who subsidized the first American journal and funded the building of laboratories to the educators, alienists, and other groups "incessantly craving," in James's words, for a science of conduct that would teach them "how to *act.*" Modern psychologists may have "recognized no nineteenth-century progenitors," but the fact remains that they possessed them. Practical psychologizing is an omnipresent social function, and the discipline that advanced its professional claims by asserting that it represented the one true science of mind soon found that by clearing the field of competitors it had inherited that function. If anything, the fact that the new psychology possessed no manifest historical linkage with the phrenological reform movement of the nineteenth century increased rather than retarded its practitioners' willingness to assert their social usefulness.

The appearance of functionalism at Chicago in the late 1890s reflected the discipline's awareness of dual sponsorship by philosophers, on the one hand, and by practical groups (primarily educators), on the other hand. Similarly, the gradual forfeiture of the subject matter of conscious experience in favor of behavioral performance in the early twentieth century testified to psychology's increasing dependence upon the patronage of nonacademic and even antiphilosophical subscribers. Ironically, the same psychologist-historians who attempt to explain this transformation in terms of the methodological problems of introspectionism roundly condemn the behaviorism that displaced introspective psychology for its scientific inconsistencies. Why psychologists should abandon one set of inconsistencies only to adopt another is a question beyond the range of internalists' explanatory framework.

Psychology's institutional support has always depended upon pure experimental research *and* unabashed application. The former endeavor legitimates the latter, and the latter pursuit justifies the former. His later career notwithstanding, Watson, prior to his forced departure from academic life, had no real interest in practical psychology. He resisted efforts to turn to educational psychology and refused to work on any committee that contained applied psychologists who "have commercialized and are commercializing and will commercialize psychology for the rest of time."[108] He wanted to work with his rats; but the professional dilemma of comparative psychology prompted him to seek a modus vivendi between his own concerns and the practical sectors of his discipline. Thorndike could criticize Watson for considering himself a heroic martyr,[109] but Thorndike was no longer a comparative researcher and was thus not susceptible to the pressures his colleague faced.

Watson secured his historical reputation as behaviorism's founder on the basis of his vigorous campaigning, not on account of his theoretical hypothesizing. In 1952 comparative psychologist Walter Hunter counted himself

among the many workers who have brought about the change from a psychology of experience to a psychology of behavior. The fundamental issue of behaviorism is not, and never was, the particular speculations of any one behaviorist—of Watson for example. Behaviorism is the point of view in psychology which holds that an adequate account can be given of psychological problems without reference to the terms consciousness and introspection.[110]

Commentators who have taken a broader view of behaviorism have seen it as an intellectual response to urbanization and to social reform, the consummate psychology for the manipulative outer-directed man, the apotheosis of the bureaucratic ideal.[111] It seems that the same might be said of phrenology. Behaviorism and phrenology certainly catered to the same social interests; both promised quick and yet scientific solutions to individual and to social problems. Writ large, the history of American academic psychology is the story of the gradual penetration by those practical categories of social thought, which had once invested phrenology with its essential meaning, into the prestigious, status-conferring world of academic science. Its history is analogous to contemporary developments within the American medical profession.[112] Yet in order to understand how this transformation occurred its history must first be written smaller. It must explain such phenomena as the arrival upon the disciplinary scene of animal psychology and the professional pressures that forced comparative researchers into alliances with proponents of utility. The broad cultural forces at work in behaviorism's ascendancy can be expressed and must be explained in terms of the social and intellectual mechanisms of the discipline's development. A nonintrospective psychology was exactly what twentieth-century applied psychologists needed; indeed, it was what they already had. But Watson's animal work and learning theory in general provided their often nonexperimental pursuits with the imprimatur of strict scientific legitimacy.

The laboratory also provided them with the rhetoric of pure science that justified the applied psychologist's penetration of virtually every aspect of modern life. "Science always endeavors to understand the laws of nature for themselves and is indifferent to the applications that may be made of them," claimed Pillsbury. "The practical psychologist," agreed Münsterberg, "ought never to forget that his psychological understanding can give him insight only into the means needed for a certain end, but cannot select the ends themselves." Watson concurred: "It must be understood at the outset . . . that psychology at present has little to do with the setting of social standards. . . . These laws of control or training must be general and comprehensive since social standards are constantly changing."[113] The rhetoric of pure science had thus been effectively translated into an argument for ideological agnosticism. Both the child and the capitalist were the psychologist's clients; the scientific norm of emotional neutrality had taught him not to distinguish between them.

Notes

Abbreviations: *AJP, American Journal of Psychology; HEP,* Edwin G. Boring, *A History of Experimental Psychology,* 2d ed. (New York: Appleton, 1950); *HPA,* Carl Murchison et al., eds., *A History of Psychology in Autobiography,* 4 vols. (Worcester, Mass.: Clark University, 1930, 1932, 1936, 1952); *JHBS, Journal of the History of the Behavioral Sciences; JPPSM, Journal of Philosophy, Psychology, and Scientific Method; PB, Psychological Bulletin; PR, Psychological Review; TCWJ,* Ralph Barton Perry, *The Thought and Character of William James,* 2 vols. (Boston: Little, Brown, 1935).

PREFACE

1. Veysey, *The Emergence of the American University* (Chicago: University of Chicago Press, 1965), p. ix.

2. See Robert Richards, "The Natural Selection Model of Conceptual Evolution," *Philosophy of Science* 44 (1977): 494–501.

3. B. F. Skinner, "Behaviorism at Fifty," *Science* 140 (1963): 951.

4. Watson, "Psychology as the Behaviorist Views It," *PR* 20 (1913): 158–77; "An Attempted Formulation of the Scope of Behavior Psychology," ibid., 24 (1917): 329–52.

5. For a somewhat fuller account of this story, see John M. O'Donnell, "The Origins of Behaviorism: American Psychology, 1870–1920" (Ph.D. diss., University of Pennsylvania, 1979).

6. Burnham, "On the Origins of Behaviorism," *JHBS* 4 (1968): 151, 150.

7. Lucille Terese Birnbaum, "Behaviorism: John Broadus Watson and American Social Thought, 1913–1933" (Ph.D. diss. University of California, Berkeley, 1964); John C. Burnham, "Psychiatry, Psychology and the Progressive Movement," *American Quarterly* 12 (1960): 457–65; David Bakan, "Behaviorism and American Urbanization," *JHBS* 2 (1966): 5–28; Kerry W. Buckley, "Behaviorism and the Professionalization of American Psychology: A Study of John Broadus Watson, 1878–1958" (Ph.D. diss., University of Massachusetts, Amherst, 1979).

CHAPTER 1

1. Useful standard histories of scientific psychology include Edwin G. Boring, *A History of Experimental Psychology,* 2d ed. (New York: Appleton, 1950), cited as *HEP;* Gardner Murphy, *An Historical Introduction to Modern Psychology* (New York: Harcourt, Brace,

1929); and Richard Müller-Freiendals, *The Evolution of Modern Psychology* (New Haven: Yale University Press, 1935).

2. John Croom Robertson, "Prefatory Words," *Mind* 1 (1876).

3. Ferrier, *On the Functions of the Brain* (London: Smith, Elder, 1876), p. 255.

4. Wundt, *Grundzüge der physiologischen Psychologie*, 2 vols. (Leipzig: W. Engelman, 1873–74); *Principles of Physiological Psychology*, trans. from the 5th German ed. (1902) by E. B. Titchener (New York: Macmillan, 1910).

5. James, "The Teaching of Philosophy in Our Colleges," *Nation* 23 (1876): 179.

6. The quote describing James's apparatus comes from Hall, who was trying to assert a priority claim to the establishment of the first "real" experimental laboratory in the country at Hopkins several years after James's innovation; Hall, *Life and Confessions of a Psychologist* (New York: Appleton, 1923), p. 218. On the priority dispute between James and Hall, see Ralph Barton Perry, *The Thought and Character of William James*, 2 vols. (Boston: Little, Brown, 1935), 2 : 7–10, cited as *TCWJ*. Despite Hall's reputation for mendacity and Harvard's "better press," there is no reason to doubt the accuracy of Hall's inventory. See Robert S. Harper, "The Laboratory of William James," *Harvard Alumni Bulletin* 52 (1949): 169–73.

7. James, *Principles of Psychology*, 2 vols. (New York: Holt, 1890).

8. Dorothy Ross, *G. Stanley Hall: The Psychologist as Prophet* (Chicago: University of Chicago Press, 1972), pp. 134–58; Hugh Hawkins, *Pioneer: A History of the Johns Hopkins University, 1874–1889* (Ithaca: Cornell University Press, 1960), pp. 187–210.

9. Robert S. Harper, "Tables of American Doctorates in Psychology," *AJP* 62 (1949): 580–81.

10. Ladd, *Elements of Physiological Psychology* (New York: Scribner's, 1887).

11. Descriptive sketches of early laboratories can be found in "Psychology in American Colleges and Universities," *AJP* 3 (1890): 275–86; William O. Krohn, "Facilities in Experimental Psychology in the Colleges of the United States," *Report of the Commissioner of Education, 1890–1891* (Washington, D.C., 1982), pp. 1139–51; E. B. Delabarre, "Les Laboratoires de Psychologie en Amérique," *L'Année Psychologique* 1 (1894): 209–55. C. R. Garvey, "List of American Psychological Laboratories," *PB* 26 (1929): 652–60, attempts a chronological ordering.

12. Burt G. Miner, "The Changing Attitude of American Universities Toward Psychology," *Science* 20 (1904): 302; Cattell, "Psychology in America," in A. T. Poffenberger, ed., *James McKeen Cattell: Man of Science*, 2 vols. (Lancaster, Pa.: Science Press, 1947), 2 : 451; Garvey, "List of American Psychological Laboratories," pp. 653–55.

13. Cattell, "Psychology in America," pp. 451, 455, 464; "Our Psychological Association and Research," in Poffenberger, ed., *Cattell*, 2 : 338.

14. Cattell, "Psychology in America," p. 462.

15. The best work in this area is Veysey, *The Emergence of the American University* (Chicago: University of Chicago Press, 1965). See also Frederick Rudolph, *The American College and University* (New York: Knopf, 1962).

16. Veysey, *Emergence*, p. 129.

17. Ibid., p. 124.

18. A. Hunter Dupree, *Science in the Federal Government: A History of Policies and Activities to 1940* (Cambridge: Belknap Press of Harvard University, 1957), p. 296.

19. See, e.g., Frank M. Albrecht, Jr., "The New Psychology in America, 1880–1895" (Ph.D. diss., Johns Hopkins University, 1960), pp. 1–12, 59–83; Veysey, *Emergence*, pp. 59, 127–28, 150–51, 167–69, 173.

20. Cattell, "The Advance of Psychology," *Science* 8 (1898): 536.

21. Albrecht, "The New Psychology" (abstract).

22. Robert A. McCaughey, "The Transformation of American Academic Life: Harvard University, 1821–1892," *Perspectives in American History* 8 (1974): 239–332, makes this critique convincingly. See also Stanley M. Guralnik, *Science and the Ante-Bellum American College* (Philadelphia: American Philosophical Society, 1975); "Sources of Misconception on the Role of Science in the Nineteenth-Century American College," *Isis* 65 (1974): 352–66; Philip J. Pauly, "G. Stanley Hall and His Successors: A History of the First Half-Century of Psychology at Johns Hopkins University" (Paper prepared for the G. Stanley Hall Centennial, Johns Hopkins University, October 1983).

23. Jastrow, "Physiological Psychology," *The Christian Union*, October 27, 1887; see also his untitled lecture on the history of American psychology delivered at The Johns Hopkins University Semicentennial Celebration, reposited in the Joseph Jastrow Papers, State Historical Society of Wisconsin, Madison, Wisconsin.

24. Buchner, "Ten Years of American Psychology: 1892–1902," *Science* 18 (1903): 241.

25. Ibid.

26. For general historical accounts of psychological "schools," see Edna Heidbreder, *Seven Psychologies* (New York: Century, 1933), and Robert S. Woodworth, *Contemporary Schools of Psychology* (New York: The Ronald Press, 1931).

27. Edwin G. Boring, "Edward Bradford Titchener, 1867–1927," *AJP* 38 (1927): 489–506.

28. Titchener, *A Textbook of Psychology*, 2 vols. (New York: Macmillan, 1909–10), 1 : 16, 19. Although Titchener's *Beginner's Psychology* (New York: Macmillan) appeared in 1915, it was really a revision of his 1896 text, *An Outline of Psychology* (New York: Macmillan). His *Textbook*, therefore, represents the last systematic compilation of his views.

29. Ibid., 1 : 20–22, 36–39, 218; "The Postulates of a Structural Psychology," *Philosophical Review* 7 (1898): 450, 465.

30. Karl E. Rothschuh, *History of Physiology*, trans. Guenter B. Risse (New York: Krieger, 1973), pp. 204–5.

31. F. A. Burtt, *The Metaphysical Foundations of Modern Thought* (New York: Harcourt, Brace, 1932), p. 30.

32. Titchener, "On 'Psychology as the Behaviorist Views It,' " *Proceedings of the American Philosophical Society* 53 (1914): 14.

33. Angell, "The Province of Functional Psychology," *PR* 14 (1907): 61–91.

34. Ibid., p. 85.

35. Ibid., p. 71.

36. Heidbreder, *Seven Psychologies*, p. 203.

37. Angell, "The Province of Functional Psychology," pp. 68, 91.

38. Ibid., p. 69.

39. Boring, *HEP*, pp. 622–23, 556.

40. Watson, in Carl Murchison et al., eds., *A History of Psychology in Autobiography*, 4 vols. (Worcester, Mass.: Clark University, 1930, 1932, 1936, 1952), 3 (1936): 276; cited as *HPA*.

41. Watson, "Psychology as the Behaviorist Views It," *PR* 20 (1913): 158.

CHAPTER 2

1. Titchener, "Wilhelm Wundt," *AJP* 32 (1921): 177.

2. This is not to say that experimental psychology in Germany quickly established itself as an independent discipline. Such institutionalization occurred first and most rap-

idly in the United States. See Mitchell G. Ash, "Experimental Psychology in Germany Before 1914: Aspects of an Academic Identity Problem," *Psychological Research* 42 (1980): 75–86; K. Danziger, "The Social Origins of Modern Psychology," in Allan R. Buss, ed., *Psychology in Social Context* (New York: Irvington, 1979), pp. 27–45.

3. William R. Woodward, "Wundt's Program for the New Psychology: Vicissitudes of Experiment, Theory, and System," in Woodward and Mitchell G. Ash, eds., *The Problematic Science: Psychology in Nineteenth-Century Thought* (New York: Praeger, 1982), pp. 167–97.

4. See W. G. Bringmann, William Balance, and Rand B. Evans, "Wilhelm Wundt, 1832–1920: A Brief Biographical Sketch," *JHBS* 11 (1975): 287–97; Boring, *HEP*, pp. 316–28.

5. See Fritz Ringer, *The Decline of the German Mandarins: The German Academic Community, 1890–1933* (Cambridge: Harvard University Press, 1969); Guenter B. Risse, "Kant, Schelling, and the Early Search for a Philosophical 'Science' of Medicine in Germany," *Journal of the History of Medicine* 27 (1972): 45–58. For more specific accounts of biological science, see Erick Nordenskiöld, *The History of Biology*, trans. Leonard B. Eyre (New York: Knopf, 1928), and Karl E. Rothshcuh, *History of Physiology*, trans. Guenter B. Risse (New York: Krieger, 1973).

6. Everett Mendelsohn, "Physical Models and Physiological Concepts: Explanation in Nineteenth-Century Biology," *British Journal for the History of Science* 2 (1965): 201–19, and David Galaty, "The Philosophical Basis of Mid-Nineteenth-Century German Reductionism," *Journal of the History of Medicine* 29 (1974): 295–316.

7. Helmholtz, "On the Conservation of Force: A Physical Memoir," in Russell Kahl, ed., *Selected Writings of Hermann von Helmholtz* (Middletown, Conn.: Wesleyan University Press, 1971), pp. 3–58.

8. Boring, *HEP*, p. 30.

9. Everett Mendelsohn, "The Biological Sciences in the Nineteenth Century: Some Problems and Sources," *History of Science* 3 (1964): 44.

10. Antonio Aliotta, *The Idealistic Reaction Against Science* (New York: Arno Press, 1975).

11. Müller, *Elements of Physiology*, trans. W. Baley, 2 vols. (London: Taylor and Walton, 1838, 1842), 2: 934.

12. Jefferson, *Selected Papers* (London: Pitman Medical, 1960), p. 116. Müller's and Jefferson's quotes have been taken from Robert M. Young, "The Functions of the Brain: Gall to Ferrier (1808–1886)," *Isis* 59 (1968): 257.

13. Wundt, *Grundzüge der physiologischen Psychologie*, 6th ed., 3 vols. (Leipzig: Engelman, 1908–11), 3 : 731. The following discussion follows Theodore Mischel, "Wundt and the Conceptual Foundations of Psychology," *Philosophy and Phenomenological Research* 31 (1970): 1–26.

14. Wundt, *Grundzüge*, 3 : 731.

15. Mischel, "Wundt," pp. 10–11.

16. Ibid., p. 11.

17. Boring, *HEP*, p. 80.

18. Fechner, *The Elements of Psychophysics*, trans. Helmut E. Adler (New York: Holt, Rinehart and Winston, 1966).

19. Ringer, *Decline*, p. 314.

20. Wundt, *Grundzüge*, 1 : 9, quoted in Mischel, "Wundt," p. 4.

21. Boring, *HEP*, pp. 327–28.

22. Ringer, *Decline*, p. 315.

23. Murphy, *Modern Psychology*, p. 165.

24. Boring, *HEP*, pp. 333–34; Woodward, "Wundt's Program for the New Psychology," p. 169.

25. Baldwin, "A Sketch of the History of Psychology," *PR* 12 (1905): 162.

26. Hall to William James, 15 February [1880], William James Papers, Houghton Library, Harvard University, Cambridge, Massachusetts.

CHAPTER 3

1. Edna Heidbreder, *Seven Psychologies* (New York: Century, 1933), pp. 94–95.

2. Gardner Murphy, *An Historical Introduction to Modern Psychology* (New York: Harcourt, Brace, 1929), pp. 46–52; Boring, *HEP*, 250–51; Titchener, "Experimental Psychology: A Retrospect," *AJP* 36 (1925): 314.

3. Preyer, *Die Seele des Kindes* (Jena: Strauss, 1881); *The Mind of the Child*, trans. by H. W. Brown (New York: Appleton, 1890); Murphy, *Modern Psychology*, 280–88; James, *Principles of Psychology*, 2 vols. (New York: Holt, 1890), 2 : 403–4; Dorothy Ross, *G. Stanley Hall: The Psychologist as Prophet* (Chicago: University of Chicago Press, 1972), pp. 124, 131; Watson, *Psychology from the Standpoint of a Behaviorist* (Philadelphia: Lippincott, 1919), pp. 194–347.

4. James to Hall, 3 September 1879, in Perry, *TCWJ*, 2 : 16; 1 : 577; Murphy, *Modern Psychology*, pp. 156–58; Boring, *HEP*, pp. 261–69.

5. Murphy, *Modern Psychology*, p. 236; Boring, *HEP*, pp. 356–61.

6. Boring to Samuel W. Fernberger, 25 February 1942, E. G. Boring Correspondence, Harvard University Archives, Cambridge, Massachusetts; Boring, *HEP*, pp. 362–71.

7. Boring, *HEP*, pp. 386–92; Murphy, *Modern Psychology*, pp. 189–99, 347–48.

8. Perry, *TCWJ*, 1 : 234–35.

9. Ibid., 2 : 5. Lotze, *Medizinsche Psychologie; Oder, Physiologie der Seele* (Leipzig: Weidmann, 1852). At the Clark University Conference in 1909, one year before his death, James confessed to the psychoanalyst Ernest Jones, "The future of psychology belongs to your work"; Jones, *The Life and Work of Sigmund Freud*, 3 vols. (New York: Basic Books, 1953–57), 2 : 57.

10. James to Thomas W. Ward [November 1868?], in Henry James, ed., *The Letters of William James*, 2 vols. (Boston: Atlantic Monthly Press, 1920), 1 : 118–19; see also Perry, *TCWJ*, 1 : 254.

11. James to parents, 3 July 1868, in Perry, *TCWJ*, 1 : 282.

12. James, review of Wundt's *Grundzüge der physiologischen Psychologie*, *North American Review* 121 (1875): 196.

13. Stumpf to James, 8 September 1886, in Perry, *TCWJ*, 2 : 67.

14. James to Stumpf, 6 February 1887, in ibid., 2 : 68.

15. Santayana to James, 3 July 1888, in ibid., 1 : 405.

16. James to Stumpf, 20 December 1892, in ibid., 2 : 181; James to Charles Sanders Peirce, 1 August 1905, in ibid., 2 : 436. Wundt's Institut returned the antipathy; see Judd, *HPA*, 2 (1932): 216. Lincoln Steffens testified to Wundt's "mental dishonesty" in *The Autobiography of Lincoln Steffens* (New York: Harcourt, Brace, 1931), pp. 150–51.

17. Judd, *HPA*, 2 (1932): 216. Judd had sent James his "Über Raumwahrnehmungen im Gebeits des Tastsinnes," *Philosophische Studien* 12 (1896): 409–63.

18. Ross, *G. Stanley Hall*, pp. 81–85; Hall to James, 26 October [1879], in Perry, *TCWJ*, 2 : 17–18; Mollie D. Boring and Edwin G. Boring, "Masters and Pupils Among the American Psychologists," *AJP* 61 (1948): 531.

19. Hall to James, 15 February [1880], William James Papers, Houghton Library, Harvard University, Cambridge, Massachusetts.

20. See, e.g., Anthony Oberschall, "The Institutionalization of American Sociology," in Oberschall, ed., *The Establishment of Empirical Sociology* (New York: Harper and Row, 1972), pp. 187–251; Dorothy Ross, "The Development of the Social Sciences," in Alexandra Oleson and John Voss, eds., *The Organization of Knowledge in Modern America, 1860–1920* (Baltimore: Johns Hopkins University Press, 1979), pp. 107–138.

21. Veysey, *The Emergence of the American University* (Chicago: University of Chicago Press, 1965), p. 129.

22. These aspects of Cattell's career are conveniently summarized in his "fairwell" speech to active work in psychology; Cattell, "The Conceptions and Methods of Psychology," *Popular Science Monthly* 66 (1904): 176–86, and reprinted in A. T. Poffenberger, ed., *James McKeen Cattell: A Man of Science*, 2 vols. (Lancaster, Pa.: Science Press, 1947), 2: 197–207.

23. Boring to Jacques Cattell, 26 January 1944, Cattell Papers, Manuscript Division, Library of Congress, Washington, D.C.

24. Michael M. Sokal, ed., *An Education in Psychology: James McKeen Cattell's Journal and Letters from Germany and England, 1880–1888* (Cambridge: M.I.T. Press, 1981), pp. 1–12. My description of Cattell's career follows Sokal, "The Education and Psychological Career of James McKeen Cattell, 1860–1904" (Ph.D. diss., Case Western Reserve University, 1972), p. 14–15, 23–38.

25. Michael M. Sokal, ed., "The Unpublished Autobiography of James McKeen Cattell," *American Psychologist* 26 (1971): 631.

26. Cattell admitted that his award was granted "by the professor of Latin, who knew even less about philosophy than I did, or the fellowship would have been given to John Dewey"; Cattell, "The Founding of the Association and of the Hopkins and Clark Laboratories," in Poffenberger, ed., *Cattell*, 2 : 501. Cattell's biographer has identified the judge as Charles D'Urban Morris, who taught a version of Common Sense Realism at Hopkins, and has suggested that Cattell's father's personal intervention with D. C. Gilman, Hopkins's president, was instrumental in his son's successful application; Sokal, ed., "Unpublished Autobiography," p. 631, editor's note 16; Sokal, "The Education and Psychological Career of Cattell," pp. 53, 63–64.

27. Cattell, "Founding of the Association," p. 501.

28. Ross, *G. Stanley Hall*, pp. 145–46.

29. Cattell, "Über die Zeit der Erkennung und Benennung von Schriftzeichen Bildern und Farben," *Philosophische Studien* 2 (1885): 635–50. Cattell abstracted his results in English under the title, "The Time It Takes to See and Name Objects," *Mind* 11 (1886): 63–65. The original work was translated by Robert S. Woodworth for inclusion in Poffenberger, ed., *Cattell*, 1 : 13–25, under the title "On the Time Required for Recognizing and Naming Letters and Words, Pictures and Colors." See Woodworth, "James McKeen Cattell, 1860–1944," *PR* 51 (1944): 201–9.

30. Quoted in Poffenberger, ed., *Cattell*, 1 : 13. Advisedly, this is Cattell's retrospective view. Sokal has shown that initially Cattell exhibited little interest in individual differences; Michael M. Sokal, "James McKeen Cattell and the Failure of Anthropometric Testing, 1890–1901," in William R. Woodward and Mitchell G. Ash, *The Prob-*

lematic Science: Psychology in Nineteenth-Century Thought (New York: Praeger, 1982), p. 326.

31. Sokal, ed., "Unpublished Autobiography," pp. 630–31.

32. Quoted in Poffenberger, ed., *Cattell,* 1 : 13.

33. Baldwin, *Between Two Wars (1861–1921),* 2 vols. (Boston: Stratford, 1926), 1 : 35.

34. Mattoon M. Curtis, "The Present Condition of German Universities," *Educational Review* 2 (1891): 39.

35. The biographical facts from which this interpretation is derived are contained in Sokal, "The Education and Psychological Career of Cattell," pp. 270–78.

36. Ibid., pp. 214–16; Michael M. Sokal, "Psychology at Victorian Cambridge—The Unofficial Laboratory of 1887–1888," *Proceedings of the American Philosophical Society* 116 (1972): 145–47.

37. Witmer to E. G. Boring, 18 March 1948, Boring Correspondence.

38. Ibid.

39. Wolfe, *AJP* 3 (1890): 277.

40. Quoted in Ludy T. Benjamin, "Psychology at the University of Nebraska, 1889–1930," *Nebraska History* 56 (1975): 376.

41. Earle D. Ross, *Democracy's College: The Land Grant Movement in the Formative Stages* (Ames, Iowa: Iowa State College, 1942), p. 115; Lawrence A. Cremin, *The Transformation of the School: Progressivism in American Education, 1876–1957* (New York: Knopf, 1961), pp. 23–57.

42. Psychologists, incidentally, resolved this dilemma after the turn of the century by declaring that "transfer of training" did not occur. There existed, in other words, no such thing as formal mental discipline; only certain laws of learning that psychologists were uniquely qualified to decipher. See Walter B. Kolesnik, *Mental Discipline in Modern Education* (Madison: University of Wisconsin Press, 1962).

43. Quoted in Benjamin, "Psychology at Nebraska," p. 376.

44. Wolfe, *AJP* 3 (1890): 277.

45. Pillsbury's paraphrase of Wolfe is in *HPA,* 2 (1932): 267. Wolfe did, in fact, publish a few redimentary experimental papers. Pillsbury's recollection, therefore, mirrors Wolfe's obscurity, not his unproductiveness.

46. Wolfe, "The New Psychology in Undergraduate Work," *PR* 2 (1895): 382–87; French, "The Place of Experimental Psychology in the Undergraduate Courses," *PR* 5 (1898): 510–12.

47. Benjamin, "Psychology at Nebraska," pp. 378–79.

48. Nebraska was no anomalous psychological wasteland. Surveys taken in 1921 and 1928 to determine "where psychologists first received their inspiration" to pursue psychology as a career both placed Nebraska third of all colleges and universities. See Samuel W. Fernberger's statistical analyses of the APA: *PB* 18 (1921): 569–72, and *PR* 35 (1928): 447–65. Ludy Benjamin has shown that six Nebraska undergraduates went on to become APA presidents; Benjamin and Amy D. Bertleson. "The Early Nebraska Laboratory, 1889–1930: Nursery for Presidents of the APA," *JHBS* 11 (1975): 142–48. Wolfe had inspired Walter Bowers Pillsbury and Madison Bentley to study at America's Wundtian stronghold, Cornell. After his departure, however, students were directed toward Columbia, Pennsylvania, and Clark, three of the country's centers of applied psychology.

49. Thus Carl Seashore at Iowa announced his priorities: "The function of psychol-

ogy was twofold, first, to promote the training of psychologists for work in schools and service centers and, secondly, to conduct research"; *HPA*, 1 (1930): 265.

50. Scripture, *HPA*, 3 (1936): 231.

51. Boring, *HEP*, 528.

52. Scripture, *Thinking, Feeling, Doing* (Meadville, Pa.: Chautauqua-Century, 1895), pp. 283, 293; *The New Psychology* (New York: Scribner's, 1897).

53. James to Josiah Royce, 18 December 1892, in Perry, *TCWJ*, 1 : 807; 2 : 145, note 12.

54. Eugene S. Mills, *George Trumbell Ladd: Pioneer American Psychologist* (Cleveland: The Press of Case Western Reserve University, 1969), pp. 218, 224; Seashore, *HPA*, 1 (1930): 250–51.

55. Scripture, *HPA*, 3 (1936): 243, 249, 251.

56. Scripture, *Thinking, Feeling, Doing*, p. 120.

57. Scripture, *HPA*, 3 (1936): 242.

58. Wundt, *Grundriss der Psychologie* (Leipzig: W. Engelmann, 1896); *Outlines of Psychology*, 3d. ed., trans. Charles Hubbard Judd (New York: Gustav E. Stechert, 1907); Judd, *HPA*, 2 (1932): 214–19; *PR* 28 (1921): 173–78.

59. Quoted in Mills, *George Trumbell Ladd*, p. 209.

60. Judd, *Psychology: General Introduction* (New York: Scribner's, 1907), p. v.

61. Judd, *PR* 28 (1921): 177.

62. The following account of Wesleyan follows Geraldine Joncich, *The Sane Positivist: A Biography of Edward L. Thorndike* (Middletown, Conn.: Wesleyan University Press, 1968), pp. 70–74.

63. Wesleyan had been in that vanguard long before the so-called postbellum "transformation" of American scholarship." See Stanley M. Guralnick, *Science and the Ante-Bellum American College*, (Philadelphia: American Philosophical Society, 1975), pp. 44–46, 67, 72, 73, 88, 113.

64. Sully, *Outlines of Psychology: with Special Reference to the Theory of Euducation* (New York: Appleton, 1884). Joncich has noted the "disproportionately large number" of Wesleyan men prominent in the field of education and educational psychology; *The Sane Positivist*, p. 73.

65. Judd, *Genetic Psychology for Teachers* (New York: Appleton, 1903); Angell, "The Province of Functional Psychology," *PR* 14 (1907): 61–91.

66. Judd, *HPA*, 2 (1932): 220, 218; Meumann, *Über Oekonomie und Technik des Lernmens* (Leipzig: W. Engelmann, 1903); Thorndike, *Educational Psychology* (New York: Lemcke and Buechner, 1903). See also the statement by Friedrich Kiesow in *HPA*, 1 (1930): 179.

67. Judd, *HPA*, 2 (1932): 221–22.

68. Witmer, "The Psychological Clinic," *Old Penn* 8 (1909): 100.

69. Judd, *HPA*, 2 (1932): 222, 224, 226.

70. Ibid., pp. 218, 219; Boring, *HEP*, p. 334.

71. Henry K. Misiak and Virginia M. Staudt, *Catholics in Psychology: A Historical Survey* (New York: McGraw-Hill, 1954), pp. 66–77.

72. A. A. Roback, *A History of American Psychology*, rev. ed. (New York: Collier, 1964), pp. 435–38.

73. Toward the end of the century, American academic life was gradually becoming isolated from Germany, its recent source of inspiration. At Catholic, the split had ecclesiastical overtones. The German clergy, hostile to American theological liberalism,

withdrew their financial support from American Catholicism's only German-oriented research university. See John Cogley, *Catholic America* (New York: Dial, 1973), pp. 198–99, and, in general, John Tracy Ellis, *The Formative Years of Catholic University in America* (Washington, D.C.: Catholic University Press, 1946).

74. Lewis M. Terman, "Frank Angell: 1857–1939," *AJP* 53 (1940): 138–40; Harper, "Tables of American Doctorates in Psychology," *AJP* 62 (1949): 579–81; Titchener to A. A. Roback, 21 September 1918, in Roback, *History of American Psychology*, p. 220.

75. Warren, *History of Association Psychology* (New York: Scribner's, 1921).

76. Warren, *HPA*, 1 (1930): 450–54, 457–58, 460, 464, 468; *PR* 28 (1921): 168.

77. Gale, "Yale Education versus Culture," *Pedogogical Seminary* 9 (1902): 3–17.

78. Minnesota psychology's chronicler has corrected the common misimpression that J. R. Angell established the laboratory there in 1892. See Miles A. Tinker, "Progress in Psychology at Minnesota (1890–1953)," unpublished typescript, n.d., Harlow Gale Papers, Archives Library, University of Minnesota, Minneapolis, p. 1.

79. David P. Kuna, "Harlow S. Gale and the Minnesota Laboratory: A False Start for Experimental Psychology" (Paper presented at the ninth annual meeting of the Cheiron Society, June 1977, University of Colorado, Boulder), p. 6.

80. Gale, "Kindergarten Psychology," unpublished paper, n.d., Gale Papers, p. 4. William James himself felt that "the 'function' of Titchener's 'scientific' psychology (which, 'structurally' considered, is a pure will-of-the-wisp) is to keep the laboratory instruments going, and to provide platforms for certain professors"; James to Mary W. Calkins, 19 September 1909, in Perry, *TCWJ*, 2 : 123.

81. See Tinker, "Progress at Minnesota," pp. 1–15.

82. See, e.g., "In Memory of Wilhelm Wundt by his American Students," *PR* 28 (1921): 178.

83. See, e.g., Boring, *HEP*, p. 347; Henryk Misiak and Virginia Staudt Sexton, *History of Psychology: An Overview* (New York: Grune and Stratton, 1966), p. 87.

84. Stratton, "Wundt and Leipzig in the Association's Early Days," *PR* 50 (1943): 68–70; *PR* 28 (1921): 170.

85. James to Howison, 2 April 1894, in Perry, *TCWJ*, 2 : 116.

86. James to Münsterberg, 21 February 1892, in ibid., 2 : 139.

87. James to Howison, 2 April 1894, in ibid., 2 : 16.

88. Roback, *History of American Psychology*, p. 482.

89. See, e.g., Stratton, "Railway Accidents and Color Sense," *Popular Science Monthly* 72 (1908): 244–52; "Some Experiments on the Perception of Movement, Color, and Direction of Lights, with Special Reference to Railway Signaling," *PR, Monograph Supplements* 10, no. 40 (1909): 84–105.

90. Stratton to Howison, 19 December 1894 and 17 January 1895, cited in Vesey, *The Emergence of the American University* (Chicago: University of Chicago Press, 1965), p. 131; Stratton, "Wundt and Leipzig," p. 69.

91. To provide closure to the James-Howison discussion it might be noted that the University of California attained significance as a research institution only after World War I. The Berkeley department produced one Ph.D. in psychology in 1899; its next, in 1921. See Harper, "Tables," pp. 580–82.

92. James R. Angell, *HPA*, 3 (1936): 6.

93. James Burrill Angell to J. R. Angell, 19 February 1892, James Rowland Angell Papers, Sterling Memorial Library, Yale University, New Haven, Connecticut.

94. James K. Angell, *HPA*, 3 (1936): 7.

95. James Burrill Angell to J. R. Angell, 10 March 1892, Angell Papers.

96. James R. Angell, *HPA*, 3 (1936): 10.

97. John Dewey to Angell, 10 May 1893, Angell Papers.

98. Matthew Hale, Jr., has also noted this fact in *Human Science and Social Order: Hugo Münsterberg and the Origins of Applied Psychology* (Philadelphia: Temple University Press, 1980), pp. 47–48.

99. Were it maintained that Angell's academic connections obviated his need to obtain the kind of certification essential to those less blessed, Cattell's career might provide adequate counterevidence.

100. Historians of higher education have claimed that it was so authorized in the doctrine of *Wissenschaft* and have tended to criticize Americans for their failure to assimilate the broad holistic aims of German scholarship, of the austere, unitary, dedicated pursuit of Truth. See, e.g., Veysey, *Emergence*, p. 127; Thomas Le Duc, *Piety and Intellect at Amherst College, 1865–1929* (New York: Columbia University Press, 1946), p. 85. By the 1870s, however, those ideals had already been compromised in Germany as scholars increasingly came to view their callings in the sober light of specialized academic careerism. See Carl Diehl, *Americans and German Scholarship, 1770–1870* (New Haven: Yale University Press, 1978), pp. 150–51.

101. Steffens, *Autobiography*, p. 151.

102. Alfred C. Raphelson, "Lincoln Steffens at Leipzig," *JHBS* 3 (1967): 38–42.

103. Jordan, "Science and the Colleges," *Popular Science Monthly* 42 (1893): 733.

CHAPTER 4

1. Angell, "The Influence of Darwin on Psychology," *PR* 16 (1909): 152.

2. Bruce Kuklick, *The Rise of American Philosophy: Cambridge, Massachusetts, 1860–1930* (New Haven: Yale University Press, 1977), p. xvii.

3. Persons, *American Minds: A History of Ideas* (New York: Holt, Rinehart and Winston, 1958), p. 189. The following exposition of the college's organization of knowledge follows Persons's account (pp. 187–200).

4. For a general view of Protestant Scholasticism, see John Dillenberger, *Protestant Thought and Natural Science* (Garden City, N.Y.: Doubleday, 1960).

5. Daniel Walker Howe, *The Unitarian Conscience: Harvard Moral Philosophy, 1805–1861* (Cambridge: Harvard University Press, 1970), p. 3. By 1825 all the major Protestant sects had established separate theological seminaries; Stanley L. Guralnick, *Science and the Ante-Bellum American College* (Philadelphia: American Philosophical Society, 1975), p. 355. The consequent secularization of the collegiate curriculum facilitated attempts to provide moral instruction increasingly compatible with natural science. See also Wilson Smith, *Professors and Public Ethics: Studies of Northern Moral Philosophers Before the Civil War* (Ithaca: Cornell University Press, 1956).

6. D. H. Meyer, *The Instructed Conscience: The Shaping of the American National Ethic* (Philadelphia: University of Pennsylvania Press, 1972), pp. 24, 4–5.

7. Ibid., p. 16.

8. This account intends not to explicate philosophical ideas but to exposit them in terms of their cultural functions. My reading of Common Sense Realism is indebted to Elizabeth Flower and Murray G. Murphey, *A History of Philosophy in America*, 2 vols. (New York: Putnam's, 1977), esp. chap. 4 and 5; and to Kuklick, *Rise of American Philosophy*, pp. 5–45.

9. Stanley L. Guralnick, "Sources of Misconception on the Role of Science in the Nineteenth-Century American College" *Isis* 65 (1974): 291.

10. Robert V. Bruce, "A Statistical Profile of American Scientists, 1846–1876," in George H. Daniels, ed., *Nineteenth-Century American Science: A Reappraisal* (Evanston, Ill.: Northwestern University Press, 1972), p. 94. This percentage contrasts with 32.2 percent who were financed by state and federal governments combined. The next-largest category (wages) is 6.3 percent.

11. Charles Weiner, "Science and Higher Education," in David D. Van Tassel and Michael G. Hall, eds., *Science and Society in the United States* (Homewood, Ill.: Dorsey, 1966), pp. 163–89.

12. "Original Papers in Relation to a Course of Liberal Education," *American Journal of Science and the Arts* 15 (1829): 197–351.

13. Guralnick, "Sources of Misconceptions on the Role of Science," pp. 353–54.

14. Walter B. Kolesnik, *Mental Discipline in Modern Education* (Madison: University of Wisconsin Press, 1962), sorts out the various meanings of mental and formal discipline.

15. Guralnick, *Science and the Ante-Bellum American College.*

16. Charles C. Gillispie, "English Ideas of the University in the Nineteenth Century," in Margaret Clapp, ed., *The Modern University* (Ithaca: Cornell University Press, 1950), pp. 38–42.

17. Quoted in Vesey, *The Emergence of the American University* (Chicago: University of Chicago Press, 1965), pp. 42–43.

18. On Paley's theological Utilitarianism in America, see Smith, *Professors and Public Ethics*, pp. 44–73.

19. Edward Hitchcock, *Reminiscences of Amherst College* (Northhampton, Mass., 1863), p. 291.

20. Edward Lurie, *Agassiz: A Life in Science*, abridged ed. (Chicago: Phoenix, 1966), pp. 300, 358.

21. Flower and Murphey, *History of Philosophy*, pp. 527–28.

22. Ibid., p. 528.

23. McCosh, *Psychology: The Cognitive Powers* (New York: Scribner's, 1888), pp. 1, 3.

24. Robert M. Young, "The Functions of the Brain: Gall to Ferrier (1808–1886)," *Isis* 59 (1968); see also his provocative extended treatment, *Mind, Brain, and Adaption in the Nineteenth Century* (Oxford: Oxford University Press, 1970).

25. Young, "Functions of the Brain," p. 257; William B. Carpenter, *Priniciples of Mental Physiology* (New York: Appleton, 1884).

26. Robert M. Young, "The Role of Psychology in the Nineteenth-Century Evolutionary Debate," in Mary Henle et al., eds., *Historical Conceptions of Psychology* (New York: Springer, 1973), p. 186.

27. Boring, *HEP*, pp. 73–74; Young, "Functions of the Brain," p. 263.

28. Ladd, *Philosophy of Mind: An Essay in the Metaphysics of Psychology* (New York: Scribner's, 1895), pp. x, 5–6.

29. Scripture, *HPA*, 3 (1936): 233.

30. Baldwin, *Between Two Wars (1861–1921)*, 2 vols. (Boston: Stratford, 1926), 1: 60.

31. See Alexander Koyré, "The Influence of Philosophic Trends on the Formation of Scientific Theories," in P. G. Frank, ed., *The Validation of Scientific Theories* (Boston: Beacon, 1953), pp. 192–203.

32. Baldwin, "Psychology Past and Present," *PR* 1 (1894): 374.

33. James, *Principles of Psychology*, 2 vols. (New York: Holt, 1890), 1: 192.

34. J. D. Y. Peel, *Herbert Spencer: The Evolution of a Sociologist* (London: Heinemann, 1971). The best account of Spencer's reception in America remains Richard Hofstadter, *Social Darwinism in American Thought*, rev. ed. (New York: Braziller, 1955).

35. Wright, "The Philosophy of Herbert Spencer," *North American Review* 100 (1865): 426. On Wright, see Edward H. Madden, *Chauncey Wright and the Foundations of Pragmatism* (Seattle: University of Washington Press, 1963); Philip P. Wiener, *Evolution and the Founders of Pragmatism* (Cambridge: Harvard University Press, 1949), pp. 31–69; and Kuklick, *Rise of American Philosophy*, pp. 63–79.

36. Hall, "Review of William James's *Principles of Psychology*," *AJP* 3 (1890): 590.

37. Henry May, *The Enlightenment in America* (New York: Oxford University Press, 1976), p. 352, and, in general, pp. 88–101, 337–57; Howe, *Unitarian Conscience*, pp. 144–48.

38. Quoted in Sheldon M. Stern, "William James and the New Psychology," in Paul Buck, ed., *Social Sciences at Harvard, 1860–1920: From Inculcation to Open Mind* (Cambridge: Harvard University Press, 1965), p. 184.

39. James, "The Teaching of Philosophy in Our Colleges," *Nation* 23 (1876): 178.

40. James to Eliot, 2 December 1875, in Perry, *TCWJ*, 2 : 11.

41. Ladd, "Psychology as So-Called 'Natural Science,' " *Philosophical Review* 1 (1892): 51–52.

42. Hall, "Review of James's *Principles*," p. 590.

43. Quoted in David Wallace, "Reflections on the Education of George Herbert Mead," *American Journal of Sociology* 72 (1967): 406.

44. For a strenuous attempt at rendering this conjunction convincing, see Joseph Ben-David, *The Scientist's Role in Society: A Comparative Study* (Englewood Cliffs, N.J.: Prentice-Hall, 1971).

45. This caricature of philosophic resistance to the new psychology stems from two sources. The first is represented by the early vituperative assaults of Hall, who in his "Philosophy in the United States" rationalized his personal difficulties in securing a permanent academic appointment in terms of opposition to his philosophic avant-gardism, thus stating his "opposition's" position in intellectually indefensible terms. The depiction also stems from autobiographical reminiscences of such psychologists as Hall, Baldwin, and Cattell, who have tended to see themselves retrospectively as Young Turks. These portrayals became entrenched in disciplinary folklore after the turn of the century when psychologists, anxious to secure departmental independence from philosophy, inferred from their own aspirations a consistent pattern of philosophical resistance to their ambitions. Thus they erroneously conflated psychology's later requirement of independence with its earlier need for recognition and assumed that conditions at both times were similar. Boring, for example, condescendingly relates McCosh's insistence that Baldwin's dissertation "refute materialism" as an example of philosophy's stubborn irrelevance and interference. Boring's assertion that Baldwin's "inclination took him to no such topic" overlooks the fact that Baldwin's entire life was involved with such refutation. See David Noble, *The Paradox of Progressive Thought* (Minneapolis: University of Minnesota Press, 1958), pp. 78–102. Boring (*HEP*, p. 530) refers to Baldwin's account in *Between Two Wars*, 1 : 20–21.

46. Persons, *American Minds*, p. 223.

47. On the reshaping of social thought in general, see Paul F. Boller, Jr., *American Thought in Transition: The Impact of Evolutionary Naturalism, 1865–1900* (Chicago: Rand-McNally, 1969); Cynthia Eagle Russett, *Darwin in America: The Intellectual Response, 1865–*

1912 (San Francisco: Freeman, 1976). On the reshaping of scientific thought, see Hamilton Cravens, *The Triumph of Evolution: American Scientists and the Heredity-Environment Controversy, 1900–1941* (Philadelphia: University of Pennsylvania Press, 1978).

48. Flower and Murphey, *History of Philosophy*, pp. xiv–xviii and chaps. 4, 5, 10, and 11.

49. Kuklick, *Rise of American Philosophy*, p. 27.

50. Angell, "The Province of Functional Psychology," *PR* 14 (1907): 73.

CHAPTER 5

1. Useful works attending to Gall's program include Owsei Temkin, "Gall and the Phrenological Movement," *Bulletin of the History of Medicine* 21 (1947): 275–321; Walther Riese and E. C. Hoff, "A History of the Doctrine of Cerebral Localization," *Journal of the History of Medicine and the Allied Sciences* 5 (1950): 5–71, 6 (1951): 429–70; and Boring, *HEP*, pp. 51–60. My interpretation of Gall is enormously indebted to Robert Young, *Mind, Brain, and Adaption in the Nineteenth Century* (Oxford: Oxford University Press, 1970) and to his briefer "The Functions of the Brain: Gall to Ferrier (1808–1886)," *Isis* 59 (1968): 251–68.

For phrenology's vogue in America, see John D. Davies, *Phrenology: Fad and Science: A Nineteenth-Century American Crusade* (New Haven: Yale University Press, 1955); Robert E. Riegel, "Early Phrenology in the United States," *Medical Life* 36 (1930): 361–76. Two retrospects of the movement are also particularly valuable: Nahum Capen, *Reminiscences of Dr. Spurzheim and George Combe* (New York: Fowler and Wells, 1881), and Nelson Sizer, *Forty Years in Phrenology* (New York: Fowler and Wells, 1882). An excellent companion to Davies's study, which concentrates on the British reception, is David DeGiustino, *Conquest of Mind: Phrenology and Victorian Social Thought* (London: Croom Helm, 1975).

David Bakan has assessed "The Influence of Phrenology on American Psychology," *JHBS* 2 (1966): 200–220, and, despite several critical reservations, I have drawn on his fertile insights repeatedly. See also Madison Bentley, "The Psychological Antecedents of Phrenology," *PR, Monographs* 21 (1916): 102–15, and, with caution, Frank M. Albrecht, Jr., "The New Psychology in America, 1880–1895" (Ph.D. diss., Johns Hopkins University, 1960), 22–37.

2. Gall, *On the Functions of the Brain and Each of Its Parts: With Observations on the Possibility of Determining the Instincts, Propensities and Talents, or the Moral and Intellectual Dispositions of Men and Animals, by the Configuration of the Head*, trans. Winslow Lewis, Jr., 6 vols. (Boston: March, Capen and Lyon, 1835).

3. Erik Nordenskiöld, *The History of Biology*, trans. by Leonard B. Eyre (New York: Knopf, 1928), p. 310.

4. Boring, *HEP*, p. 57.

5. Young, "Functions of the Brain," pp. 256–57, 266; Boring, *HEP*, 62–70.

6. Gall, *On the Functions of the Brain*, 3 : 157.

7. Ibid., pp. 158–59.

8. See Ferrier's acknowledgment of the accuracy of Gall's criticisms in his *The Functions of the Brain*, 2d ed. (London: Smith, Elder, 1878), p. 269.

9. Gall, *On the Functions of the Brain*, 3 : 160.

10. Ibid., p. 157.

11. Young, "Functions of the Brain," p. 266.

12. Temkin, "Gall and the Phrenological Movement," p. 292. Gall's comment is quoted in Young, "Functions of the Brain," p. 254.

13. David Hume, *A Treatise of Human Nature*, ed. L. A. Selby-Bigge (Oxford: Clarendon, 1896), p. xxiii.

14. Comte, *Philosophie Positive*, in Stanislav Andreski, ed., *The Essential Comte*, trans. Margaret Clarke (London: Croom Helm, 1974), pp. 32–33.

15. Quoted in Bakan, "The Influence of Phrenology," pp. 209–10.

16. Cattell, "The Conceptions and Methods of Psychology," *Popular Science Monthly* 66 (1904): 179–80; Michael M. Sokal, "The Education and Psychological Career of James McKeen Cattell, 1860–1904" (Ph.D. diss., Case Western Reserve University, 1972), pp. 29–30, 300.

17. Watson in *HPA*, 3 (1936): 274, 276; Watson, *Psychology from the Standpoint of a Behaviorist*, p. vii. John C. Burnham has also noted this connection in "On the Origins of Behaviorism," *JHBS* 4 (1968): 143–51, 148–49.

18. Meyer, *The Fundamental Laws of Behavior* (Boston: Badger, 1911), pp. vx, 2.

19. Meyer, *Psychology of the Other One: An Introductory Text-Book* (Columbia, Mo.: Missouri Book Co., 1921).

20. Watson, *Behaviorism* (New York: People's Institute, 1924), p. 10. See also Münsterberg, *Psychology: General and Applied* (New York: Appleton, 1914), p. 2.

21. Caldwell, *Elements of Phrenology* (Lexington, Ky.: Meriwether, 1824).

22. See, e.g., Boring, *HEP*, pp. 640–41; Knight Dunlap, "The Case Against Introspection," *PR* 19 (1912): 404–13.

23. If true, it is one of the ironies of the history of science that the psychology division of Cornell's Department of Philosophy, which Wundt's archdisciple Titchener commandeered, was explicitly created, according to Bakan, "to accumulate evidence in behalf of phrenology"; Bakan, "The Influence of Phrenology," p. 202. See Morris Bishop, *A History of Cornell* (Ithaca: Cornell University Press, 1962), p. 277.

24. Gall, *On the Functions of the Brain*, 3 : 166–67.

25. Titchener, "The Postulates of a Structural Psychology," *Philosophical Review* 7 (1898): 450.

26. Hamilton Cravens and John C. Burnham, "Psychology and Evolutionary Naturalism in American Thought, 1890–1940," *American Quarterly* 23 (1971): 635–57.

27. McDougall, *An Introduction to Social Psychology* (London: Methuen, 1908); Bernard Hollander, "McDougall's Social Psychology Anticipated One Hundred Years: A Contribution to the History of Philosophy," *The Ethiological Journal* 9 (1924): 1–20. Hollander, incidentally, was a twentieth-century phrenologist whose *Mental Functions of the Brain* (London: Grant Richards, 1901) he alternatively titled *The Revival of Phrenology*. See John Henry Bridges, *Illustrations of Positivism*, ed. H. Gordon Jones (London: Watts, 1915), pp. 57, 68–69.

28. Watson, *Behavior: An Introduction to Comparative Psychology* (New York: Holt, Rinehart and Winston, 1914). See Richard Herrnstein's Introduction to the 1967 Holt, Rinehart and Winston republication, reprinted in Mary Henle et al., eds., *Historical Conceptions of Psychology* (New York: Springer, 1973), pp. 98–115, esp. pp. 102–3.

29. Yerkes, "Behaviorism and Genetic Psychology," *JPPSM* 14 (1917): 155; "The Harvard Laboratory of Animal Psychology and the Franklin Field Station," *Journal of Animal Behavior* 4 (1914): 176–84, 181.

30. Temkin, "Gall and the Phrenological Movement," p. 284.

31. Young, "Functions of the Brain," p. 254; Temkin, "Gall and the Phrenological

Movement," pp. 281–83, 292; James R. Angell, "The Province of Functional Psychology," *PR* 14 (1907): 63, 64.

32. Dallenbach, "The History and Derivation of the Word 'Function' as a Systematic Term in Psychology," *AJP* 26 (1915): 473–84, 484. Bakan, "The Influence of Phrenology," has cited this study.

33. Boring, *HEP*, 642; "The Influence of Evolutionary Theory Upon American Psychological Thought," *Evolutionary Thought in America*, ed. Stow Persons (New Haven: Yale University Press, 1950), p. 288; Edna Heidbreder, *Seven Psychologies* (New York: Century, 1933), p. 239; Willard Harrell and Ross Harrison, "The Rise and Fall of Behaviorism," *Journal of General Psychology* 18 (1938): 367–421, 369–70.

34. Bakan, "The Influence of Phrenology," p. 210; Young, "Functions of the Brain," p. 254; Bain, *Logic*, rev. ed. (New York: Appleton, 1884), p. 517.

35. James, *Principles of Psychology* 2 vols. (New York: Holt, 1890), 1 : 28; T. A. Hyde, quoted in Perry, *TCWJ*, 2 : 51.

36. William Sheldon, *The Varieties of Human Physique* (New York: Harper's, 1940), p. 12; cited in Bakan, "The Influence of Phrenology," p. 201. See also Ernst Kretschmer, *Physique and Character* (New York: Harcourt, Brace, 1925).

37. It should be obvious that the term "useful" is being employed here in a distinctive sense. The introspective psychology of the Common Sense Realists sought to provide very valuable insights into the nature of self. Nevertheless, it appeared useless to the solutions of a wide variety of problems advancing to the forefront of contemporary social concern.

38. Capen, *Reminiscences*, p. 221; quoted in Bakan, "The Influence of Phrenology," p. 210.

39. Cattell, "Conceptions and Methods," p. 185. Cattell went on to say: "I see no reason why the application of systematized knowledge of the control of human nature may not in the course of the present century accomplish results commensurate with the nineteenth century applications of physical science to the material world" (p. 186).

40. Hall, "Practical Relations Between Psychology and the War," *Journal of Applied Psychology* 1 (1917): 9–16, 11; Dorothy Ross, *G. Stanley Hall: The Psychologist as Prophet* (Chicago: University of Chicago Press, 1972), p. 76.

41. Meyer, *Fundamental Laws*, pp. 239–41, wherein he cites his indebtedness to the Chicago sociologist Bernard; L. L. Bernard, *Transition to an Objective Standard of Social Control* (Chicago: University of Chicago Press, 1911).

42. Bakan, "The Influence of Phrenology," p. 212.

43. It is useful in this regard to note that in contemporary medical parlance "empiricism" was synonymous with charlatanism.

44. Bakan, "The Influence of Phrenology," p. 211.

45. Madeleine Stern, *Heads and Headlines: The Phrenological Fowlers* (Norman: University of Oklahoma Press, 1971).

46. Well into the twentieth century, academic psychologists continued to tar their competition with the brush of phrenological quackery. See Guenter B. Risse, "Vocational Guidance During the Depression: Phrenology versus Applied Psychology," *JHBS* 12 (1976): 130–40; Dallenbach, "Phrenology versus Psychoanalysis," *AJP* 48 (1955): 511–25.

47. James, "A Plea for Psychology as a 'Natural Science,' " *Philosophical Review* 1 (1892): 146–53, 148.

48. Combe, *Notes on the United States of North America during a Phrenological Visit in*

1838–1840 (Edinburgh: Stewart, 1841). Arthur E. Fink, *Causes of Crime: Biological Theories in the United States, 1800–1915* (Philadelphia: University of Pennsylvania Press, 1938), pp. 11–12, discusses the respectability of phrenology's adherents.

49. Davies, *Phrenology*, p. 172.

50. For a more detailed look at this reception, see John M. O'Donnell, "The Origins of Behaviorism: American Psychology, 1870–1920" (Ph.D. diss., University of Pennsylvania, 1979), pp. 212–21.

51. Maurice Mandelbaum has noted that throughout the nineteenth century "political and social theory proceeded on the assumption that it was through psychology—i.e., through an analysis of the needs and capacities of individual human beings—that one could both understand and evaluate the forms of institutions which characterized social life"; *History, Man, and Reason: A Study in Nineteenth-Century Thought* (Baltimore: Johns Hopkins University Press, 1971), p. 163.

52. Stow Persons, *The Decline of American Gentility* (New York: Columbia University Press, 1973); George Fredrickson, *The Inner Civil War: Northern Intellectuals and the Crisis of the Union* (New York: Harper and Row, 1965), esp. chap. 13, "Science and the New Intellectuals," pp. 199–216. This phenomenon—the connection between professionalization, science, and reform—which Fredrickson examines in the period of the new psychology's ascendancy, nevertheless possessed antebellum roots during the time of phrenology's popularity. See John Higham, "From Boundlessness to Consolidation: The Transformation of American Culture, 1848–1860" (Ann Arbor: William L. Clements Library, 1969), and John L. Thomas, "Romantic Reform in America, 1815–1865," *American Quarterly* 17 (1965): 656–81.

53. Boring, *HEP*, p. 507.

54. Davies, *Phrenology*, p. 50.

55. Münsterberg, *Psychology and Industrial Efficiency* (Boston: Houghton Mifflin, 1913), pp. 636–82.

56. One could object that this dichotomy constitutes an overdrawn caricature of mental and moral philosophy, that the Realists were not oblivious to questions of individual differences. In 1840, for example, Bowdoin's Thomas Upham published *Outlines of Imperfect and Disordered Mental Action* (New York: Harper & Brothers, 1840), an early treatise on abnormal psychology. Yet Upham relied upon a conception of mental faculties affected by bodily states and drew upon the positivistic medical inquiries of Rush and later phrenologists. Often, the extent of the moral philosophers' utilitarian concerns reflected either the extent to which phrenological categories of thought had infiltrated Realism or the extent to which it challenged Realism to relevance, as in the case of Noah Porter. In his 1868 *Human Intellect* (New York: Scribner's, 1868), the Yale philosopher described psychology as "propaedeutic to other areas of human conduct," "a basis for the applied discipline of education," and "an adaptive science" (p. 13).

57. Carroll C. Pratt, "Faculty Psychology," *PR* 36 (1929): 142–71; Boring, *HEP*, pp. 329–38, 384–85.

58. Bain, *The Senses and the Intellect* (London: Parker, 1855), and *The Emotions and the Will* (London: Parker, 1859).

59. Robert Thomson, *The Pelican History of Psychology* (Harmondsworth, England: Penguin, 1968), pp. 27–30.

60. Youmans, Introduction to Alexander Bain, *Mental Science: A Compendium of Psychology and the History of Philosophy* (New York: Appleton, 1868), pp. 5–8.

61. Titchener, "Wilhelm Wundt," *AJP* 32 (1921): 177; Flugel is quoted in Thomson, *The Pelican History*, p. 30.

62. Bain, *On the Study of Character, Including an Estimate of Phrenology* (London: Parker, 1861); Young, "Functions of the Brain," p. 259.

63. The best short sketch of Bain's theory of movement is in Young, *Mind, Brain, and Adaptation,* pp. 101–33.

64. Young, "Functions of the Brain," p. 260; Spencer, *Principles of Psychology,* 2 vols., 3d ed. (London: Williams and Norgate, 1881).

65. George B. Denton, "Early Psychological Theories of Herbert Spencer," *AJP* 32 (1921): 5–15.

66. Stow Persons, *American Minds: A History of Ideas* (New York: Holt, Rinehart and Winston, 1958), p. 236.

67. Mann, "Fourth Annual Report" (1840), in Lawrence A. Cremin, ed., *The Republic and the School: Horace Mann on the Education of Free Men* (New York: Teachers College Press, 1957), p. 52; Mann, *A Few Thoughts for a Young Man . . .* (Boston: Ticknor, Reed and Fields, 1850), p. 83; Merle Curti, *The Social Ideas of American Educators* (New York: Scribner's, 1935), pp. 101–38; Merle Curti, "Human Nature in American Thought: The Age of Reason and Morality, 1750–1860," *Political Science Quarterly* 68 (1953): 354–75, 361–63; Lawrence A. Cremin, *The Transformation of the School: Progressivism in American Education, 1876–1957* (New York: Random House, 1964), pp. 90–126; Charles Everett Strickland, "The Child and the Race: The Doctrine of Recapitulation and Culture Epochs in the Rise of the Child-Centered Ideal in American Educational Thought, 1875–1900" (Ph.D. diss., University of Wisconsin, 1963); Robert E. Gringer, *A History of Genetic Psychology: The First Science of Human Development* (New York: Wiley, 1967).

68. *Criminal Man: According to the Classification of Cesare Lombroso* (New York: Putnam 1911). See also Mark H. Haller, *Eugenics: Hereditarian Attitudes in American Thought* (New Brunswick: Rutgers University Press, 1963), pp. 15, 40–42; Fink, *Causes of Crime,* pp. 99–150; Hans Kurella, *Cesare Lombroso: A Modern Man of Science,* trans. M. Eden Paul (London: Bebman, 1911).

69. See, e.g., Haller, *Eugenics,* pp. 17–20, and Charles E. Rosenberg, *No Other Gods: On Science and American Social Thought* (Baltimore: Johns Hopkins University Press, 1976), p. 42.

70. On the intellectual, ideological, and professional conflicts between neurologists and alienists, see Charles E. Rosenberg, *The Trial of Assassin Guiteau: Psychiatry and Law in the Gilded Age* (Chicago: University of Chicago Press, 1968). On moral treatment, see Norman Dain, *Concepts of Insanity in the United States, 1789–1865* (New Brunswick, N.J.: Rutgers University Press, 1964). On the institutional aspects of the alienists' failure, see Gerald N. Grob, *Mental Institutions in America: Social Policy to 1875* (New York: Free Press, 1973) and "Rediscovering Asylums: The Unhistorical History of the Mental Hospital" in Morris J. Vogel and Charles E. Rosenberg, eds., *The Therapeutic Revolution: Essays in the Social History of American Medicine* (Philadelphia: University of Pennsylvania Press, 1979), pp. 135–57.

71. Horace W. Magoun, "Darwin and Concepts of Brain Function," in J. F. Delafresnaye, ed., *Brain Mechanisms and Learning* (Oxford: Blackwell, 1961), p. 17; Nathan G. Hale, Jr., *Freud and the Americans: The Beginnings of Psychoanalysis in the United States, 1876–1917* (New York: Oxford University Press, 1971), pp. 54, 56; Young, "Functions of the Brain," pp. 260–62; Rosenberg, *The Trial of Assassin Guiteau,* p. 247.

72. Haller, *Eugenics,* pp. 21–57; John Higham, *Strangers in the Land: Patterns of American Nativism, 1860–1925* (New Brunswick: Rutgers University Press, 1963), and Barbara Miller Solomon, *Ancestors and Immigrants: A Changing New England Tradition* (Cambridge: Harvard University Press, 1956), remain excellent standard accounts.

73. Haller, *Eugenics*, pp. 8–20; Ruth Schwartz Cowan, "Francis Galton's Statistical Ideas: The Influence of Eugenics," *Journal of the History of Biology* 5 (1972): 389–412; Higham, *Strangers in the Land*, pp. 135–36; John S. Haller, Jr., *Outcasts from Evolution: Scientific Attitudes of Racial Inferiority, 1859–1900* (New York: McGraw-Hill, 1975; first published by the University of Illinois Press, 1971).

74. William Stanton, *The Leopard's Spots: Scientific Attitudes Toward Race in America, 1815–1859* (Chicago: University of Chicago Press, 1960), pp. 20, 29, 35–38.

75. Heidbreder, *Seven Psychologies*; Robert S. Woodworth, *Contemporary Schools of Psychology* (New York: The Ronald Press, 1931). The quotation is from Boring, *HEP*, p. 460.

76. The fullest exposition of the new psychology is Hall, "The New Psychology," *Andover Review* 3 (1885): 120–35, 239–48. See also his "Philosophy in the United States," *Mind* 4 (1879): 89–105, esp. pp. 93–94, 104, 105.

77. See Gladys Bryson's trio of articles: "The Emergence of the Social Sciences from Moral Philosophy," *International Journal of Social Ethics* 42 (1932): 302–23; "The Comparable Interests of the Old Moral Philosophy and the Modern Social Sciences," *Social Forces* 11 (1932): 19–27; and "Sociology Considered as Moral Philosophy," *Sociological Review* 24 (1932): 26–36. On the search for an "inductive ethics," see David B. Potts, "Social Ethics at Harvard, 1881–1931: A Study in Academic Activism," in Paul Buck, ed., *Social Sciences at Harvard, 1860–1920: From Inculcation to Open Mind* (Cambridge: Harvard University Press, 1965), pp. 91–128.

78. William James, "The Teaching of Philosophy in Our Colleges," *Nation* 23 (1876): 178.

79. Brian Mackenzie, "Darwinism and Positivism as Methodological Influences on the Development of Psychology," *JHBS* 12 (1976): 330–37, 334.

80. One need only look at the first volume of Hall's *American Journal of Psychology* to appreciate the breadth of the new psychology's concerns. Other examples include Cattell, "Mental Tests and Measurements," *Mind* 15 (1890): 373–81; Cattell and Livingston Farrand, "Physical and Mental Measurements of the Students of Columbia University," *PR* 3 (1896): 618–48; J. Allan Gilbert, "Researches on the Mental and Physical Development of School Children," *Studies from the Yale Psychological Laboratory* 2 (1894): 40–100; Hall, "The Contents of Children's Minds," *Princeton Review* 11 (1883): 249–72; "Laura Bridgman," *Mind* 4 (1880): 149–72; "Laboratory of the McLean Hospital, Somerville, Massachusetts," *American Journal of Insanity* 51 (1895): 358–64; Linus Ward Kline, "Methods in Animal Psychology," *AJP* 10 (1899): 256–79; Hall, "Recent Researches on Hypnotism," *Mind* 6 (1881): 98–104; Ladd, "Contributions to the Psychology of Visual Dreams," *Mind*, n.s., 1 (1892): 299–304; Mary Calkins, "Statistics of Dreams," *AJP* 5 (1893): 311–43.

81. Herbert Nichols, "The Psychology Laboratory at Harvard," *McClure's* 1 (1893): 407.

82. James, "A Plea for Psychology as a 'Natural Science,' " p. 153.

CHAPTER 6

1. William James, "The Teaching of Philosophy in Our Colleges," *Nation* 23 (1876): 178.

2. Ibid.

3. This phenomenon—the relationship between professional advancement and conscription of scientific procedures and models—has been amply documented for such fields as medicine, psychiatry, political science, sociology, philosophy, agriculture, and social work. See William G. Rothstein, *American Physicians in the Nineteenth Century: From Sects to Science* (Baltimore: Johns Hopkins University Press, 1972); Charles E. Rosenberg, *The Trial of Assassin Guiteau: Psychiatry and Law in the Gilded Age* (Chicago: University of Chicago Press, 1968); Edward A. Purcell, Jr., *The Crisis of Democratic Theory: Scientific Naturalism and the Problem of Value* (Lexington: University of Kentucky Press, 1973); Thomas L. Haskell, *The Emergence of Professional Social Science: The American Social Science Association and the Nineteenth-Century Crisis of Authority* (Urbana: University of Illinois Press, 1977); Bruce Kuklick, *The Rise of American Philosophy: Cambridge, Massachusetts, 1860–1930* (New Haven: Yale University Press, 1977); Margaret W. Rossiter, *The Emergence of Agricultural Science: Justus Liebig and the Americans, 1840–1880* (New Haven: Yale University Press, 1975); Roy Lubove, *The Professional Altruist: The Emergence of Social Work as a Career* (Cambridge: Harvard University Press, 1965).

4. Robert A. McCaughey, "Transformation of American Academic Life: Harvard University, 1821–1892," *Perspectives in American History* 8 (1974): 243–55.

5. Ibid., pp. 254–74.

6. Richard Hofstadter, *Anti-Intellectualism in American Life* (New York: Knopf, 1963), pp. 145–71; Stow Persons, *The Decline of American Gentility* (New York: Columbia University Press, 1973), pp. 109–13, 179–202; Jurgen Herbst, *The German Historical School in American Scholarship* (Ithaca: Cornell University Press, 1965); Carl Diehl, *Americans and German Scholarship, 1770–1870* (New Haven: Yale University Press, 1978).

7. Haskell, *Emergence of Professional Social Science*, p. 65.

8. George H. Daniels, *Science in American Society: A Social History* (New York: Knopf, 1971), pp. 174–205; Charles E. Rosenberg, *The Cholera Years: The United States in 1832, 1849 and 1868* (Chicago: University of Chicago Press, 1962), esp. pp. 192–225; "Science, Technology, and Economic Growth: The Case of the Agricultural Experiment Station Scientist, 1875–1914," in George H. Daniels, ed., *Nineteenth-Century American Science, A Reappraisal* (Evanston, Il.: Northwestern University Press, 1972), pp. 181–209; Rossiter, *Emergence of Agricultural Science*.

9. Bruce, "A Statistical Profile of American Scientists, 1846–1876."

10. Haskell, *Emergence of Professional Social Science*, p. 68; George H. Daniels, *Science in the Age of Jackson* (New York: Columbia University Press, 1968), p. 34.

11. McCaughey, "Transformation of American Academic Life," pp. 266–67.

12. Quoted in ibid., p. 310.

13. James to Daniel Coit Gilman, 18 April 1881, quoted in Jackson I. Cope, "William James's Correspondence with Daniel Coit Gilman, 1877–1881," *Journal of the History of Ideas* 12 (1951): 627. See also James to G. Stanley Hall, 9 October [1909?], William James Papers, Houghton Library, Harvard University, Cambridge, Massachusetts.

14. In addition to Perry's intellectual biography, see Gay Wilson Allen, *William James* (New York: Random House, 1967).

15. George Fredrickson, *The Inner Civil War: Northern Intellectuals and the Crisis of the Union* (New York: Harper and Row, 1965), p. 175.

16. James, "Louis Agassiz," in *Memories and Studies* (London: Longmans, Green, 1911), p. 6; Perry, *TCWJ*, 1 : 208.

17. James to Thomas Ward, [12] September 1867, quoted in Perry, *TCWJ*, 1 : 244. See Robert J. Richards, "The Personal Equation in Science: William James's Psycho-

logical and Moral Uses of Darwinian Theory," *Harvard Library Bulletin* 30 (October 1983): 387–425.

18. Daniels, *Science in American Society*, pp. 171–72.

19. James to Holmes, 15 May 1868, quoted in Perry, *TCWJ*, 1 : 275–76.

20. James, diary entry, 10 April 1873, quoted in ibid., 1 : 343.

21. Ibid., 1 : 250.

22. James to Thomas Ward, 9 October [1868], quoted in ibid., 1 : 287.

23. James to Robert James, 27 January 1868, quoted in ibid., 1 : 259.

24. Quoted in ibid., 2 : 12.

25. James, diary entry, 10 February 1873, quoted in ibid., 1 : 335. Henry James, Sr., noted at the time that his son "has been shaking off his respect for men of mere science as such"; ibid., 1 : 339–40.

26. Ibid., 1 : 339–41, 343; Overseers' Report, 1 November 1873, p. 5, Harvard University Archives.

27. Perry, *TCWJ*, 2 : 10; Robert S. Harper, "That Early Laboratory of William James," MS copy, Harvard University Archives, pp. 12, 21; Sheldon Stern, "William James and the New Psychology," in Paul Buck, ed., *Social Sciences at Harvard, 1860–1920: From Inculcation to Open Mind* (Cambridge: Harvard University Press, 1965), pp. 182–86; James to D. C. Gilman, 23 April 1877, quoted in Cope, "Correspondence," p. 613.

28. Hugh Hawkins, *Between Harvard and America: The Educational Leadership of Charles W. Eliot* (New York: Oxford University Press, 1972), pp. 29–30, 33–36; Kuklick, *The Rise of American Philosophy*, pp. 129–39.

29. Eliot, "The New Education: Its Organization," *Atlantic Monthly* 23 (1869): 203–20, 358–67.

30. Ibid., p. 366.

31. Eliot, "Inaugural Address," in Samuel Eliot Morison, ed., *The Development of Harvard University Since the Inauguration of President Eliot, 1869–1929* (Cambridge: Harvard University Press, 1930), p. lx.

32. Eliot, "The New Education," p. 215.

33. Eliot, "Inaugural Address," p. lix; Richard Hofstadter and DeWitt Hardy, *The Development and Scope of Higher Education in the United States* (New York: Columbia University Press, 1955), pp. 98–99.

34. McCaughey, "Transformation of American Academic Life," pp. 274–78.

35. Eliot, "Inaugural Address," p. lxxiv.

36. Ibid., p. lxii.

37. McCaughey, "Transformation of American Academic Life," p. 284. Detailed analysis of the economic context of Harvard's plight can be found in Seymour E. Harris, *The Economics of Harvard* (New York: McGraw-Hill, 1970), pp. 39–66.

38. For a novelistic account of student attitudes toward collegiate philosophy during the period, see Owen Wister, *Philosophy 4: A Story of Harvard University* (New York: Macmillan, 1911).

39. Stern, "William James and the New Psychology," pp. 184, 186.

40. McCaughey, "Transformation of American Academic Life," pp. 245, 278–79, 282.

41. W. B. Cannon, "Henry Pickering Bowditch, 1840–1911," *Memoirs of the National Academy of Science* 17 (1924): 183–96; Perry, *TCWJ*, 1 : 249.

42. James to Eliot, 2 December 1895, quoted in Perry, *TCWJ*, 2 : 11.

43. Eliot, "Inaugural Address," pp. lxii, lx.

44. Eliot, The New Education," p. 367.

45. Eliot, "Inaugural Address," p. lxi. When in 1875 Charles Loring Jackson asked for relief time from teaching one class in order to conduct publishable investigations in organic chemistry, Eliot bluntly refused his request with the remark, "I can't see that that will serve any useful purpose here"; Henry James, *Charles W. Eliot: President of Harvard University, 1869–1909*, 2 vols. (Boston: Houghton Mifflin, 1930), 2 : 19. James understood Eliot's aims far better than his chemist colleague.

46. See, e.g., Eliot to James, 20 May 1894, quoted in ibid., 2 : 86–87.

47. James to Howison, 2 April 1894, quoted in Perry, *TCWJ*, 2 : 116–17; James, "The Teaching of Philosophy in Our Colleges," pp. 179, 178.

48. James to Eliot, 20 October 1889, Eliot Papers, Harvard University Archives.

49. Perry, *TCWJ*, 2 : 138–40, 144; Stern, "William James and the New Psychology," p. 222.

50. James to Ladd, 4 April 1888, in Ladd's unpublished autobiography; quoted in Eugene S. Mills, *George Trumbell Ladd: Pioneer American Psychologist* (Cleveland: The Press of Case Western Reserve University, 1969), p. 104. One must infer from Mills's preface that this 794-page manuscript remains in his personal possession; Ladd, *Elements of Physiological Psychology* (New York: Scribner's, 1887).

51. Titchener, "George Trumbell Ladd," *AJP* 32 (1921): 600.

52. Mills, *Ladd*, pp. 14–36.

53. Ladd, autobiography, in Mills, *Ladd*, pp. 42–43; Donald Scott, *From Office to Profession: The New England Ministry, 1750–1850* (Philadelphia: University of Pennsylvania Press, 1978).

54. Ladd, "The New Theology," *New Englander* 35 (1876): 660–94, 679.

55. Mills, *Ladd*, p. 64.

56. Ibid., p. 65.

57. See esp. Ladd, *The Unknown God of Herbert and the Promise and Potency of Professor Tyndall* (Milwaukee: Hauser, 1878); "Final Purpose in Nature," *New Englander* 38 (1879): 677–700.

58. Daniel Day Williams, *The Andover Liberals: A Study in American Theology* (New York: Columbia University Press, 1941).

59. George Peterson, *The New England College in the Age of the University* (Amherst, Ma.: Amherst College Press, 1964), p. 243.

60. Mills, *Ladd*, p. 81.

61. Joseph Blau, *Men and Movements in American Philosophy* (New York: Prentice-Hall, 1952), pp. 102–109; Herbert W. Schneider, *A History of American Philosophy* (New York: Columbia University Press, 1946), pp. 245–46; D. H. Meyer, *The Instructed Conscience: The Shaping of the American National Ethic* (Philadelphia: University of Pennsylvania Press, 1972), pp. 46, 4–6; Noah Porter, *The Human Intellect* (New York: Scribner's, 1868) and *Elements of Intellectual Science* (New York: Scribner's, 1871); Morris, "Friedrich Adolf Trendelenberg," *New Englander* 33 (1874): 287–336.

62. Porter, *The Human Intellect*, p. 662.

63. Schneider, *History of American Philosophy*, p. 246.

64. See Ladd's autobiographical account of his relationship with Porter and his reasons for studying psychology in Mills, *Ladd*, pp. 70–71.

65. Quoted in Mills, *Ladd*, p. 81.

66. Ladd, autobiography, in ibid., p. 102.

67. Ladd, *Elements of Physiological Psychology* (New York: Scribner's, 1887), p. iii.

68. Laurence Veysey, *The Emergence of the American University* (Chicago: University of Chicago Press, 1965), pp. 24, 50–51; Hugh Hawkins, "Three Presidents Testify," *American Quarterly* 11 (1959): 101.

69. C. W. Eliot to D. C. Gilman, 9 March 1880, quoted in Veysey, *Emergence*, p. 50.

CHAPTER 7

1. See Dorothy Ross, *G. Stanley Hall: The Psychologist as Prophet* (Chicago: University of Chicago Press, 1972), pp. 3–14.

2. Mark Hopkins, *Lectures on Moral Science* (Boston: Gould and Lincoln, 1862). See D. H. Meyer, *The Instructed Conscience: The Shaping of the American National Ethic* (Philadelphia: University of Pennsylvania Press, 1972), pp. 16–17.

3. Frederick Rudolph, *Mark Hopkins and the Log: Williams College, 1836–1872* (New Haven: Yale University Press, 1956), pp. 225–31.

4. Ross, *G. Stanley Hall*, p. 29; Thomas Le Duc, *Piety and Intellect at Amherst College, 1865–1929* (New York: Columbia University Press, 1946), pp. 14, 51–52, 85.

5. Ross, *G. Stanley Hall*, p. 33.

6. Ibid., pp. 34–35.

7. Ibid., pp. 35–49.

8. Ibid., pp. 50–61.

9. Hall, "College Instruction in Philosophy," *Nation* 23 (September, 1876): 180.

10. Ibid.

11. William James, "The Teaching of Philosophy in Our Colleges," *Nation*, 23 (September, 1876): 178.

12. James to D. C. Gilman, 23 April 1877, in Jackson I. Cope, "William James's Correspondence with Daniel Coit Gilman," *Journal of the History of Ideas* 12 (1951): 613–14.

13. Ross, *G. Stanley Hall*, pp. 70–72, 79–80.

14. Hugh Hawkins, *Pioneer: A History of the Johns Hopkins University, 1874–1889* (Ithaca: Cornell University Press, 1960), pp. 3–10.

15. Ibid., pp. 14–18; Laurence Veysey, *The Emergence of the American University* (Chicago: University of Chicago Press, 1965), p. 159; Abraham Flexner, *Daniel Coit Gilman: Creator of the American Type of University* (New York: Harcourt, Brace, 1946).

16. Albert Lanphier Hammond, "Brief History of the Department of Philosophy, 1876–1938" (Lanier Room, Eisenhower Library, Johns Hopkins University), p. 8.

17. Hugh Hawkins, *Pioneer*, p. 13; Hawkins "Three Presidents Testify," *American Quarterly* 11 (1959): 99–119.

18. Robert A. McCaughey, "The Transformation of American Academic Life: Harvard University, 1821–1892," *Perspectives in American History* 8 (1974): 289.

19. Frank M. Albrecht, Jr., "The New Psychology in America" (Ph.D. diss., Johns Hopkins University, 1960)," p. 79; Walter Rogers, *Andrew D. White and the Modern University* (Ithaca: Cornell University Press, 1942), p. 80; G. Stanley Hall, *Life and Confessions of a Psychologist* (New York: Appleton, 1923), p. 230.

20. Henry James, *Charles W. Eliot: President of Harvard University, 1869–1909*, 2 vols. (Boston: Houghton Mifflin, 1930), 2 : 14.

21. Ibid., 2 : 19–20; Hawkins, *Pioneer*, p. 77.

22. Hammond, "Brief History of the Department of Philosophy," p. 5.

23. Gilman, *The Launching of a University and Other Papers* (New York: Dodd, Mead, 1906), p. 20; Albrecht, "The New Psychology," p. 114.

24. Quoted in Veysey, *Emergence*, p. 50.

25. Quoted in Hawkins, *Pioneer*, pp. 70–71.

26. Quoted in Fabian Franklin, *The Life of Daniel Coit Gilman* (New York: Dodd, Mead, 1910), p. 221.

27. Gilman, *Launching of a University*, p. 23.

28. Hall, "Philosophy in the United States," *Mind* 4 (1879): 89–105, 96–97, 98.

29. Hawkins, *Pioneer*, p. 193; Ross, *G. Stanley Hall*, p. 135.

30. Hall to D. C. Gilman, 5 January [1881], quoted in Ross, *G. Stanley Hall*, pp. 138–39.

31. Hall to D. C. Gilman, 18 February [1879], quoted in Hawkins, *Pioneer*, p. 194.

32. James to D. C. Gilman, 18 February [1879], quoted in Cope, "Correspondence," p. 623.

33. James Eliot Cabot, e.g., spoke for Harvard's Overseers when he depreciated "the mere historical retailing of opinions"; see William Stern, "William James and the New Psychology" in Paul Buck, ed., *Social Sciences at Harvard, 1860–1920: From Inculcation to Open Mind* (Cambridge: Harvard University Press, 1965), p. 188.

34. Hall to Charles Eliot Norton, 3 February 1879, quoted in Ross, *G. Stanley Hall*, p. 79; Hall, *Life and Confessions*, p. 215.

35. Hall, *Life and Confessions*, p. 215; Ross, *G. Stanley Hall*, p. 106.

36. Ibid., pp. 112–13; Hawkins, *Pioneer*, p. 202; James to D. C. Gilman, 18 July 1880, quoted in Cope, "Correspondence," p. 624.

37. Peirce to D. C. Gilman and trustees, 8 February 1884, quoted in Hawkins, *Pioneer*, p. 196.

38. Max Fisch and Jackson I. Cope, "Peirce at the Johns Hopkins University," *Studies in the Philosophy of Charles Sanders Peirce*, 1st series, ed. Philip Wiener and Frederic H. Young (Cambridge: Harvard University Press, 1952), p. 285.

39. Gilman, "Annual Address to the University," *Johns Hopkins Circular* 4 (1885): 48–49.

40. Hall, "The New Psychology," *Andover Review* 3 (1885): 120–35, 239–48.

41. Ibid., pp. 125, 127.

42. E. A. Andres, "William Keith Brooks," *Science* 28 (1908): 777–86; Ross, *G. Stanley Hall*, p. 153; Hawkins, *Pioneer*, pp. 144–45. For the pervasiveness of "biologism" at Hopkins, see ibid., pp. 300–303.

43. Hall, "The New Psychology," pp. 121–22, 126, 128.

44. Ibid., p. 122.

45. Peirce, "Questions Concerning Certain Faculties Claimed for Man," *Journal of Speculative Philosophy* 2 (1868): 103–14; reprinted in Philip P. Wiener, ed., *Charles S. Peirce: Selected Writings* (New York: Dover, 1958), pp. 15–38, esp. p. 33. Peirce repeated this claim at Hopkins; see *Johns Hopkins Circular* 1 (1879–82): 18.

46. Peirce, "The Fixation of Belief," *Popular Science Monthly* 12 (1877): 1–15; reprinted in Weiner, ed., *Charles S. Peirce*, pp. 91–112; Peirce to D. C. Gilman, 13 September 1877, quoted in Cope, "Correspondence," p. 615.

47. Hall, "The New Psychology," p. 133.

48. Hall, *Aspects of German Culture* (Boston: Osgood, 1881), p. 297.

49. Hall, "The New Psychology," pp. 123–24, 126.

50. Ibid., pp. 129, 130. For an example of what Joseph Blau, in his *Men and Move-*

ments in American Philosophy (New York: Prentice–Hall, 1952), p. 102, calls "the psychologizing of philosophy," see Dewey, "The Psychological Standpoint," *Mind* 11 (1886): 1–19, and "Psychology as Philosophic Method," ibid., pp. 153–73.

51. Veysey, *Emergence*, pp. 57–251.

52. Hawkins, *Pioneer*, p. 295; David Hollinger, "American Cultural Critics and the Search for a Scientific Conscience: From Andrew Dickson White to Robert K. Merton" (Paper delivered at the first annual meeting of the Social Science History Association, University of Pennsylvania, 1976), pp. 9–10.

53. Hall, "Research—The Vital Spirit of Teaching," *Forum* 17 (1894): 558–70.

54. Mary W. Calkins, "Experimental Psychology at Wellesley," *AJP* 5 (1892): 127–28; Hall, "Psychology in American Colleges and Universities," *AJP* 3 (1890): 275–86; H. K. Wolfe, "The New Psychology in the Undergraduate Work," *PR* 2 (1895): 382–87.

55. Hall, "The New Psychology as a Basis of Education," *Forum* 17 (1894): 713.

56. J. M. Baldwin, *Between Two Wars (1861–1921)* (Boston: The Stratford Co., 1926), 2 vols, 1 : 62–63.

57. Ladd, *Essays on Higher Education* (New York: Scribner's, 1899), pp. 25, 81–82, 131–32.

58. James to C. W. Eliot, 2 December 1875, quoted in Perry, *TCWJ*, 1 : 11; Hall, "Psychological Literature," *AJP* 1 (1887): 162–64; Ladd to Hall, 30 November 1887, G. Stanley Hall Papers, Clark University Archives, Goddard Library, Worcester, Massachusetts.

59. See, e.g., William O. Krohn, "Facilities in Experimental Psychology in the Colleges of the United States," *Report of the Commissioner of Education, 1890–1891* (Washington, D.C., 1892), p. 1151.

60. Ross, *G. Stanley Hall*, pp. 155–57; Seashore, *HPA* 1 (1930): 248.

61. Ross (*G. Stanley Hall*, p. 187) considers Jastrow an experimentalist, but he was contemporarily regarded as a popularizer, advocate of applied psychology, and disciplinary interpreter of Freudianism. He claimed that the professor "must teach and preach, talk and write, lead and cooperate, invent and apply, go in for research and popularity all at once" ("An American Academician," *Educational Review* 41 [1911]: 29). His own career was much akin to Hall's. The other Americans were Patrick, Dewey, and J. H. Hyslop—philosophers all—and W. H. Burnham, who specialized in pedagogy and mental hygiene.

62. This pattern persisted into the twentieth century. In 1906 the APA Council recommended the ouster of any member who had not been engaged in active research for a period of five years or more; Samuel W. Fernberger, "The American Psychological Association: A Historical Summary, 1892–1930," *PB* 29 (1932): 23. The move was unsuccessful.

63. Charles E. Rosenberg, *No Other Gods: On Science and American Social Thought* (Baltimore: Johns Hopkins University Press, 1976), p. 15; George H. Daniels, *Science in American Society: A Social History* (New York: Knopf, 1971), p. 274.

64. Cattell, "Address of the President Before the American Psychological Association, 1895," *PR* 3 (1896): 148.

65. Veysey, *Emergence*, pp. 77–78, 156; Daniels, *Science in American Society*, p. 275; Robert Wiebe, *The Search for Order, 1877–1920* (New York: Hill and Wang, 1967), p. 129; Howard S. Miller, *Dollars for Research: Science and Its Patrons in Nineteenth-Century America* (Seattle: University of Washington Press, 1970), pp. 181–84; James, "The

Teaching of Philosophy," p. 178; Hall to James, 15 February 1880, William James Papers, Houghton Library, Harvard University, Cambridge, Massachusetts.

66. For a typical example of the problems researchers encountered at small colleges, see Raymond Dodge, *HPA*, 1 (1930): 107–8.

67. Sanford's official status was recognized only in 1892.

68. Quoted in Veysey, *Emergence*, p. 159.

69. Franklin, *The Life of Daniel Coit Gilman*, pp. 122–59; Hawkins, *Pioneer*, p. 19; Veysey, *Emergence*, p. 160.

70. Quoted in ibid., p. 159.

71. Hall, "The University Idea," *Pedagogical Seminary* 15 (1908): 104; "Some Possible Effects of the War on American Psychology," *PB* 16 (1919): 48.

72. Hall, "The New Psychology," p. 127.

73. Ibid., p. 128; Ross, *G. Stanley Hall*, pp. 159–61.

74. Hall, "The New Psychology," p. 128.

75. Albrecht, "The New Psychology," pp. 122–23.

76. Ross, *G. Stanley Hall*, p. 159.

77. Hall, "The New Psychology," p. 248; *Johns Hopkins University Circular* 6 (1887): 114.

CHAPTER 8

1. Donald H. Meyer has applied the term "scientific humanism" to Hall's effort to bring science to the rescue of a traditional mental and moral philosophy which focused roundly on human nature, assumed that the human mind possessed moral attributes, and insisted that psychology should include the study of values; "The Scientific Humanism of G. Stanley Hall," *Journal of Humanistic Psychology* 11 (1971): 201–13. The designation consistently suits James and Ladd.

2. Ralph Barton Perry, "Psychology," in Samuel E. Morison, ed., *The Development of Harvard University Since the Inauguration of President Eliot, 1869–1929* (Cambridge: Harvard University Press, 1930), p. 216; J. M. Baldwin, "Psychology Past and Present," *PR* 1 (1894): 381–82; James McKeen Cattell, "Address of the President Before the American Psychological Association, 1895," *PR* 3 (1896): 146.

3. Angell, *HPA*, 3 (1930): 25; Boring, *HEP*, p. 529; Pillsbury, "The Psychology of Edward Bradford Titchener," *Philosophical Review* 37 (1928): 107.

4. Baldwin, *Between Two Wars*, 1 : 77.

5. Robert M. Yerkes, "Psychology in Its Relations to Biology," *JPPSM* 7 (1910): 113–24.

6. James, *Principles of Psychology*, 2 vols; (New York, Holt, 1890); Ladd, "Psychology as So-Called 'Natural Science,' " *Philosophical Review* 1 (1892): 24–53.

7. Hall, "Review of William James's *Principles of Psychology*," *AJP* 3 (1890): 589, 585–87, 591.

8. Ladd, "Psychology as So-Called 'Natural Science,' " pp. 31, 51–52.

9. Ladd, "Is Psychology a Science?" *PR* 1 (1894): 393.

10. William James, "A Plea for Psychology as a 'Natural Science,' " *Philosophical Review* 1 (1892): 146.

11. James, *Principles of Psychology*, 1 : 182.

12. James, "Plea for Psychology," pp. 151, 152.

13. Ibid., p. 153.

14. Ladd, "Is Psychology a Science?" p. 395.

15. Ladd, "President's Address Before the New York Meeting of the American Psychological Association," *PR* 1 (1894): 2, 5.

16. Ladd, *Elements of Physiological Psychology* (New York: Scribner's, 1887), p. 1; Ladd, "President's Address," p. 6.

17. James, *Psychology: Briefer Course* (New York: Holt, 1892), p. 1; *Principles of Psychology*, 1 : 185, 182.

18. James, "Plea for Psychology," p. 149.

19. Ladd, *Philosophy of Mind: An Essay in the Metaphysics of Psychology* (New York: Scribner's, 1895), pp. x, 5–6, 344.

20. Ibid., p. 17; "President's Address," p. 6. The hortatory tone of Ladd's pronouncements suggests that his conception was already under attack.

21. James, "Plea for Psychology," p. 149.

22. Ibid., pp. 147–48.

23. Ibid., p. 148. Cf. James McKeen Cattell's statement a decade later: "I see no reason why the application of a systematized knowledge to the control of human nature may not in the course of the present century accomplish results commensurate with the nineteenth century applications of physical science to the material world"; "Conceptions and Methods of Psychology," *Popular Science Monthly* 66 (1904): 186.

24. James, "Plea for Psychology," p. 148.

25. Ibid., pp. 148–50. See also [Hall], "Psychological Literature," *AJP* 1 (1887): 162–64.

26. James, "Plea for Psychology," pp. 149, 153.

27. Daniels, *Science in American Society: A Social History* (New York: Knopf, 1971), p. 275; Rosenberg, *No Other Gods: On Science and American Social Thought* (Baltimore: Johns Hopkins University Press, 1976), p. 18.

28. Laurence Veysey, *The Emergence of the American University*. (Chicago: University of Chicago Press, 1965), pp. 138–39.

29. Ladd, "The Essentials of a Modern Liberal Education," *Educational Review* 10 (1895): 237–38.

30. Ladd, "President's Address," p. 18.

31. Ibid., p. 11.

32. Cattell, "Progress of Psychology," in Albert T. Poffenberger, ed., *James McKeen Cattell: Man of Science*, 2 vols. (Lancaster, Pa.: Science Press, 1947) 2 : 49–50; Ladd, "President's Address," p. 19.

33. Ladd, "President's Address," pp. 7, 21; Cattell, "Progress of Psychology," p. 51.

34. Titchener, "The Past Decade in Experimental Psychology," *Lectures and Addresses Delivered Before the Departments of Psychology and Pedagogy in Celebration of the Twentieth Anniversary of the Opening of Clark University, September, 1909* (Worcester, Mass.: Clark University, 1910), pp. 160–62.

35. Münsterberg, "Psychology and Education," *Educational Review* 16 (1898): 117.

36. Scripture, "Methods of Laboratory Mind-Study," *Forum* 17 (1894): 728.

37. Cattell, "Conceptions and Methods," p. 185.

38. This political transformation has been examined in the voluminous literature of political history that stemmed from two seminal works: Eric F. Goldman, *Rendezvous with Destiny: A History of Modern American Reform* (New York: Knopf, 1952), and Richard Hofstadter, *The Age of Reform* (New York: Knopf, 1955). For the occurrence of this shift within the American scientific community in general, see Ronald C. Tobey, *The*

American Ideology of National Science, 1919–1930 (Pittsburgh: University of Pittsburgh Press, 1971), esp. pp. 3–19. For psychology in particular, see John C. Burnham, "Psychiatry, Psychology and the Progressive Movement," *American Quarterly* 12 (1960): 457–65. For an account of this transformation occurring within philosophy, psychology's sponsor, see David W. Noble, *The Paradox of Progressive Thought* (Minneapolis: University of Minnesota Press, 1958); within education, psychology's newer patron, see Raymond E. Callahan, *Education and the Cult of Efficiency* (Chicago: University of Chicago Press, 1962). In every case, this shift was under way in the 1890s.

39. Bryan, "A Plea for Special Child Study," *Proceedings of the International Congress of Education, 1893* (New York: Little and Co., 1894), p. 778.

40. Cattell, "Address, of the President," p. 144; Lloyd, "Some Unscientific Reflections About Science," *PR* 8 (1901): 175; Dewey, "Psychology and Social Practice," *PR* 7 (1900): 119.

41. Robert S. Harper, "Tables of American Doctorates in Psychology," *AJP* 62 (1949): 580–81; Frank M. Albrecht, Jr., "The New Psychology in America," (Ph.D. diss., Johns Hopkins University, 1960), p. 154; Thaddeus Bolton to E. C. Sanford, 26 April 1924, G. Stanley Hall Papers, Goddard Library, Clark University, Worcester, Massachusetts.

42. Dorothy Ross, *G. Stanley Hall: The Psychologist as Prophet* (Chicago: University of Chicago Press, 1972), p. 167.

43. Jastrow claimed that the *Journal's* highly technical nature was deliberately intended "to frighten off the dilettante psychologists who regard the possession of a mind as a sufficient stock in trade for pursuing their calling"; *Christian Union*, 15 March 1888; see also ibid., 24 November 1887.

44. Ladd, "President's Address," p. 19; James to Croom Robertson, 9 November 1887, in Perry, *TCWJ*, 2 : 85.

45. Hugh Hawkins, *Pioneer: A History of the Johns Hopkins University, 1874–1889* (Ithaca: Cornell University Press, 1960), pp. 109–10; Ross, *G. Stanley Hall*, p. 179.

46. Hall to D. C. Gilman, draft, 13 March 1888, Hall Papers.

47. Veysey, *Emergence*, pp. 165–67; Ross, *G. Stanley Hall*, pp. 186–219.

48. Hall, *Life and Confessions of a Psychologist* (New York: Appleton, 1923), pp. 295–97; Ross, *G. Stanley Hall*, pp. 220–30.

49. Ross, *G. Stanley Hall*, pp. 279–81; Joseph F. Kett, "Science and Sentiment: The American Child Study Movement, 1880–1910" (Paper delivered before the Organization of American Historians, April 1970); Charles E. Strickland, "The Child and the Race: The Doctrine of Recapitulation and Culture Epochs in the Rise of the Child-Centered Ideal in American Educational Thought, 1875–1900" (Ph.D. diss., University of Wisconsin, 1963).

50. Cursory accounts of the APA's formation can be found in [Jastrow], "The American Psychological Association," *Science* 20 (1892): 104; [Cattell], *Proceedings of the American Psychological Association* (New York: Macmillan, 1894), pp. 1–2; Cattell, "Our Psychological Association and Research," *Science* 45 (1917): 275–84; Samuel W. Fernberger, "The American Psychological Association, 1892–1942," *PR* 50 (1943): 33–60; Wayne Dennis and Edwin C. Boring, "The Founding of the APA," *American Psychologist* 7 (1952): 95–97.

51. Fernberger, "The American Psychological Association: A Historical Summary, 1892–1930," *PB* 29 (1932): 22.

52. The papers are abstracted in [Cattell], *Proceedings*, a twenty-nine-page pamphlet

that has been reproduced with an introduction by Michael M. Sokal in *American Psychologist* 28 (1973): 277–92. Subsequent references will use the original pagination preserved in the reproduction.

53. Cattell, *Proceedings*, pp. 3–4.

54. Ibid., pp. 6–7.

55. Ibid., p. 8. See also Jastrow, "The Section of Psychology," in *World's Columbian Exposition: Official Catalog*, pt. 12 (Chicago, 1893), pp. 50–60, and Baldwin, "Psychology Past and Present," pp. 377–81, for full descriptions of the purposes of the exhibit.

56. Cattell, *Proceedings*, pp. 4–5, 10.

57. Ibid., p. 11. This is essentially the stance Ladd took in his presidential address the following year and that Cattell attacked in his address two years later.

58. Ibid.

59. Woodworth, *HPA*, 2 (1932): 379.

60. Fullerton, "Psychology and Physiology," *PR* 3 (1896): 2.

61. Scripture, "The Problem of Psychology," *Mind* 16 (1891): 308–9.

62. Cattell, "Progress of Psychology," p. 49.

63. Münsterberg, "Danger from Experimental Psychology," *Atlantic Monthly* 81 (1898): 159–67; Münsterberg to C. W. Eliot, 1 March 1903, Charles W. Eliot Papers, Harvard University Archives, Cambridge, Massachusetts.

64. Cattell, *Proceedings*, p. 8.

65. Perry, "Psychology," in Morison, ed., *Development of Harvard*, p. 216.

66. Knight Dunlap, *HPA*, 2 (1932): 42.

67. Seashore, *Pioneering in Psychology* (Iowa City: University of Iowa, 1942), p. 8; *HPA*, 1 (1930): 260.

68. Dunlap, *HPA*, 2 (1932): 42. Dunlap, ibid., p. 41, relates Münsterberg's admiration of his ability to "tinker," thus reflecting one difference between the first and second generations of experimentalists. Inspecting a pendulum Dunlap had constructed, his director declared, "I could write a book of 300 pages easier than I could make that"—a claim he verified almost annually. Like gentlemen, philosophers did not work with their hands.

69. Seashore, *Pioneering in Psychology*, pp. 11–13; Ladd, *Elements of Physiological Psychology* (New York: Scribner's, 1887).

70. See, e.g., Dunlap, *HPA*, 2 (1932): 35; Lewis Terman, ibid., p. 302; R. S. Woodworth, ibid., p. 361; R. M. Yerkes, ibid., p. 385; H. H. Carr, *HPA*, 3 (1936): 70; E. L. Thorndike, ibid., p. 265.

71. Dunlap, *HPA* 2 (1932): 40–41.

72. Watson, *HPA*, 3 (1936): 274.

73. Audrey B. Davis and Uta C. Merzbach, *Early Auditory Studies: Activities in the Psychological Laboratories of American Universities* (Washington, D.C.: Smithsonian Institution, 1973), pp. 4–10; Robert C. Davis, "The Brass Age of Psychology," *Technology and Culture* 11 (1970): 604–12.

74. Scripture, "Accurate Work in Psychology," *AJP* 6 (1894): 427–30.

75. Woodworth, *HPA*, 2 (1932): 370.

76. See, e.g., Lightner Witmer, *Analytical Psychology* (Boston: Ginn, 1902), p. 108.

77. Münsterberg, in Cattell, *Proceedings*, p. 11.

78. Seashore, *HPA*, 1 (1930): 261–62; Albrecht, "The New Psychology," p. 152.

79. Carr, *HPA*, 3 (1936): 73.

80. Angell, ibid., p. 30; Seashore, ibid., pp. 231, 264; Edward Franklin Buchner, "A Quarter Century of Psychology in America: 1878–1903," *AJP* 14 (1903): 414.

81. Tolman, *HPA*, 4 (1952): 323.

82. Baldwin, "Psychology Past and Present," p. 382.

83. Münsterberg, in Cattell, *Proceedings*, p. 11.

84. James McKeen Cattell, "Mental Tests and Measurements" *Mind* 15 (1890): 373–81; Cattell and Farrand, "Physical and Mental Measurements of the Students of Columbia University," *PR* 3 (1896): 618–47; Sokal, "The Education and Psychological Career of James McKeen Cattell, 1860–1904" (Ph.D. diss., Case Western Reserve University, 1972), pp. 477–81; Geraldine Joncich, *The Sane Positivist: A Biography of Edward L. Thorndike* (Middletown, Conn.: Wesleyan University Press, 1968) pp. 113–16, 220–22.

85. John Dewey and James Alexander McLellan, *Applied Psychology: An Introduction to the Principles and Practice of Education* (Boston and New York: Educational Publishing Co., 1889). The best account of Dewey's early career is Neil Couglan, *Young John Dewey: An Essay in American Intellectual History* (Chicago: University of Chicago Press, 1975). See also George Dykhuizen, *The Life and Mind of John Dewey* (Carbondale: Southern Illinois University Press, 1973), and Darnell Rucker, *The Chicago Pragmatists* (Minneapolis: University of Minnesota Press, 1969).

86. Jastrow, *HPA*, 1 (1930): 142; "The Statistical Study of Mental Development," *Transactions of the Illinois Society of Child-Study* 2 (1897): 100–108; Bagley, "On the Correlation of Mental and Motor Abilities in School Children," *AJP* 12 (1901): 193–205. Bagley collaborated with S. S. Colvin on one of the first "behavioristic" textbooks in educational psychology, *Human Behavior: A First Book in Psychology for Teachers* (New York: Macmillan, 1913).

87. Seashore, *Pioneering in Psychology*, pp. 6–8; Gilbert, "Experiments on the Muscular Sensitiveness of School Children," *Studies from the Yale Psychological Laboratory* 1 (1893): 80–87; "Researches upon School Children and College Students," *University of Iowa Studies in Psychology* 1 (1897): 1–39.

88. Albert Fishlow, "Levels of Nineteenth-Century American Investment in Education," *Journal of Economic History* 26 (1966): 418–36; Jason R. Robarts, "The Quest for a Science of Education in the Nineteenth Century," *History of Education Quarterly* 8 (1968): 431–46.

89. E. F. Buchner, "Ten Years of American Psychology, 1892–1902," *Science* 18 (1903): 238; Ross, *G. Stanley Hall*, p. 282.

90. Cattell, "Address of the President," p. 144.

91. Witmer, "The Organization of Practical Work in Psychology," *PR* 4 (1897): 116–17; "Practical Work in Psychology," *Pediatrics* 2 (1896): 462–71.

92. John M. O'Donnell, "The Clinical Psychology of Lightner Witmer: A Case Study of Institutional Innovation and Intellectual Change," *JHBS* 15 (1979): 3–17.

93. See the APA Clinical Section's "Guide to the Psychological Clinics in the United States," reprinted in *Psychological Clinic* 23 (1935): 9–140; Theodate L. Smith, "The Development of Psychological Clinics in the United States," *Pedagogical Seminary* 21 (1914): 143–53.

94. Joncich, *The Sane Positivist*, pp. 173, 177–81; Arthur G. Powell, "Speculations on the Early Impact of Schools of Education on Educational Psychology," *History of Education Quarterly* 11 (1971): 406–12.

95. These data have been extrapolated from William E. Story and Louis N. Wilson,

eds., *Clark University, 1889–1899: Decennial Celebration* (Worcester, Mass.: Norwood, 1899). The staff, fellows, and scholars of the departments of psychology and pedagogy are listed on pp. 119–22, and their curricula vitae can be found on pp. 459–584.

96. Henry J. Perkinson, *The Imperfect Panacea: American Faith in Education, 1865–1965* (New York: Random House, 1968).

97. Harper, "Tables" pp. 580–81. Sufficient numbers of Clark doctorates were nonexperimental.

98. James to Howison, 2 April 1894, in Perry, *TCWJ*, 2 : 116; Seashore, *HPA*, 1 (1930): 253; Pillsbury, *HPA*, 2 (1932): 271; Raphelson, "Psychology at the University of Michigan, Volume I: History of the Department of Psychology, 1852–1950," p. 12; Raphelson Papers, Archives of the History of American Psychology.

99. Seashore, *Pioneering in Psychology*, p. 16; *HPA*, 1 (1930): 262.

100. Pillsbury's activity exemplifies the first motive; see Raphelson, "Psychology at Michigan," p. 16. The second motive is exhibited at almost every state and midwestern university; see, e.g., Darnell Rucker, *The Chicago Pragmatists* (Minneapolis: University of Minnesota Press, 1969), pp. 4–5, 83–85. Witmer at Pennsylvania represents the third motive; see O'Donnell, "The Clinical Psychology of Lightner Witmer," p. 8.

101. Carr, *HPA*, 3 (1936): 73.

102. Baldwin, Cattell, and Jastrow, "Physical and Mental Tests," *PR* 5 (1898): 172–79; Sanford, "The Philadelphia Meeting of the American Psychological Association," *Science* 3 (1896): 119–21; Baldwin et al., "Preliminary Report of the Committee on Physical and Mental Tests," *Science* 5 (1897): 211–14; Münsterberg, "Danger from Experimental Psychology," *Atlantic Monthly* 81 (1898): 159–67; Münsterberg, "The New Psychology," in *The Old Psychology and the New*, ed. L. Dunton (Boston: New England Publishing Co., 1895), pp. 14–15.

103. Jastrow, "Some Currents and Undercurrents in Psychology," *PR* 8 (1901): 24. Other specific rebuttals of Münsterberg's viewpoint include Cattell, "Professor Münsterberg on 'The Danger from Experimental Psychology,'" *PR* 5 (1898): 411–13; Thorndike, "What Is a Psychical Fact?" ibid., pp. 645–50; Dewey, "Psychology and Social Practice," *PR* 7 (1900): 105–24.

104. Scripture, "Methods of Laboratory Mind-Study," pp. 724–25; Bryan and N. Harter, "Studies in the Physiology and Psychology of the Telegraphic Language," *PR* 4 (1897): 27–53; "Studies on the Telegraphic Language; the Acquisition of a Hierarchy of Habits," *PR* 6 (1899): 346–75; Witmer, "The Psychological Clinic," *Old Penn* 8 (1909): 100; Seashore, *Pioneering in Psychology*, p. 16.

105. Bentley, *HPA*, 3 (1936): 63.

106. Jerome S. Bruner and Gordon W. Allport, "Fifty Years of Change in American Psychology," *PR* 37 (1940): 757–76, esp. 764–65. In this most exhaustive and sophisticated content analysis of psychological literature, the publications from the year 1888 were added to those of 1898 in order to procure a larger sample. This addition would suppress the percentages for the categories "application" and "child subjects," which would have been underrepresented in 1888.

107. Cattell, "Address of the President," p. 134.

108. A. C. Armstrong, Jr., "Philosophy in American Colleges," *Educational Review* 13 (1897): 10–22.

CHAPTER 9

1. Boring, *HEP*, p. 506; Robert M. Young, "The Functions of the Brain: Gall to Ferrier (1808–1886)," *Isis* 59 (1968): 254.

2. James R. Angell, "The Province of Functional Psychology," *PR* 14 (1907): 70.

3. Robert E. Grinder, *A History of Genetic Psychology: The First Science of Human Development* (New York: Wiley, 1967); Erika Apfelbaum, "Prolegomena for a History of Social Psychology: Some Hypotheses Concerning Its Emergence in the 20th Century and Its Raison d'Etre" (Paper presented at the tenth annual meeting of Cheiron, Wellesley College, Wellesley, Massachusetts, June 1978).

4. Boring, *HEP*, pp. 447–48.

5. Hall, "The New Psychology," *Andover Review* 3 (1885): 123.

6. Hall, *Life and Confessions of a Psychologist* (New York: Appleton, 1923), pp. 363–65.

7. Henry Drummond, *The Ascent of Man* (New York: Pott, 1894); G. J. Romanes, *Mental Evolution in Animals* (New York: Appleton, 1884); *Mental Evolution in Man* (New York: Appleton, 1889); Dorothy Ross, *G. Stanley Hall: The Psychologist as Prophet* (Chicago: University of Chicago Press, 1972), p. 262.

8. Hall, "Editorial," *AJP* 7 (1896): 8; "Modern Methods in the Study of the Soul," *Christian Register* 75 (1896): 131–33, and cited in Ross, *G. Stanley Hall*, p. 263.

9. [Hall], "Historical Sketch of the Work in General Psychology," and supplementary remarks, in William E. Story and Louis N. Wilson, eds., *Clark University, 1889–1899: Decennial Celebration* (Worcester, Mass.: Norwood, 1899), pp. 122–47.

10. Ibid., pp. 141–42.

11. Ibid.

12. Ibid., pp. 139–40.

13. For an able discussion of this episode, which led to the creation of the *Psychological Review*, see Ross, *G. Stanley Hall*, pp. 235–42.

14. Terman, *HPA*, 2 (1932): 314, 317–18.

15. Taber to W. B. Pillsbury, 12 May 1914, Walter B. Pillsbury Collection, Bentley Historical Library, University of Michigan, Ann Arbor.

16. Hall to Martin L. Reymert, 21 July 1919, G. Stanley Hall Papers, Goddard Library, Clark University, Worcester, Massachusetts.

17. Hall, "Historical Sketch," p. 141.

18. Grinder, *History of Genetic Psychology*, p. 206.

19. E. B. Titchener to J. McK. Cattell, 31 July 1903, James McKeen Cattell Papers, Manuscript Division, Library of Congress, Washington, D.C.

20. Geraldine Joncich, *The Sane Positivist: A Biography of Edward L. Thorndike* (Middletown Conn.: Wesleyan University Press, 1968), p. 98.

21. Charles E. Strickland, "The Child and the Race: The Doctrine of Recapitulation and Culture Epochs in the Rise of the Child-Centered Ideal in American Educational Thought, 1875–1900," (Ph.D. diss.: University of Wisconsin, 1963).

22. Morgan, *Introduction to Comparative Psychology* (London: Scott, 1894); Boring, *HEP*, p. 475; Robert Thomson, *The Pelican History of Psychology*, pp. 119–22.

23. W. S. Small, "Experimental Studies of the Mental Processes of the Rat," *AJP* 11 (1900): 133–65; 12 (1901): 205–39; L. W. Kline, "Suggestions toward a Laboratory Course in Comparative Psychology," *AJP* 10 (1899): 399–430; A. J. Kinnamon, "Mental Life of Two *Macacus Rhesus* Monkeys in Captivity," *AJP* 13 (1902): 98–148, 173–218; J. P. Porter, "The Habits, Instincts, and Mental Processes of Spiders . . . ," *AJP* 17 (1906):

306–57; H. B. Davis, "The Raccoon: A Study in Animal Intelligence," *AJP* 18 (1907): 447–89; E. J. Swift, "Studies in the Psychology and Physiology of Learning," *AJP* 14 (1903): 201–51; L. Ellison, "Consciousness in Relation to Learning," *AJP* 22 (1911): 158–213.

24. George W. Stocking, Jr., "Lamarckianism in American Social Science, 1890–1915," in *Race, Culture, and Evolution: Essays in the History of Anthropology* (New York: The Free Press, 1968), pp. 234–69, esp. pp. 254–55; Waldo Shumway, "The Recapitulation Theory," *Quarterly Review of Biology* 7 (1932): 93–99.

25. Ross, *G. Stanley Hall*, p. 350.

26. Hall to William A. White, 11 December 1912, Hall Papers.

27. Sully, *Outlines of Psychology: With Special Reference to the Theory of Education* (New York: Appleton, 1884).

28. Thorndike, *HPA*, 3 (1936): 263–65; Joncich, *The Sane Positivist*, pp. 72–75, 97–98, 103.

29. Thorndike, *HPA*, 3 (1936): 265; "Animal Intelligence: An Experimental Study of the Associative Processes in Animals," *PR, Monograph Supplements* 2 (1898); Joncich, *The Sane Positivist*, pp. 74–75.

30. Pavlov, *Lectures on Conditioned Reflexes* (New York: International Publishers, 1923; first published in Petrograd, 1923), preface.

31. Baldwin, *Mental Development in the Child and the Race* (New York: Macmillan, 1895).

32. Fay Berger Karpf, *American Social Psychology: Its Origins, Development, and European Background* (New York: McGraw-Hill, 1932); Vahan D. Sewny, *The Social Theory of James Mark Baldwin* (New York: Kings Crown, 1945).

33. James Mark Baldwin, *HPA*, 1 (1930): 1–4; *Between Two Wars (1861–1921)* (Boston: The Stratford Co., 1926), 1 : 21, 40 and passim.

34. Baldwin, "Psychology Past and Present," *PR* 1 (1894): 367–68; *Handbook of Psychology*, 2 vols. (New York: Holt, 1889, 1891).

35. Ibid., p. 368.

36. Baldwin, "Types of Reaction," *PR* 2 (1895): 259–73.

37. Boring, *HEP*, pp. 413–14, 436.

38. Madison Bentley, *HPA*, 1 (1930): 54.

39. Baldwin, *HPA*, 1 (1930): 4.

40. Quoted in Henry James, ed., *The Letters of William James*, 2 vols. (Boston: Atlantic Monthly Press, 1920), 2 : 54.

41. Baldwin, *Mental Development*, p. 2.

42. Baldwin, "Consciousness and Evolution," *Science* 2 (1895): 219–23; "Physical and Social Heredity," *American Naturalist* 30 (1896): 422–28; *Development and Evolution* (New York: Macmillan, 1902).

43. Baldwin, *HPA*, 1 (1930) : 6; *Development and Evolution*, appendix A.

44. R. Jackson Wilson, *In Quest of Community: Social Philosophy in The United States, 1860–1920* (New York: Wiley and Sons, 1968), p. 72.

45. Baldwin to H. B. Fine, 20 September 1903, quoted in *Between the Wars*, 2 : 256–57.

46. Baldwin, "History of Psychology," *PR* 12 (1905): 159.

47. J. B. Watson in mimeographed *Journal of the Psychology Club*, 1st number (May 1950), in John B. Watson Papers, Library of Congress.

48. James, "The Chicago School," *PB* 1 (1904): 1.

49. Darnell Rucker, *The Chicago Pragmatists* (Minneapolis: University of Minnesota,

1969). An excellent account of Chicago functionalism is in Edna Heidbreder, *Seven Psychologies* (New York: Century, 1933), pp. 201–33.

50. For intellectual and institutional background, see Rucker, *Chicago Pragmatists;* Neil Coughlan, *Young John Dewey: An Essay in American Intellectual History* (Chicago: University of Chicago Press, 1975); Alfred C. Raphelson, "The Pre-Chicago Association of the Early Functionalists," *JHBS* 9 (1973): 115–22; Morton G. White, *The Origin of Dewey's Instrumentalism* (New York: Columbia University Press, 1943); and John M. O'Donnell, "The Origins of Behaviorism: American Psychology, 1870–1920" (Ph.D. diss., University of Pennsylvania, 1979), pp. 444–53.

51. Quoted in Rucker, *Chicago Pragmatists*, p. 30.

52. Angell and Moore, "Reaction-Time: A Study in Attention and Habit," *PR* 3 (1896): 245–58.

53. A. A. Roback, *A History of American Psychology*, rev. ed. (New York: Collier, 1964), p. 240.

54. Angell and Moore, "Reaction-Time," p. 253.

55. Dewey, "Reflex Arc Concept in Psychology," *PR* 3 (1896): 357–70.

56. The definition is Harvey Carr's; see Heidbreder, *Seven Psychologies*, p. 219.

57. Angell, "Province of Functional Psychology," p. 30.

58. Rucker, *Chicago Pragmatists*, pp. 59–60.

59. Titchener, "The Postulates of a Structural Psychology," *Philosophical Review* 7 (1898): 453; see also "Structural and Functional Psychology," ibid., 8 (1899): 290–99.

60. Rucker, *Chicago Pragmatists*, pp. 83–106, wherein the connection between Dewey's theories and those informing the child-study movement are noted. The similarities between "progressive education" and the ideas of the phrenologically oriented nineteenth-century educators has been examined by Lawrence A. Cremin, *The Transformation of the School: Progressivism in American Education, 1876–1957* (New York: Random House, 1964), p. 126.

61. E. G. Boring, "The Influence of Evolutionary Theory Upon American Psychological Thought" in Stow Persons, ed., *Evolutionary Thought in America* (New Haven: Yale University Press, 1950), pp. 273–74; *HEP*, pp. 551–52.

62. Angell, "Province of Functional Psychology," pp. 62–64.

63. Ibid., p. 65.

64. Ibid., pp. 65, 66.

65. Ibid., p. 73.

66. Ibid.

67. Ibid., pp. 71, 69, 72.

68. See, e.g., William James, *Principles of Psychology*, 2 vols. (New York: Holt, 1890), 2: 486–593; Baldwin, "Consciousness and Evolution," p. 223; James R. Angell, "The Influence of Darwin on Psychology," *PR* 16 (1909): 157.

69. Joncich, *The Sane Positivist*, p. 412.

70. Ibid., pp. 69, 70, 76.

71. John B. Watson, "Psychology as the Behaviorist Views It," *PR* 20 (1913): 158, 165–66.

CHAPTER 10

1. Arthur Koestler, *The Ghost in the Machine* (New York: Macmillan, 1967), pp. 15 ff.

2. Willard Harrell and Ross Harrison, "The Rise and Fall of Behaviorism," *Journal*

of General Psychology 18 (1938): 371; Edna Heidbreder, *Seven Psychologies* (New York: Century, 1933), p. 236; Watson, *Behaviorism* (New York: People's Institute, 1924), p. ix; "Psychology as the Behaviorist Views It," *PR* 20 (1913): 175.

3. C. J. Warden, "The Development of Modern Comparative Psychology," *Quarterly Review of Biology* 3 (1928): 486–522; W. Mills, "Some Aspects of the Development of Comparative Psychology," *Science* 19 (1904): 745–57; Boring, *HEP*, pp. 472–76, 622–31; C. Lloyd Morgan, *An Introduction to Comparative Psychology* (London: Walter Scott, 1894); Watson, *Animal Education: An Experimental Study of the Psychical Development of the White Rat* (Chicago: University of Chicago Press, 1903).

4. Heidbreder, *Seven Psychologies*, p. 236.

5. Carr, *HPA*, 3 (1936): 79.

6. Buchner, "Psychological Progress in 1908," *PB* 6 (1909): 10.

7. Jerome S. Bruner and Gordon W. Allport, "Fifty Years of Change in American Psychology," *PR* 37 (1940): 758, 764.

8. Watson to R. M. Yerkes, 13 December 1909, Yerkes Papers, Yale Medical Library, New Haven, Connecticut.

9. And this includes both Porter *and* Sanford at Clark. The others were Watson, Yerkes, L. W. Cole, and M. F. Washburn. To determine this figure, Cattell's entries were checked against the APA's *Directory* listing of psychologists and their academic titles, the *Psychological Index*'s list of publications, and the compilation of comparative psychology facilities contained in C. J. Warden and L. H. Warner, "The Development of Animal Psychology in the United States During the Last Three Decades," *PR* 34 (1927): 196–205.

10. Titchener to Yerkes, 11 January 1907, Yerkes Papers. For insights into Titchener's antipathy toward animal research, see Boring, "Titchener's Experimentalists," *JHBS* 3 (1967): 323, and Titchener to Boring, 9 May 1927, Boring Correspondence, Harvard University Archives, Cambridge, Massachusetts. See also his 1909 correspondence with Adolf Meyer, The Adolf Meyer Corrrespondence, Adolf Meyer Archive, The Alan Chesney Medical Archives, The Johns Hopkins Medical Institutions, Box I/3832/folders 1–7.

11. Watson to Yerkes, 6 February 1910, and Yerkes to C. J. Herrick, 18 August 1911, Yerkes Papers.

12. See, e.g., Titchener, *A Beginner's Psychology* (New York: Macmillan, 1915), pp. 13–14, 267. In 1908 Titchener's student Mary Floy Washburn published *The Animal Mind* (New York, Macmillan), which attempted to follow Titchener's restrictions. Her methods were the exception that proved the rule. The following year Madison Bentley revived course work in comparative psychology at Cornell, but after his departure in 1912, Titchener discontinued the offering; see T. A. Ryan, "Psychology at Cornell After Titchener" (Unpublished paper, Department of Psychology, Cornell University, Ithaca, New York), p. 12.

13. Robert S. Woodworth, *Contemporary Schools of Psychology* (New York: The Ronald Press, 1931), p. 56.

14. See, e.g., Hall to W. A. White, 11 December 1912, G. Stanley Hall Papers, Goddard Library, Clark University, Worcester, Massachusetts; and Hall to Yerkes, 18 May and 7 July 1915, Yerkes Papers.

15. James, *Principles of Psychology*, 2 vols. (New York: Holt, 1890), 2 : 688.

16. See Conway Zirkle, "The Knowledge of Heredity Before 1900," in L. C. Dunn,

ed., *Genetics in the 20th Century* (New York: Macmillan, 1951), pp. 53 ff.; Dunn, *A Short History of Genetics* (New York: McGraw-Hill, 1965).

17. Watson to Yerkes, 29 October 1909, Yerkes Papers.

18. James, *Principles of Psychology*, 2 : 391–92; E. L. Thorndike, "Animal Intelligence: An Experimental Study of the Associative Processes in Animals, *PR, Monograph Supplements* 2 (1898): 105 ff; John B. Watson, *Behavior: An Introduction to Comparative Psychology* (New York: Holt, 1914), pp. 44, 53, 109.

19. Watson to Yerkes, 4 March 1912, Yerkes Papers.

20. Geraldine Joncich, *The Sane Positivist: A Biography of Edward L. Thorndike* (Middletown, Conn.: Wesleyan University Press, 1968), p. 418.

21. Yerkes to Cattell, 2 April 1910; Cattell to Yerkes, 5 April 1910, Yerkes Papers.

22. From the beginnings of animal psychology's development in the universities, comparative psychologists were forced to look beyond normal sources for funding; see G. S. Hall to D. C. Gilman, 7 April 1902, and Hall to George F. Hoar, 24 September 1902, Hall Papers.

23. Münsterberg to C. W. Eliot, 17 October 1898, Charles W. Eliot Papers, Harvard University Archives, Cambridge, Massachusetts.

24. The following paragraphs on Watson's early years have benefited from Kerry W. Buckley's careful study, "Background for Behaviorism: John Broadus Watson and Patterns of Social Mobility in Greenville, South Carolina" (Paper presented at the tenth annual meeting of Cheiron, Wellesley College, Wellesley, Massachusetts, June 1978).

25. Buckley, "Background for Behaviorism," p. 12; Lucille T. Birnbaum, "Behaviorism: John Broadus Watson and American Social Thought, 1913–1933" (Ph.D. diss., University of California, Berkeley, 1964), pp. 14–15; Watson to Thomas W. Harrell and Ross Harrison, 16 June 1936, Harrell Papers, Archives of the History of American Psychology.

26. Buckley, "Background for Behaviorism," pp. 3–6; Watson, *HPA*, 3 (1936): 271.

27. Birnbaum, "Behaviorism," p. 23; Buckley, "Background for Behaviorism," p. 9.

28. Buckley, "Background for Behaviorism," pp. 13–14; Watson, *HPA*, 3 (1936): 271, 272.

29. Watson to Harper, 20 July 1900, quoted in Buckley, "Background for Behaviorism," p. 1.

30. Ibid., p. 11; Watson, *HPA*, 3 (1936): 272. Distaste for convention, however, does not imply dispensation from dogmatism, as Adolf Meyer pointedly suggested to Watson; Meyer to Watson, 29 May 1916 and 3 June 1916, Meyer Correspondence.

31. Watson, *HPA* 3 (1936): 274, 276.

32. Donald H. Barron, "H. H. Donaldson," *Dictionary of American Biography*, supplement 2, pp. 156–57; Donaldson, "Anatomical Observations on the Brain of Laura Bridgman," *AJP* 3 (1890): 293–342; 4 (1891): 248–94. Hall, "Laura Bridgman," *Mind* 4 (1879): 149–72; Dorothy Ross, *G. Stanley Hall: The Psychologist as Prophet* (Chicago: University of Chicago Press, 1972), p. 78. Donaldson, diaries, 1892–93, and "For My Boys" (typescript autobiography), pp. 79–102, Donaldson Papers, American Philosophical Society, Philadelphia.

33. Watson, *HPA*, 3 (1936): 274.

34. Donald Fleming, "Introduction" in Loeb, *The Mechanistic Conception of Life* (Cambridge: Belknap Press of Harvard University, 1964; originally published in 1912), pp. vii–xli.

35. Angell, *HPA*, 3 (1936): 12; Watson, ibid., p. 273; Watson to Loeb, 2 January 1914, Loeb Papers, Manuscript Division, Library of Congress.

36. Watson, *Animal Education, An Experimental Study on the Psychical Development of the White Rat* (Chicago: University of Chicago Press, 1903), pp. 7, 86.

37. Watson, *HPA*, 3 (1936): 276. An associate of Watson at Chicago, Walter Van Dyke Bingham recalled that Watson "used to have trouble making consistent introspective reports"; *HPA*, 4 (1952): 7. One commentator speculates that behaviorists' supposed anti-intellectualism stemmed from lack of verbal fluency; David Bakan, "Behaviorism and American Urbanization," *JHBS* 2 (1966): 20–21.

38. Watson, "Psychology as the Behaviorist Views It," p. 168.

39. Watson, *Psychology from the Standpoint of a Behaviorist*, 2d ed. (Philadelphia: Lippincott, 1924), p. viii; *HPA*, 3 (1936): 275, 276. Harvey Carr substantiates Watson's chronology in ibid., p. 76. See also J. C. Burnham, "On the Origins of Behaviorism," *JHBS* 4 (1968): 148.

40. Cattell, "The Conceptions and Methods of Psychology," *Popular Science Monthly* 66 (1904): 180; Burnham, "On the Origins of Behaviorism," pp. 148–49.

41. Watson, *HPA*, 3 (1936): 275; "Kinaesthetic and Organic Sensations: Their Role in the Reactions of the White Rat to the Maze," *PR, Monograph Supplements* 33 (1907).

42. Watson to Yerkes, 23 May 1905 and 9 August 1906, Yerkes Papers. Commentators have subsequently and incorrectly interpreted this revision as an indication of Watson's subscription to Loeb's neuromechanistic reductionist views. For a corrective to this view, see Burnham, "On the Origins of Behaviorism," pp. 146–47.

43. Watson to Yerkes, 26 August 1904, Yerkes Papers.

44. Idem, 17 June 1905; Watson, "The Need for an Experimental Station for the Study of Certain Problems in Animal Behavior," *PB* 3 (1906): 149–56.

45. Watson to Yerkes, 21 March 1906, Yerkes Papers.

46. Watson, *HPA*, 3 (1936): 275.

47. Watson to Yerkes, 6 November 1906 and 5 March 1907, Yerkes Papers; Watson, *HPA*, 3 (1936): 277; Yerkes, *HPA*, 2 (1932): 393. Personal concerns also influenced Watson's decision to move; see Watson to Adolf Meyer, 13 August [1920], Meyer Correspondence.

48. Watson to Yerkes, 19 November 1907, Yerkes Papers.

49. Idem, 26 August 1904.

50. Idem, 27 May 1908.

51. Yerkes to Perry, 4 December 1928, Yerkes Papers.

52. Yerkes, *HPA*, 2 (1932): 381–82, 386–89; "Early Days of Comparative Psychology," *PR* 50 (1943): 75; Royce to Eliot, 7 May 1906, Eliot Papers.

53. Thorndike to Yerkes, 25 February 1899, Yerkes Papers.

54. Thorndike, *HPA*, 3 (1936): 264–65; Yerkes, "Early Days of Comparative Psychology," *PR* 50 (1943): 74; Joncich, *The Sane Positivist*, pp. 88–89.

55. Thorndike, *HPA*, 3 (1936): 395, 396.

56. Münsterberg to Eliot, 6 April, 15 April, and 13 December 1902, Eliot Papers.

57. Roswell P. Angier to Yerkes, 17 May 1905, Yerkes Papers; Edwin B. Holt to C. W. Eliot, 11 December 1906, Eliot Papers.

58. Royce to Eliot, 7 May 1906, Eliot Papers; reprinted in John Clendenning, ed., *The Letters of Josiah Royce* (Chicago: University of Chicago Press, 1970), pp. 499–501.

59. Kuklick, *Rise of American Philosophy: Cambridge, Massachusetts, 1860–1930* (New Haven: Yale University Press, 1977), pp. 255–56.

60. Münsterberg to C. W. Eliot, 26 April 1908, Eliot Papers.

61. Idem, 5 May 1908; Eliot to Münsterberg, 18 June 1908, Eliot Papers.

62. Robert M. Yerkes, *HPA*, 2 (1932): 390–91; Yerkes, "Testament" (typescript autobiography), p. 133, Yerkes Papers, Yale Medical Library, New Haven, Connecticut.

63. Münsterberg to Yerkes, 30 January, 19 December, and 21 December 1911, Yerkes Papers.

64. Yerkes, "Testament," p. 140.

65. Watson to Yerkes, 26 February 1913, Yerkes Papers.

66. L. W. Cole to Yerkes, 25 June and 8 July 1908, 10 October 1911, and 8 September 1914; Yerkes to Arthur H. Daniels, 29 August 1912, Yerkes Papers; Cole, "Adding Upward and Downward," *Journal of Educational Psychology* 3 (1912): 83–94.

67. Haggerty to Yerkes, 15 August 1909; Lindley to Yerkes, 6 June 1909; Haggerty to Yerkes, 17 March 1910, 5 October 1912, and 25 May 1916, Yerkes Papers.

68. Besides Cole and Haggerty, Yerkes' list included the following Ph.D.'s: J. C. Bell, F. S. Breed, C. S. Berry, K. T. Waugh, C. E. Kellogg, S. L. Pressey, and H. E. Burtt. Among them, they published only six postdoctoral animal studies. Interestingly, the students who remained in comparative psychology the longest, H. C. Bingham and C. A. Coburn, were masters of arts. Upon returning to Harvard to receive doctorates (in other words, after securing professional tickets to upward mobility), they too entered applied fields.

69. Angier to Yerkes, 26 September 1912. Frost was able to reinstate himself briefly at Yale before leaving the profession to become an industrial management consultant. See also E. B. Holt to Yerkes, 18 March 1912, Yerkes Papers.

70. Yerkes, *HPA*, 2 (1932): 390; Hamilton to Yerkes, 15 October 1912, Yerkes Papers.

71. Dunlap, *HPA*, 2 (1932): 43–44.

72. Buchner, "Psychological Progress in 1910," *PB* 8 (1911): 3.

73. Watson to A. O. Lovejoy, 18 April [1910], Arthur Oncken Lovejoy Papers, Eisenhower Library, The Johns Hopkins University; Watson to Adolf Meyer, 14 November [1912], Meyer Correspondence.

74. Watson to Yerkes, 1 September 1909 and 6 February [1910], Yerkes Papers.

75. Watson to Lovejoy, 17 April [1910], Lovejoy Papers; Philip J. Pauly, "G. Stanley Hall and his Successors, A History of the First Half-Century of Psychology at Johns Hopkins University" (Paper presented at the G. Stanley Hall Centennial, Johns Hopkins University, October 1983).

76. Yerkes, "Psychology and Its Relations to Biology," *JPPSM* 7 (1910): 113.

77. See Titchener to K. Dunlap, 22 November 1911, Dunlap Papers, Archives of the History of American Psychology.

78. Yerkes, "Psychology in Its Relations to Biology," pp. 114–16.

79. Ibid., pp. 120, 122, 119.

80. Yerkes was sensitive to this criticism; see *HPA*, 2 (1932): 396; Yerkes to Watson, 30 October 1915; Watson to Yerkes, 12 May 1916; and Yerkes to Watson, 16 May 1916, Yerkes Papers.

81. Yerkes, "Psychology in Its Relations to Biology," pp. 118–19.

82. Yerkes, "Comparative Psychology: A Question of Definitions," *JPPSM* 10 (1913): 581; "The Harvard Laboratory of Animal Psychology and the Franklin Field Station," *Journal of Animal Behavior* 4 (1914): 180, 183; Yerkes to H. S. Jennings, 19 February 1912, and Yerkes to Watson, 13 October 1915, Yerkes Papers.

83. Yerkes, "Psychology in Its Relations to Biology," p. 119.

84. Watson to Yerkes, 29 October [1909], Yerkes Papers.

85. Watson, review of Jennings's *Behavior of the Lower Organisms, PB* 4 (1907): 288–91; Watson to Yerkes, 2 October 1907; 29 September, 30 November, and 6 December 1908, Yerkes Papers. See also Burnham, "On the Origins of Behaviorism," pp. 146–47.

86. Watson to Yerkes, 29 October [1909], Yerkes Papers.

87. Idem, 6 February [1910], Yerkes Papers.

88. Idem, 5 March 1907; Adolf Meyer to Watson, 11 January 1912, Meyer Correspondence; Cedric Larson and John J. Sullivan, "Watson's Relations to Titchener," *JHBS* 1 (1965): 338–54. John Burnham has alternately proposed that Watson refrained from announcing his manifesto until he had "solved the problem of the higher thought processes" in terms of "a stimulus-response model of implicit speech mechanisms in associative memory"; "On the Origins of Behaviorism," p. 150. Burnham follows Albert E. Goss, "Early Behaviorism and Verbal Mediating Responses," *American Psychologist* 16 (1961): 285–98, who maintains that this theory was, in Burnham's words, "so basic that the movement could not have existed without it." It seems apparent, however, that this theory was the weakest aspect of Watson's formulation which few psychologists—even those who called themselves behaviorists—accepted.

89. Warren, *HPA,* 1 (1930): 462–63; Watson to J. M. Cattell, 10 January 1913, Cattell Papers.

90. Watson to Yerkes, 21 May 1912, Yerkes Papers.

91. Birnbaum, "Behaviorism," p. 33; Watson, "Content of a Course in Psychology for Medical Students," *PB* 9 (1912): 89–90; Meyer, "The Value of Psychology in Psychiatry," *Journal of the American Medical Association* 58 (1912): 911–14.

92. Quoted in Alfred Lief, *The Common Sense Psychiatry of Dr. Adolf Meyer* (New York: McGraw-Hill, 1948), pp. 87, 143. Meyer, it should be noted, was not enamored with Watson's peculiar formulations; see his handwritten notes in reaction to Watson's "Psychology as the Behaviorist Views It" in Box I/3974, folder 4, Meyer Correspondence. A trustworthy account of the relationship between Watson and Meyer is Ruth Leys, "Meyer, Watson, and the Dangers of Behaviorism," *JHBS* 20 (1984): 128–49.

93. Yerkes, "Testament," p. 142.

94. Watson to Yerkes, 21 February 1912, Yerkes Papers.

95. Yerkes, "Comparative Psychology in Relation to Medicine," *Boston Medical and Surgical Journal* 169 (1913): 779–81.

96. In 1916 he played this card. That year the philosophical faculty was forced to relocate and because of its "chronic state of poverty . . . was not able to provide adequate space" for the psychological laboratories; Dunlap, *HPA,* 2 (1932): 46–47. Meyer furnished Watson with a "magnificent suite" containing "animal quarters" and "a nice operating room in the clinic"; Watson to Yerkes, 7 February 1916, Yerkes Papers; Adolf Meyer to Yerkes, 10 April 1916, Meyer Correspondence.

97. Idem, 12 December 1912 and 12 March 1913, Yerkes Papers; Warren, *HPA,* 1 (1930): 462.

98. When, e.g., in 1943 seventy prominent psychologists were asked to rank-order the twenty-five articles they considered to have had the greatest impact upon them and upon psychology at large, "Psychology as the Behaviorist Views It" was their overwhelming first choice; Herbert S. Langfeld, "Fifty Volumes of the *Psychological Review,*" *PR* 50 (1943): 152. The results of such a poll taken, say, in 1917 or 1927 would have

revealed a quite different picture. During World War II psychologists chose the article which historically validated their contemporary activities. See also B. F. Skinner, *About Behaviorism* (New York: Knopf, 1974), pp. 1–6.

99. Watson, "Psychology as the Behaviorist Views It," pp. 158. 159, 163.

100. Ibid., pp. 159–62; Watson to Paul Thomas Young, 14 August 1917, Young Papers, Archives of the History of American Psychology.

101. Angell, "Behavior as a Category of Psychology," *PR* 20 (1913): 268.

102. Yerkes, "Comparative Psychology: A Question of Definitions," pp. 581–82; H. R. Marshall, "Is Psychology Evaporating?" *JPPSM* 10 (1913): 710–16.

103. James, "What the Will Effects," *Scribner's* 3 (1888): 240.

104. Eliott P. Frost, "Can Biology and Physiology Dispense with Consciousness?" *PR* 19 (1912): 246–52; Watson, "Psychology as the Behaviorist Views It," pp. 166–67; Karl E. Rothschuh, *History of Physiology*, trans by Guenter B. Risse (New York: Krieger, 1973), p. 241.

105. Watson to Loeb, 2 January 1914, Loeb Papers.

106. Watson, review of Jennings, p. 291; "Psychology as the Behaviorist Views It," pp. 167, 162, 176–77.

107. Ibid., p. 175.

108. Ibid., p. 169.

109. Ibid., pp. 168–69.

110. See also Watson, *Behavior*, pp. 46–48, 201–2.

111. See, e.g., Cattell, "Conceptions and Methods"; William James, "Does 'Consciousness' Exist?" *JPPSM* 1 (1904): 477–91; Thorndike, "The Study of Consciousness and the Study of Behavior," *PB* 8 (1911): 39; "Ideo-Motor Action," *PR* 30 (1913): 91–106; W. B. Pillsbury, *The Essentials of Psychology* (New York: Macmillan, 1911); Max Meyer, *The Fundamental Laws of Human Behavior* (Boston: R. G. Badger, 1911); William McDougall, *Psychology: The Study of Behavior* (London: Williams and Norgate, 1912); K. Dunlap, "The Case Against Introspection," *PR* 19 (1912): 240–45; Maurice Parmelee, *The Science of Human Behavior: Biological and Psychological Foundations* (New York: Macmillan, 1913).

112. Titchener, "On 'Psychology as the Behaviorist Views It,' " *Proceedings of the American Philosophical Society* 53 (1914): 1–17, is the most devastating retort. Franz Samelson, "Reactions to Watson's Behaviorism: The Early Years" (paper presented at the tenth annual meeting of Cheiron, Wellesley College, Wellesley, Massachusetts, June 1978), provides a compilation of the responses to Watson's paper.

113. See Walter S. Hunter, "An Open Letter to the Anti-Behaviorists," *PR* 19 (1922): 307–8; Boring, *HEP*, p. 645.

114. Hamilton to Yerkes, 20 August 1913, 3 January 1916, Yerkes Papers; Yerkes, "Behaviorism and Genetic Psychology," *JPPSM* 14 (1917): 155.

115. Burnham, "On the Origins of Behaviorism," p. 145.

116. Ibid., p. 150; Samelson, "Reactions to Watson's Behaviorism: The Early Years," pp. 10, 22.

117. F. L. Wells, "Dynamic Psychology," *PB* 10 (1913): 434. This passage has been cited by Burnham ("On the Origins of Behaviorism," p. 150), who has suggested that "the evolution of Watson's thinking, on the one hand, is not necessarily relevant to the origins of behaviorism, on the other hand." Social historians concerned with the implications of behaviorism for social thought have explained the origins of Watson's thinking in terms of his religious ideology and have sought to explain the acceptance of be-

haviorism in terms of its compatability with American culture, particularly in terms of the promise of behaviorism for social control. See, e.g., Birnbaum, "Behaviorism," passim; Paul G. Creelan, "Watsonian Behaviorism and the Calvinist Conscience," *JHBS* 10 (1974): 95–118; Bakan, "Behaviorism and American Urbanization"; Burnham, "Psychiatry, Psychology and the Progressive Movement," *American Quarterly* 12 (1960): 457–65. Psychologists have tended to concentrate on the "internal" scientific antecedents of Watsonianism; e.g., Woodworth, *Contemporary Schools of Psychology*, pp. 111–16; Boring, *HEP*, pp. 620–41; Richard J. Herrnstein, Introduction to the reprint edition of Watson, *Behavior* (New York: Holt, Rinehart and Winston, 1967). Burnham ("On the Origins of Behaviorism," p. 150) suggests that the historian inspect "the actions of the psychological community," the focus of the next chapter.

118. Looking at these individuals through an examination of their published responses, Samelson has mistakenly concluded that there was no behavioristic movement in the second decade of the twentieth century; "Reactions to Watson's Behaviorism: The Early Years," p. 23 and, in general, Samelson, "The Struggle for Scientific Authority: The Reception of Watson's Behaviorism, 1913–1920," *JHBS* 17 (1981): 399–425.

CHAPTER 11

1. Krueger, "New Aims and Tendencies in Psychology," *Philosophical Review* 22 (1913): 252, 264, 259–60.

2. Ibid., p. 257.

3. McDougall, *Introduction to Social Psychology*, 8th ed. (Boston: Luce, 1914), p. 15.

4. Ibid., p. 6.

5. Watson, "The Image and Affection in Behavior," *JPPSM* 10 (1913): 422.

6. Watson, "Psychology as the Behaviorist Views It," *PR* 20 (1913): 169–70.

7. Titchener, "On 'Psychology as the Behaviorist Views It,' " *Proceedings of the American Philosophical Society* 53 (1914): 14.

8. Watson, "Psychology as the Behaviorist Views It," p. 169.

9. Hollingworth's several published articles were collected in *The Influence of Caffeine on Efficiency* (New York: Science Press, 1912).

10. Jastrow, "Varieties of Psychological Experience," *PR* 24 (1917): 263.

11. See Samuel P. Hays, *Response to Industrialism, 1885–1914* (Chicago: University of Chicago Press, 1957); Samuel Haber, *Efficiency and Uplift: Scientific Management in the Progressive Era, 1890–1920* (Chicago: University of Chicago Press, 1964); David F. Noble, *America By Design: Science, Technology, and the Rise of Corporate Capitalism* (New York: Knopf, 1977).

12. Daniels, *Science in American Society: A Social History* (New York: Knopf 1971), p. 290 and, in general, pp. 288–315.

13. Walter Lippmann, *Drift and Mastery* (New York: Kennerley, 1914); L. L. Bernard, *The Transition to an Objective Standard of Social Control* (Chicago: University of Chicago Press, 1911); Simon Patten, *The New Basis of Civilization* (New York: Macmillan, 1907).

14. Ronald C. Tobey, *The American Ideology of National Science, 1919–1930* (Pittsburg, Pa.: University of Pittsburg Press, 1971), pp 3–19.

15. Dewey, "Psychological Doctrine and Philosophical Teaching," *JPPSM* 11 (1914): 505, 508.

16. Dewey, "The Need for Social Psychology," *PR* 24 (1917): 270, 272, 275–77.

17. Watson, "An Attempted Formulation of the Scope of Behavior Psychology," *PR* 24 (1917): 329.

18. Quoted in Eric F. Goldman, *Rendezvous with Destiny: A History of Modern American Reform* (New York: Knopf, 1952), p. 123.

19. Laurence Veysey, *The Emergence of the American University* (Chicago: University of Chicago Press, 1965), p. 283.

20. Christian A. Ruckmich, "The History and Status of Psychology in the United States," *AJP* 23 (1912): 523.

21. Veysey, *Emergence*, p. 283.

22. Frederick Rudolph, *The American College and University* (New York: Knopf, 1962), pp. 355–65.

23. Hall to Meyer, 15 June 1900, G. Stanley Hall Papers, Goddard Library, Clark University, Worcester, Massachusetts.

24. Meyer, *The Fundamental Laws of Behavior* (Boston: Richard G. Badger, 1911); Pillsbury, *HPA*, 2 (1932): 292; P. Bordwell, et al., "Academic Freedom at the University of Missouri . . . ," *Bulletin of the American Association of University Professors* 16 (1930): 143–76.

25. Cited in David Bakan, "The Influence of Phrenology on American Psychology," *JHBS* 2 (1966): 208.

26. Parmelee, *The Science of Human Behavior: Biological and Psychological Foundations* (New York: Macmillan, 1913).

27. Weiss, "The Relation Between Functional and Behavior Psychology," *PR* 24 (1917): 353–55; Birnbaum, "Behaviorism: John Broadus Watson and American Social Thought, 1913–1933" (Ph.D. diss., University of California, Berkeley, 1964), pp. 93–94. For a similar upbraiding of functionalism for wasting its time on the mind-body relationship, see midwesterner G. A. Tawney's "Consciousness in Psychology and Philosophy," *JPPSM* 8 (1911): 197–203. Birnbaum ("Behaviorism," p. 207) has called behaviorists "regional radicals," a designation explicable, I believe, in terms of regional pressures toward application of psychological knowledge.

28. This group included F. N. Maxfield, the Witmerian clinician; H. H. Goddard, a leader of the American eugenics movement; S. L. and L. C. Pressey, a noted team of intelligence testers; and H. E. Burtt, a former student of comparative psychology.

29. Hall to Meyer, 15 June 1900, Hall Papers; Jastrow to "My dear Folks," 9 September 1888, Jastrow Papers, Perkins Library, Duke University, Durham, North Carolina; *HPA*, 1 (1930): 150; Adams, quoted in Veysey, *Emergence* p. 104.

30. Lincoln Steffens, "Sending a State to College," *American Magazine* 67 (1909); 349–64; J. David Hoeveler, Jr., "The University and the Social Gospel: The Intellectual Origins of the 'Wisconsin Idea,' " *Wisconsin Magazine of History* 59 (1976): 282–98.

31. Jastrow, *HPA* 1 (1930): 155; Merle Curti and Vernon Cartensen, *University of Wisconsin: A History, 1848–1925*, 2 vols. (Madison: University of Wisconsin Press, 1949), 1: 545; 2: 334.

32. Ibid., 1 : 281; John Bascom, *Science of the Mind* (New York: Putnam, 1881); *Comparative Psychology: Growth and Grades of Intelligence* (New York: Putnam, 1878); Dorothy Ross, *G. Stanley Hall: The Psychologist as Prophet* (Chicago: University of Chicago Press, 1972), pp. 24–25; Jastrow, *HPA*, 1 (1930): 154–55.

33. Seashore, *Pioneering in Psychology* (Iowa City: University of Iowa Press, 1942), pp. 15, 2–5.

34. Seashore, *HPA*, 1 (1930): 254; Audrey B. Davis and Uta C. Merzbach, *Early*

Auditory Studies: Activities in the Psychology Laboratories of American Universities (Washington, D.C.: Smithsonian Institution Press, 1975), pp. 32, 23–25.

35. Seashore, *Pioneering in Psychology*, passim; *HPA*, 1 (1930): 260–86; "The Consulting Psychologist," *Ppoular Science Monthly* 78 (1911): 283–96; Seashore et al., "Report of the Committee of the American Psychological Association on the Teaching of Psychology," *Psychological Monographs* 12 (1910): 1–93; "The Measure of a Singer," *Science* 35 (1912): 201; Robert S. Harper, "Tables of American Doctorates in Psychology," *AJP* 62 (1949): 582–83.

36. See Miles A. Tinker, "Progress in Psychology at Minnesota (1890–1953)," Harlow Gale Papers, Archives Library, University of Minnesota, Minneapolis, Minnesota. A most revealing portrait of Minnesota psychology just prior to World War I is contained in folders 220–223 of the Robert M. Yerkes Papers, Yale Medical Library, New Haven, Connecticut; John Dashiell, *Fundamentals of Objective Psychology* (Cambridge, Mass: The Riverside Press, 1928).

37. Elliot to Yerkes, 8 November 1918, Yerkes Papers; Elliott, *HPA*, 4 (1952): 85.

38. Starbuck, *The Psychology of Religion: An Empirical Study of the Growth of Religious Consciousness* (London: Scott, 1899); Starbuck to William James, 20 July 1903, William James Papers, Houghton Library, Harvard University, Cambridge, Massachusetts; Seashore, *Pioneering in Psychology*, p. 21. For an analogous situation, see E. F. Buchner to G. S. Hall, 11 August 1902 and 12 January 1903, Hall Papers.

39. Ludy T. Benjamin, "Psychology at the University of Nebraska, 1889–1930," *Nebraska History* 56 (1975): 384.

40. Cattell, "Statistics of American Psychologists," *AJP* 14 (1903): 591.

41. Ruckmich, "History and Status of Psychology," pp. 528–29, 523.

42. Cattell, "Statistics of American Psychologists," p. 591; Ruckmich, "History and Status of Psychology," p. 530; Cattell, "Our Psychological Association and Research," in Albert T. Poffenberger, ed., *James McKeen Cattell: Man of Science*, 2 vols. (Lancaster, Pa.: Science Press, 1947), 2 : 339.

43. Cattell, "Statistics of American Psychologists," p. 591; Ruckmich, "History and Status of Psychology," p. 530; Cattell, "Our Psychological Association and Research," in Poffenberger, ed., *Cattell*, 2 : 339.

44. Veysey, *Emergence*, p. 176; Mark A. May, "A Retrospective View of the Institute of Human Relations at Yale," *Behavior Science Notes* 6 (1971): 141–72; Paul S. Achilles, "The Role of the Psychological Corporation in Applied Psychology," *AJP* 50 (1937): 229–47.

45. Jacob Z. Jacobson, *Scott of Northwestern: The Life Story of a Pioneer in Psychology and Education* (Chicago: Mariano, 1951), pp. 70 ff.; Leonard W. Ferguson, *The Heritage of Industrial Psychology* (n.p., 1963–65), p. 4; Seashore, "The Tonoscope," *Psychological Monographs* 16 (1914): 1–12; Hollingworth, "Memories of the Early Development of the Psychology of Advertising," *PB* 35 (1938): 309; "Years at Columbia" (typescript autobiography, Hollingworth Papers, Nebraska State Historical Society, Lincoln, Nebraska), pp. 56–68.

46. Angell, *HPA*, 3 (1936): 38, 15.

47. Bingham, *HPA*, 4 (1952): 9.

48. Dodge, *HPA*, 2 (1932): 107, 121. Dodge prepared the way for his applied work by pleading for objectivism; "The Theory and Limitations of Introspection," *AJP* 23 (1912): 214–29.

49. Alexandra Lee Levin, "The Jastrows in Madison: A Chronicle of University Life,

1880–1890," *Wisconsin Magazine of History* 46 (1963): 249; [Jastrow], "The Status of the American Professor," *Educational Review* 16 (1898): 417–34; "Practical Aspects of Psychology," ibid., 17 (1899): 135–53; *Fact and Fable in Psychology* (Boston: Houghton Mifflin, 1900); *HPA*, 1 (1930): 156.

50. Hollingworth, "Years at Columbia," pp. 48, 56.

51. Sarton to Loeb, 14 December 1916; Loeb to Sarton, 16 December 1916, Jacques Loeb Papers, Manuscript Division, Library of Congress, Washington, D.C.

52. See Birnbaum, "Behaviorism," p. 66. Münsterberg's *Psychology: General and Applied* (New York: Appleton, 1914) represents the most thorough example of his scope. For his "humanitarian" justifications for applied psychology, see pp. vii, 2–4, 341–50. Matthew Hale, Jr., *Human Science and Social Order: Hugo Münsterberg and the Origins of Applied Psychology* (Philadelphia: Temple University Press, 1980) has sensitively related Münsterberg's applied endeavors to his social thought, and Bruce Kuklick, *The Rise of American Psychology: Cambridge, Massachusetts, 1860–1930* (New Haven: Yale University Press, 1977), pp. 198–214, has placed his applied psychology and his behaviorism within the context of his systematic philosophy.

53. Robert M. Yerkes, "Testament" (typescript autobiography), p. 167 Yerkes Papers; *HPA*, 2 (1932): 392; Yerkes to J. B. Johnston, 16 March 1917, Yerkes Papers.

54. Dunlap, *HPA*, 2 (1932): 40, 42; R. M. Elliott, ibid., p. 79.

55. Dunlap, *HPA*, 2 (1932): 44.

56. Watson to Yerkes, 28 September 1909 and 11 November 1909, Yerkes Papers; Dunlap, *HPA*, 2 (1932): 45, 44; Watson, *HPA*, 3 (1936): 277.

57. Even in the area of academic teaching, psychologists were beginning by 1910 to emphasize behavioral notions. Teachers of elementary courses felt that "psychology is not best taught to beginners as the study of human *consciousness* but as the study of human *nature and behavior.*" Twentieth-century students were finding "the practical, social, moral and educational bearing of psychology" much more useful than its philosophic aspects. In normal schools, introspection was almost never used; observation of children was preferred. In general, students tended to regard introspection as requiring "either an abnormal gift of some sort or years of toilsome training"; see Seashore et al., "Report on the Teaching of Psychology," pp. 7, 64; Ruckmich, "History and Status of Psychology," p. 531.

58. These figures were extrapolated from the listings of the second edition of *American Men of Science (AMS)*. While the derived total sample represents 85.8 percent of the APA's total membership, it is nevertheless representative, for, unlike the APA's *Directory*, *AMS* eliminated the least distinguished 14 percent whose inclusion in the *Directory* still by 1910 was a function of membership and certification, not scientific contribution. At a time when certain applied interests were in some sectors disparaged, psychologists were more likely to acknowledge such interests in *AMS* than in their own official register.

Incidentally, there were American women of science too. Contrary to its title, *AMS* included nineteen women psychologists (10 percent of the sample); ten of them listed applied concerns, a ratio consonant with their male counterparts' choices.

59. Thorndike, *Animal Intelligence: An Experimental Study of the Associative Processes in Animals* in *Columbia Contributions to Education,* vol. 4, (New York: Macmillan, 1911); *Educational Psychology;* Vol. 1: *The Original Nature of Man;* Vol. 2: *The Learning Process;* Vol. 3: *Mental Work and Fatigue and Individual Differences* (N.Y.: Teachers College Press, 1913, 1914). See Joncich, *The Sane Positivist,* pp. 282–355 and 409–29.

60. Thorndike, "The Foundations of Educational Achievement," quoted in Joncich, ed., *Psychology and the Science of Education; Selected Writings of Edward L. Thorndike* (New York: Teachers College Press, 1962), p. 11.

61. Hollingworth, "Recent Applications of Experimental Psychology," *Arizona Journal of Education* 1 (1910): 103, quoted in David Phillip Kuna, "The Psychology of Advertising, 1896–1916" (Ph.D. diss., University of New Hampshire, 1976), p. 292.

62. Ogden, "The Relation of Psychology to Philosophy and Education," *PR* 20 (1913): 181. Ogden's remarks were contained in his presidential address to the Southern Society for Philosophy and Psychology. Watson was elected president the following year.

63. Arthur G. Powell, "Speculations on the Early Impact of Schools of Education on Educational Psychology," *History of Education Quarterly* 11 (1971): 408; Clarence E. Ragsdale, *Modern Psychologies and Education* (New York: Macmillan, 1932), pp. 52–56, 168–214.

64. Leonard V. Koos, *Trends in American Higher Education* (Cambridge: Harvard University Press, 1926), p. 3; Lance E. Davis et al., *American Economic Growth* (New York: Harper and Row, 1972), p. 661; Marjorie Rankin, *Trends in Educational Occupations* (New York: Teachers College Press, 1930), p. 1.

65. Robert L. Church, "Educational Psychology and Social reform in the Progressive Era," *History of Education Quarterly* 11 (1971): 400–401; David B. Tyack, *The One Best System* (Cambridge: Harvard University Press, 1974).

66. See, e.g., E. D. Starbuck to William James, 23 August 1902; James to G. S. Hall, 25 November [1909?], James Papers.

67. These figures were extrapolated from data supplied in Ruckmich, "History and Status of Psychology," pp. 524–27.

68. Ibid., p. 522; M. E. Haggerty to Yerkes, 15 March 1917, Yerkes Papers; Thorndike, "The Contributions of Psychology to Education," *Journal of Educational Psychology* 1 (1910): 8; E. C. Sanford, "Experimental Pedagogy and Experimental Psychology," ibid., pp. 590–95.

69. Haggerty to Yerkes, 5 October 1912, Yerkes Papers.

70. Church, "Educational Psychology and Social Reform."

71. General historical accounts of clinical psychology include John M. Reisman, *The Development of Clinical Psychology* (New York: Appleton-Century-Crofts, 1966); C. M. Louttit, "The Nature of Clinical Psychology," *PB* 36 (1939): 361–89; Robert A. Brotemarkle, "Clinical Psychology, 1896–1946," *Journal of Consulting Psychology* 11 (1947): 1–14; Robert I. Watson, "A Brief History of Clinical Psychology," *PB* 50 (1953): 321–46. For brief sketches of Witmer and his clinic, see Joseph Collins, "Lightner Witmer: A Biographical Sketch," in Robert A. Brotemarkle, ed., *Clinical Psychology: Studies in Honor of Lightner Witmer* (Philadelphia: University of Pennsylvania Press, 1931), pp. 3–9, and Samuel W. Fernberger, "History of the Psychological Clinic," in ibid., pp. 10–36. See also John M. O'Donnell, "The Clinical Psychology of Lightner Witmer: A Case Study of Institutional Innovation and Intellectual Change," *JHBS* 15 (1979): 3–17.

72. Witmer, "The Psychological Clinic," *Old Penn* 8 (1909): 100; Arthur Holmes, *The Conservation of the Child: A Manual of Clinical Psychology Presenting the Examination and Treatment of Backward Children* (Philadelphia: Lippincott, 1912), pp. 28–29; Witmer, "Practical Work in Psychology," *Pediatrics* 2 (1896): 116–17; Witmer et al., *The Special Class For Backward Children* (Philadelphia: The Psychological Clinic Press, 1911); Fernberger, "History of the Psychological Clinic," pp. 14, 15; Edward Potts Cheyney, *His-*

tory of the University of Pennsylvania (Philadelphia: University of Pennsylvania Press, 1940), pp. 353–55, 401.

73. These records have been microfilmed and surveyed. See Murray Levine and Julius Wishner, "The Case Records of the Psychological Clinic at the University of Pennsylvania (1896–1961)," *JHBS* 13 (1977): 59–66.

74. Witmer, "The Analytical Diagnosis," *Psychological Clinic* 14 (1922): 130; "Performance and Success: An Outline of Psychology for Diagnostic Testing and Teaching," ibid., 12 (1919): 148; O'Donnell, "Clinical Psychology of Lightner Witmer," pp. 9–12.

75. Frederich Maria Urban to S. W. Fernberger, 25 November 1919, Urban Correspondence, University of Pennsylvania Archives, Philadelphia.

76. Charles E. Rosenberg has stated that after 1900 "the reformist in temperament tended, as their emotional position dictated, to dissociate behavioral characteristics entirely from a possible genetic basis"; Charles E. Rosenberg, *No Other Gods: On Science and American Social Thought* (Baltimore: Johns Hopkins University Press, 1976), p. 10.

77. Witmer, "Criminals in the Making," *Psychological Clinic* 4 (1911): 231–32.

78. J. E. W. Wallin, *The Mental Health of the School Child* (New Haven: Yale University Press, 1914), pp. 22–120; Theodate L. Smith, "The Development of Psychological Clinics in the United States," *Pedagogical Seminary* 21 (1914): 143–53; Louttit, "Nature of Clinical Psychology," p. 372.

79. Witmer, "Criminals in the Making," p. 232.

80. Weidensall, "Criminology and Delinquency," *PB* 10 (1913): 232.

81. Nathan G. Hale, Jr., *Freud and the Americans: The Beginnings of Psychoanalysis in the United States, 1876–1917* (New York: Oxford University Press, 1971), p. 72.

82. For an account of the conference, see ibid., pp. 3–23.

83. Adolf Meyer, "The Role of Habit-Disorganizations," *Nervous and Mental Disease Monograph Series No. 9*, 1 (1912); "Objective Psychology or Psychobiology," *Journal of the American Medical Association* 65 (1915): 860–62; William A. White, "Childhood: The Golden Period for Mental Hygiene," *Mental Hygiene* 4 (1920): 261–62, 266; "The Behavioristic Attitude," ibid., 5 (1921): 1–18.

84. Hamilton, "An Experimental Study of an Unusual Type of Reaction in a Dog," *Journal of Comparative Neurology and Psychology* 17 (1907): 329–41; "Perseverance Reactions in Primates and Rodents," *Behavior Monographs* 3 (1916). Hamilton to Yerkes, 22 April 1914, 22 December 1914, and 17 May 1922, Yerkes Papers. Yerkes wrote the Forword to Hamilton's *Objective Psychopathology* (St. Louis, Mo.: Mosby, 1925).

85. Watson, "Behavior and the Concept of Mental Disease," *JPPSM* 13 (1916): 589–96; Frink, *Morbid Fears and Compulsions* (New York: Moffat, Yard, 1918); Hale, *Freud and the Americans*, pp. 335, 358, 386, 388.

86. [Hall], "Twentieth Anniversary of Clark University," *Nation* 89 (1909): 285.

87. See, e.g., K. Dunlap, *Mysticism, Freudianism and Scientific Psychology* (St. Louis, Mo.: Mosby, 1920). It seems probable that Freudianism served in some instances to push psychologists toward more biologically based conceptions of their subject matter; see Watson, "Does Holt Follow Freud?" *JPPSM* 14 (1917): 85–93.

88. For insights into this conflict, see Seashore, *Pioneering in Psychology*, pp. 128–34; Thomas Verner Moore, "A Century of Psychology in Relation to Psychiatry," in *One Hundred Years of American Psychiatry*, ed. J. K. Hall et al. (New York: Columbia University Press, 1944), pp. 468–77; William J. Goode, "Encroachment, Charlatanism, and the Emerging Profession: Psychology, Sociology, and Medicine," *American Sociological*

Review 25 (1960): 907–13; John C. Burnham, "The Struggle between Physicians and Paramedical Personnel in American Psychiatry, 1917–1941," *Journal of the History of Medicine and Allied Sciences* 29 (1974): 93–106; J. E. W. Wallin, "A Note on the Origin of the APA Clinical Section," *American Psychologist* 16 (1961): 256–58.

89. Shepherd Ivory Franz, "Psychology and Psychiatry," *PB* 14 (1917): 228.

90. Hollingworth, "Judgments of Persuasiveness," *PR* 18 (1911): 234–35.

91. Quoted in Kuna, "The Psychology of Advertising," p. 293.

92. Watson, *HPA*, 3 (1936): 280.

93. For general portraits of these movements, see Donald S. Napoli, *The Architects of Adjustment: The History of the Psychological Profession in the United States* (Port Washington, New York: Kennikat, 1980); Donald K. Pickens, *Eugenics and the Progressives* (Nashville: Vanderbilt University Press, 1968), chap. 7; Ferguson, *Heritage of Industrial Psychology;* Loren Baritz, *Servants of Power: A History of the Use of Social Sciences in American Industry* (Middletown, Conn.: Wesleyan University Press, 1960); Stuart Ewen, *Captains of Consciousness: Advertising and the Social Roots of Consumer Culture* (New York: McGraw-Hill, 1976); A. Michal McMahon, "An American Courtship: Psychologists and Advertising Theory in the Progressive Era," *American Studies* 13 (1972): 5–18.

94. The great majority of applied psychologists received training at the major centers of educational psychology: Chicago, Columbia, and Clark. From 1900 until the United States entry into the Great War, these three institutions produced more than half (177) of all the American doctorates in psychology (334); Harper, "Tables," p. 581.

95. Warren, "The Mental and the Physical," *PR* 21 (1914): 79–100. Warren is quoted in M. E. Haggerty, "The Twenty-second Annual Meeting of the American Psychological Association," *JPPSM* 11 (1914): 87.

96. Walter B. Pillsbury, *The Essentials of Psychology* (New York: Macmillan, 1911), pp. 1–2.

97. Watson, "Psychology as the Behaviorist Views It," pp. 165–66; A. C. Raphelson, "Psychology at Michigan: 1880 to 1950" (Address delivered to the Department of Psychology Sesquicentennial Colloquium, University of Michigan, Ann Arbor, 1967), p. 6; Titchener to Yerkes, 13 August 1911, Yerkes Papers.

98. Dunlap, *HPA*, 2 (1932): 45; *A System of Psychology* (New York: Scribner's 1912). Dunlap preserved *his* scientific conscience two years later in *An Outline of Psychobiology* (Baltimore: The Johns Hopkins University, 1914).

99. Warren, *HPA*, 1 (1930): 462.

100. Hall, "Some Possible Effects of the War on American Psychology," *PB* 16 (1919): 48.

101. See John M. O'Donnell, "The Crisis of Experimentalism in the 1920s: E. G. Boring and His Uses of History," *American Psychologist* 34 (1979): 289–95.

102. Bartlett, *HPA*, 3 (1936): 40; Terman, *HPA*, 2 (1932): 325.

103. Much of this treatment is self-congratulatory; psychologists portrayed their warwork as so completely successful that historians have been inclined to accept their assessments uncritically. See, e.g., Yerkes, ed., *The New World of Science: Its Development During the War* (New York: Century, 1920); Thomas M. Camfield, "Psychologists at War: The History of American Psychology and the First World War" (Ph.D. diss., University of Texas, Austin, 1969); Ferguson, *Heritage of Industrial Psychology*, pp. 101–39. For more critical accounts, see Daniel J. Kevles, "Testing the Army's Intelligence: Psychologists and the Military in World War I," *Journal of American History* 55 (1968):

565–81, and Franz Samelson, "World War I Intelligence Testing and the Development of Psychology," *JHBS* 13 (1977): 274–82.

104. Cattell, "Retrospect: Psychology as a Profesion," *Journal of Consulting Psychology* 1 (1937): 1; Cattell "Address of the President Before the American Psychological Association, 1895," *PR* 3(1896): 136. Angell, *HPA*, 3 (1936): 16; Tolman, *HPA*, 4 (1952): 327–28; Dodge, *HPA*, 1 (1930): 117, and quoted in Yerkes, "Report of the Psychology Committee of the National Research Council," *PR* 26 (1919): 107; Yerkes, *HPA*, 2 (1932): 399.

105. Yerkes, *HPA*, 2 (1932): 399.

106. See folder 11, Yerkes Papers.

107. Napoli, *Architects of Adjustment*, p. 8.

108. Watson to Yerkes, 19 April 1917, Yerkes Papers.

109. Thorndike, "Watson's 'Behavior,' " review, *Journal of Animal Behavior* 5 (1915): 467.

110. Hunter, *HPA*, 4 (1952): 186.

111. David Bakan, "Behaviorism and American Urbanization," *JHBS* 2 (1966): 5–28; John C. Burnham, "Psychiatry, Psychology and the Progressive Movement," *American Quarterly* 12 (1960): 457–65; "The New Psychology: From Narcissism to Social Control," in *Change and Continuity in Twentieth-Century America: The 1920s*, ed. John Braeman et al. (Columbus: Ohio State University Press, 1968), pp. 351–98. A study which relates these broad pressures to behaviorism through a biographical analysis of Watson is Kerry Buckley, "Behaviorism and the Professionalization of American Psychology: A Study of John Broadus Watson, 1878–1958" (Ph.D. diss., University of Massachusetts, Amherst, 1982).

112. See, e.g., William G. Rothstein, *American Physicians in the Nineteenth Century: From Sects to Science* (Baltimore: Johns Hopkins University Press, 1972).

113. Pillsbury, *Essentials of Psychology*, p. 2; Münsterberg, *Psychology: General and Applied*, p. 350; Watson, "An Attempted Formulation of the Scope of Behavior Psychology," pp. 329–30.

Index

Adams, Charles K., 217
Adler, Mortimer, 171
Agassiz, Louis, 94, 96, 97
American Association for the Advancement of Science, 94
American Journal of Psychology, 3, 142, 144, 163
American Men of Science, 212, 287n.58
American Psychological Association (APA), 3, 141; founding of, 143-44; first meeting of, 144-46; and Watson, 201
Andover Theological Seminary, 106
Angell, Frank, 26, 43, 48
Angell, James Burrill, 48
Angell, James Rowland, career of, 48-49; on Darwinism, 52, 159; on behaviorism, 178; on comparative psychology, 177-78; on functionalism, 11-12, 172, 175-77; on phrenology, 74-75; on structuralism, 160; on teaching and research, 223; on American psychology, 131; on WW I, 239; mentioned, 40, 65, 152, 172, 187-89, 201
Animal psychology. *See* Comparative psychology.
Applied psychology, 128, 131-41, 152-58; and introspection, 41; and phrenology, 78-79; and positivism, 87; and education 118-19, 226-32; and genetic psychology, 160; and behaviorism, 237
Armstrong, Andrew C., 40, 166
Arps, George F., 216
Associationism, 16, 79-80
Avenarius, Richard, 37

Bagley, William Chandler, 153
Bain, Alexander, on phrenology, 75; influence of, on American psychology, 80-83; mentioned, 16, 40, 107, 121, 131, 171
Baldwin, James Mark, 44, 131-32, 151, 190; on Wundt, 23-24; on positivism, 60; career of, 167-68; theory of, 168-71; mentioned, 4, 33, 172, 173, 197
Bartlett, Frederick Charles, 238
Bascom, John, 217
Becker, Carl, 126
Beer, Thomas, 205
Behaviorism, of Watson, x-xi, 12-13, 178, 179, 191-211; of Gall, 67-68, 74, 76; of M. Meyer, 72; of McDougall, 74; of Yerkes, 74, 192; of Bain, 80-81; of James, 133, 136; of Thorndike, 166-67, 227-29; of A. Meyer, 202; of Witmer, 233; and comparative psychology, 179-80; and psychiatry, 235-36; and applied psychology, 237; Koestler on, 179; Titchener on, 210
Bell, Charles, 18, 59
Bentley, Madison, 157, 220
Bernard, Luther Lee, 76
Bernheim, Hippolyte, 44
Bethe, Albrecht, 205
Binet, Alfred, 184
Bingham, Walter Van Dyke, 223
Biology, 17, 176, 188, 204-205. *See* Evolution, Darwinism.
Boas, Franz, 152, 164, 166
Boring, Edwin G., 4; on J. McKeen Cat-